The Most Amazing Story

SECOND EDITION

Cover Art

By Mary Nazworth

Dedication

This curriculum is dedicated in a special way to my grandchildren, but in reality it is dedicated to all children of the world.

The Most Amazing Story

SECOND EDITION

Distributed by Wanda Nazworth and

DM2 International Inc.

Disciple Makers Multiplied

PO Box 3570

Harlingen, TX 78551

For more information:

Email: wnazworth@gmail.com

www.DM2USA.org

Acknowledgments

When I began writing this curriculum, my desire was to provide moms with a Bible story book that went beyond simply telling Bible stories to giving children an understanding of God's over-all plan as revealed through the pages of the Bible. As it turned out, I ended up doing most of the writing while simultaneously teaching the material in Sunday school, resulting in a multi-purpose curriculum.

I want to thank my children, first of all, for sacrificing mom-time and putting up with me through six years of working on this material! I also want to thank Nancy Hughes, my long-term fellow Sunday school teacher, for her encouragement and invaluable input, especially in the activities. Thank you, too, to the friends and family members who have taken the time to edit the material: MelRae Ambs, Donna Barkman, Doug and Della Davis, Carissa Robinson. Finally, a special thanks to my wonderful husband, Bret Nazworth, for encouraging me to persevere. Without him, I probably would have quit working on this many times.

Most of all, I give all the glory for this curriculum to God, as it is His incredible and amazing story I am telling!

My joy will truly be fulfilled if, through this material, children around the world come to a clear and accurate understanding of the Bible and its main message, the Gospel of Jesus Christ.

Wanda D. Nazworth

Copyright

Scripture passages quoted are from the New King James Version, 1997, Thomas Nelson, Inc.

Coloring pages by Jim LeGette

Contents

Curriculum Synopsis 11

Old Testament Lessons 15

1. The Most Wonderful Letter 17
2. Who is God? 23
3. In the Beginning 29
4. A Wonderful World 35
5. Mission Completed 41
6. Special Helpers 47
7. The Rebel Angel 53
8. The First Parents 59
9. Separated 65
10. Consequences 73
11. Banished 79
12. An Unacceptable Offering 85
13. Noah 93
14. The Terrible Flood 99
15. God's Promises 103
16. Confusion 109
17. A Great Nation 117
18. Fire from Heaven 123
19. More than the Stars 129
20. Helpless 135
21. Twins 141
22. Jealous Brothers 149
23. The King's Dream 157
24. Suffering in Egypt 163
25. Rescued by a Princess 169
26. I AM 175

27. Let My People Go   183

28. When I See the Blood   191

29. Trapped   199

30. Hungry and Thirsty   205

31. A New Agreement   213

32. Ten Rules   219

33. A Broken Agreement   227

34. A Beautiful Tent   233

35. Forgiveness   241

36. Spies   247

37. Snakes   253

38. Canaan at Last   259

39. False Gods   267

40. A Trumpet and a Pitcher   275

41. Tricked   283

42. A Giant   295

43. An Awesome Temple   303

44. Cry Louder!   309

45. Swallowed by a Fish   317

46. A Burning Fiery Furnace   325

47. In the Lions' Den   333

48. God's Plans   339

    New Testament Lessons   346

49. A Special Baby   347

50. Immanuel: God with Us   353

51. A Preacher in the Desert   361

52. Good News for Everyone   367

53. God's Lamb   375

54. Satan Tries to Trick Jesus   381

55. Jesus Teaches and Heals   389

56. A Visitor at Night   397

57. Two Sick Men   403

58. Hypocrites   411

59. Supernatural Power   417

60. Bread that Gives Eternal Life   425

61. Dirty on the Inside   433

62. Who is Jesus?   441

63. The Good Shepherd   449

64. Little Children   457

65. Riches are Tricky   461

66. A Dead Man Comes Back to Life   469

67. The Last Passover   479

68. Condemned   487

69. Executed   497

70. Alive!   503

71. Accepted   513

72. Eternal Life   517

73. Jesus is the Only Door   523

74. Jesus our Substitute   527

75. The Last Passover Lamb   533

76. Friends, not Enemies   537

77. Redeemed   545

78. Declared Righteous   551

79. Safe and Secure   557

80. A New Identity   565

   Appendix   571

Curriculum Synopsis

Worldview

This curriculum is based on the belief that the Bible is God's unfolding revelation of who He is and how He desires to relate to mankind.

This curriculum is different from most in that it does not focus on the good behavior of the child. It is not designed to teach children to act and/or talk like good Christians. We believe that teaching with a focus on good character, behavior, and vocabulary often results merely in outward change. When this occurs, it leads either to pride or defeat, and sadly fails to address the child's real spiritual needs. If the heart of the child is changed by the truth of the Word of God, then the conduct of the child will be changed as well.

A Four-Fold Goal

- To give children a biblical understanding of who God is.
- To accurately present God's plan of salvation.
- To provide a global understanding of God's eternal plan for humankind from a true-grace perspective, as revealed in the Word of God.
- To effectively communicate a biblical worldview in order to prepare children to stand firmly in the truth amidst all the deceptive philosophies of the culture.

Methodology

To accomplish this four-fold goal, the lessons begin in Genesis and move through key sections of the Bible. They are set up to teach God's character and His plan for humanity by continually reiterating and reviewing the following basic worldview truths:

God (Father, Son, and Holy Spirit)
- The God of the Bible is the only true and living God.
- There is only one God who exists as three persons: God the Father, God the Son, and God the Holy Spirit.
- God has always existed by His own power; He does not need anything.
- God is a spirit being.
- God is the Creator of the world and all that is in it; therefore, all things belong to God and God is the highest authority.
- God is all-powerful; nothing is too hard for Him.
- God is everywhere all the time.
- God knows everything.

- God is perfect and everything He does is perfect in every way.
- God is a God of order.
- God is the One who gives life.
- God does not change; He is always the same.
- God is faithful; He always finishes what He starts.
- God always tells the truth; He keeps His promises.
- God always fulfills His plans; no one can stop God.
- God is a personal being; He communicates with people.
- God speaks to us through His Word, the Bible.
- God is a God of love, mercy, and grace.
- God is not partial.
- God cannot sin.

Jesus Christ
- Jesus Christ is God.
- Jesus Christ is a human being.
- Since Jesus Christ is God, He has all the attributes of God. Jesus is all-powerful, He knows everything, He loves people, etc.
- Jesus Christ is perfect in every way; He never sinned.
- Jesus Christ is the only Savior.
- Jesus Christ will someday be king forever.

Angels
- God created angels.
- God's purpose for angels was for them to be His helpers and messengers.
- Angels are spirits.
- God made angels strong and smart, but they are not as strong and smart as God.
- When God made the angels, they were perfect in every way.

Satan
- Satan and his demons are God's enemies.
- Satan is a liar and a murderer who seeks to destroy people.
- Satan's helpers are the fallen angels called demons.
- God is stronger than Satan and his demons; they can never win against God.

- Someday God will cast Satan and his demons into the Lake of Fire where they will be for eternity.

People

- All people come from Adam and are born separated from God.
- The spirit of every person in Adam's family is dead to God.
- All people are born sinners and commit sin.
- All people are born under Satan's dominion.

God's World

- God created the earth especially for mankind.

Mankind's Dilemma

- No one in Adam's family is acceptable to God.
- It is impossible for anyone in Adam's family to please God or pay for sin.
- The penalty for sin is separation from God forever in a terrible place of suffering (the Lake of Fire).
- At the moment of death, a person goes immediately to either Heaven or Hell (and ultimately to the Lake of Fire).

God's Plan

- From the beginning of time, God planned to send the Savior to save mankind from death and make him acceptable to God.
- Only God is able to save people from Satan and death and make them acceptable to Him.
- God saves only those who believe Him.

General Uses

These lessons can be used in a classroom setting (e.g., Sunday school), as a home Bible study, as homeschool Bible curriculum, or as true stories simply to be read aloud. They are flexible enough to be used with a wide range of ages, from preschoolers to teenagers.

It is my desire that the material be easily and accurately understood by all. With that in mind, we have sought to keep the terminology both clear and uncomplicated. In creating this curriculum, my intention was to make the material understandable to those with minimal knowledge of the Bible and to make it adaptable to any language and/or culture.

Sunday school curriculum

This is a user-friendly Sunday school curriculum; very little preparation is needed on the part of the teacher. The lessons are written in such a way that the teacher can simply read them to the class, if necessary. The curriculum was created with this simplicity for two reasons: (1) to ensure that even young people can begin to teach, and (2) to ensure that the important worldview truths brought out in the lessons are not overlooked.

Another unique benefit of this book when used as a Sunday school curriculum is that it can be repeated several times with the same group of children because the concepts are foundational and can be understood in more depth each time the curriculum is repeated. The first time children go through the material they may be very young and only retain the basics; however, each additional time they review the material they retain more, until finally they become so familiar with the lessons they can teach them themselves.

A third beneficial aspect of this curriculum is that it can be used in a multilevel classroom, much like the one-room schools of old.

Furthermore, the lessons and activities are designed simply enough that they can be used with small or large groups of children in remote settings, such as in developing countries, where there may be limited supplies and materials.

Finally, a word of instruction on how to use the lessons. Lessons are typically concise enough to be presented in a 15-20 minute time period. The memory verses, along with the review questions and activities, are designed to enforce the key concepts of the lesson.

The Most Amazing Story

Old Testament

1
The Most Wonderful Letter

Introduction to the Bible

Memory Verse

All Scripture is given by inspiration of God …. 2 Timothy 3:16a

Lesson

Have you ever gotten a letter or a birthday card in the mail? It is fun to receive mail, isn't it? When you get a letter in the mail, you open it in excitement to see what it says.

Did you know that many years ago Someone really important wrote you a special letter? You may have seen this letter on a bookshelf in your home, or in a store, or in the library. Even though this letter was written long ago, there are many copies of the letter still in existence today. You can buy a copy at almost any bookstore. By now you have probably guessed what this letter is. It is the Bible.

The Bible is a long letter written to every person in the world. The author of the Bible is God. God wrote you a letter because He wants you to get to know Him, and because He has some important news for you.

Even though the Bible is God's letter, God did not write it with His own hands. Instead, God chose about 40 men to write for Him. These writers were called prophets. A prophet was someone who spoke to people for God. God would give a message to the prophet, then the prophet would communicate God's message to the people.

God had several ways of communicating to the prophets what He wanted them to write. Sometimes He talked to the prophets in a voice they could hear. Other times He talked to the prophets through special dreams. Still other times, God simply put His words into their thoughts.

The Bible tells us the prophets were always careful to write exactly what God told them to write. The prophets never changed anything God said. They never added their own ideas or explanations; they never left anything out.

 ...knowing this first, that no prophecy of Scripture is of any private interpretation, for prophecy never came by the will of man, but holy men of God spoke as they were moved by the Holy Spirit. 2 Peter 1:20-21

It took God more than 1,500 years to write the Bible! That is a long time. The reason it took so long is because the Bible tells the true story of what God did over the space of hundreds of years. The Bible is God's history book.

The first prophets wrote the beginning of God's story, but these prophets died before the story was complete. So, God used another group of prophets to write more of His story. In the end, it took 40 prophets to write the whole story of the Bible.

And do you know what is so amazing about the Bible? All of it agrees.

Have you ever heard about the same event from two or three different people? Every person seems to have his or her own version of what really happened. But the Bible is not like that. Even though 40 men, who lived at different times and in different places, wrote the Bible over a space of more than 1,500 years, the whole Bible agrees. '

Do you know why every part of the Bible agrees? It is because the Bible has only one author, and that is God. God always tells the truth; He does not change. That is why one part of the Bible never says the opposite of another part.

...God, who cannot lie... Titus 1:2

When the Bible was first written, it did not look anything like a modern-day Bible. For one thing, the paper used by the prophets was different from the paper we have today. The prophets wrote on either papyrus or leather.

Papyrus is a plant that grows near the Nile River in Egypt. To make paper out of papyrus, the inside part of the plant was cut into thin strips. These strips were placed side by side. A second layer of strips, facing the other direction, was laid across the first layer. As these layers of papyrus dried, they stuck together to form sheets of paper.

Leather "paper" was made by drying and scraping animal skins.

Finally, the leather or pieces of papyrus were connected to make one long strip of paper that was rolled up from both ends to make a scroll.

Unfortunately, with the passing of time, the leather and papyrus became brittle and cracked. When this happened, new copies had to be made. Since there were no copy machines or printers in those days, special men called scribes copied the scrolls by hand.

Because the scribes respected God, they were extremely careful when they made copies of His words. If a scribe found even a tiny mistake in the copy he was making, he would throw it out and start over again! The copy had to be exactly the same as the original scroll.

As you can imagine, it took many years to make just one copy of a scroll. Thankfully, God protected many of these scrolls so that they are still in existence today. Scholars have found that the Bibles we have today say the same thing as the scrolls did long ago.

Nowadays, the Bible is not copied by hand. Today, computers and printers make it possible to print millions of Bibles in a short amount of time.

The Bible has two parts to it: the Old Testament and the New Testament. There are 39 books in the Old Testament and 27 books in the New Testament, for a total of 66 books.

The prophets who wrote the books of the Old Testament spoke Hebrew. Therefore, the Old Testament was written in the Hebrew language. The New Testament was written in Greek.

The Bible has been translated into numerous languages so that people all over the world can know what God has to say to them. The Bible is for all people. God wants everyone to get to know Him. He wants everyone to hear the good news He has for us.

Questions

1. To whom did God write His letter, the Bible? *He wrote it to every person in the world, including you.*

2. What was God's reason for writing us a letter? *God wrote us a letter because He wants us to get to know Him. God also has some really good news for us.*

3. What were the men called who wrote God's words in the Bible? *They were called prophets.*

4. How many prophets did God use to write His letter? *God used about 40 prophets.*

5. Did the prophets write exactly what God wanted them to write, or did they add some of their own ideas? *They wrote exactly what God said to write.*

6. How long did it take for the entire Bible to be written? *It took more than 1,500 years.*

7. How can the whole Bible agree when it was written by so many different men? *It all agrees because there is only one author, and that is God.*

8. Is every part of the Bible true? *Yes, the Bible is God's Word, and God always tells the truth.*

9. The Bible is divided into two parts. What are these two parts called? *They are called the Old Testament and the New Testament.*

10. Does the Bible say the same thing today as what the prophets wrote in the scrolls long ago? *Yes, God has protected His message so that it still says the same thing it did in the beginning when the prophets first wrote it down.*

How to Find a Verse in the Bible

The books of the Bible are divided into chapters and verses. Years after the prophets wrote down God's words on scrolls, Bible scholars added chapters and verses to help readers find their place. The chapters and verses act like street addresses to help you find your way around the Bible.

All through this book, there will be quotes from the Bible like the one below.

In the beginning God created the heavens and the earth.
Genesis 1:1

At the end of each quote you will see what is called a reference that looks like this: **Genesis 1:1**. Just like an address tells you where someone lives, the reference tells you where you can find the quote in the Bible.

A reference has three parts. The first part is the name of the book. The reference above tells you that the quote is found in the book of Genesis. The number right after the name of the book is the chapter number, which is chapter 1 in the above example. The second number is the verse number. In our example, the verse number is also 1. This tells us that the above quote is found in the first verse of the first chapter of the book of Genesis.

Let's say you want to find this quote in the Bible. The first thing you need to do is locate the book of Genesis. A good way to do this is to look in the table of contents at the front of the Bible. Once you have located the book of Genesis, you'll see a big number 1 right at the beginning of the book. This big number stands for Chapter One. Right at the first of Chapter One you'll see another number 1, a little smaller than the first 1. The small number 1 is the number of the verse. You will see that there are many verses in Chapter One. At the end of Chapter One, you'll see a big 2 for Chapter Two. Chapter Two also has many verses.

You will find that every book in the Bible is numbered in this same way. Once you understand how it works, it will be easy for you to find any of the verses quoted in these lessons.

Biblical Worldviews

- God is the author of the Bible.
- God is a personal being; He communicates with people.
- God always tells the truth.
- God does not change; the whole Bible has the same message.
- God protected the Bible so that it still says the same thing it did in the beginning.

Activity 1: Handmade Scroll

Supplies:

- One heavy 8 ½" by 14" piece of paper per student
- Pencils, crayons
- Sponge, paint, and yarn (optional)

Instructions:

- Students place their papers lengthwise in front of them.
- Students write 2 Timothy 3:16a across the length of their papers.
- They may use crayons to decorate the background.
- Optional: Cut out sponge in shape of small cross, about 3x2 inches. Students dip cross in paint and sponge paint onto paper around verse.
- Scrolls are now complete—students simply roll the paper into a scroll and secure with a piece of yarn or with the tassel from Activity 2 below.

Activity 2: Handmade Scroll Tassel

Supplies:

- Three strands of yarn (1 yard long) of different colors per student.

Instructions:

- Students work in groups of two, taking turns to help each other.
- To make a tassel, students put three strands together.
- One student holds one end while the other student holds the other end and takes a few steps back.
- One student twists the strands over and over, while the other holds her end tightly.
- When sufficiently twisted, one student drops her end, creating a homemade tassel. This tassel may be used to tie around the scroll.

Extra Bible References

Genesis 2:4; Numbers 12:6-8, 23:19; Deuteronomy 18:18; 1 Samuel 15:29; Isaiah 40:8; Jeremiah 9:23-24; 36:2, 6; Luke 4:17; Romans 1:2; 2 Timothy 3:16; Hebrews 1:1, 12; 6:18

2
Who is God?
Characteristics of God

Memory Verse

Before the mountains were brought forth, or ever You had formed the earth and the world, even from everlasting to everlasting, You are God. Psalm 90:2

Lesson

What is God like? What does God do? Where does God live? To find out what God is like, we must read the letter He wrote us. These are the first words in the Bible:

In the beginning God... Genesis 1:1a

God was alive in the beginning. Before the earth or the universe existed, God was there.

Before the mountains were brought forth, or ever You had formed the earth and the world, even from everlasting to everlasting, You are God. Psalm 90:2

God exists from "everlasting to everlasting." This means there was never a time in the past when God was not alive, and there will never be a time in the future when God will die. God never had a beginning; He was never born. And God will never have an end; He will never die.

"I am the Alpha and the Omega, the Beginning and the End," says the Lord, "who is and who was and who is to come, the Almighty." Revelation 1:8

You and I are not like God. Everything in the world has a beginning, even you. If you are nine years old, you were born nine years ago. You have not always existed the way God has. You came into the world as a baby. Now you are growing up. Someday you will get old, and then one day you will die.

But God does not grow old. God will never change. He has always been exactly the same as He is right now, and He will keep on being the same forever.

...they will be changed. But You are the same, and Your years will not fail. Hebrews 1:12

God does not need sunshine, food, water, or air like you and I do. God lived perfectly fine, all alone, before any of these existed. You and I would die without food, water, and air, but God stays alive by His own power.

The Bible says that God is spirit. This means God does not have a body made of skin and bones like humans do.

God is Spirit... John 4:24

Even though God does not have a body and cannot be seen, God is a real person. God is not simply an invisible force. The Bible says God is a personal being.

God has a personality; He likes some things and does not like other things. God makes decisions. God is intelligent. He has feelings. God wants to have a relationship with people; He wants us to get to know Him just like we would get to know a friend.

The LORD your God in your midst, the Mighty One, will save; He will rejoice over you with gladness, He will quiet you with His love, He will rejoice over you with singing. Zephaniah 3:17

The Bible also says God is everywhere at the same time.

Sometimes it would be great if you could be in two places at once, wouldn't it? Let's say your family is going to the beach and your best friend is having a birthday party on the same day. Wouldn't it be nice to be able to do both things? Of course, that is impossible because you can only be in one place at a time.

Only God is everywhere all the time. Right now, God is in His home in Heaven and He is in the room where you are. God is in the far-away land of Africa and at your grandparent's home - all at the same time!

Where can I go from Your Spirit? Or where can I flee from Your presence?

If I take the wings of the morning, and dwell in the uttermost parts of the sea, even there Your hand shall lead me, and Your right hand shall hold me. Psalm 139:7, 9-10

Wherever you go, God is already there. It is impossible to hide from God.

"Am I a God near at hand," says the LORD, "and not a God afar off? Can anyone hide himself in secret places, so I shall not see him?" says the LORD; "Do I not fill heaven and earth?" says the LORD. Jeremiah 23:23-24

Even though God is everywhere at the same time, God is not in everything, nor is everything God.

The Bible says there is only one God.

I am the LORD, and there is no other; there is no God besides Me. Isaiah 45:5a

God is the highest ruler. He has authority over every person and government on Earth. No one can tell God what to do. God does whatever He decides to do. If God does not allow something to happen, it cannot happen. No one is greater than God!

That they may know that You, whose name alone is the LORD, are the Most High over all the earth. Psalm 83:18

This awesome God wrote you a wonderful letter because He wants you to get to know Him. God wants to be your friend.

Questions

1. When did God come into being? *God does not have a beginning; He was never born. God has always lived.*

2. Will God ever die? *No, God will never die.*

3. What are some things you need in order to stay alive? *You need sunshine, food, water, and air.*

4. What does God need in order to stay alive? *God does not need anything. God lived long before there was any food, water, or air. God stays alive by His own power.*

5. Does God have a body like you and I do? *No, God does not have a body like ours; God does not have a body made of skin and bones. God is spirit.*

6. Is God a real person, or is He simply a force? *God is an intelligent personal being who has feelings and makes decisions. You can get to know God just like you get to know a friend.*

7. Why is it impossible to hide from God? *You cannot hide from God because God is everywhere at all times.*

8. How can you get to know God? *You can learn about God by reading His letter, the Bible. In the Bible, God tells us what He is like.*

9. How many Gods are there? *There is only one God – the one we read about in the Bible.*

10. Who is in charge of the whole world? *God is. God is higher than all kings and governments. God does whatever He decides and no one can stop Him.*

Biblical Worldviews

- God has always existed. He was never born and He will never die.
- God does not change; He is always the same.
- God does not need anything to stay alive; He lives by His own power.
- God is spirit.
- God is a personal being; He is not simply some kind of force.
- God is everywhere at all times.
- There is only one God.
- No one is greater than God.

Activity: Make a Chart

Supplies:

- "Attribute" printouts, one per student (see appendix page 572)
- Blank sheet of paper, one per student
- Glue
- Scissors

Instructions:

- Students fold blank sheet of paper in half vertically to make a line down the center, and then open paper up again.
- Students label one side of the paper with their name.
- They label the other side "God."
- Then they cut out the attribute boxes.
- Finally, students glue the appropriate attributes under the corresponding headings on their papers.

Extra Bible References

Deuteronomy 6:4; Nehemiah 9:6; Psalms 83:18; 86:10; 97:9; 103:19; 145:3, 13; 147:5; Isaiah 45:5-6; 46:9-10; Jeremiah 10:6, 10; Acts 17:24-25; Colossians 1:16-17; 1 Timothy 1:17; James 1:17; Revelation 22:13

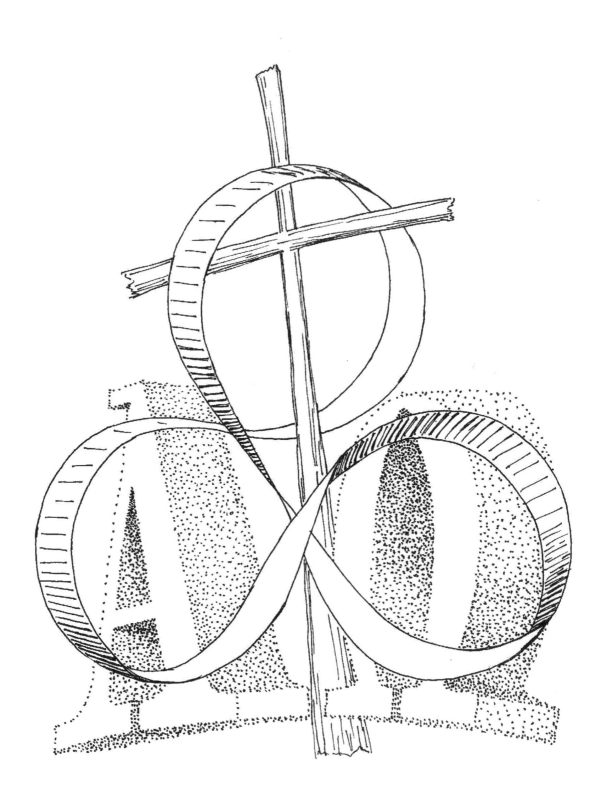

3
In the Beginning
Creation Part I

Memory Verse

Before the mountains were brought forth, or ever You had formed the earth and the world, even from everlasting to everlasting, You are God. Psalm 90:2

Lesson

Where do all the things we see around us come from? How did the sun and moon get up in the sky? How did plants, trees, and animals come into being?

Many years ago, I lived in the Amazon rainforest in South America. I lived in a village of tribal people called the Yanomamo. The Yanomamo hunt for food with long bows and arrows. Many Yanomamo families live together in one huge round house that only has a roof around the edge. In the middle it is open to the sky.

The Yanomamo believe that fish came from chips of wood. They say that long ago a man was chopping down a tree when some of the wood chips landed in the water nearby and turned into fish. The Yanomamo have many other interesting stories, too, about how things came into being in the beginning.

In other parts of the world, there are people who believe that an explosion out in the universe got everything started. They say that an explosion caused tiny one-celled creatures to start growing and changing. After billions of years, birds, animals, and people slowly began to develop.

So how can we know the truth about where plants, animals, and people came from? Was anyone alive in the beginning to see what really happened?

The Bible says that God was there in the beginning. In the beginning of time, before anything existed, God was alive. Since God was there, He knows how everything came to be.

In His letter, the Bible, God tells us the true story of how the world and everything in it began.

In the beginning God created the heavens and the earth.
Genesis 1:1

The Bible says that the Creator of the world is God.

The earth was without form, and void; and darkness was on the face of the deep. And the Spirit of God was hovering over the face of the waters. Genesis 1:2

Before God formed the earth and filled it with life, there was only darkness, water, and endless emptiness. In the darkness, God the Holy Spirit hovered over the water, ready to release His great power.

Then God spoke.

Then God said, "Let there be light"; and there was light.

And God saw the light, that it was good; and God divided the light from the darkness.

God called the light Day, and the darkness He called Night. So the evening and the morning were the first day. Genesis 1:3-5

How could God make the light appear simply by declaring, "Let there be light"? You or I could not do that. Not even the most intelligent scientist could do that. Only God is powerful enough to create light just by speaking. Nothing is too hard for God. With His powerful voice God made light shine out of the darkness.

Who taught God to make light? After all, everyone has to be taught, right? When you were small you did not know how to read or write. Someone had to teach you. Someone had to teach you how to tie your shoes. Almost everything you know, you were taught. So, who taught God all that He knows? The Bible says God did not have a teacher.

Who has directed the Spirit of the LORD, or as His counselor has taught Him? ...Who taught Him knowledge, and showed Him the way of understanding? ...Have you not known? Have you not heard? The everlasting God, the LORD, the Creator of the ends of the earth, neither faints nor is weary. His understanding is unsearchable. Isaiah 40:13-14, 28

> **The Spirit of God**
>
> Even though there is only one God, He exists as three persons: the Father, the Son, and the Holy Spirit. God the Father is God, God the Son is God, and God the Holy Spirit is God. All three are one and the same God.

God does not need anyone to teach Him. God does not need anyone to counsel Him or give Him advice. God knows and understands everything. He always has.

The Bible says that the light God made was good. The light God made did not flicker on and off. It did not grow dim like flashlights do when the batteries are low. The light God made shone brightly because everything God does is the best.

...His work is perfect... Deuteronomy 32:4

After God made the light, He separated the light from the darkness. God made it to be dark at night and light during the day. Every night when it gets dark, you can be sure it will be light again in the morning.

When morning dawned on the second day, God continued His work of creating the world.

Then God said, "Let there be a firmament in the midst of the waters, and let it divide the waters from the waters."

Thus God made the firmament, and divided the waters which were under the firmament from the waters which were above the firmament; and it was so.

And God called the firmament Heaven. So the evening and the morning were the second day. Genesis 1:6-8

Firmament is a long word that simply means empty space. In the beginning there was water everywhere, but on day two God moved the water aside to form an empty space in the middle of the water. God called this empty space Heaven; we call it "sky." The sky itself was dry, with water above and below it.

On day three, God gathered together the water that was below the sky to create Planet Earth.

Then God said, "Let the waters under the heavens be gathered together into one place, and let the dry land appear"; and it was so. And God called the dry land Earth, and the gathering together of the waters He called Seas. And God saw that it was good. Genesis 1:9-10

After God gathered together the water, He caused dry land to appear on the earth.

By the end of day three, everything had changed! No longer was there only darkness and water everywhere. Now there was night and day; and in the daytime, there was light. In the middle of all the water, there was now a huge dry space called the sky. Below the sky was the beginning of a new planet – Planet Earth.

The Bible says that every day when God looked at what He had done that day, He was happy. Everything was turning out just the way He wanted it.

Questions

1. Why is God the only One who can tell us how everything came into being in the beginning? *God is the only One who knows how everything came into being in the beginning because He was the only One there to see what really happened.*

2. What was the earth like in the beginning? *In the beginning there was only darkness and water everywhere. The earth had no shape, and it was empty.*

3. In the darkness, who was hovering over the water? *God the Holy Spirit was hovering over the water, ready to release His great power to create the world.*

4. How was it possible for God to make the light shine just by speaking? *God can do anything; He has all power to do whatever He wants.*

5. Who taught God how to make light? *No one did. God knows everything.*

6. What did God do on the second day? *On the second day of creation, God made a big empty space in the water called the sky.*

7. On the third day, what did God make? *On the third day, God made Planet Earth.*

8. When God looked at His work, was He happy with all He had made? *Yes, God was happy. All God's work was good because God is perfect. God cannot make anything bad.*

Biblical Worldviews

- God existed before anything else existed.
- God exists by His own power.
- There is only one God who exists in three persons: God the Father, God the Son, and God the Holy Spirit.
- God is the Creator.
- God can do anything; nothing is too hard for Him.
- God knows everything.
- God is perfect.
- God is a God of order.

Activity: Memory Verse Mobile

Supplies:

- Two regular-sized sturdy paper plates per student
- "Coloring Picture" printouts, one per student (see appendix page 573)
- "Memory Verse" printouts, one per student (see appendix page 574)
- Glue or double sided tape
- Stapler
- Scissors
- Crayons
- Hole punch
- String or yarn, cut into 8" segments, one piece per student
- Aluminum foil (optional)

Instructions:

- Students color the picture.
- Students cut out the memory verse and coloring picture.
- Staple or glue paper plates together to form a hollow area on the inside.
- Optional: Students cover this paper plate mobile with aluminum foil.
- Students glue or tape the memory verse to one side of the paper plate mobile.
- Students then glue or tape the colored picture to the other side of the mobile.
- Now punch a hole through the top of the paper plates.
- Students thread yarn through the hole at the top of the mobile to make a hanging.
- Optional: Students can make a tassel for their mobile using the tassel directions from Lesson 1.

Extra Bible References

Job 38:1-21; Psalms 18:30, 19:1-4, 24:1-2, 33:6-9, 95:3-5, 104:30; Proverbs 3:19; Isaiah 6:3, 45:7, 48:12-13; Jeremiah 10:12-13, 32:17; Romans 1:20, 11:33; Colossians 1:16; Hebrews 1:10, 11:3; 2 Peter 3:5

The Trinity: Genesis 1:26, 3:22; Matthew 28:18-19; 2 Corinthians 13:14; Ephesians 1:17; 2:13, 18; Hebrews 9:14

4
A Wonderful World
Creation Part II

Memory Verse

Ah, Lord GOD! Behold, You have made the heavens and the earth by Your great power and outstretched arm. There is nothing too hard for You. Jeremiah 32:17

Lesson

On the third day, after God made dry land appear, He spoke again. Suddenly, something incredible happened. Like fireworks in the night sky, the land burst into color!

Then God said, "Let the earth bring forth grass, the herb that yields seed, and the fruit tree that yields fruit according to its kind, whose seed is in itself, on the earth"; and it was so.

And the earth brought forth grass, the herb that yields seed according to its kind, and the tree that yields fruit, whose seed is in itself according to its kind.

And God saw that it was good. So the evening and the morning were the third day. Genesis 1:11-13

At God's command, plants sprung up everywhere! Simply by speaking God made palm trees, oak trees, fruit trees, herbs, and flowers. God made more kinds of trees and plants than you could ever imagine. Only God has the power to do that.

God made the plants and flowers pretty so we could enjoy them. God also made plants to give us food, medicine, and oxygen.

God wanted there to always be lots of plants on the earth, so He made a way for them to produce more of their own kind by giving them seeds. Inside each seed, God put the beginning of a new plant.

God is a God of order. He gave apple seeds to apple trees and tomato seeds to tomatoes. It would be confusing if you planted an apple seed and up came a banana plant. Thankfully, that is not the way God created plants and seeds. God made seeds to produce only their own kind.

At the end of day three when God looked over the land, He was pleased. The dry land was covered with beautiful plants, flowers, and trees of all colors and shapes.

Now that the earth was full of plants, it was time for God to fill the universe.

Then God said, "Let there be lights in the firmament of the heavens to divide the day from the night; and let them be for signs and seasons, and for days and years; and let them be for lights in the firmament of the heavens to give light on the earth"; and it was so.

Then God made two great lights: the greater light to rule the day, and the lesser light to rule the night. He made the stars also.

God set them in the firmament of the heavens to give light on the earth, and to rule over the day and over the night, and to divide the light from the darkness.

And God saw that it was good. So the evening and the morning were the fourth day. Genesis 1:14-19

God filled the universe with lights.

Even though God had already made light, on day four He created the sun, moon, and stars. The sun, moon, and stars help us keep track of time. The sun comes up every morning to let us know that a new day has started. The phases of the moon help us keep track of months. There are always 28 days from one full moon to the next. The stars change, too, depending on the season. Every season a different set of stars is visible in the sky.

Only God could have thought of all those details! At the end of day four when God looked at the universe, He was pleased with His work.

On day five God made living creatures to fill the sky and the oceans.

Then God said, "Let the waters abound with an abundance of living creatures, and let birds fly above the earth across the face of the firmament of the heavens."

So God created great sea creatures and every living thing that moves, with which the waters abounded, according to their kind, and every winged bird according to its kind. And God saw that it was good.

And God blessed them, saying, "Be fruitful and multiply, and fill the waters in the seas, and let birds multiply on the earth."

So the evening and the morning were the fifth day. Genesis 1:20-23

God created millions of sea creatures. He made whales, sharks, and dolphins. He made stingrays, sea horses, crabs, and fish. God made huge sea animals and tiny ones. He made sea creatures of all colors and shapes.

God created countless birds of every color, shape, and size, too. He made eagles, owls, sparrows, robins, seagulls and all kinds of beautiful parrots. Everywhere on Earth birds fly in the sky.

On day six, God made the animals that live on land.

Then God said, "Let the earth bring forth the living creature according to its kind: cattle and creeping thing and beast of the earth, each according to its kind"; and it was so.

And God made the beast of the earth according to its kind, cattle according to its kind, and everything that creeps on the earth according to its kind.

And God saw that it was good. Genesis 1:24-25

God made camels that can survive in the desert with only a little bit of water. He made kangaroos that carry their babies in pouches. He made polar bears that live in the snow and sleep all winter long. He made all the animals you see at the zoo. He made goats, cows, and pigs. God also made dogs, cats, and hamsters.

God made all the animals to be able to have babies. Every day more baby fish, birds, and land animals are born into the world. God is so awesome; He thought about everything!

Why did God make such a great variety of animals, birds, and sea creatures? Why did He make so many flavors of fruits and vegetables? Why did He make so many colors of flowers?

God did it for us, because He loves us! God could have made only two or three animals. He could have made everything the same color. Instead of making apples, bananas, oranges, kiwis, and grapes, He could have made only bananas.

But God knew you and I would get tired of eating only bananas all the time. So He made lots of different fruits. He made many kinds of vegetables. He made many colors of flowers and many different animals. God wanted to give us a place to live that would be interesting and exciting. He wanted us to have a beautiful world to enjoy.

No one is like God. No one could create the world and everything in it simply by speaking. Only God has the power and knows how to create a world out of nothing!

Great is our Lord, and mighty in power; His understanding is infinite. Psalm 147:5

Questions

1. How did God create the plants and animals? *God spoke the plants and animals into being with His powerful voice.*

2. What did God give to plants so they could produce more plants just like themselves? *God gave plants seeds. Inside every seed God put the beginning of a new plant just like the one it came from.*

3. How did God know how to make the sun, moon, stars, and all the plants and animals? *God knows how to do everything. There is nothing God does not know.*

4. Why did God make so many different kinds of plants and animals? Why did He make so many lovely colors, smells, and tastes? *God made so many different kinds of plants and animals because He wanted us to have an interesting, exciting, and beautiful place to live.*

5. What did God put in the sky on the fourth day so that we could keep track of days, months, and years? *God put the sun, moon, and stars up in the sky.*

6. Can you hide from God? *No, you could never hide from God because God is everywhere all of the time.*

7. Was there anything wrong with any part of the world God made? *No, everything God made was perfect because God is perfect.*

Biblical Worldviews

- God is the Creator of everything.
- God can do anything; nothing is too hard for Him.
- God knows everything.
- God is everywhere all the time.
- God is perfect.
- God is a God of order.
- God is a God of love.

Activity: Creation Story Board

Supplies:

- "Days of Creation" printouts, one per student (see appendix page 575)
- Crayons, markers or colored pencils
- Old magazine pictures or stickers (optional)
- Construction paper (optional)
- Glue or tape (optional)

Instructions:

- Students draw, color, and/or use stickers and magazine cutouts to illustrate in each box what happened on each day of creation.
- Optional: Once the student has finished coloring and designing each box, he may cut out the boxes and glue or tape them in the correct order onto the construction paper, or staple them together to make a mini-booklet.

Extra Bible References

Deuteronomy 32:4; 2 Samuel 22:31; Psalms 29:3-9, 99:3-5, 104:19-23, 119:68; Isaiah 40:25-26; Jeremiah 32:27; Romans 1:20, 25

5
Mission Completed
Creation of Man

Memory Verse

Ah, Lord GOD! Behold, You have made the heavens and the earth by Your great power and outstretched arm. There is nothing too hard for You. Jeremiah 32:17

Lesson

God made the world and everything in it especially for people.

For thus says the LORD, who created the heavens, who is God, who formed the earth and made it…who formed it to be inhabited: "I am the LORD, and there is no other." Isaiah 45:18

Finally, when everything was ready, God made a man.

And the LORD God formed man of the dust of the ground, and breathed into his nostrils the breath of life; and man became a living being. Genesis 2:7

When God made the sun, the moon, the stars, and all the plants and animals, He simply spoke and they appeared. But when God made the first human being, He took some dirt and carefully shaped a body.

Have you ever shaped animals or people out of clay? When you finished, did the animal or person you made start walking around or talking? Of course not! It was not alive.

But God can do something no one else can do. The Bible says God breathed into the man's nostrils and "the man became a living being." God can give life.

When God breathed into the man, He gave the man a soul and a spirit. This soul and spirit was what made the man a living human being.

Every living person has a soul and a spirit. Even though your soul and spirit are invisible, they are the real you. Your body is simply the house where your soul and spirit live. Your soul and spirit give life to your body. If your soul and spirit were to leave your body, your body would die.

As you can see, God made man different from the animals.

> Then God said, "Let Us make man in Our image, according to Our likeness...So God created man in His own image; in the image of God He created him... Genesis 1:26a, 27a

> To whom was God speaking when He said, "Let Us make man in Our image"?
>
> Remember how there is only one God who exists as three persons? It was these three: God the Father, God the Son, and God the Holy Spirit who decided together to make mankind in their image, or likeness.

The Bible says God made people "in the image of God." God made the invisible part of us – our soul and spirit – to be like Him. Just like God has a mind, feelings, and the ability to make decisions, He wanted you and me to have a mind, feelings, and the ability to make decisions.

God gave us a mind so we could think and learn. God wanted to be able to communicate with us. He wanted us to be able to read and understand His letter, the Bible. God wanted us to be able to get to know Him. That is why God gave us a mind.

> But let him who glories glory in this, that he understands and knows Me, that I am the Lord... Jeremiah 9:24a

Of course, no person is as intelligent as God, but God did make us smarter than the animals.

God also gave us feelings. Did you know God has feelings? God loves. He gets happy and sad. God wanted us to be able to express feelings the way He does. He wanted us to be able to love and adore Him.

> The Lord has appeared of old to me, saying: "Yes, I have loved you with an everlasting love; therefore with lovingkindness I have drawn you." Jeremiah 31:3

Another way God made people like Himself is that He gave us the ability to make decisions. God made decisions when He created the world. He decided what color to make bananas and how long to make the giraffe's neck.

God could have made us robots that would do only what He programmed us to do. But He wanted us to love Him from our hearts because we wanted to love Him. He did not want us to worship Him simply because we were programmed to do so.

God is Spirit, and those who worship Him must worship in spirit and truth. John 4:24

Finally, God's creation was done. In six days God had transformed the formless, dark emptiness into a beautiful, bright world full of all types of plants and animals. Only God could create such an incredible world. And to think, He did it all for us.

Then God saw everything that He had made, and indeed it was very good. So the evening and the morning were the sixth day.

Thus the heavens and the earth, and all the host of them, were finished. Genesis 1:31-2:1

God always finishes whatever He starts. You and I sometimes start something and then change our minds. Have you ever started to play a game and then gotten tired of it before you were done? Or maybe you started to paint a picture and then set it aside because you did not like the way it was turning out. God is not like that. If God starts a project, He always completes it.

In six days God created the whole world and everything in it. So what do you think He did on the seventh day? The Bible says that on the seventh day God rested.

And on the seventh day God ended His work which He had done, and He rested on the seventh day from all His work which He had done.

Then God blessed the seventh day and sanctified it, because in it He rested from all His work which God had created and made. Genesis 2:2-3

| Sanctify – to set apart |

Do you think God rested on the seventh day because He was worn out from making the world? After all, it could not have been easy putting the planets up in the sky or making so many different kinds of plants, fish, birds, and animals.

No, God was not tired. God never gets tired.

Have you not known? Have you not heard? The everlasting God, the LORD, The Creator of the ends of the earth, neither faints nor is weary. Isaiah 40:28a

God did not rest on the seventh day because He was worn out. He rested because He was done with everything He had planned to do. God finished His work, so He took a break.

The Bible says God "blessed the seventh day and sanctified it." God set the seventh day of every week apart as a special day for remembering that He is the Creator of the world.

The whole world belongs to God because He is the Creator. Since God is the owner of the world, He is the One in charge. God is the highest authority; He is over all the governments of the world.

Questions

1. For whom did God make the world and everything in it? *God made the world for people.*

2. Name some ways God made people to be like Him? *God gave us a mind so we could get to know Him, He gave us feelings so we could love Him, and He gave us the ability to make choices.*

3. Who is the only One who can give life? *God is the only One who can give life.*

4. When God starts to do something, does He always finish it? *Yes, God always finishes every project He starts.*

5. Does God sometimes mess up on a project? *No, God is perfect. Everything He does is good and perfect in every way.*

6. Was God exhausted when He finished creating the world and everything in it? *No, God does not get tired or weary.*

7. What was so special about the seventh day of the week? *It was the day God rested after He finished creating the world. God set the seventh day apart as a holiday for people to remember that He is the Creator.*

8. Why is God the One in charge of the world? *God is in charge of the world because He made it. Everything and everyone belong to Him.*

Biblical Worldviews

- God is the Creator of the world and all people.
- Since God is the Creator, He is the owner and the One in charge.
- God always finishes whatever He starts.
- God is the One who gives life to all people.

- God made people in His likeness; He made people to be more intelligent than the animals.
- God is a personal being; He wants to have a relationship with us.
- There is only one God who exists as God the Father, God the Son, and God the Holy Spirit.
- God is a God of love.
- God is perfect.
- God can do anything; nothing is too hard for Him.

Activity 1: Clay Person

Supplies:

- Clay or play dough

Instructions:

- Each student shapes a person out of clay.
- Have a discussion time. Ask students if they could make the person they formed come alive. Talk about how God breathed life into the first man. Talk about how God made the man in His image.

Activity 2: Drawing of Person

Supplies:

- Pencil
- Paper, one sheet per student
- Crayons

Instructions:

- Each student draws a person, attempting to make the person look as life-like as possible.
- Students color their pictures.
- Students write Genesis 2:7 above, or underneath, the picture.
- Have a discussion time. Ask students if they could make the person they drew come alive. Talk about how God breathed life into the first man. Talk about how God made the man in His image.

Extra Bible References

Deuteronomy 30:19-20; 1 Chronicles 29:11-12; Nehemiah 9:6; Job 12:10, 33:4; Psalms 18:30, 24:1-2, 33:11, 97:9, 100:3, 115:3, 119:73, 135:5-6, 139:13-17, 145:3-7; Proverbs 6:16; Isaiah 42:5, 44:24, 45:18; Jeremiah 9:23-24; Zephaniah 3:17; Matthew 23:37; Luke 19:41; John 3:16, 4:23-24; Acts 17:24-25, 28; 1 Corinthians 10:26; Philippians 3:10; 1 John 4:7–10

6
Special Helpers
Creation of Angels

Memory Verse

For by Him all things were created that are in heaven and that are on earth, visible and invisible... All things were created through Him and for Him. Colossians 1:16

Lesson

Did you know that while God was creating the earth there were angels cheering Him on?

"Where were you when I laid the foundations of the earth? ...

When the morning stars sang together...?" Job 38:4a, 7a

In this verse God calls the angels morning stars. The Bible says that when God started making the earth, the angels sang together.

Where did these angels come from? The Bible says God created the angels before He made the earth.

For by Him all things were created that are in heaven and that are on earth, visible and invisible...All things were created through Him and for Him. Colossians 1:16

God made the angels to be His helpers. He wanted them to go wherever He sent them and do whatever He asked them to do.

Bless the LORD, you His angels, who excel in strength, who do His word, heeding the voice of His word. Psalm 103:20

Was it wrong for God to decide what the angels should do? No, since God created the angels, He could choose how He wanted to use them.

It's kind of like when you color a picture. If you color it, it's yours, right? You can do whatever you want with it. You can give it away, or you can keep it for yourself. That is how it was with God and the angels. Since God made the angels, He could use them in any way He decided.

God is the Creator of everything in the world. He is the One who gives life to every living creature. Since everything that exists is made by God, God owns it all. He is the greatest.

The earth is the Lord's, and all its fullness, the world and those who dwell therein. For He has founded it upon the seas, and established it upon the waters. Psalm 24:1-2

But even though it was right for God to tell the angels what to do, He did not force them to do what He wanted. God let the angels decide whether or not they would do what He said.

How would you like it if you had a friend who always did whatever you wanted? You would think she really liked you. But what if you found out she was only being kind because her parents told her she had to be nice to you? Would you like that? Wouldn't you rather have a friend who decided on her own to be your friend?

In the same way, God wanted each angel to make his own decision about whether or not he would follow God. God wanted the angels to obey Him because they wanted to, not because He made them obey Him.

The Bible says that angels are spirits. That means angels are invisible to people on Earth. Just like we can't see God, we can't see angels either, because angels do not have bodies made of skin and bones like we do.

Since angels do not have bodies like we do, it's easy for them to move about. Angels do not need to go through a door in order to get into a room; they just go right through the wall! They don't have to walk, or ride in a car, or fly in an airplane to get to their destination. In the blink of an eye they simply appear wherever they want to go.

Are they not all ministering spirits…? Hebrews 1:14a

But even though angels are spirits, they are not everywhere at once like God is. Angels can only be in one place at a time.

God made the angels to be strong and smart. Angels are stronger and smarter than people, but they are weaker and less intelligent than God.

Bless the LORD, you His angels, who excel in strength, who do His word… Psalm 103:20a

What is man that You are mindful of him...For You have made him a little lower than the angels... Psalm 8:4-5a

Since God is completely good and perfect in every way, the angels He created were perfect, too. There was nothing wrong with any of them.

You might mess up on a project or make a bad grade on a test. You mess up because you are not perfect. But God is perfect; He never messes up on anything. Everything about the angels was good and right.

He is the Rock, His work is perfect... Deuteronomy 32:4a

When God created the angels, He made so many you could never count them all.

But you have come to...the city of the living God...to an innumerable company of angels... Hebrews 12:22

Can you imagine how powerful God is to be able to make that many angels? Nothing is too hard for God.

The Bible says when God first made the angels they lived with Him in Heaven.

...but are like angels of God in heaven. Matthew 22:30b

Even though God is everywhere all the time, Heaven is God's home.

Look down from Your holy habitation, from heaven... Deuteronomy 26:15a

Heaven is a wonderful and beautiful place; there is no sickness, no suffering, and no sadness. There is only love and kindness. Everything in Heaven is good.

God made the angels to be His special helpers. The angels were perfect and lived with God in His perfect home. Everything was wonderful!

Questions

1. Is God greater than the angels? *Yes, God is greater than the angels because He is the One who made them and gave them life.*

2. When God made the angels, what did He want the angels to do? *He wanted angels to be His workers; He wanted them to do whatever He said.*

3. Why was it okay for God to tell the angels what to do? *Since God created the angels, they belonged to Him and He had the right to tell them what to do.*

4. Did God force the angels to follow Him? *No, He gave them a choice.*

5. Do angels have bodies like you and I do? *No, angels are spirits.*

6. Can angels be everywhere at the same time? *No, they can only be in one place at a time.*

7. Are angels strong and smart? *Yes, angels are very strong and very smart. The Bible says that angels are both stronger and smarter than people, but they are not as smart and strong as God.*

8. When God first made the angels, was there any part of them that was bad? *No, God made the angels perfect in every way.*

9. How could God make so many angels? *God can do anything; nothing is too hard for Him.*

10. Where did the angels live when God first made them? *They lived with God in Heaven.*

Biblical Worldviews

- God made the angels to be His special helpers.
- Angels are powerful and smart, but not as powerful or smart as God.
- Angels are spirits.
- When God first created the angels they were perfect in every way.
- God can do anything; nothing is too hard for Him.
- Since God is the Creator, He is the One in charge.
- God is perfect.

Activity: Angel Worksheet

Supplies:

- "Angel" printouts, one per student (see appendix page 576)
- Pencil or colored marker
- Crayons
- Glitter and glue (optional)

Instructions:

- Students complete "Angel" worksheet. Fill in blanks to say: God made angels to be His helpers.
- Decorate in any way desired.

Extra Bible References

Genesis 2:1; Deuteronomy 32:4; 2 Samuel 22:31; 1 Chronicles 29:11-12; Nehemiah 9:6; Psalms 91:11, 103:20-22, 148:2; Isaiah 45:12; Matthew 25:31; Mark 13:27; John 1:3; Acts 17:24; Colossians 2:18; 2 Thessalonians 1:7; Hebrews 1: 6-7, 14; 1 Peter 3:22; 2 Peter 2:10-11; Revelation 4:11, 10:6, 22:8-9

7
The Rebel Angel
Lucifer's Rebellion

Memory Verse

A haughty look, a proud heart...are sin. Proverbs 21:4

Lesson

All the angels in Heaven were wonderful, but there was one angel who was especially beautiful and intelligent. His name was Lucifer. The name Lucifer means shining star.

The Bible says that Lucifer was a cherub. A cherub is a type of angel. In the Bible we read that cherubim did the work of guarding and protecting.

But even though God made Lucifer perfect in every way, something terrible happened.

Thus says the Lord GOD: "You were the seal of perfection, full of wisdom and perfect in beauty...You were the anointed cherub who covers; I established you; you were on the holy mountain of God...you were perfect in your ways from the day you were created, till iniquity was found in you...you became filled with violence within, and you sinned; ...your heart was lifted up because of your beauty; you corrupted your wisdom for the sake of your splendor..."
Ezekiel 28:12b—17a

Lucifer started thinking he really was beautiful. Instead of being thankful to God, Lucifer decided he did not need God. He thought he could be great and important without God. This kind of thinking is called being proud.

In the Bible, God says being proud is wrong.

A haughty look, a proud heart...are sin. Proverbs 21:4

Remember how God let the angels choose whether or not they would do what He wanted? When Lucifer became proud, he chose not to obey God anymore.

...you have said in your heart: "I will ascend into heaven, I will exalt my throne above the stars of God; I will also sit on the mount of the congregation on the farthest sides of the north; I will ascend above the heights of the clouds, I will be like the Most High."
Isaiah 14:13-14

Can you count how many times Lucifer said, "I will," in the verses above? He said it five times! Lucifer decided to do what he wanted rather than what God wanted him to do. Lucifer decided he wanted to "be like the Most High." Lucifer wanted to be the one in charge. Many angels followed Lucifer in this rebellion.

> **Rebellion - to go against the one in charge**

But God would not allow Lucifer to take His place.

...are You not God in heaven, and do You not rule over all the kingdoms of the nations, and in Your hand is there not power and might, so that no one is able to withstand You? 2 Chronicles 20:6b

Even though many angels joined Lucifer, they could not overthrow God. Since God created the angels, He is much more powerful than they are. Even if all the angels joined together, they would not be stronger than God.

Everyone proud in heart is an abomination to the LORD; though they join forces, none will go unpunished. Proverbs 16:5

> **Abomination – horrible or sickening**

God is perfect; He is completely good. Anything sinful or bad is sickening to Him. God could not allow the proud and rebellious angels to stay in Heaven, so He threw them out.

How you are fallen from heaven, O Lucifer, son of the morning! Isaiah 14:12a

When God threw Lucifer out of Heaven, Lucifer's name changed to Satan. The angels who followed Lucifer came to be known as demons. Now Satan and his demons live in the air above the earth. To this day, they continue fighting against God.

And He said to them, "I saw Satan fall like lightning from heaven." Luke 10:18

The name Satan means enemy. When Lucifer rebelled against God, he became God's enemy. That is why God changed his name to Satan.

Another name for Satan is the devil. The name devil means accuser. One of the ways Satan tries to hurt people is by accusing them. That means Satan reminds people of all the bad things they have done to make them feel miserable and hopeless.

> ...your adversary the devil walks about like a roaring lion, seeking whom he may devour. 1 Peter 5:8b

Adversary - enemy

Our enemy, the accuser, wanders about the earth looking for someone he can trick and destroy.

But God will not let Satan and his demons go on doing their evil work forever. When God threw Satan and his demons out of Heaven, He made a special place just for them:

> ...the everlasting fire prepared for the devil and his angels...
> Matthew 25:41b

Someday God is going to throw Satan and his followers into this everlasting fire, known as the Lake of Fire.

> The devil, who deceived them, was cast into the lake of fire and brimstone...And...will be tormented day and night forever and ever.
> Revelation 20:10

Satan and his demons will not escape from this terrible place of suffering. When God throws them into the Lake of Fire, they will be there forever, locked up in torment. Never will they be able to hurt people again.

Questions

1. What does the name Lucifer mean? *It means shining star.*

2. Who made Lucifer beautiful and wise? *God did.*

3. Was there anything bad about Lucifer when God created him? *No, He was perfect in every way.*

4. What wrong thoughts did Lucifer begin to have? *He started getting proud about how beautiful he was. He started thinking he was great, and he wanted to take God's place.*

5. Could Lucifer and all his followers overthrow God? *No, God is more powerful than all the angels put together. He is the highest ruler.*

6. Can anyone who is evil live with God in Heaven? *No, God is perfect. Sin is sickening to God; He cannot allow anything bad or sinful to live with Him in Heaven.*

7. What does the name Satan mean? *It means enemy.*

8. What does the name devil mean? *It means accuser.*

9. What are Satan and his demons doing right now? *They are roaming around the earth looking for someone to hurt and destroy.*

10. What will happen to Satan and his demons someday? *God is going to throw them into the Lake of Fire where they will suffer forever and ever.*

Biblical Worldviews

- Satan is a created being.
- Since God is the Creator, He is the highest authority and the One in charge. No one is greater than God.
- God is stronger than Satan and all his demons put together; Satan can never win against God.
- God can do anything; nothing is too hard for Him.
- God is perfect; He will not allow anything sinful into Heaven.
- God created a place of eternal suffering for Satan and his angels.

Activity: Bible Bingo

Supplies:
- Bingo cards and game tokens (Any set will do. You can buy an inexpensive set at the dollar store.)

Instructions:
- Give each student a bingo card and some tokens.
- Ask a question from the lesson review and call on a student to answer it. If the student answers it correctly, she calls the bingo square she wants to cover. Everyone else who has that square covers it as well.
- Continue to ask questions, calling on a different student each time. Allow everyone to answer at least one question and pick at least one bingo square.
- The game is over when the first student shouts BINGO because she has covered a complete row with tokens, either vertically, horizontally, or diagonally.
- Play the game several times until everyone has had a turn answering a question and/or all the questions from the review have been asked and answered.

Extra Bible References

Deuteronomy 32:17, 39; 1 Chronicles 29:11, 12; 2 Chronicles 20:6; Job 1:7;
Psalms 24:3-5, 8; 33:11; 97:9; Proverbs 16:5; Jeremiah 10:6; Ezekiel 28:11-19;
Daniel 4:35, 37; Habakkuk 1:13; Matthew 5:48, 25:41; Luke 4:8, 13, 36; 8:12, 30; 9:1;
Matthew 10:18, 22:31; Acts 5:3, 13:10; 1 Corinthians 4:7; 2 Corinthians 4:4;
Ephesians 6:12; 2 Timothy 2:26; Revelation 12:4; 20:1-3, 7-10

8
The First Parents
Adam and Eve Part I

Memory Verse

The earth is the Lord's, and all its fullness, the world and those who dwell therein.
Psalm 24:1

Lesson

Remember the man God made on the last day of creation? God named this man Adam. God made a special home for Adam. It was called the Garden of Eden. This was the most wonderful garden imaginable. All kinds of friendly animals wandered among the trees and flowers. There was a river running through the garden, and fruit trees of every sort grew everywhere.

The LORD God planted a garden eastward in Eden, and there He put the man whom He had formed.

And out of the ground the LORD God made every tree grow that is pleasant to the sight and good for food....

Now a river went out of Eden to water the garden...

the LORD God took the man and put him in the garden of Eden to tend and keep it. Genesis 2:8-9a, 10a, 15

God did not ask Adam where he wanted to live or what kind of work he wanted to do. God simply put Adam in the Garden of Eden and made him to be the caretaker.

Was it okay for God to make these decisions for Adam? Yes, it was. Just like God had the right to decide what the angels would do, it was perfectly okay for God to decide where Adam would live and what his work would be. After all, God was the One who created Adam. Adam belonged to God in the same way the angels belonged to Him.

But although God could do with Adam whatever He wanted, God loved Adam and always did what was best for him. Since God created Adam, He knew what Adam needed.

Adam was pleased with everything God did for him; he loved his home and enjoyed taking care of the garden.

But God knew there was one more thing Adam needed.

And the LORD God said, "It is not good that man should be alone; I will make him a helper comparable to him." Genesis 2:18

God knew Adam needed a partner, so He gave Adam a second job to do.

Now the Lord God had formed out of the ground all the beasts of the field and all the birds of the air. He brought them to the man to see what he would name them; and whatever the man called each living creature, that was its name.

So the man gave names to all the livestock, the birds of the air and all the beasts of the field. But for Adam no suitable helper was found. Genesis 2:19-20

Adam's job was to give names to all the birds and animals. This was a huge task, but when God made Adam, He made him incredibly intelligent. One by one, as God brought them to him, Adam gave each bird and animal its own special name.

As Adam worked, he noticed something - every animal had a partner. For every male animal there was a female of the same kind. This made Adam want a partner too.

But only God could provide a partner for Adam. God made Adam fall into a deep sleep.

And the LORD God caused a deep sleep to fall on Adam, and he slept; and He took one of his ribs, and closed up the flesh in its place. Then the rib which the LORD God had taken from man He made into a woman, and He brought her to the man.

And Adam said: "This is now bone of my bones and flesh of my flesh; she shall be called Woman, because she was taken out of Man." Genesis 2:21-23

While Adam slept, God took out one of his ribs. From this rib, God made a partner for Adam. Only God could do that! God is the only One who can create a living person.

Not only did God decide where Adam would live and what kind of work he would do, God decided who Adam's partner would be. The partner God gave Adam was perfect. Adam named her Eve.

...Adam called his wife's name Eve... Genesis 3:20

Adam loved Eve very much. After all, Eve came from his body and was made in God's likeness just like he was. She had an intelligent mind, she had emotions, and she could make decisions. Eve was the partner and friend Adam needed.

The Bible says that Adam and Eve did not wear any clothes.

And they were both naked, the man and his wife, and were not ashamed. Genesis 2:25

Since Adam and Eve did not know anything bad, being naked did not embarrass them.

God talked to Adam and Eve and told them what He had planned for them.

Then God blessed them, and God said to them, "Be fruitful and multiply; fill the earth and subdue it; have dominion over the fish of the sea, over the birds of the air, and over every living thing that moves on the earth." Genesis 1:28

God made the earth especially for people. He wanted Adam and Eve to have lots of children so there would be people everywhere. God put Adam and Eve and their children in charge of the earth and everything on it.

Since the earth belongs to God, He could do with it whatever He wanted.

The earth is the LORD's, and all its fullness, the world and those who dwell therein. Psalm 24:1

Adam and Eve lived a long time and had a lot of children, just like God wanted.

...the days of Adam were eight hundred years; and he had sons and daughters. Genesis 5:4b

This is what the Bible says:

...Adam called his wife's name Eve, because she was the mother of all living. Genesis 3:20

61

All people on Earth, including you and me, come from Adam and Eve.

Remember

God wanted Adam and Eve to have a family. He wanted Adam and Eve's children to have families too. It was God's plan for a man and a woman to get married and have children.

Since God made the earth especially for people, He wanted people to live everywhere on the earth. God put people in charge of the earth. He made plants, animals, and natural resources for our use and enjoyment. God wants us to take good care of everything He made for us.

Questions

1. Was it right for God to put Adam in the garden and give him a job without asking him first? *Yes, God could do whatever He wanted with Adam. God was the One who made Adam and gave him life; Adam belonged to God.*

2. Did God know what Adam needed? *Yes, God formed Adam and knew all about him. God knew what Adam needed even better than Adam did.*

3. Who was the only One who could provide a wife for Adam? *Only God could provide a wife for Adam because only God can make a living being. God is the only Life-Giver.*

4. Was anything wrong with the things God provided for Adam? *No, everything God gave Adam was good and perfect in every way. The garden was a wonderful place to live. Adam liked his work, and he loved his wife.*

5. Why were Adam and Eve not embarrassed when they were naked? *They were not embarrassed because they didn't have any bad thoughts.*

6. Why did God make both a man and a woman? *God wanted there to be families on the earth. He wanted a man to marry a woman; He wanted them to have children.*

7. What was God's plan for Adam and Eve and their children? *He wanted them to fill the earth and rule over it.*

8. Did God tell Adam and Eve what He wanted them to do, or did God just leave them to guess about what He wanted? *God communicated with them. He told them what His plans were for them.*

9. Who do all people in the world come from? *Everyone comes from Adam and Eve.*

Biblical Worldviews

- God is the only Life-Giver.
- People are helpless; they need God.
- God is a God of love; He cares about people.
- God can do anything; nothing is too hard for Him.

- God had a plan for people.
- God made the earth and everything on it for people to use and enjoy.
- God is perfect.
- God is a personal being; He communicates with people.
- Since God is the Creator, He is the One in charge.

Activity: Bible Hangman

Supplies:

- Chalkboard or dry erase board
- Chalk or dry erase markers

Instructions:

- Draw a large hangman tree on the board.
- Draw lines and spaces under the tree to correspond to the letters and spaces of the key phrase.

Example:

— — —   — — — — — — —   — — — —
— — —   — — — — —   — — —   — — — — —
— — — —   — —   — — — —   — — —
— — — —   — — —   — — — —   — — — —
— —.

- **Key phrase**: God created Adam and Eve and wanted them to fill the earth and rule over it.
- **Optional key phrase for younger students**: God created Adam and Eve.
- Ask the lesson review questions, one at a time. Call on one student or one team to answer each question.
- If answer is correct, the student or team gets to pick a letter, i.e., the letter b.
- If the letter picked is in the key phrase, the teacher fills it in on the board each time it occurs.
- If the letter picked is not in the key phrase, the teacher draws one part of a stick figure on the hangman tree, i.e., a head, an arm, a stick body, etc.
- When a student (or team) thinks he knows the key phrase, he may try to solve the puzzle on his turn. The game is over when a student or team solves the puzzle or the teacher draws all the parts of the stick man, whichever comes first.

Extra Bible References

Genesis 2:24; 1 Chronicles 29:11-12; Nehemiah 9:6; Psalms 8:6-8, 24:1-2, 95:6, 100:3; Psalm 119:73; Isaiah 42:5; 45:9, 12; Jeremiah 27:5; 32:27; Zechariah 12:1; Acts 17:26; 1 Corinthians 10:26; Matthew 6:8; Philippians 4:19; Hebrews 2:5-7; James 1:17

9
Separated
Adam and Eve Part II

Memory Verse

The earth is the Lord's, and all its fullness, the world and those who dwell therein.
Psalm 24:1

Lesson

In the middle of the garden where Adam and Eve lived, God put two special fruit trees. One of these trees was The Tree of Life. The other was The Tree of the Knowledge of Good and Evil.

The Tree of Life was also in the midst of the garden, and The Tree of the Knowledge of Good and Evil...

And the LORD God commanded the man, saying, "Of every tree of the garden you may freely eat; but of The Tree of the Knowledge of Good and Evil you shall not eat, for in the day that you eat of it you shall surely die." Genesis 2:9b, 16-17

God wanted Adam and Eve to eat from The Tree of Life; eating from The Tree of Life would cause Adam and Eve to live forever. God wanted Adam and Eve to live.

But God did not want Adam and Eve to eat from The Tree of the Knowledge of Good and Evil. God told Adam that if they ate from this tree they would certainly die.

This did not mean Adam and Eve would immediately fall over dead if they ate from The Tree of the Knowledge of Good and Evil, but it did mean they would immediately become separated from God. To become separated from God is to die spiritually.

If Adam and Eve became separated from their Creator and the One who had given them life, their bodies would slowly start to get old. Then one day they would die. When they died, their soul and spirit would go to the terrible place of suffering where they would remain separated from God forever and ever. This is what would happen to Adam and Eve if they ate from The Tree of the Knowledge of Good and Evil.

Why did God put one forbidden tree in the garden? Why was there one tree from which Adam and Eve were not allowed to eat? It was because God wanted Adam and Eve to have a choice. He wanted them to be able to decide if they would believe Him or not. If Adam and Eve believed God, they would do what He said. If they disbelieved God, they would eat.

God's enemy Satan saw this as his chance to destroy Adam and Eve; he came up with a plan to get Adam and Eve to go against what God said. Satan wanted Adam and Eve to die.

Now the serpent was more cunning than any beast of the field which the LORD God had made. And he said to the woman, "Has God indeed said, 'You shall not eat of every tree of the garden'?"
Genesis 3:1

Satan decided to hide inside one of the smartest animals of all - the snake; when the snake started talking to her, Eve did not seem surprised.

Satan made it sound like God was being unfair by not letting them eat from *all* the trees!

And the woman said to the serpent, "We may eat the fruit of the trees of the garden; but of the fruit of the tree which is in the midst of the garden, God has said, 'You shall not eat it, nor shall you touch it, lest you die.'" Genesis 3:2-3

God had not said Adam and Eve would die if they *touched* the fruit; He said they would die if they ate the fruit.

Then the serpent said to the woman, "You will not surely die. For God knows that in the day you eat of it your eyes will be opened, and you will be like God, knowing good and evil." Genesis 3:4-5

Satan told Eve God was lying. He said it was not true that they would die if they ate from The Tree of the Knowledge of Good and Evil. He said that if they ate the fruit from that tree their eyes would be opened and they would find out things only God knows.

Eve started thinking that maybe Satan was right. "God must be keeping something good from us," she thought.

So when the woman saw that the tree was good for food, that it was pleasant to the eyes, and a tree desirable to make one wise, she

took of its fruit and ate. She also gave to her husband with her, and
he ate. Genesis 3:6

Eve looked at the tree. The fruit looked delicious and she would love to be as smart as God! The more she thought about it, the better it looked. Finally, Eve took a fruit from the tree and bit into it. She gave some to Adam too.

Satan did not make Adam and Eve rebel against God. They had a choice. They should have believed God, but instead they chose to believe Satan.

Then the eyes of both of them were opened, and they knew that they were naked; and they sewed fig leaves together and made themselves coverings.

And they heard the sound of the LORD God walking in the garden in the cool of the day, and Adam and his wife hid themselves from the presence of the LORD God among the trees of the garden. Genesis 3:7-8

As soon as Adam and Eve ate the fruit, their eyes were opened and they realized they were naked. Suddenly, they were embarrassed. But this time, instead of depending on God to solve their problems, Adam and Eve tried fixing things on their own. They tried to cover their nakedness by making clothes out of leaves.

That afternoon when God came to visit, Adam and Eve hid from Him. What happened? Why were Adam and Eve suddenly afraid of God?

Adam and Eve hid from God because they had died just like God said they would. They had become separated from God. Adam and Eve's relationship with God had ended.

Adam and Eve should have believed God. After all, God was the One who had given them life and every good thing they could ever want. God was their friend. Had He not put them in a beautiful garden filled with fruit trees and flowers and animals of every kind? Their loving Creator would not lie to them!

But sadly, Adam and Eve believed Satan instead of God. When they did, they joined Satan's side, and Satan began to tell them what to do. Because Adam and Eve were now on Satan's side, and because they were dead to God, Adam and Eve were no longer able to please God.

What a sad story! Was there any hope Adam and Eve's friendship with God could be restored? Or had Satan won his battle against God by gaining control over God's people?

Remember

Satan is a liar and a murderer.

...the devil...was a murderer from the beginning, and does not stand in the truth, because there is no truth in him. When he speaks a lie, he speaks from his own resources, for he is a liar and the father of it. John 8:44

Just like Satan tricked Eve, he tries to trick you so that you will not believe God. Satan uses whatever tactic he thinks will work on you. He may use magazines, textbooks, teachers at school, T.V. shows, or even friends and family.

If you are not sure about what God says in the Bible, you will easily believe Satan's lies. That is why you need to know what God says.

Remember, God made you and He loves you. God always tells the truth. God wants to save you from death; He wants you to live with Him forever. If you hear or read anything that disagrees with what God says in the Bible, you can be sure it comes from Satan. Satan wants to destroy you; he wants you to be separated from God forever in the terrible place of suffering.

Questions

1. What two special trees did God put in the middle of the garden? *God put The Tree of Life and The Tree of the Knowledge of Good and Evil in the middle of the garden.*

2. Of all the trees in the garden, from which one tree did God tell Adam and Eve not to eat? *The only tree from which God told Adam and Eve not to eat was The Tree of the Knowledge of Good and Evil.*

3. Why did God put one forbidden tree in the garden? *God put just one not-allowed tree in the garden to give Adam and Eve a choice of whether they would believe Him or not. If Adam and Eve believed God, they would do as He said. If they did not believe Him, they would eat from the tree.*

4. What did God say would happen to Adam and Eve if they ate from The Tree of the Knowledge of Good and Evil? *God said they would die. If Adam and Eve ate from The Tree of the Knowledge of Good and Evil, they would become separated from God. To be separated from God meant they would die spiritually; it meant their relationship with God would end.*

5. If Adam and Eve became separated from God, what would happen to their bodies? *Their bodies would get old and die.*

6. What would happen to Adam and Eve's soul and spirit (their real selves) when their bodies died? *Their real selves – their soul and spirit – would go to the terrible place of suffering where they would be separated from God forever.*

7. What did Satan say would happen to Adam and Eve if they ate from The Tree of the Knowledge of Good and Evil? *Satan said Adam and Eve would not die. Satan said that if Adam and Eve ate from The Tree of the Knowledge of Good and Evil their eyes would be opened and they would be like God.*

8. Who was telling the truth, God or Satan? *God was. God told Adam and Eve the truth because He loved them and did not want them to die. Satan lied to them because he wanted them to eat the fruit and die.*

9. When Adam and Eve believed Satan instead of God, whose side did they join? *They joined Satan's side.*

10. After Adam and Eve became separated from God, could they do anything to please God? *No, when Adam and Eve became separated from God, they were no longer able to please God.*

11. How can you keep from being tricked by Satan? *You can keep from being tricked by Satan's lies if you know and believe what God says in the Bible. God is the One who loves you and tells you the truth.*

Biblical Worldviews

- God gives people a choice about who they will believe.
- Satan fights against God. He is a liar. He hates people.
- God is a God of love.
- God is a personal being; He communicates with people.
- God tells the truth.
- God says the penalty for sin is death.
- There is a place of eternal suffering.

Activity: Adam and Eve Skit

Supplies:
- Four student volunteers

Instructions:
- Optional: a large potted tree and a fake snake for props.
- Students act out the scene from the garden with Adam and Eve and the serpent. You may use the attached script or let students make up their own script. There are four parts: the narrator, Adam, Eve, and the voice of the serpent.
- Discuss skit, emphasizing key points from the lesson.

Adam and Eve Skit (by Nancy Hughes)

Narrator #1: Despite everything God had done for Adam and Eve, they were not satisfied. Let's travel back in time and see for ourselves the sad events that unfolded that day long ago in the Garden of Eden.

Serpent: Eve, oh Eve, my dear friend Eve. There you are. I've been looking all over the place for you. Did God really tell you that you can't eat from all the trees in the garden? Oh, my poor Eve. How sad, how very sad! That's terrible, just terrible.

Eve: Oh, we can eat fruit from all the trees in the garden except from this one tree right here. God said if we eat from it we will die.

Serpent: Oh, Eve, my dear Eve. You've got to be kidding. Interesting… very interesting. Did God really tell you that you're going to die? Ha – God doesn't want you to eat it because He knows that when you do, your eyes will be opened. Yes, when you eat it, Eve, then you will be like God.

(Eve looks at the fruit, pondering what the serpent said.)

Serpent: Just look at this tree, Eve. It has great fruit on it. It tastes soooo good, better than anything you've ever tasted or experienced before. Look, just look how beautiful it is. Beautiful, just like you, my dear Eve. And remember, once you eat it you will be soooo wise, not like the uh…. dummy you are now.

Eve: What if he's right? Just think of everything I might be missing out on. Maybe God doesn't have my best interest in mind after all. Maybe I would be wise, even wiser than God. Maybe my new friend here is right.

Eve: Oh Adam, Adam, come here. (Adam joins her.) Look. (She bites into apple.) Take some. (She gives to Adam.) Eat. (Adam eats too.)

Narrator #1: So we see that on a day in history many thousands of years ago, Adam and Eve chose to trust Satan rather than God. And when they did, their choice ruined everything!

Extra Bible References

> Numbers 22:28; Ezekiel 18:20; Psalms 19:7-11; 33:4; 119:142, 151, 160; Isaiah 59:2; Zechariah 3:1; Mark 4:15, 7:21-23; Acts 5:3, 26:18; Romans 6:23, 8:6-8; 2 Corinthians 1:20, 2:11, 4:4, 11:13-14; Ephesians 2:1-2; 2 Thessalonians 1:8-9; 2 Thessalonians 2:9; Titus 1:2; 1 John 5:19, 3:8

10
Consequences
Adam and Eve Part III

Memory Verse

Therefore, just as through one man sin entered the world, and death through sin, and thus death spread to all men, because all sinned— Romans 5:12

Lesson

Even though Adam and Eve hid from God, God saw them. He knew where Adam and Eve were, and He knew what they had done. God called to Adam to see what he would say.

Then the LORD God called to Adam and said to him, "Where are you?" So he said, "I heard Your voice in the garden, and I was afraid because I was naked; and I hid myself."

And He said, "Who told you that you were naked? Have you eaten from the tree of which I commanded you that you should not eat?"

Then the man said, "The woman whom You gave to be with me, she gave me of the tree, and I ate."

And the LORD God said to the woman, "What is this you have done?"

The woman said, "The serpent deceived me, and I ate." Genesis 3:9-13

Since Adam belonged to God, it was right for God to question Adam about what he had done. But instead of admitting he had done wrong, Adam blamed God and Eve. It was God's fault for giving Eve to him, and Eve's fault for handing him the fruit.

Eve did not admit she was wrong either. She said it was the snake's fault.

So God spoke to the snake.

So the LORD God said to the serpent: "Because you have done this, you are cursed more than all cattle, and more than every beast of the field; on your belly you shall go, and you shall eat dust all the days of your life." Genesis 3:14

Because the snake allowed Satan to use it, God put a curse on all snakes. Remember how snakes were the smartest of all the animals? Now God made snakes to be the lowest of all the animals. God cursed all snakes so that from then on they would have to crawl on their bellies in the dust.

Since Adam and Eve had joined Satan's side, all their children would now be born on Satan's side too. This must have made Satan happy! Now he was in charge of God's people.

But, no one can defeat God, not even Satan. God told Satan that one day the Child of a woman would destroy his power over mankind.

And I will put enmity between you and the woman, and between your seed and her Seed; He shall bruise your head, and you shall bruise His heel. Genesis 3:15

> Seed - child, or children

Even though God told Adam not to eat the fruit from The Tree of the Knowledge of Good and Evil, God knew Adam and Eve would eat it. This did not make God happy, but God knows everything. He knew Adam and Eve would believe Satan's lie, and He already had a plan for setting mankind free from Satan and death.

God told Satan there would be a battle between Satan and his children and the Child of a woman. God said Satan would bruise the Child's heel, but the Child would bruise Satan's head.

In God's plan, a woman would one day have a special Child who would save people from Satan's dominion. This Child would be called the Savior. Even though Satan would try to hurt the Savior, the Savior would win. By bruising Satan's head, the Savior would destroy Satan's power over mankind.

God had clearly told Adam they were not to eat from The Tree of the Knowledge of Good and Evil. He had warned him what would happen if they did. God was Adam and Eve's Maker. He loved them and gave them everything good. He would never lie to them. Adam and Eve should have believed God. When they purposefully did the very thing God had told them not to do, they deserved to be separated from God forever, but God was merciful to them. Instead of immediately sending them to the terrible place of suffering, He showed them grace by promising to send a Savior to free them from Satan's control.

> Mercy - not getting the punishment you deserve
>
> Grace - getting a gift when you deserve to get in trouble
>
> If a thief breaks into your house and your parents do not call the police that is mercy. But if your parents give the thief some food and extra money to help him out that is grace.
>
> Grace is even better than mercy.

Even though God showed Adam and Eve mercy and grace, they still had to face the consequences of going against what God said. The end result of sin is always death.

For the wages of sin is death... Romans 6:23a

God told Eve that because of what she had done, she, and all women after her, would suffer pain whenever their babies were born.

To the woman He said: "...in pain you shall bring forth children..." Genesis 3:16a

Because Adam ate from The Tree of the Knowledge of Good and Evil, even after God had clearly told him not to, God cursed the earth he had made for Adam and his children.

Then to Adam He said, "Because you have heeded the voice of your wife, and have eaten from the tree of which I commanded you, saying, 'You shall not eat of it': "Cursed is the ground for your sake; in toil you shall eat of it all the days of your life. Both thorns and thistles it shall bring forth for you, and you shall eat the herb of the field. In the sweat of your face you shall eat bread till you return to the ground, for out of it you were taken; for dust you are, and to dust you shall return." Genesis 3:17-19

Thorns and thistles started to grow everywhere. Bugs and plants became poisonous. Animals became mean. And now, instead of simply picking fruit from a tree, God said Adam would have to work hard to provide food for his family.

Because Adam went against God, pain and suffering entered the perfect world God had made. God had wanted Adam and Eve to live forever, but now Adam and Eve's bodies began to grow old. Someday their bodies would die and turn into dust again.

What terrible consequences resulted from Adam and Eve not believing God! All Adam and Eve's children would suffer because of what Adam and Eve had done. I am sure Adam and Eve wished many times they had believed God instead of Satan.

Remember

Adam and Eve did what God had said not to do. The Bible says that breaking God's rules is sin.

...sin is lawlessness. 1 John 3:4b

Just like God knew what Adam and Eve had done, God knows everything you have done too. Nothing is hidden from God; He sees everything. God knows all the things you have done that are displeasing to Him.

And there is no creature hidden from His sight, but all things are naked and open to the eyes of Him to whom we must give account. Hebrews 4:13

Sin always results in death. All who sin will be separated from God forever in the terrible place of suffering when their life on Earth is over.

The soul who sins shall die. Ezekiel 18:4b.

But God is loving and full of grace. From the beginning of time, He planned to send a Savior to rescue all people, including you and me, from the terrible death penalty we deserve for our sin.

Questions

1. Could Adam and Eve hide from God? *No, Adam and Eve could not hide from God because God is everywhere and knows everything.*

2. Why did God have the right to question Adam and Eve about what they had done? *God had the right to question Adam and Eve because He created them; Adam and Eve belonged to God.*

3. Who did God plan to send to rescue people from Satan's dominion? *God's plan was to send a Savior to rescue people from Satan's control.*

4. Does God always complete His plans? *Yes, God always does what He plans to do.*

5. How did God show mercy to Adam and Eve? *God did not send them to the terrible place of suffering right away.*

6. How did God show grace to Adam and Eve? *God promised to send a Savior who would rescue them from Satan.*

7. What happened to the perfect earth because of what Adam did? *God cursed the ground so that it started to produce thorns and thistles. Bugs and plants became poisonous, animals became mean, sickness and death entered the world, and people had to start working hard in order to produce enough food to eat.*

8. What is sin? *Sin is breaking God's rules.*

9. What is the penalty for sin? *The penalty for sin is death.*

10. Does God know everything you have ever done? *Yes, God sees and knows everything. He knows all you have done that is displeasing to Him.*

Biblical Worldviews

- God is everywhere at all times.
- God knows everything. He knows what will happen in the future.
- Since God created people, it is right for him to question them about what they have done.
- All people are sinners.
- God says that the penalty for going against what He says is death; it is separation from God forever in the terrible place of suffering.
- Satan fights against God, but God always wins.
- God is loving, merciful, and gracious.
- God's plan for mankind was to send the Savior.
- God is a personal being; He communicates with people.

Activity: Bible Hangman

Supplies:

- Chalkboard or dry erase board
- Chalk or dry erase markers

Instructions:

- Draw a large hangman tree on the board.
- Draw lines and spaces under the tree to correspond to the letters and spaces of the key phrase.
- **Key phrase**: God is a God of love and He always keeps His promises.
- **Optional key phrase for younger students**: God keeps His promises.
- Ask the lesson review questions, one at a time. Call on one student or one team to answer each question.
- If answer is correct, the student or team gets to pick a letter, i.e., the letter b.
- If the letter picked is in the key phrase, the teacher fills it in on the board each time it occurs.
- If the letter picked is not in the key phrase, the teacher draws one part of a stick figure on the hangman tree, i.e., a head, an arm, a stick body, etc.
- When a student (or team) thinks he knows the key phrase, he may try to solve the puzzle on his turn. The game is over when a student or team solves the puzzle or the teacher draws all the parts of the stick man, whichever comes first.

Activity 2: Mercy and Grace Skit

Supplies:

- Groups of students (two or three per group)
- Props (optional)
- Construction paper
- Marker

Instructions:

- Divide students into groups.
- Each group comes up with a story where someone does something deserving of punishment but ends up receiving both mercy and grace.
- Each group makes two signs out of construction paper, one that has MERCY written on it in big letters and one with GRACE written on it.
- Groups take turns acting out their stories.
- When group acts out the part where the guilty one receives mercy, the sign that says "mercy" is held up.
- When group acts out the part where the guilty one receives grace, the sign that says "grace" is held up.
- Discuss: What is mercy? What is grace?

Extra Bible References

Joshua 23:14; 2 Samuel 14:14; 1 Chronicles 29:11-12; Psalms 5:4, 139:7-13, 145:8; Proverbs 15:3; Isaiah 7:14, 43:11; Jeremiah 23:23-24; Ezekiel 18:20, 33:11; Luke 1:26-35, 4:5-6; John 12:31; Romans 8:20-22; Galatians 3:10, 13, 16, 19; 1 Peter 1:20; Hebrews 2:14-15, 4:13; 1 John 3:8, 5:19

11
Banished
Adam and Eve Part IV

Memory Verse

Therefore, just as through one man sin entered the world, and death through sin, and thus death spread to all men, because all sinned— Romans 5:12

Lesson

Remember when Adam and Eve ate the fruit and realized they were naked? What did they do? Did they ask God for clothes? No, they sewed fig leaves together to make their own clothes. Instead of depending on God to take care of them, like they had always done, Adam and Eve tried to fix what they had done on their own.

God did not accept the clothes Adam and Eve made. Now that they were separated from Him, it was impossible for Adam and Eve to do anything to please God.

Also for Adam and his wife the LORD God made tunics of skin, and clothed them. Genesis 3:21

In His mercy, God made clothes for Adam and Eve. God was the only One who could make acceptable clothes for them, but in order to do so He had to kill an animal. Because Adam and Eve did what God told them not to do, an innocent animal had to die. God wanted Adam and Eve to understand that sin causes death.

For the wages of sin is death... Romans 6:23

When Adam and Eve ate from The Tree of the Knowledge of Good and Evil, they became sinners. Now that they were sinful, God no longer wanted Adam and Eve to eat from The Tree of Life. God did not want sinful people to live forever in a sinful state.

Then the LORD God said, "Behold, the man has become like one of Us, to know good and evil. And now, lest he put out his hand and take also of The Tree of Life, and eat, and live forever"— therefore the LORD God sent him out of the garden of Eden to till the ground from which he was taken. Genesis 3:22-23

79

Remember what happened to Lucifer and his followers when they rebelled against God? God threw them out of Heaven. God is absolutely perfect. No one sinful can live with God.

> For You are not a God who takes pleasure in wickedness, nor shall evil dwell with You. Psalm 5:4

When Adam and Eve rebelled against God, they also had to leave God's presence; they could not continue to live in the garden.

> So He drove out the man; and He placed cherubim at the east of the garden of Eden, and a flaming sword which turned every way, to guard the way to The Tree of Life. Genesis 3:24

There was no way for Adam and Eve to sneak past the cherubim and the flaming sword. They could not get to The Tree of Life to eat from it. There was nothing they could do now to get eternal life.

After Adam and Eve left the garden, Eve became pregnant. In great pain, she gave birth to her first son. Eve named her baby Cain.

> **Cherubim is plural for cherub. Lucifer was a cherub. Cherubim are angels whose special job is to guard and protect.**

> Now…Eve…conceived and bore Cain, and said, "I have acquired a man from the LORD." Genesis 4:1

Eve knew God is the One who gives life. She knew God was the One who had given life to both her and Adam. When Cain was born, Eve believed it was God who made him and gave him to her.

> He gives to all life, breath, and all things. Acts 17:25b

Soon Eve had another baby.

> Then she bore again, this time his brother Abel. Genesis 4:2a

Because Adam and Eve had believed Satan instead of God, they became separated from God and had to leave the Garden of Eden. Now they were under Satan's dominion. Since Adam and Eve were now God's enemies; all their children were born enemies of God too. All of Adam and Eve's children were born on Satan's side and were sinners separated from God just like their parents.

Remember

Because all people come from Adam, all people are sinners. The penalty for sin is death.

...through one man sin entered the world, and death through sin, and thus death spread to all men, because all sinned— Romans 5:12

When Adam and Eve ate from The Tree of the Knowledge of Good and Evil, they became separated from God and were banished from the Garden of Eden. Because of their sin, they would have to be separated from God forever in the terrible place of suffering.

Because you were born into Adam's family, you were born a sinner just like your father, Adam. You were born separated from God. There is nothing you can do to please God or make Him accept you. Just like Adam and Eve could not get back into the garden to eat from The Tree of Life, there is nothing you can do to get eternal life. Only God can save you from eternal death. Only He can make you acceptable to Him so that you can live with Him forever.

Questions

1. When Adam and Eve realized they were naked, did they ask God to make clothes for them? *No, Adam and Eve tried to fix the problem on their own by sewing fig leaves together to make clothes for themselves.*

2. Was God pleased with the clothes Adam and Eve made? *No, the clothes Adam and Eve made for themselves were not acceptable to God.*

3. Who was the only One who could make acceptable clothes for Adam and Eve? *Only God could make coverings for Adam and Eve that He would accept.*

4. How did God make acceptable clothes for Adam and Eve? *God made acceptable clothes for Adam and Eve by killing an animal and making clothes out of the animal's skin.*

5. What is the penalty for doing what God says not to do, or sinning? *The penalty for sin is death.*

6. Why did God not let Adam and Eve eat from The Tree of Life? *God did not want sinful people to live forever in their sinful condition.*

7. Was there any way for Adam and Eve to sneak past God's angels and get back into the garden? *No, there was nothing Adam and Eve could do to get to The Tree of Life.*

8. Who gave life to Cain and Abel? *God did. God is the One who gives life.*

9. Into whose family were you born? *You were born into Adam's family.*

10. Is there anything you can do to make yourself acceptable to God so that you can live with Him forever? *No, only God can make you acceptable to Him. Only God can save you from death and give you eternal life.*

Biblical Worldviews

- Since all people are born into Adam's family, all people are sinners separated from God.
- The penalty for sin is death.
- No one in Adam's family is able to please God, or save himself, or do anything at all to gain eternal life.
- Only God can make a person acceptable to Him.
- Only God can save a person from death and give eternal life.

Activity: Bible Tic-Tac-Toe

Supplies:

- Chalkboard or dry erase board
- Chalk or dry erase markers

Instructions:

- Draw a large tic-tac-toe on the board.
- Divide students into two teams.
- Ask review questions and let each team take turns trying to answer a question. If the team answers the question correctly, they get to put an "X" or an "O" on the board. The first team to get three in a row, horizontally, vertically, or diagonally, wins.
- Play several times until students have answered all the review questions.

Extra Bible References

Exodus 34:6; 2 Samuel 14:14; Psalm 5:4-6, 86:15; Isaiah 59:2; Romans 3:10-18, 4:5; Ephesians 2:1-3; Colossians 1:21

12
An Unacceptable Offering
Cain and Abel

Memory Verse

There is a way that seems right to a man, but its end is the way of death.
Proverbs 14:12

Lesson

Adam and Eve most certainly told Cain and Abel about the beautiful garden where they used to live. Cain and Abel must have heard the sad story of how their parents had to leave the garden and about how God killed an animal to make acceptable clothes for them. Cain and Abel knew about the promise of a Savior.

Because Adam and Eve had joined Satan's side, Cain and Abel were born on Satan's side too. Cain and Abel were sinners separated from God. But even though Cain and Abel were under Satan's dominion, God was still their rightful owner because He was the One who made them.

God loved Cain and Abel and showed them how they could come to Him. In the same way God had killed an animal to make acceptable clothes for Adam and Eve, God wanted Cain and Abel to kill an animal, and then bring it to Him.

Cain and Abel wanted God to accept them, so they each brought God an offering. Abel killed a lamb and brought the parts of it to God just like God wanted. But Cain decided to come to God in his way; he brought God some food he had planted.

The Bible says God accepted Abel and his offering, but He did not accept Cain and his offering.

Now Abel was a keeper of sheep, but Cain was a tiller of the ground. And in the process of time it came to pass that Cain brought an offering of the fruit of the ground to the LORD. Abel also brought of the firstborn of his flock and of their fat.

And the LORD respected Abel and his offering, but He did not respect Cain and his offering. And Cain was very angry...

So the LORD said to Cain, "Why are you angry? ...If you do well, will you not be accepted?" Genesis 4:2b-7a

God gave Cain a second chance. He told Cain that if he did "well" he too would be accepted. Cain knew how God wanted him to come to Him, but Cain had his own ideas. When God did not accept his offering, Cain became angry.

The Bible says that Abel offered the right sacrifice because he believed God. Cain did not offer the right sacrifice because he did not believe God. Cain trusted in himself and brought God food from his garden rather than killing a lamb.

By faith Abel offered to God a more excellent sacrifice than Cain...Hebrews 11:4a

> **Faith – to have faith in God means you believe God**

It made Cain angry that God accepted Abel's sacrifice and not his. He wanted God to accept his offering even though it was not what God had shown him to do. The more he thought about it, the angrier he became.

Now Cain talked with Abel his brother; and it came to pass, when they were in the field, that Cain rose up against Abel his brother and killed him. Then the LORD said to Cain, "Where is Abel your brother?"

He said, "I do not know. Am I my brother's keeper?" Genesis 4:8-9

God was Cain's rightful owner; it was right for God to question Cain about his actions. But instead of admitting he was wrong, Cain retorted, "Am I responsible for my brother?"

Because Cain killed Abel, God made it so he could not be a farmer any more. God said that when Cain planted seeds, they would not grow. Cain would be forced to wander about the earth.

And He said, "What have you done? The voice of your brother's blood cries out to Me from the ground. So now you are cursed from the earth, which has opened its mouth to receive your brother's blood from your hand. When you till the ground, it shall no longer yield its strength to you. A fugitive and a vagabond you shall be on the earth." Genesis 4:10-12

It was wrong for Cain to take his brother's life. God is the One who gives life to people; only He has the right to decide how long a person should live.

And Cain said to the LORD, "My punishment is greater than I can bear! Surely You have driven me out this day from the face of the ground; I shall be hidden from Your face; I shall be a fugitive and a vagabond on the earth, and it will happen that anyone who finds me will kill me." Genesis 4:13-15

Now that he had killed Abel, Cain was scared someone might try to kill him, so God graciously put a mark of protection on Cain.

Then Cain went out from the presence of the LORD... Genesis 4:16a

But no matter how kind God was to Cain, Cain never changed his mind; he never came to believe God. In the end, Cain quit caring about God altogether.

The history of the Bible tells us that Cain's children were just like Cain; they did not care about God either. The only thing Cain's descendants cared about was having a good life.

After Cain killed Abel, God gave Eve another son in place of Abel.

> Punishment is the penalty for breaking a law or rule.
>
> When a person breaks the speed limit, he or she must pay a fine. There is a penalty for breaking the law.
>
> In the same way, there is a penalty for going against what God wants; the Bible calls this penalty "punishment."

And... [Eve] bore a son and named him Seth, "For God has appointed another seed for me instead of Abel, whom Cain killed." Genesis 4:25b

Seth believed God just like Abel had. The Bible tells us that later on the promised Savior came from Seth's family line.

Remember

Just like Cain and Abel, you were born into Adam's family. Because you were born into Adam's family, you are a sinner who is separated from God.

Yet there is good news. In the same way God showed Cain and Abel how to come to Him, He has made a way for you to come to Him too. In the Garden of Eden, God promised to send a Savior who would make a way for the whole world to be rescued from Satan and death.

> I, even I, am the LORD, and besides Me there is no savior.
> Isaiah 43:11

Don't be like Cain who tried to come to God according to his own ideas. Believe God like Abel did!

Questions

1. Did Cain know how God wanted him to come to Him? *Yes, Cain knew; God had shown him. God always communicates with people what He wants them to do. Cain knew what to do so that God would accept him.*

2. How did God want Cain and Abel to come to Him to be made acceptable? *He wanted them to kill an animal and bring the parts of it to Him.*

3. What did Cain offer to God? *Cain offered God some food he had grown in his fields.*

4. Why did Cain not come to God in the way God had shown him to come? *Cain thought he could be accepted by God according to his own ideas. He did not believe God.*

5. Did God give Cain a chance to change his mind and come to Him in the right way? *Yes, God told Cain that if he did what was right he would also be accepted.*

6. Why is murder wrong? *Since God is the One who gives life to people, He is the only One with the right to decide when someone should die.*

7. What happened to Cain's family? *Since Cain stopped caring about God, his family did not care about God either. Cain's family lived only to please themselves.*

8. What was the name of the son God gave Eve to replace Abel? *His name was Seth.*

9. Who is the only One who can save you from Satan and death? *Only God can make a way for you to come to Him and be saved from death.*

Biblical Worldviews

- God is a personal being; He communicates with people.
- God is the Creator and Owner of mankind.
- All people are born into Adam's family. This means all people are born sinners separated from God and under Satan's dominion.
- It is impossible for sinful people to please God.
- Only God can provide a way for people to be saved.
- The only way to please God is to believe Him.
- God is a God of love; He is merciful.
- God is everywhere at all times.
- God knows everything.
- It is wrong to murder. As the One who gives life, only God has the right to decide when someone should die.

Activity: Cain and Abel Skit

Supplies:

- Four student volunteers: two narrators, Cain, and Abel
- Four copies of the script (below)
- Although no other supplies are needed, you can use a toy lamb (for Abel's sacrifice) and a bowl of fruit (for Cain's sacrifice) if you have them.

Instructions:

- Students act out the skit.
- Students who are watching the skit discuss which actor is Cain, which one is Abel, and why. Have them discuss why God accepted Abel and his sacrifice and not Cain and his sacrifice.

Cain and Abel Skit (by Nancy Hughes)

<u>Narrator #1</u>: Let's travel back in time and see if you can guess which one of Adam and Eve's children trusted God and which one didn't.

(With their sacrifices, Cain and Abel enter stage from opposite sides and come to center)

<u>Cain</u>: (with chest sticking out in a proud, self-assured manner)

This sacrifice is fresh and new

I picked it with my hands.

I dug the fields and planted it

And with it here I stand.

What can I give to God?

Of course I have the very best.

Through my hard work and effort

I'm sure I'll pass His test!

What can I give to God?

The real question is:

What will He give to me?

Since He sees all my work

Rewards I'm sure to see

What can I give to God?

I'm sure I'll beat my brother's plan.

Those animals are so disgusting

With my fine fruit

I'll be the best man.

Abel: (with humility, yet sincerity in what he is saying)

Lord, this sacrifice reminds me of

The mess my sin has made

And once again I'm forced to know;

The price that must be paid.

Without death there is no life.

I would be doomed to die,

But this lamb's blood covers me

And through faith I'm free.

Lord, Thy work alone on my behalf

Is all I'm trusting in.

I know someday you'll finish it

And save me from my sin

Without death there is no life.

I would be doomed to die.

But this lamb's blood covers me

And through faith I'm free.

Narrator #2:

You see, Cain and Abel were born outside the garden; they were born sinners separated from God. Like their parents Adam and Eve, no amount of good works could make them acceptable to God. Cain thought he could please God according to his own ideas, but by refusing to do things God's way, he missed the whole point. The whole point of the sacrifice was to show that SIN BRINGS DEATH.

But Cain refused to believe God and acknowledge that he deserved death for his sin. Let me ask you this: Which plan do you think did a better job of showing that people needed a substitute to die in their place – the fruit sacrifice or the animal sacrifice?

Narrator #1:

It always looks better at first glance to do things our way, but God's plans are always best. The Bible tells us that Cain was miserable after his sacrifice. But instead of doing what was right, Cain made things even worse. He became angry because things had worked out better for Abel than for him. Cain's jealously grew and finally he became so angry he struck his brother Abel and killed him.

Narrator #2:

It was the first time one person killed another person, and God was greatly displeased. As far as we know, Cain never came to trust God. How sad Adam and Eve must have been to lose both their sons this way. Sin always brings sadness and death.

Extra Bible References

Genesis 4:16-24, 9:6; Exodus 34:19; Leviticus 17:11; Psalms 51:3-5, 100:3;
Psalm 139:7-13; Proverbs 15:3; Isaiah 43:7, 11; 59:2; 64:6; Ezekiel 18:4, 33:11;
Daniel 4:37; Romans 3:23; 4:5; 5:12; 6:23; 8:6-8; 10:11-13, 17; 13:4; 1 Timothy 2:4;
James 1:15; Hebrews 4:13; 9:22; 11:1-6, 39, 40; 1 John 3:12

13
Noah
Part I

Memory Verse

"For I have no pleasure in the death of one who dies," says the Lord God. "Therefore turn and live!" Ezekiel 18:32

Lesson

Adam and Eve lived hundreds of years and had lots of children and grandchildren.

After he begot Seth, the days of Adam were eight hundred years; and he had sons and daughters. So all the days that Adam lived were nine hundred and thirty years; and he died. Genesis 5:4-5

With the passing of time, there began to be a lot of people on the earth. But sadly, Adam and Eve's children and grandchildren did not care about God. Instead, they followed their own evil desires and the ways of Satan.

The Bible describes how they acted:

...although they knew God, they did not glorify Him as God, nor were thankful....who exchanged the truth of God for the lie, and worshiped and served the creature rather than the Creator...being filled with all unrighteousness...full of envy, murder, strife, deceit, evil-mindedness; they are...haters of God, violent, proud, boasters, inventors of evil things, disobedient to parents...untrustworthy, unloving, unforgiving, unmerciful... Romans 1: 21, 25, 29-31

Adam and Eve's descendants turned away from God because they were separated from God. They were born on Satan's side and they did what he wanted them to do. They were sinners.

Even though the people in the world at this time knew about God, they stopped honoring Him as the all-powerful, all-knowing Creator of the world. The people stopped being thankful to God. In their foolish thinking they began to believe lies about God. They were cruel and committed murder, they gossiped, and the children disobeyed their parents.

God saw how evil everyone had become.

Then the LORD saw that the wickedness of man was great in the earth, and that every intent of the thoughts of his heart was only evil continually. And the LORD was sorry that He had made man on the earth, and He was grieved in His heart.

So the LORD said, "I will destroy man whom I have created from the face of the earth, both man and beast, creeping thing and birds of the air, for I am sorry that I have made them." Genesis 6:5-7

God saw what was happening on the earth. He knew what the people were thinking. He knew their thoughts were "only evil continually." It made God sad that the people He created had turned away from Him. Because of their sin, the people would have to die.

But there was one man who still believed in the one true God. His name was Noah.

Noah was a just man, perfect in his generations. Genesis 6:9a

Noah was born into Adam's family just like everyone else. He too was a sinner separated from God, but there was one difference between Noah and all the other people in the world. Noah believed God. He was like Abel. He knew God was the only One who could save him from sin and death.

...Noah...became heir of the righteousness which is according to faith. Hebrews 11:7

The Bible says that even though Noah was a sinner, he received the gift of "righteousness" because of his faith in God. Just like Abel, God accepted Noah because Noah believed Him.

Righteous = Just = Perfect = Acceptable to God

And God said to Noah, "...Make yourself an ark of gopher wood; make rooms in the ark, and cover it inside and outside with pitch. And this is how you shall make it: The length of the ark shall be three hundred cubits [450 feet long], its width fifty cubits [75 feet wide], and its height thirty cubits [45 feet high]. You shall make a window for the ark...and set the door of the ark in its side. You shall make it with lower, second, and third decks. And behold, I Myself am bringing

floodwaters on the earth, to destroy from under heaven all flesh in which is the breath of life; everything that is on the earth shall die. But I will establish My covenant with you; and you shall go into the ark—you, your sons, your wife, and your sons' wives with you."
Genesis 6:13-18

God was going to send a flood to destroy all life on Earth, but because Noah believed God, God promised to protect him.

God gave Noah careful instructions about how to build a boat that would keep him and his family safe. God told Noah to make the boat three stories high and very long – just as big as a modern day cargo ship. God also told Noah to put only one door in the boat.

Noah had never seen a flood; he had never seen rain.

For the LORD God had not caused it to rain on the earth...but a mist went up from the earth and watered the whole face of the ground. Genesis 2:5-6

But even though Noah had never seen rain, he believed God would do what He said. Noah believed God was going to send a flood to cover the earth.

Noah believed that God was the only One who could save him and his family from death. He knew that only God could show him how to build a boat that would keep him and his family safe. That is why Noah followed God's instructions instead of his own ideas.

Thus Noah did; according to all that God commanded him, so he did. Genesis 6:22

Remember

Remember how Cain tried to come to God according to his own ideas? Cain did not believe God; he thought he could make up his own way of coming to God, but God did not accept Cain or his offering.

Abel, on the other hand, did believe God. Just like Noah, Abel believed that God was the only One who could show him how to be saved from death. That is why Abel came to God in the way God had shown him to come.

Just like Abel and the people in Noah's day, you also should die, because the penalty for sin is death. But God does not want you to be separated from Him.

"For I have no pleasure in the death of one who dies," says the Lord God. "Therefore turn and live!" Ezekiel 18:32

Only God can make a way for you to be saved. Remember how in the Garden of Eden God promised to send a Savior who would make a way for all people to be saved from Satan, sin, and death. This was God's plan all along; He planned for the Savior to make a way for you to be made acceptable to Him and saved from the death penalty you deserve for your sin.

Believe God and come to Him in His way, by trusting in the promised Savior. All who trust in the Savior to rescue them from death will be saved and will live with God forever.

Questions

1. Why did Adam and Eve's children reject God? *Adam and Eve's children turned away from God because they were sinners separated from God.*

2. What were the people like in the days of Noah? *The people in Noah's day did not honor God as the all-powerful, all-knowing Creator of the world. They were not thankful to God, they believed lies about God, they were cruel and murdered, they gossiped, and the children did not obey their parents!*

3. Was Noah a sinner like everyone else? *Yes, Noah was born into Adam's family just like everyone else. He, too, was a sinner separated from God.*

4. Who was the only One who could save Noah and his family from the flood? *Only God could save Noah and his family from the flood.*

5. Why did God save Noah from the flood? *God rescued Noah because Noah believed God.*

6. Why did Noah build the boat exactly like God said? *Noah built the boat exactly like God said because Noah believed God was the only One who could show him how he could be saved from death.*

7. Is God happy about people being separated from Him? *No, God does not want people to be separated from Him; God wants all people to live with Him forever.*

8. What is the penalty for sin? *The penalty for sin is death; it is separation from God forever in the terrible place of suffering.*

9. Can you save yourself from this death penalty? *No, there is nothing you can do to free yourself from the death penalty you deserve.*

10. Who is the only One who can save you from death? *Only God can make a way for you to escape being separated from Him forever.*

11. Who did God say He would send to make a way for you to be saved from Satan, sin, and death? *In the Garden of Eden, God promised to send a Savior who would make a way for us to be rescued from Satan and death.*

Biblical Worldviews

- Since all people are born into Adam's family, all people are sinners who cannot please God.
- God is everywhere at all times.
- God knows everything.
- The penalty for sin is death.
- God is the only One who can save us from the death we deserve.
- God is a personal being; He communicates with people.
- God is a God of love.
- God saves only those who believe Him.

Activity: Bible Bingo

Supplies:

- Bingo cards and game tokens (Any set will do. You can buy an inexpensive set at the dollar store.)

Instructions:

- Give each student a bingo card and some tokens.
- Ask a question from the lesson review and call on a student to answer it. If the student answers it correctly, she calls the bingo square she wants to cover. Everyone else who has that square covers it as well.
- Continue to ask questions, calling on a different student each time. Allow everyone to answer at least one question and pick at least one bingo square.
- The game is over when the first student shouts BINGO because she has covered a complete row with tokens, either vertically, horizontally, or diagonally.
- Play the game several times until everyone has had a turn answering a question and/or all the questions from the review have been asked and answered.

Extra Bible References

Psalms 5:4-6; Isaiah 43:11, 53:6; Ezekiel 18:4, 33:11; Matthew 24:37-39; Mark 7:21-23; Luke 17:26-27; Romans 1:18-32, 3:10-18, 4:1-7, 5:12, 8:6-8; Galatians 5:19-21; Hebrews 4:13, 11:1-7; 2 Peter 2:4-11

14
The Terrible Flood
Noah Part II

Memory Verse

"For I have no pleasure in the death of one who dies," says the Lord God. "Therefore turn and live!" Ezekiel 18:32

Lesson

It took many years to finish building the huge boat. All the while they were building, Noah preached to the people. Even though the people did not care about God, God still cared about them. He used Noah to warn them about what would happen if they refused to believe Him.

The Bible calls Noah a preacher of righteousness.

Noah...a preacher of righteousness... 2 Peter 2:5

Noah warned the people that if they did not change their minds about God and about their sin God would send a terrible flood to destroy them. But not one person paid attention to the warning. No one believed God would send a flood. The people just kept on partying and having a good time.

But God always does what He says He will do; He always tells the truth. God told the truth when He said Adam and Eve would die if they ate from The Tree of the Knowledge of Good and Evil, and God was telling the truth when He said He would destroy the world with a flood.

When the boat was finally finished, Noah gathered his family, and together with the animals, they entered the boat. Then God closed the one and only door.

Suddenly, great fountains of water spewed up out of the earth. At the same time, rain started to pour down from the sky. How surprised the unbelieving people must have been!

In the six hundredth year of Noah's life...all the fountains of the great deep were broken up, and the windows of heaven were opened...

On the very same day Noah and Noah's sons, Shem, Ham, and Japheth, and Noah's wife and the three wives of his sons with them, entered the ark—they and every beast after its kind, all cattle...every creeping thing that creeps on the earth...every bird of every sort. And they went into the ark to Noah, two by two...male and female of all flesh, went in as God had commanded him; and the LORD shut him in.

Now the flood was on the earth forty days. The waters increased and lifted up the ark, and it rose high above the earth...and the ark moved about on the surface of the waters. And the waters prevailed exceedingly on the earth, and all the high hills under the whole heaven were covered...So He destroyed all living things which were on the...ground: both man and cattle, creeping thing and bird of the air. They were destroyed from the earth. Only Noah and those who were with him in the ark remained alive. And the waters prevailed on the earth one hundred and fifty days. Genesis 7:11-24

For forty days and nights, the water got higher and higher until even the tallest mountains on Earth were covered.

Only God could make such an immense flood that it would wipe out all life on Earth. Only God is that powerful!

God is in charge of the world. He can do whatever He wants with the earth and those living on it, because He made it and He owns it all.

The heavens are Yours, the earth also is Yours; the world and all its fullness, You have founded them. Psalm 89:11

Once the flood started, it was too late for people to change their minds. No matter how hard they screamed and banged on the door, Noah could not let them in. Once God shut the door, it could not be opened, and there was no other way to get into the boat.

Noah and his family were safe on the inside, but everyone on the outside died; all who did not believe God drowned and went to the terrible place of suffering to be separated from God forever.

Remember

In the same way God spoke through Noah to warn the people about the coming flood, He speaks to people today through the Bible to warn them that they will die if they do not trust in Him. God wants everyone to know the truth so they can be saved from death.

...God our Savior...desires all men to be saved and to come to the knowledge of the truth. 1 Timothy 2:4

God does not want you to be separated from Him forever. He wants you to believe Him the way Noah did. God promises that all who believe in Him will not perish, but will live with Him forever.

...whoever believes in Him should not perish but have everlasting life. John 3:16

Questions

1. Why did God decide to destroy all life on Earth? *God destroyed all life on Earth because of the wickedness of the people. Everyone, except Noah and his family, had turned away from God. The people only thought about evil things all the time.*

2. Who did God use to warn the people about the coming flood? *God used Noah. All the while Noah and his sons were building the boat, Noah warned the people.*

3. Did any of the people come to believe God? *No, no one believed God. They did not believe God would send a flood to punish them for their sin.*

4. Does God always do what He says He will do? *Yes, no matter how long it takes, God always does what He says He will do.*

5. After God shut the door to the boat, was there any way for the people to be saved from death? *No, once God shut the door, it was too late. No one could open the door and there was no other way into the boat.*

6. Who is in charge of the world? *God is, because He is the Creator of the world and everything in it.*

7. How does God communicate with you and me? *He communicates with us through His words in the Bible.*

8. What is God's promise to those who trust in Him to save them from sin and death? *God promises that those who trust in Him will not be separated from Him in the terrible place of suffering but will have eternal life.*

Biblical Worldviews

- The payment for sin is death.
- All people are sinners.
- God is a personal being; He communicates with people.
- God tells the truth.
- God is a God of love; He is patient with sinners, giving them time to change their minds.
- Since God is the Creator, He is the highest authority and the One in charge.
- God can do anything; nothing is too hard for Him.
- There is a terrible place of suffering where all who do not believe God will be separated from Him forever.
- God saves only those who believe Him.

Activity: Drawing with Door

Supplies:

- Pencil, crayons, or colored pencils
- Paper, one sheet per student
- Small amount of brown construction paper to make doors
- Glue or double-sided tape

Instructions:

- Students draw the flood scene and Noah's Ark on the paper, making sure to leave room for the one door.
- Students use brown construction paper to cut out a door for the boat.
- Students glue or tape their door onto Noah's boat.
- Students label their drawings with these words: One Door.

Extra Bible References

Psalms 29:10, 89:11, 104:6-9, 107:23-30, 135: 5-7, 147:18, 148:4-5; Isaiah 43:11; Ezekiel 18:20, 33:11; Amos 4:13; John 3:17-18, 14:6, 16:7-10; 1 Peter 3:20; 2 Peter 2:4-9, 3:3-10; Revelation 20:15

15
God's Promises
Noah Part III

Memory Verse

That they may know that You, whose name alone is the Lord, are the Most High over all the earth. Psalm 83:18

Lesson

For a year the water covered the earth. As Noah and his family floated alone month after month, they may have wondered if God had forgotten them.

But God did not forget about Noah.

Then God remembered Noah, and every living thing, and all the animals that were with him in the ark. And God made a wind to pass over the earth, and the waters subsided. Genesis 8:1

God had promised to keep Noah and his family safe, and He did. In His perfect time, He sent a wind over the earth to dry up the water.

In the same way God caused the water to cover the earth; God now caused the wind to blow so the water would go down. As the Creator of the world, God can make the wind and the water do whatever He decides.

And in the second month...the earth was dried.

Then God spoke to Noah, saying, "Go out of the ark, you and your wife, and your sons and your sons' wives with you. Bring out with you every living thing of all flesh that is with you: birds and cattle and every creeping thing that creeps on the earth, so that they may abound on the earth, and be fruitful and multiply on the earth."

So Noah went out, and his sons and his wife and his sons' wives with him. Every animal, every creeping thing, every bird, and whatever creeps on the earth, according to their families, went out of the ark. Genesis 8:14-19

The entire time Noah and his family were on the boat, God lovingly cared for them. No one died of sickness or hunger; everyone survived.

Then Noah built an altar to the LORD, and took of every clean animal and of every clean bird, and offered burnt offerings on the altar. And the LORD smelled a soothing aroma.

Then the LORD said in His heart, "I will never again curse the ground for man's sake, although the imagination of man's heart is evil from his youth; nor will I again destroy every living thing as I have done." Genesis 8:20-21

After the flood, Noah built an altar to offer sacrifices to God.

Noah was like Abel. He believed God and came to God in the way God had shown – by killing an animal.

God was pleased with Noah's offering. He promised never to send a worldwide flood again.

> God set apart certain animals as "clean" animals. By clean animals God did not mean animals that had been washed. The animals God called clean were the ones that were acceptable as sacrifices. For example, God accepted sheep, goats, and pigeons as sacrifices, but He did not accept camels, rabbits, or pigs. God called camels, rabbits, and pigs "unclean" animals.

Then God spoke to Noah and to his sons with him, saying: "And as for Me, behold, I establish My covenant with you and with your descendants after you...Never again shall all flesh be cut off by the waters of the flood; never again shall there be a flood to destroy the earth."

And God said: "This is the sign of the covenant which I make between Me and you, and every living creature that is with you, for perpetual generations: I set My rainbow in the cloud, and it shall be for the sign of the covenant between Me and the earth. It shall be, when I bring a cloud over the earth, that the rainbow shall be seen in the cloud; and I will remember My covenant which is between Me and you and every

living creature of all flesh; the waters shall never again become a
flood to destroy all flesh." Genesis 9:8-15

In the beginning, God told Adam and Eve to have lots of children. God wanted people to be everywhere on the earth. But when Adam and Eve's children completely rejected God, God destroyed them.

After the flood, God told Noah and his sons to "be fruitful and multiply, and fill the earth." This was the same command God had given to Adam and Eve. God wanted Noah and his descendants to have many children so that the earth would become full of people once more.

So God blessed Noah and his sons, and said to them: "Be fruitful and multiply, and fill the earth. And the fear of you and the dread of you shall be on every beast of the earth, on every bird of the air, on all that move on the earth, and on all the fish of the sea. They are given into your hand. Every moving thing that lives shall be food for you. I have given you all things, even as the green herbs."
Genesis 9:1—3

God made the world and all the plants and animals for people. God wants us to take good care of the world, use its resources, and enjoy all He has given us.

Remember

Every time you see a rainbow, God wants you to remember His promise to Noah. The rainbow should remind you that God keeps His promises.

You can depend on God. God always tells the truth. Everything written in the Bible is true.

The entirety of Your word is truth... Psalm 119:160a

God does everything He says He will do. In the Garden of Eden, God said He would send the Child of a woman to destroy Satan's rule over mankind. God planned to send a Savior to rescue us from Satan and the death penalty we deserve for our sin. God never forgot His plan. In His perfect time, He sent the Savior just like He said He would.

Questions

1. Did God forget about Noah and his family when they were in the boat? *No, God remembered Noah and his family. He kept them safe just as He promised He would.*

2. Why could God tell the wind and the water what do? *God can control the wind, the water, and all of nature because He is the One who created everything.*

3. What did Noah's sacrifice show about his belief in God? *Noah's sacrifice showed that Noah believed God.*

4. For whom did God make the earth and everything on it? *He made it all for people.*

5. Will God ever destroy the whole earth with a flood again? *No, God promised He would never destroy the whole earth with a flood again.*

6. After the flood, what did God tell Noah to do? *God told Noah to have many children and "fill the earth." God wanted people to spread out everywhere over the whole earth.*

7. Did God have the right to put people in charge of the earth? *Yes, God made the earth and the people on it; He can do with them whatever He decides.*

8. What does God want us to remember whenever we see a rainbow? *He wants us to remember His promise to never again destroy the whole earth with a flood. He also wants us to remember that He always keeps His promises.*

Biblical Worldviews

- God always does what He says; He keeps His promises. You can depend on God.
- God is a God of love; He is merciful.
- God is a personal being; He communicates with mankind.
- The only way to please God is to believe Him.
- As the Creator of everything, God is the highest authority over all humanity and all nature.
- God made the earth for people to use, enjoy, and care for.

Activity: Rainbow Picture with Bible Verse

Supplies:

- Pencil, crayons, colored pencils or markers
- Blank paper, one per student
- Cotton balls
- Glue

Instructions:

- Students draw and color an ark with a rainbow over it.
- Students may wish to color the rainbow using the correct sequence of colors. The top of the rainbow is red, followed by orange, yellow, green, blue, indigo, and violet at the bottom.
- Using glue, students may attach cotton balls in the sky to resemble white puffy clouds.

107

- Students write the memory verse above or below the rainbow.

- Optional: Students write "God Keeps His Promises" above or below the rainbow.

Extra Bible References

Genesis 6:18; Leviticus 1:10, 14; 11:1-23, 29, 30, 46, 47; 20:25; Joshua 23:14;
1 Kings 8:56; Psalms 8:6-8, 9:10, 33:4, 104:6-9, 115:16, 147:18, 148:4-5; Isaiah 45:18;
Isaiah 46:11; Romans 3:10-17

16
Confusion
Tower of Babel

Memory Verse

That they may know that You, whose name alone is the Lord, are the Most High over all the earth. Psalm 83:18

Lesson

After the flood, Noah's sons had many children, grandchildren, and great-grandchildren. Soon there were a lot of people on the earth again.

God told Noah and his sons to "fill the earth," because He wanted there to be people everywhere.

So God blessed Noah and his sons, and said to them: "Be fruitful and multiply, and fill the earth." Genesis 9:1

But the people in Noah's family did not want to be separated from each other. Instead of spreading out like God said, everyone stayed together.

Now the whole earth had one language and one speech. And it came to pass, as they journeyed from the east, that they found a plain in the land of Shinar, and they dwelt there.

And they said, "Come, let us build ourselves a city, and a tower whose top is in the heavens; let us make a name for ourselves, lest we be scattered abroad over the face of the whole earth." Genesis 11:1-2, 4

Noah's descendants (his children, grandchildren, and great-grandchildren) decided to settle in the land of Shinar. Here they planned to build both a city where they could all live together and a tall tower that would reach way up into the sky.

What a foolish decision! Noah's descendants should have known they could never get away with going against God. After all, they had heard how the people in Noah's day were destroyed by a terrible flood when they rebelled against God.

> Shinar was in Mesopotamia, which today is the country of Iraq.

But Noah's descendants were born into Adam's family, and just like their father, Adam, they were born sinners under Satan's dominion.

Remember when Lucifer decided to do what he wanted instead of what God wanted? Lucifer became Satan, God's enemy. It was Satan who was leading these people to do what they wanted instead of what God wanted.

Of course, God knew what the people were thinking and planning. He knows everything!

> But the LORD came down to see the city and the tower which the sons of men had built. And the LORD said, "Indeed the people are one and they all have one language, and this is what they begin to do; now nothing that they propose to do will be withheld from them. Come, let Us go down and there confuse their language, that they may not understand one another's speech."
>
> So the LORD scattered them abroad from there over the face of all the earth, and they ceased building the city. Therefore its name is called Babel, because there the LORD confused the language of all the earth; and from there the LORD scattered them abroad over the face of all the earth. Genesis 11:5-9

Did you know there are many people like the Yanomamo? There are many groups of people living far away in the jungles and rainforests of the world. These people have never seen a car or been in a store.

And yet, even though they do not have internet or know how to read, most of these people know about the flood that covered the earth long ago. That is because the flood really did happen just like the Bible says.

Noah's sons told their children about the flood. They in turn told their children, and so on. In this way the story was passed on to people all around the world.

Of course, since it was not written down, the details of the story changed over time. But it is certainly amazing that many people groups, who have never read the Bible, know about a world-wide flood!

Who was God talking with when He said, "Come, let Us go down and there confuse their language"? Remember, the only true and living God exists in three persons. These three persons - God the Father, God the Son, and God the Holy Spirit - decided together to confuse the language of the people.

Because everyone spoke the same language, people easily worked together as a team. The people thought that by working together they could accomplish anything; they thought that together they could fight against God and win. But no one can win against God. God confused their language so they could no longer work together.

You can imagine what happened when everyone suddenly started speaking different languages! The workers could not understand what their bosses told them to do. Since no one understood each other, it became impossible to get any work done, and they were forced to stop building the tower.

Because God confused the language of the people, the name of that place where they lived came to be called Babel.

No one gets away with going against God. When Satan tried to take God's place, God threw him out of Heaven. When Adam and Eve went against what God said, they were separated from God and had to leave the garden and The Tree of Life. When Cain did things his own way, God caused the seeds he planted not to grow so that he had to wander about looking for food. In Noah's day, God destroyed everyone who did not believe Him with a terrible flood.

The LORD brings the counsel of the nations to nothing; He makes the plans of the peoples of no effect. The counsel of the LORD stands forever, the plans of His heart to all generations. Psalm 33:10-11

> **Interesting Facts**
>
> In Hebrew (the language the Old Testament was written in) the word babel means confusion, and in the Babylonian language it means "the gate of gods."
>
> The city in Mesopotamia where the Tower of Babel was built came to be called Babylon.
>
> The people of Babylon built many towers like the one we read about in the Bible. On top of these towers they built temples for worshiping the sun, moon, and stars. We know about these temple-towers because archaeologists have dug them up in the country of Iraq. They call the towers "ziggurats."
>
> The Bible indicates that false religions began in Babylon.

Remember

Many people do not believe God is the Creator of the world; they do not believe that God has the authority to tell them what to do. They think they can do whatever they want and get away with it. They act just like the people did at the tower of Babel.

But no matter what people think, God is real, and the Bible is true. The Bible says that the penalty for sin is death.

The soul who sins shall die. Ezekiel 18:4b.

Because of the things you have done that displease God, you deserve to be separated from God forever. There is nothing you can do to make God save you from death. There is no religion that can save you. All mankind's ideas about how to get to Heaven only lead to death.

There is a way that seems right to a man, but its end is the way of death. Proverbs 16:25

God is the only One who can save you from Satan, sin, and death.

I, even I, am the LORD, And besides Me there is no savior. Isaiah 43:11

Questions

1. What did God tell Noah and his sons to do? *God told Noah and his sons to have many children and "fill the earth."*

2. Did Noah's descendants spread out all over the earth like God told them to? *No, they all decided to live in the same place.*

3. Did Noah's descendants think they could go against God and get away it? *Yes, even though they knew God had destroyed the people in Noah's day with a flood because of their wickedness, they still thought they could get away with going against God.*

4. Did God know that the people were not following His directions? *Yes, God is everywhere. He sees and knows everything.*

5. What did God do to make the people fill the earth like He had told them to do? *He gave them all different languages so they could not continue building and were forced to spread apart.*

6. What happened to Lucifer when he tried to take God's place in Heaven? *God threw him and all the angels who followed him out of Heaven.*

7. What happened to Adam and Eve when they believed Satan instead of believing God? *They became separated from God. They had to leave the Garden of Eden and The Tree of Life.*

8. What happened to the people in Noah's day when they ignored God? *They were all destroyed by a terrible flood.*

9. Who is in charge of the world? *God is. He is the Creator of the world and everything in it. He makes His own decisions and can do what He decides with His creation.*

10. Is there any religion that can keep you from being separated from God forever in the terrible place of suffering? *No, God is the only One who can save you from death. In the Bible, God tells you how to be saved. Religions offer you man's ideas. You cannot be saved according to man's ideas.*

Biblical Worldviews

- God is the Creator of the world; therefore He is the highest authority.
- God is a personal being; He communicates with people and tells them what He wants them to do.
- Everything God says in the Bible is true.
- God is everywhere all the time.
- God knows everything.
- All people are sinners.
- No one can go against what God says and win.
- The penalty for sin is death; it is separation from God forever in the terrible place of suffering.
- There is only one true and living God who exists in three persons.
- Religion cannot save you from being separated from God forever in the terrible place of suffering.

Activity 1: Tower of Babel Skit

Supplies:
- Student volunteers
- Bricks or blocks, optional

Instructions:
- Students divide into one or more large groups. There should be at least five or six students in each group.
- Each group takes a turn acting out the building of the city and the tower. At first, all actors speak the same language and work together to stack the blocks, but then their languages are changed and everything becomes a confusion. Everyone speaks gibberish and they cannot work together. Soon they begin to move away from each other.
- Discuss skit students acted out, emphasizing how no one gets away with going against what God says. Sooner or later, all sin leads to death.

Activity 2: Tower of Babel Paper Cups Race

Supplies:

- Large paper, plastic, or Styrofoam cups – about 10 cups for each group of students
- Stop watch, optional

Instructions:

- Divide students into groups with 3-5 members each.
- Part One: Students work together in complete silence while building a tower with the cups. The first team to build the highest tower wins. Teacher may use stop watch to time students.
- Part Two: Students do the same activity, but this time they speak to each other while building the tower. Once again, teacher may use stop watch.
- Teacher and students then compare the times and quality of work for parts one and two, noting that it is easier to work together and accomplish goals if students can talk to one another.

Extra Bible References

1 Chronicles 29:11; Psalms 2:1-6, 28:5, 83:18; Proverbs 15:3, 16:5; Isaiah 40:15, 43:11; Isaiah 46:9-10, 53:6; Jeremiah 10:6, 50:38; Daniel 4:35, 37; Ephesians 2:1-3; Romans 1:18-23, 3:10-18, 5:12, 8:6-8; Hebrews 4:13; Revelation 17:5, 18:21

17
A Great Nation
God Chose Abram

Memory Verse

Indeed I have spoken it; I will also bring it to pass. I have purposed it; I will also do it. Isaiah 46:11b

Lesson

Even after God destroyed everyone on Earth with a terrible flood and confused the language of the people at the Tower of Babel, most people did not believe He was the only true God.

But there was one man who did believe in God. His name was Abram. Abram lived in the city of Ur in Mesopotamia, not too far from the Tower of Babel. Ur was a rich and important city, but the people there, including Abram's family, worshiped false gods.

Your fathers, *including* Terah, the father of Abraham...served other gods. Joshua 24:2b

Ever since Adam and Eve joined Satan's side, people kept turning away from God. Cain and his family, the people at the time of the flood, and the people at the Tower of Babel all turned away from God. Even though God created the world just for them, they were not thankful to Him. They did not care about God at all and became more and more wicked.

But God is a God of love. Even though most people did not care about Him, He cared about them and still planned to send the Savior. God always keeps His promises no matter what people do.

God chose Abram to play an important part in His plan. He told Abram to move away from his homeland because He was going to make him into a great nation.

Now the Lord had said to Abram: "Get out of your country, from your family and from your father's house, to a land that I will show you. I will make you a great nation; I will bless you and make your name great; and you shall be a blessing. I will bless those who bless you, and I will curse him who curses you; and in you all the families of the earth shall be blessed." Genesis 12:1-3

Was it okay for God to have a plan for Abram's life? Yes, it was. God created Abram; it was okay for God to decide what Abram should do. But even still, God let Abram choose whether or not he would believe Him and do what He said.

Even though Abram and his wife Sarai had never been able to have children, God said a great nation would come from Abram.

...Sarai was barren; she had no child. Genesis 11:30

God promised to treat Abram and his children well and to protect them from their enemies.

Most importantly, God promised Abram that through him all the families of the earth would be blessed. Everyone on Earth was going to receive kindness and help through Abram because the promised Savior was going to come from Abram's nation.

Abram trusted God. Even though he did not know where he was going, the Bible says that by faith Abram packed up his belongings to follow God's leading.

By faith Abraham obeyed when he was called to go out to the place which he would receive as an inheritance. And he went out, not knowing where he was going. Hebrews 11:8

Abram had a nephew named Lot. Lot's dad had died, so Abram took Lot with him on his journey.

So Abram departed as the LORD had spoken to him, and Lot went with him. And Abram was seventy-five years old when he departed from Haran. Then Abram took Sarai his wife and Lot his brother's son, and all their possessions that they had gathered, and the people whom they had acquired in Haran, and they departed to go to the land of Canaan. So they came to the land of Canaan.

Then the LORD appeared to Abram and said, "To your descendants I will give this land." And there he built an altar to the LORD, who had appeared to him. Genesis 12:4-5, 7

Abram and Lot were rich. They had lots of animals and servants. It was hard for them to move. There were no moving vans or trailers to carry their animals and all their belongings. Everyone had to walk. Can you imagine that? All the cows, sheep, donkeys and camels, all the servants and their children, everyone had to make the long, dusty trip on foot.

Finally Abram's family and servants arrived at their destination – the land of Canaan. When they got there, God told Abram He was going to give this land to Abram's descendants. Then Abram built an altar to God. Since Abram believed God, he came to God by offering animal sacrifices just like Abel and Noah did.

The people of Canaan were giant and powerful. They lived in huge, walled cities. The Bible says they worshiped false gods and did many horrible things.

> ...the people who dwell in the land are strong; the cities are fortified and very large...all the people... in it are men of great stature...giants... Numbers 13:28, 32-33

> ...the Canaanites...have iron chariots and are strong... Joshua 17:18b

> ... all their abominations [horrors] which they have done for their gods... Deuteronomy 20:18

The people of Canaan were like the people in Noah's day; they were wicked and did not care at all about the true and living God. The Bible says they were ruining the land with their sickening behavior. God knew that one day He would have to destroy them.

> For the land is defiled; therefore I visit the punishment of its iniquity upon it, and the land vomits out its inhabitants. Leviticus 18:25

Since God is the Creator of the world, He can do with it what He chooses. God had the authority to give this land to whomever He decided. Someday, God would give this land to Abram's descendants.

> I have made the earth, the man and the beast that are on the ground, by My great power and by My outstretched arm, and have given it to whom it seemed proper to Me. Jeremiah 27:5

Remember

Long before you were born, God planned to send a Savior to rescue mankind from Satan and eternal death. God always does whatever He plans to do. God chose Abram to be an important part of His plan. Someday a great nation would come from Abram. The Savior, who would bring God's kindness and help to all the families of the earth, would come from this nation.

He indeed was foreordained before the foundation of the world...
1 Peter 1:20a

Questions

1. After God showed His great power at the flood and at the Tower of Babel, did the people begin to worship God? *No, instead of worshiping the true and living God, they worshiped false gods.*

2. Was God still planning to send the Savior, even though people always turned away from Him and acted wickedly? *Yes, God still loved people even though they kept turning away from Him. In His mercy and grace, He still planned to send the Savior.*

3. What did God tell Abram to do? *He told Abram to leave his family and his homeland to move to an unknown land.*

4. Why was it okay for God to tell Abram what to do? *God could tell Abram what to do because He created Abram.*

5. Could Abram have chosen not to do what God said? *Yes, Abram could choose whether or not He would believe God and do what God said.*

6. What promises did God make to Abram? *God told Abram He would make him into a great nation, that He would protect him from his enemies, that He would give the land of Canaan to his descendants, and, most importantly, that the Savior would come from his nation.*

7. Did Abram believe these promises? *Yes, Abram believed God and left his home to go wherever God led him.*

8. Can you trust God to keep His promises? *Yes, God always does what He says He will do. You can depend on God.*

9. What were the Canaanites like? *The Canaanites worshiped false gods and did many horrible and sickening things. They did not care about the true and living God.*

10. Was it right for God to give the Canaanites' land to Abram's descendants? *Yes, it was, because God created the earth and everything on it. It all belongs to Him so He can do with it whatever He pleases.*

Biblical Worldviews

- The God of the Bible is the only true and living God.
- God's great plan was to send the Savior to rescue mankind from Satan, sin, and death.
- No matter what, God always accomplishes His plans and keeps His promises.
- God is a personal being; He communicates with people.
- All people are sinners.
- The payment for sin is death.
- God is a God of love.
- Since God created the world and everything in it, it all belongs to Him and He can do with it whatever He pleases.
- The only way to please God is to believe Him.

Activity: Bible Tic-Tac-Toe

Supplies:

- Chalkboard or dry erase board
- Chalk or dry erase markers

Instructions:

- Draw a large tic-tac-toe on the board.
- Divide students into two teams.
- Ask review questions and let each team take turns trying to answer a question. If the team answers the question correctly, they get to put an "X" or an "O" on the board. The first team to get three in a row, horizontally, vertically, or diagonally, wins.
- Play several times until you have used all the review questions.

Extra Bible References

Genesis 11:10-32, 12:1-5, 13:2; Leviticus 18:28-30; Deuteronomy 9:4; Psalm 9:10; Psalms 83:18, 89:11; Isaiah 46:8-11; Acts 7:2-3; Romans 1:1-2, 23-25; Galatians 3:8; Galatians 5:19-21; Ephesians 1:4, 2:1-5; Hebrews 11:8-10; 2 Peter 3:9

18
Fire from Heaven

Lot

Memory Verse

Indeed I have spoken it; I will also bring it to pass. I have purposed it; I will also do it.
Isaiah 46:11b

Lesson

When Abram moved to Canaan, he took his nephew Lot with him. Lot was rich like Abram.

Lot also, who went with Abram, had flocks and herds and tents.
Genesis 13:5

Lot believed in God the same way Abel and Noah did. Lot knew he was a sinner separated from God, but he trusted in God to save him and make him acceptable to God.

Because Lot trusted in God to save him, God gave Lot the gift of righteousness. That is why the Bible calls Lot a "righteous man." Even though Lot was a sinner, in God's eyes Lot was righteous and acceptable to Him because he had trusted in God to save him from sin and death.

...Lot...that righteous man...2 Peter 2:7-8

In Canaan, Lot lived with his uncle Abram, but because they owned so many animals, it soon became impossible for Lot and Abram to live in the same place.

Now the land was not able to support them, that they might dwell together, for their possessions were so great that they could not dwell together. And there was strife between the herdsmen of Abram's livestock and the herdsmen of Lot's livestock.
Genesis 13:6-7a

The workers who took care of Lot's animals and those who took care of Abram's animals started to argue because there was not enough food and water for all the animals.

So Abram said to Lot, "Please let there be no strife between you and me, and between my herdsmen and your herdsmen; for we are brethren. Is not the whole land before you? Please separate from me. If you take the left, then I will go to the right; or, if you go to the right, then I will go to the left." Genesis 13:8-9

Abram did not want there to be an argument between him and his nephew. He decided it would be best for one of them to move to another spot. After all, there was lots of land from which to choose. Kindly, Abram let Lot have first choice.

And Lot lifted his eyes and saw all the plain of Jordan, that it was well watered everywhere...like the garden of the Lord...Then Lot chose for himself all the plain of Jordan, and Lot journeyed east.

And they separated from each other. Abram dwelt in the land of Canaan, and Lot dwelt in the cities of the plain and pitched his tent even as far as Sodom. But the men of Sodom were exceedingly wicked and sinful against the Lord. Genesis 13:10-13

Without asking God what to do, Lot decided to move near the Jordan River since he could see there was lots of water and green grass in that place for his animals.

Lot did not know that the people living by the Jordan River, in the cities of Sodom and Gomorrah, were "exceedingly wicked and sinful against the Lord." If he would have asked God, God would have shown him not to move there. In the end, Lot's decision turned out to be a very bad one.

After Lot moved to the Jordan River, God sent angels to talk to Abram. Even though angels are invisible, they can take on the form of a person to deliver a message to someone on Earth. The angels who appeared to Abram looked like men, but Abram knew they were sent by God. The angels told Abram about something God was planning to do:

And the Lord said, "Because the outcry against Sodom and Gomorrah is great, and because their sin is very grave, I will go down now and see..." Then the men turned away from there and went toward Sodom... Genesis 18:20-22a

The people of Sodom and Gomorrah had completely turned away from God. God saw how wicked they were. They were mean and hateful and selfish.

After talking to Abram, the angels went to Sodom.

Now the two angels came to Sodom in the evening...

Then the men said to Lot, "Have you anyone else here? Son-in-law, your sons, your daughters, and whomever you have in the city--take them out of this place! For we will destroy this place, because the outcry against them has grown great before the face of the Lord, and the Lord has sent us to destroy it."

So Lot went out and spoke to his sons-in-law, who had married his daughters, and said, "Get up, get out of this place; for the Lord will destroy this city!" But to his sons-in-law he seemed to be joking.

When the morning dawned, the angels urged Lot to hurry, saying, "Arise, take your wife and your two daughters who are here, lest you be consumed in the punishment of the city." And while he lingered, the men took hold of his hand, his wife's hand, and the hands of his two daughters, the Lord being merciful to him, and they brought him out and set him outside the city. So it came to pass, when they had brought them outside, that he said, "Escape for your life! Do not look behind you nor stay anywhere in the plain. Escape to the mountains, lest you be destroyed."

Then the Lord rained brimstone and fire on Sodom and Gomorrah, from the Lord out of the heavens. So He overthrew those cities, all the plain, all the inhabitants of the cities, and what grew on the ground.

But his [Lot's] wife looked back behind him, and she became a pillar of salt. Genesis 19:1, 12-17, 24-26

God is the highest authority and judge. He is the One who decides what should happen to sinners. He has declared that the penalty for sin is death.

Lift up Thyself, Thou judge of the earth; render to the proud their due reward. Psalm 94:2

125

Remember what happened in Noah's day? Even though the people thought they could get away with their evil behavior, the judge of the universe declared them guilty and sentenced them to death.

No one in Sodom and Gomorrah paid any attention to the one true God either. They thought they could be as wicked as they wanted and God would not do anything about it, but they also received the death sentence for their wicked deeds.

Yet God protected Lot, just like He had protected Noah, because Lot believed in God.

Sadly, Lot's wife did not listen to God. She looked back, even though God had warned her and her family not to. Because she did not believe God's words, Lot's wife became a pillar of salt.

As soon as Lot was far enough away, God caused burning sulfur to rain down on Sodom and Gomorrah. Burning sulfur is like the melted rock that flows from a volcano. The sight was terrifying. Both cities were completely destroyed. Even the land around them was burned up. No one escaped; everyone died.

God is the Creator of the world. The whole world and all people belong to Him; therefore, He can do whatever He chooses with His creation.

Remember

The penalty for sin is death. Since we are all sinners, there is nothing we can do to escape from the death sentence we deserve.

 The soul who sins shall die. Ezekiel 18:4b

Only God can save us from having to be separated from Him forever in the terrible place of suffering. Remember how He saved Noah from the flood? Noah was a sinner. He deserved to die, but God saved Noah because Noah believed Him. It was the same with Lot. Even though Lot was a sinner, God gave Lot the gift of righteousness because Lot trusted in Him. Before God destroyed Sodom and Gomorrah, He rescued Lot.

Even though the penalty for sin is death, God promises to save all who trust in Him. That is why, from the beginning, He planned to send the Savior to make a way for people to be rescued from sin and death.

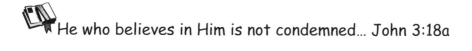He who believes in Him is not condemned... John 3:18a

Questions

1. Why did Lot decide to move close to the Jordan River? *Lot chose to move close to the Jordan River because he saw there was lots of water and green grass there for his animals.*

2. What were the people like who lived near the Jordan River? *The people were very wicked. None of them believed in God.*

3. Who is the highest authority and judge? *God is the highest authority and judge.*

4. What does God say must happen to sinners? *God says the penalty for sin is death; it is separation from God forever in the terrible place of suffering.*

5. Why did God rescue Lot? *God sent angels to rescue Lot because Lot had trusted in God to save him from the death penalty he deserved for his sin.*

6. Why did God turn Lot's wife into a pillar of salt? *God turned Lot's wife into a pillar of salt because she looked back even though God said not to.*

7. What did God do to the cities of Sodom and Gomorrah? *He rained burning sulfur, which is like the melted rock in a volcano, down on Sodom and Gomorrah so that they were totally destroyed.*

8. Was there any way for the people of Sodom and Gomorrah to escape God's punishment? *No, no one was able to escape; everyone died.*

9. Who was the only One who could rescue Lot from death? *Only God could deliver Lot from death.*

10. Who is the only One who can rescue you from the death penalty you deserve for your sin? *Only God can deliver you from the death penalty you deserve.*

Biblical Worldviews

- God is a personal being; He communicates with people.
- God is everywhere; He knows everything.
- Since God is the Creator, He is the highest authority and judge.
- All people are sinners.
- The penalty for sin is death.
- We cannot save ourselves. Only God can save us.
- God saves only those who believe in Him.
- Those who do not believe God will be separated from Him forever in the terrible place of suffering, from which there will be no escape.

Activity: Bible Hangman

Supplies:

- Chalkboard or dry erase board
- Chalk or dry erase markers

Instructions:

- Draw a large hangman tree on the board.
- Draw lines and spaces under the tree to correspond to the letters and spaces of the key phrase.
- **Key phrase**: Even though Lot was a sinner, God rescued Lot because Lot believed God.
- **Key phrase for younger students**: God sees everything.
- Ask the lesson review questions, one at a time. Call on one student or one team to answer each question.
- If answer is correct, the student or team gets to pick a letter, i.e., the letter b.
- If the letter picked is in the key phrase, the teacher fills it in on the board each time it occurs.
- If the letter picked is not in the key phrase, the teacher draws one part of a stick figure on the hangman tree, i.e., a head, an arm, a stick body, etc.
- When a student (or team) thinks he knows the key phrase, he may try to solve the puzzle on his turn. The game is over when a student or team solves the puzzle or the teacher draws all the parts of the stick man, whichever comes first.
-

Extra Bible References

Psalms 11:6, 83:18, 94:1-2; Proverbs 3:5-6, 14:12; Isaiah 46:9-10; Ezekiel 16:49-50; Ezekiel 18:20, 38:22; Luke 17:28-33; Romans 3:10-18, 5:12; Philippians 2:3; 2 Peter 2:6-9; 1 John 2:15-17; Revelation 20:14-15

19
More than the Stars
God's Promises to Abram

Memory Verse

And he believed in the Lord, and He accounted it to him for righteousness. Genesis 15:6

Lesson

After Lot moved away, God promised to give Abram more children than he could possibly count. God told Abram that one day all the land he could see in every direction would belong to his children. Someday God would give the land of Canaan to Abram's descendants just as He had promised Abram when he first arrived.

And the Lord said to Abram, after Lot had separated from him: "Lift your eyes now and look from the place where you are-- northward, southward, eastward, and westward; for all the land which you see I give to you and your descendants forever. And I will make your descendants as the dust of the earth; so that if a man could number the dust of the earth, then your descendants also could be numbered. Arise, walk in the land through its length and its width, for I give it to you." Genesis 13:14-17

Year after year, Abram and Sarai waited for God to do what He promised and give them many descendants, but nothing happened. No children were born to them. Abram began to wonder if God meant what He said.

...Abram said, "Look, You have given me no offspring..." Genesis 15:3

But God assured Abram He had not forgotten His promise.

And behold, the word of the Lord came to him, saying, "...one who will come from your own body shall be your heir." Then He brought him outside and said, "Look now toward heaven, and count the stars if you are able to number them." And He said to him, "So shall your descendants be."

God is the One who gives life. He is the One who breathed life into Adam. He is the One who made Eve out of Adam's rib. Nothing is impossible for God.

Even though Abram and Sarai were old and unable to have children, God was going to give them a son, and from this son would come countless descendants. God said that just like it is impossible to count all the stars in the sky, it would be impossible to count all the children that were going to be born into Abram's family.

Abram believed God would do what He promised; He believed God would give him a son. He believed that from this son would come many descendants and that one of these descendants would be the Savior who would save him from the death penalty he deserved for his sin.

And he believed in the Lord, and He accounted it to him for righteousness. Genesis 15:4-6

When Abram "believed in the Lord," God gave him the gift of His righteousness, or His perfect goodness. This gift made Abram acceptable to God. Even though Abram still sinned sometimes, he was now no longer separated from God. Since Abram had God's righteousness, he would live with God in Heaven when he died.

God talked to Abram about something that was going to happen to his descendants after his death.

Then He said to Abram: "Know certainly that your descendants will be strangers in a land that is not theirs, and will serve them, and they will afflict them four hundred years. And also the nation whom they serve I will judge; afterward they shall come out with great possessions.

Now as for you, you shall go to your fathers in peace; you shall be buried at a good old age. But in the fourth generation they shall return here, for the iniquity of the Amorites is not yet complete." Genesis 15:13-16

God knows what will happen in the future. God told Abram his descendants would be slaves in another country for four hundred years. After that, He would free them from their misery and send them back to Canaan with great riches.

131

God was not going to give the land of Canaan to Abram's children until "the iniquity of the Amorites" was "complete." The Amorites lived in the land of Canaan. God was not going to take their land from them until their iniquity (their sin) had reached its limit.

Remember how God gave the people in Noah's day time to change their minds? All during the many years it took Noah and his sons to build the boat, Noah warned the people that God would destroy them if they did not turn to Him. But finally, when not one person believed God, God sent the flood.

God was patient with the Canaanites too. Because He loved them, He gave them time to change their minds about Him and about their evil behavior. But even though God was giving them a chance to change their minds, He knew what would happen in the end. God knew that after four hundred years the Canaanites would be more wicked than ever, and He would have to destroy them.

Because of God's plan to make Abram's family into a great nation, God gave new names to Abram and Sarai. This is what God told Abram:

> No longer shall your name be called Abram, but your name shall be Abraham; for I have made you a father of many nations...
>
> As for Sarai your wife, you shall not call her name Sarai, but Sarah shall be her name. And I will bless her and also give you a son by her...and she shall be a mother of nations; kings of peoples shall be from her. Genesis 17:5, 15-16

Abram's new name, Abraham, meant "father of a great number of people." Sarai's new name, Sarah, meant "royal princess." Many children and a great nation would come from Abraham and Sarah.

God kept His promise to Abraham; He made Abraham into a great nation and Abraham became famous. Did you know the people living in Israel today are Abraham's descendants? We hear about the nation of Israel on the news all the time, even though Abraham has been gone for three thousand years!

Remember

Only righteous, or perfect, people can live with God. But just like all of Adam and Eve's children, you are a sinner and cannot do anything to make yourself acceptable to God.

The Bible says God cannot allow sinful people to live with Him in Heaven. So what are you going to do?

> For You are not a God who takes pleasure in wickedness, nor shall evil dwell with You. Psalm 5:4

Remember what God did for Abraham? When Abraham believed God, God gave him the gift of righteousness. This gift of righteousness made Abraham acceptable to God.

> But to him who...believes on Him...his faith is accounted for righteousness... Romans 4:5

Only God can make you acceptable to Him. He promised to send the Savior to make a way for you to be able to live with Him in Heaven. Trust in God to rescue you from sin and death!

Questions

1. After Lot moved away, what did God say He would give to Abraham? *God said He would give Abraham more children than he could count and that He would give them the land of Canaan.*

2. Who gives life to every person? *God does.*

3. What special person was going to be one of Abraham's descendants? *The Savior was going to be one of Abraham's descendants.*

4. Was Abraham a sinner? *Yes, he was.*

5. When did God give Abraham the gift of righteousness? *God gave Abraham the gift of righteousness when Abraham believed in Him. Abraham trusted in God to send the Savior to save him from the death penalty he deserved for his sin.*

6. What did God tell Abraham would happen to his descendants after his death? *God told Abraham that his descendants would be slaves in another country for four hundred years. After that time, God said He would free Abraham's descendants and send them back to Canaan with great riches.*

7. Why did God wait four hundred years to give the land of Canaan to Abraham's descendants? *God is loving and patient. He wanted to give the Canaanites a chance to believe in Him.*

8. Who is the only One who can make you acceptable to God? *Only God can make you acceptable to Him.*

9. Who did God promise to send to rescue you from sin and death? *God promised to send the Savior to rescue you from sin and death.*

10. What is the only way for you to please God? *The only way for you to please God is to believe Him.*

Biblical Worldviews

- God keeps His promises; you can depend on God to do what He says He will do.
- God is the One who gives life.
- All people are sinners.
- The penalty for sin is death.
- Only God can make people acceptable to Him; only He can give righteousness.
- God saves only those who believe in Him.
- God knows everything; He knows the future.
- God is a God of love; He is merciful and patient.
- God had a plan for saving people through the Savior.

Activity: Count the Stars Picture

Supplies:

- Paper, one piece per student
- Pencil, crayons or colored pencils
- Lots and lots of gold or silver star stickers

Instructions:

- Students draw and color an outdoor night scene with Abraham in it.
- Students fill the night sky with star stickers. They can use as many stars as they can.
- Students write out Genesis 15:6 on the front or back of the paper.

Extra Bible References

Genesis 18:25; Exodus 32:13; Leviticus 18:24-25; Numbers 23:19; Deuteronomy 18:12; Isaiah 46:8-10; John 3:18, 8:56-59; Acts 10:34; Romans 2:11, 4:1-25; Galatians 3:6-9; 1 Timothy 2:4; James 4:12; Hebrews 11:6, 8-16, 39-40; 1 Peter 4:5; 2 Peter 3:9

20
Helpless
Abraham and Isaac

Memory Verse

I, even I, am the Lord, and besides Me there is no savior. Isaiah 43:11

Lesson

When Abraham was 100 years old and Sarah 90, God gave them a baby boy! God kept His promise to Abraham.

Abraham and Sarah named their baby Isaac.

And the Lord visited Sarah as He had said, and the Lord did for Sarah as He had spoken. For Sarah conceived and bore Abraham a son in his old age...And Abraham called the name of his son who was born to him--whom Sarah bore to him--Isaac. Genesis 21:1-3

Abraham and Sarah had waited a long time for this baby. They loved Isaac. Abraham believed that through Isaac God was going to give him countless descendants.

But then God asked Abraham to do something unthinkable.

Now it came to pass after these things that God tested Abraham, and said to him, "Abraham!" And he said, "Here I am." Then He said, "Take now your son, your only son Isaac, whom you love, and go to the land of Moriah, and offer him there as a burnt offering on one of the mountains of which I shall tell you." Genesis 22:1-2

God hates murder. He does not want people to sacrifice children, or adults, to false gods. This is the only time God ever asked a parent to sacrifice a child. God had an important reason for asking Abraham to sacrifice Isaac. Later on, you will see what an incredible sacrifice God made for you and me.

Abraham must have wondered what God was thinking. How could God keep His promise to give him many descendants if he killed his only son? Do you think Abraham trusted God and did what God asked, or not?

135

God was the One who gave Isaac life. Abraham knew Isaac really belonged to God. If God wanted to take Isaac's life, He could. And so, early the next morning, Abraham and Isaac left to go to the place God told Abraham to go.

So Abraham rose early in the morning and saddled his donkey, and took two of his young men with him, and Isaac his son; and he split the wood for the burnt offering, and arose and went to the place of which God had told him. Then on the third day Abraham lifted his eyes and saw the place afar off.

And Abraham said to his young men, "Stay here with the donkey; the lad and I will go yonder and worship, and we will come back to you." So Abraham took the wood of the burnt offering and laid it on Isaac his son; and he took the fire in his hand, and a knife, and the two of them went together. Genesis 22:3-6

When they neared the place where God had said for Abraham to sacrifice Isaac, Abraham and Isaac went on alone without their servants. Abraham told the servants, "**We** will come back to you." Abraham believed that both he and Isaac would return.

The Bible says Abraham believed that even if he killed Isaac, God was able to bring him back to life again.

By faith Abraham, when he was tested, offered up Isaac, and he who had received the promises offered up his only begotten son...concluding that God was able to raise him up, even from the dead... Hebrews 11:17-19

When Abraham and Isaac came to the place where God had said for him to sacrifice Isaac, Abraham built an altar. Then Abraham tied up his only son and laid him on top of the wood.

Then they came to the place of which God had told him. And Abraham built an altar there and placed the wood in order; and he bound Isaac his son and laid him on the altar, upon the wood. And Abraham stretched out his hand and took the knife to slay his son. Genesis 22:9-10

Isaac was tied with ropes; he could not move. He could not get off the altar. There was nothing he could do to save himself from certain death.

137

Then Abraham lifted his knife.

But the Angel of the Lord called to him from heaven and said, "Abraham, Abraham!"

So he said, "Here I am."

And He said, "Do not lay your hand on the lad, or do anything to him; for now I know that you fear God, since you have not withheld your son, your only son, from Me."

Then Abraham lifted his eyes and looked, and there behind him was a ram caught in a thicket by its horns. So Abraham went and took the ram, and offered it up for a burnt offering instead of his son. And Abraham called the name of the place, The-Lord-Will-Provide; as it is said to this day, "In the Mount of The Lord it shall be provided."
Genesis 22:11-14

Only God could make a way for Isaac to be set free. In His love, God provided a ram (a boy sheep) to be sacrificed in Isaac's place.

The only kind of sacrifice God would accept in the place of Isaac was a perfect one. Since the ram was caught by its horns, it did not have any scratches or bruises. God provided a perfect lamb to die in place of Isaac.

Abraham named the place where God provided the ram for Isaac "The-Lord-Will-Provide".

So Abraham returned to his young men, and they rose and went together to Beersheba; and Abraham dwelt at Beersheba.
Genesis 22:19

Abraham trusted God. He was not like Adam and Eve who believed Satan instead of God. He was not like Cain, or the people at the Tower of Babel, who thought their way was better than God's way.

Instead, Abraham believed God and did what God asked. God did not let Abraham down. He provided a way of escape for Isaac so Isaac did not have to die. God was still going to give Abraham many children just as He promised, and one of those children was going to be the Savior.

Remember

Did you know you are a lot like Isaac when he was on the altar? Isaac could not get free because he was tied with ropes. Isaac could do nothing to escape; he was going to die.

Your sin is like those ropes tied around Isaac. Just like the ropes held Isaac on the altar, your sin keeps you bound up for death. There is nothing you can do to escape.

For the wages of sin is death... Romans 6:23a

But just like God was the only One who could make a way for Isaac to be saved from death, God is the only One who can rescue you from death. On the mountain, God provided a perfect male sheep to die in Isaac's place. God has provided for you, too, by promising to send the Savior to rescue you from sin and death.

I, even I, am the LORD, and besides Me there is no savior.
Isaiah 43:11

Questions

1. Does God always do what He promises to do? *Yes, God always keeps His promises.*

2. Is anything too hard for God? *No, nothing is too hard for God.*

3. How old were Abraham and Sarah when Isaac was born? *Abraham was 100 years old and Sarah was 90.*

4. Why was it okay for God to tell Abraham to sacrifice Isaac? *God could tell Abraham to sacrifice Isaac because Isaac belonged to God. God is the One who gave Isaac life.*

5. When God asked Abraham to sacrifice his only son, did Abraham think God had changed His mind about giving him many descendants? *No, Abraham trusted God. He knew God always does what He says He will do. Abraham believed that if he killed Isaac, God could bring him back to life again.*

6. In what way are you like Isaac on the altar? *Just like Isaac could not free himself from death because of the ropes that held him on the altar, you cannot escape from death because of your sin. The Bible says that because of your sin you must die.*

7. Who was the only One who could provide a way for Isaac to escape death? *God was the only One who could make a way for him to be saved.*

8. What did God provide for Isaac? *God provided a perfect male lamb to die in Isaac's place.*

9. Who is the only One who can provide a way for you to escape death? *Only God can make a way for you to escape death.*

10. Who did God say would come from Abraham's descendants to help all the families of the earth? *God promised Abraham that the Savior would be one of his descendants and would bring God's kindness and help to all people in the world.*

Biblical Worldviews

- God keeps His promises.
- Nothing is too hard for God.
- Since God is the One who gives life to people, they rightfully belong to Him and it is okay for Him to tell them what they should do.
- God is a personal being; He communicates with people.
- The only way to please God is to believe Him.
- All people are sinners and the penalty for sin is death.
- We cannot save ourselves. Only God can save us.
- Since God is perfect, He only accepted a perfect sacrifice to take Isaac's place.
- God had a plan to send the Savior to rescue people from Satan, sin, and death.

Activity: Clay or Play Dough Sculpture

Supplies:
- Modeling clay, play-dough, or miniature marshmallows
- Wooden or cardboard base
- White glue and glue gun
- Cotton balls
- Photocopy of memory verse (optional)

Instructions:
- Students shape four legs and a head out of modeling clay or play-dough (or they may use miniature marshmallows for the legs and head, although the model won't last as long).
- If using modeling clay, each leg should be about the size of a miniature marshmallow and the head should be about the size of a very small grape.
- If using modeling clay, bake according to package directions.
- Students use glue to attach legs to the cardboard or wooden base. (The teacher may choose to do this part with a glue gun; do not allow children to use glue gun.)
- Students glue together large cotton balls to create the lamb's body.
- Students glue body onto legs. Then glue on the head.
- Students either write out memory verse or cut out and glue a photocopy of the verse onto the base of the model.

Extra Bible References

Leviticus 22:24; Psalm 9:10, 24:1, 115:3; Isaiah 42:5; Jeremiah 32:17; Luke 1:37; Acts 17:25; 2 Corinthians 5:21; Hebrews 11:17-19

21
Twins
Esau and Jacob

Memory Verse

> *I, even I, am the Lord, and besides Me there is no savior. Isaiah 43:11*

Lesson

When Isaac was forty years old, Abraham decided he should get married. In those days, parents usually decided who their children would marry. Abraham did not want Isaac to marry a Canaanite woman, so he sent his servant to his homeland, Mesopotamia, to find a wife for Isaac.

...Abraham said to the oldest servant of his house, who ruled over all that he had, "...go to my country and to my family, and take a wife for my son Isaac." Genesis 24:2-4

In Mesopotamia, God led Abraham's servant to a woman named Rebekah. The servant took Rebekah to Isaac in Canaan. Isaac and Rebekah got married, but Rebekah was unable to have children. The Bible says, "She was barren."

Finally, Isaac prayed for Rebekah and she became pregnant with twins.

Isaac was forty years old when he took Rebekah as wife...Now Isaac pleaded with the LORD for his wife, because she was barren; and the LORD granted his plea, and Rebekah his wife conceived. But the children struggled together within her; and she said, "If all is well, why am I like this?" So she went to inquire of the LORD.

And the LORD said to her: "Two nations are in your womb, two peoples shall be separated from your body; one people shall be stronger than the other, and the older shall serve the younger." Genesis 25:20-23

When Rebekah asked God why the twins inside of her were fighting, God said that someday the twins would both become great nations. The nation from the younger son would be greater than the nation from the older one.

The day came for the babies to be born.

So when her days were fulfilled for her to give birth, indeed there were twins in her womb. And the first came out red. He was like a hairy garment all over; so they called his name Esau. Afterward his brother came out, and his hand took hold of Esau's heel; so his name was called Jacob. Isaac was sixty years old when she bore them.

So the boys grew. And Esau was a skillful hunter, a man of the field; but Jacob was a mild man, dwelling in tents. And Isaac loved Esau because he ate of his game, but Rebekah loved Jacob.
Genesis 25:24-28

Even though Jacob and Esau were twins, Esau was older because he was born first. In Abraham and Isaac's time, to be the oldest in the family was a special honor. When the dad died, the oldest son would get twice as much of his dad's possessions as the other sons. For example, he would get ten sheep while each of his brothers would get only five sheep. This was called his birthright.

The oldest son also received an important blessing, or a special promise of good things to come, from his father.

Remember all the promises God made to Abraham? God promised to give Abraham countless descendants. God promised to give the land of Canaan to Abraham's descendants, and He promised Abraham that the Savior would come from his family. This last promise was the most important one.

When Abraham died, he passed these promises on to Isaac as part of Isaac's blessing and birthright. Isaac planned to pass them on to his oldest son Esau; but Esau did not care about God and His promises.

One day when Jacob and Esau were grown, Esau came home from hunting tired and hungry.

Now Jacob cooked a stew; and Esau came in from the field, and he was weary. And Esau said to Jacob, "Please feed me with that same red stew, for I am weary."...

But Jacob said, "Sell me your birthright as of this day."

And Esau said, "Look, I am about to die; so what is this birthright to me?"

Then Jacob said, "Swear to me as of this day."

So he swore to him, and sold his birthright to Jacob. And Jacob gave Esau bread and stew of lentils; then he ate and drank, arose, and went his way. Thus Esau despised his birthright. Genesis 25:29-34

All Esau could think about was how hungry he was. He gladly sold Jacob his birthright in exchange for a bowl of stew! Esau did not care about his birthright, but Jacob did.

Later, when Isaac was about to die, Jacob sneakily took Esau's blessing too.

Now it came to pass, when Isaac was old and his eyes were so dim that he could not see, that he called Esau his older son and said to him, "My son....Behold now, I am old. I do not know the day of my death...go out to the field and hunt game for me. And make me savory food, such as I love, and bring it to me that I may eat, that my soul may bless you before I die."

Now Rebekah was listening when Isaac spoke to Esau his son...So Rebekah spoke to Jacob her son, saying, "Indeed I heard your father speak to Esau your brother, saying, 'Bring me game and make savory food for me, that I may eat it and bless you in the presence of the LORD before my death.' Now...I will make savory food...for your father, such as he loves. Then you shall take it to your father, that he may eat it, and that he may bless you before his death."
Genesis 27:1-10

Then Rebekah took the choice clothes of her elder son Esau...and put them on Jacob her younger son. And she put the skins of the...goats on his hands and on the smooth part of his neck. Then she gave the savory food and the bread, which she had prepared, into the hand of her son Jacob.

So he went to his father and said, "My father."

And he said, "Here I am. Who are you, my son?"

143

Jacob said to his father, "I am Esau your firstborn...please arise, sit and eat of my game, that your soul may bless me." Genesis 27:15-19

Isaac said to Jacob, "Please come near, that I may feel you, my son, whether you are really my son Esau or not." So Jacob went near to Isaac his father, and he felt him and said, "The voice is Jacob's voice, but the hands are the hands of Esau." And he did not recognize him, because his hands were hairy like his brother Esau's hands; so he blessed him. Genesis 27:21-23

Now it happened, as soon as Isaac had finished blessing Jacob...that Esau his brother came in from his hunting.

And his father Isaac said to him, "Who are you?"

So he said, "I am your son, your firstborn, Esau."

Then Isaac trembled exceedingly, and said, "Who? Where is the one who hunted game and brought it to me? I ate all of it before you came, and I have blessed him—and indeed he shall be blessed."

When Esau heard the words of his father, he cried with an exceedingly great and bitter cry... Genesis 27:30-34a

Even though Esau sold his birthright to Jacob, he was angry when Jacob took his blessing too. But the Bible says that Esau was a profane person and really did not care about God and His promises.

...lest there be any...profane person like Esau, who for one morsel of food sold his birthright. For you know that afterward, when he wanted to inherit the blessing, he was rejected...though he sought it diligently with tears. Hebrews 12:16-17

Just like Cain, Esau became so angry with his brother he wanted to kill him.

So Esau hated Jacob because of the blessing with which his father blessed him, and Esau said in his heart, "The days of mourning for my father are at hand; then I will kill my brother Jacob." Genesis 27:41

Rebekah sent Jacob to her home in Mesopotamia to get away from Esau. It was a long journey that took many days. One night as Jacob slept, God spoke to him in a dream.

Now Jacob...came to a certain place and stayed there all night, because the sun had set. And he took one of the stones of that place and put it at his head, and he lay down in that place to sleep. Then he dreamed, and behold, a ladder was set up on the earth, and its top reached to heaven; and there the angels of God were ascending and descending on it.

And behold, the LORD stood above it and said: "I am the LORD God of Abraham your father and the God of Isaac; the land on which you lie I will give to you and your descendants. Also your descendants shall be as the dust of the earth; you shall spread abroad to the west and the east, to the north and the south; and in you and in your seed all the families of the earth shall be blessed. Behold, I am with you and will keep you wherever you go, and will bring you back to this land; for I will not leave you until I have done what I have spoken to you."
Genesis 28:10-15

Today God does not communicate with us through dreams. Everything God wants to say to us has already been recorded in the Bible. But the Bible was not yet written when Jacob lived on Earth. That is why God spoke to him in a dream.

God promised to protect Jacob and one day take him back to Canaan. God promised Jacob he would receive all the promises made to Abraham, his grandfather. Jacob's descendants would be more than could be counted, God was going to give them the land of Canaan, and one of his descendants was going to bring God's kindness and help to all the families of the earth.

Someday Jacob's descendants would become a great nation. From this nation would come the promised Savior, and just like the ladder in Jacob's dream made a bridge from Earth to Heaven, the Savior would make a way for people on Earth to go to Heaven. Through this promised Savior, God would bless all people by making a way for them to live with God forever.

God had told Rebekah that her younger son would be greater than his older brother. Even before Jacob and Esau were born, it was God's plan for Jacob, not Esau, to receive the promises made to Abraham. But rather than taking matters into his own hands, Jacob should have trusted in God. He should not have tried to trick Esau.

Remember

Esau did not care about what would happen to him when he died. He only cared about right now. He wanted to do whatever made him happy, even if it was wrong.

Many people are like Esau. They only care about being happy and having fun right now. They do not think about what will happen when their life on Earth is over.

But the Bible says the payment for sin is separation from God forever in the terrible place of suffering. If you do not trust in the Savior while you are still alive on Earth, you will have to be separated from God forever.

You need to trust in the Savior to rescue you from death. Only the promised Savior can make a way for you to be acceptable to God so that you can live with Him forever when you die.

...whoever believes in Him should not perish but have everlasting life. John 3:16b

God promises that whoever believes in Him will not be separated from Him in the place of suffering but will have everlasting life with Him.

Questions

1. Why were the twins fighting inside Rebekah? *God said they were fighting because one day they would both become great nations, and the nation from the younger son would be greater than the nation from the older son.*

2. What promises did God make to Abraham? *God promised to give Abraham countless children, God promised to give Abraham's family the land of Canaan, and, most importantly, God promised that the Savior would come from Abraham's family.*

3. Was God going to keep these promises, even though they did not come true during Abraham's lifetime? *Yes, no matter how long it takes, God always keeps His promises. God does everything He plans to do.*

4. Who did Abraham pass the promises on to? *Abraham passed the promises on to his son, Isaac.*

5. Did Esau care about God? *No, the Bible says Esau was a profane person. He did not care about God or His promises.*

6. What did Jacob see in his dream? *Jacob saw a ladder that reached from Earth to Heaven. He saw God standing at the top of the ladder.*

7. How does this ladder remind us of the promised Savior? *The promised Savior was going to make a way for people on Earth to go to Heaven and be with God.*

8. What did God promise Jacob in his dream? *God promised to be with Jacob and take him safely back to Canaan. God also promised Jacob he would receive all the promises made to Abraham, his grandfather.*

9. Why is it important for you to think about what will happen to you after you die? *It is important because the Bible says that when people die they go either to Heaven or to the terrible place of suffering. If you trust in God to save you, you will go to Heaven when you die; but if you do not trust in God while you are alive on Earth, you will be forever separated from God in the place of suffering.*

Biblical Worldviews

- God is the One who gives life.
- God knows everything; He knows what will happen in the future.
- God is a personal being; He communicates with people.
- God speaks to us through the Bible.
- God always does what He plans to do; God keeps His promises.
- All people are sinners.
- God saves only those who believe Him.
- God planned to send the Savior; God always completes His plans.

Activity: Blessing Skit

Supplies:

- Four student volunteers
- Although no other supplies are needed, you can use a large pot and a piece of animal fur for props if you have them.

Instructions:

- Have student volunteers play the parts of Isaac, Rebecca, Esau, and Jacob as they act out the story of Jacob and Esau.
- If you have more than four students who want to act, divide them into more than one group and let each group act it out while the other students watch.
- Discuss skit emphasizing key points from the lesson.

Extra Bible References

Exodus 32:13; 2 Chronicles 21:8; Psalm 33:11; Isaiah 46:10; John 1:51, 14:6; Romans 9:10-14; 1 Timothy 2:5; 1 Peter 1:10-12, 20-21; Hebrews 11:9-10, 13-21; Hebrews 11:39-40, 12:16-17

22
Jealous Brothers
Joseph Part I

Memory Verse

There are many plans in a man's heart, nevertheless the LORD's counsel—that will stand. Proverbs 19:21

Lesson

Jacob lived in Mesopotamia for a long time. God took care of Jacob just like He promised and gave him many children and lots of riches.

... [Jacob] became exceedingly prosperous, and had large flocks, female and male servants, and camels and donkeys. Genesis 30:43

Finally God said it was time for Jacob to return to Canaan.

...Then the LORD said to Jacob, "Return to the land of your fathers and to your family, and I will be with you." Genesis 31:3

Then Jacob rose...to go to his father Isaac in the land of Canaan. Genesis 31:17-18

Jacob, who was also called Israel, had twelve sons. His favorite son was Joseph. Jacob made a lovely, colorful coat for Joseph.

Now Israel loved Joseph more than all his children...he made him a tunic of many colors. But when his brothers saw that their father loved him more than all his brothers, they hated him and could not speak peaceably to him. Genesis 37:3-4

Jacob and his sons were sinners. Jacob was wrong to love Joseph more than his other sons, and it was wrong for Joseph's brothers to hate him.

One night Joseph had a dream. He told his dream to his brothers.

Now Joseph had a dream, and he told it to his brothers; and they hated him even more. So he said to them, "Please hear this dream which I have dreamed: There we were, binding sheaves in the field. Then behold, my sheaf arose and also stood upright; and indeed your sheaves stood all around and bowed down to my sheaf."

And his brothers said to him, "Shall you indeed reign over us? Or shall you indeed have dominion over us?" So they hated him even more for his dreams and for his words.

Then he dreamed still another dream and told it to his brothers, and said, "Look, I have dreamed another dream. And this time, the sun, the moon, and the eleven stars bowed down to me."

So he told it to his father and his brothers; and his father rebuked him and said to him, "What is this dream that you have dreamed? Shall your mother and I and your brothers indeed come to bow down to the earth before you?" And his brothers envied him, but his father kept the matter in mind. Genesis 37:5-11

God gave these dreams to Joseph. God wanted Joseph to know that someday he would rule over his family. Of course, when Joseph told his dreams to his brothers, it made them jealous and they hated him even more.

One day Jacob sent Joseph to check on his brothers who were out in the field caring for their sheep.

Then he said to him, "Please go and see if it is well with your brothers and well with the flocks, and bring back word to me." Genesis 37:14a

Now when they saw him afar off...they conspired against him to kill him...

But Reuben heard it... and said, "Let us not kill him...but cast him into this pit..."...

So...when Joseph had come to his brothers...they stripped Joseph of his tunic... of many colors...Then they took him and cast him into a pit...

151

And they sat down to eat a meal. Then they lifted their eyes and looked, and there was a company of Ishmaelites, coming from Gilead with their camels...on their way...down to Egypt...so the brothers... lifted him out of the pit, and sold him to the Ishmaelites for twenty shekels of silver. And they took Joseph to Egypt...

So [his brothers] took Joseph's tunic, killed a kid of the goats, and dipped the tunic in the blood. Then they...brought it to their father and said, "We have found this. Do you know whether it is your son's tunic or not?"

And he recognized it and said, "It is my son's tunic. A wild beast has devoured him. Without doubt Joseph is torn to pieces." Then Jacob tore his clothes...and mourned for his son many days. Genesis 37:18-34

Joseph's brothers sold him to some traders going to Egypt. In Egypt, one of Pharaoh's officers bought Joseph as a slave.

...Potiphar, an officer of Pharaoh, captain of the guard...bought him from the Ishmaelites...

> **Pharaoh – an Egyptian king**

The LORD was with Joseph, and he was a successful man...And his master saw that the LORD was with him... So...he made him overseer of his house, and all that he had he put under his authority. Genesis 39:1-4

God was with Joseph even though he was in a strange place far from home. Joseph did his work so well that Potiphar put him in charge of everything he owned. But then Potiphar's wife lied about Joseph. She told Potiphar that Joseph had fallen in love with her. Of course, this was not true.

So it was, when his master heard the words which his wife spoke...that his anger was aroused. Then Joseph's master took him and put him into the prison, a place where the king's prisoners were confined... But the LORD was with Joseph and showed him mercy, and He gave him favor in the sight of the keeper of the prison. And the keeper of the prison committed to Joseph's hand all the prisoners who were in the prison...and whatever he did, the LORD made it prosper. Genesis 39:19-23

Even in prison, God was with Joseph so that Joseph was put in charge of all the prisoners.

One day, two of Pharaoh's officers were thrown into the prison with Joseph.

It came to pass after these things that the butler and the baker of the king of Egypt offended their lord, the king of Egypt. And Pharaoh was angry with his two officers, the chief butler and the chief baker. So he put them in...prison, the place where Joseph was confined...

Then the butler and the baker...had a dream, both of them...And Joseph came in to them in the morning and looked at them, and saw that they were sad. So he asked..., "Why do you look so sad today?"

And they said to him, "We each have had a dream, and there is no interpreter of it."

So Joseph said to them, "Do not interpretations belong to God? Tell them to me, please."

Then the chief butler told his dream to Joseph, and said to him, "Behold, in my dream a vine was before me, and in the vine were three branches; it was as though it budded, its blossoms shot forth, and its clusters brought forth ripe grapes. Then Pharaoh's cup was in my hand; and I took the grapes and pressed them into Pharaoh's cup, and placed the cup in Pharaoh's hand."

And Joseph said to him, "This is the interpretation of it: The three branches are three days. Now within three days Pharaoh will...restore you to your place, and you will put Pharaoh's cup in his hand according to the former manner, when you were his butler. But remember me when it is well with you, and please show kindness to me; make mention of me to Pharaoh, and get me out of this house. For indeed I was stolen away from the land of the Hebrews; and also I have done nothing here that they should put me into the dungeon."

When the chief baker saw that the interpretation was good, he said to Joseph, "...in my dream...there were three white baskets on my head. In the uppermost basket were all kinds of baked goods for Pharaoh, and the birds ate them out of the basket on my head."

So Joseph answered and said, "This is the interpretation of it: The three baskets are three days. Within three days Pharaoh will...hang you on a tree; and the birds will eat your flesh from you."

Now it came to pass on the third day, which was Pharaoh's birthday, that he made a feast for all his servants...Then he restored the chief butler to his butlership again...But he hanged the chief baker, as Joseph had interpreted to them. Yet the chief butler did not remember Joseph, but forgot him. Genesis 40:1-23

When the baker and the butler told their dreams to Joseph, Joseph trusted in God to give him the meaning of the dreams. God knows everything; He showed Joseph what the dreams meant. Of course, everything happened exactly like Joseph said. Pharaoh released the butler, but the baker he put to death.

When the butler returned to Pharaoh's palace, he forgot about Joseph. But God did not forget about him. At the perfect time, God did for Joseph exactly what He said He would do. God always accomplishes His plans.

Remember

Even before you were born, when you were still inside your mom, God formed you. He made you just the way He wanted you to be, and He is One who gave you life. God loves you and cares about you just like He loved Joseph and cared about him.

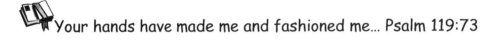Your hands have made me and fashioned me... Psalm 119:73

God wants you to trust in Him. Even though Joseph's brothers hated him, and Potiphar's wife lied about him, Joseph still trusted in God. He knew that in His time, God would do what He promised.

In the Garden of Eden, God promised to send the Savior. Later, God told Abraham that the Savior would come from his family and bring God's kindness and help to all people. God wants you to trust in the Savior to rescue you from sin and death so that you will not be separated from Him forever in the terrible place of suffering.

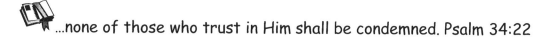 ...none of those who trust in Him shall be condemned. Psalm 34:22

God promises that everyone who trusts in Him will be saved from death.

Questions

1. How did God take care of Jacob in Mesopotamia? *He gave him many children and made him rich. He took care of him just like He promised.*

2. How many sons did Jacob have? *Jacob had twelve sons.*

3. Who was Jacob's favorite son? *Joseph was Jacob's favorite son.*

4. Why were Joseph's brothers angry with him? *They were angry with Joseph because their dad loved Joseph more than he loved them and because Joseph dreamed he would rule over them someday.*

5. What happened in Joseph's dreams? *First Joseph dreamed that his brothers' bundles of grain bowed down to his bundle. In his second dream, the sun, moon, and eleven stars bowed down to him.*

6. Who gave these dreams to Joseph? *God gave these dreams to Joseph.*

7. What did Joseph's brothers do to him? *They sold Joseph to traders going to Egypt.*

8. What did Jacob think happened to Joseph? *He thought a wild animal had killed him.*

9. What terrible thing happened to Joseph while he was working for Potiphar? *Potiphar threw Joseph in prison because of the lie Potiphar's wife told him.*

10. Did Joseph stop trusting God because of all the terrible things that happened to him? *No, even though everything seemed to go wrong, Joseph still trusted in God.*

Biblical Worldviews

- God is a personal being; He communicates with people.
- God keeps His promises.
- All people are sinners.
- God works out everything according to His plan.
- God knows everything.
- God is a God of love.
- God saves only those who believe Him.

Activity: Memory Verse Ball

Supplies:

- One or more mid-size balls

- Copy of memory verse: "And those who know Your name will put their trust in You; For You, LORD, have not forsaken those who seek You." Psalm 9:10

Instructions:

- Depending on the number of students, students either divide into teams, or form one large circle.

- Students then practice the memory verse while throwing the ball to each other and catching it.

- For example: The teacher says the first part of the verse to be memorized. Then she throws the ball to one of the students, who repeats word for word what she just said and throws the ball to another student. Go around until everyone has had a chance to catch the ball and say the first part of the verse. Now add the second part of the verse and do the same thing. Then add the third part and so on until each student has memorized the entire verse, including the reference.

- If students have been working in small groups, they now come together to form a large circle and each one recites the verse and reference in front of the entire class with or without the balls.

Extra Bible References

1 Chronicles 29:12; Isaiah 42:9, 46:10; Acts 10:34; Romans 2:11, 3:9-12

23
The King's Dream
Joseph Part II

Memory Verse

There are many plans in a man's heart, nevertheless the LORD's counsel—that will stand. Proverbs 19:21

Lesson

One night long after Joseph told the butler and baker the meaning of their dreams, the king of Egypt had a dream.

Then it came to pass, at the end of two full years, that Pharaoh had a dream; and behold, he stood by the river. Suddenly there came up out of the river seven cows, fine looking and fat…Then…seven other cows came up after them out of the river, ugly and gaunt…And the ugly…cows ate up the seven…fat cows…

Pharaoh…dreamed a second time; and suddenly seven heads of grain came up on one stalk, plump and good. Then behold, seven thin heads, blighted by the east wind, sprang up after them. And the seven thin heads devoured the seven plump and full heads…

Now it came to pass in the morning that [Pharaoh] …was troubled, and he…called for all the magicians of Egypt and all its wise men. And Pharaoh told them his dreams, but there was no one who could interpret them for Pharaoh. Genesis 41:1-8

None of the magicians or wise men in all of Egypt could tell the king what his dream meant. Then the king's butler remembered Joseph.

Then the chief butler spoke to Pharaoh, saying: "I remember… When Pharaoh was angry with his servants, and put me in custody in the house of the captain of the guard, both me and the chief baker, we each had a dream in one night…Now there was a young… man with

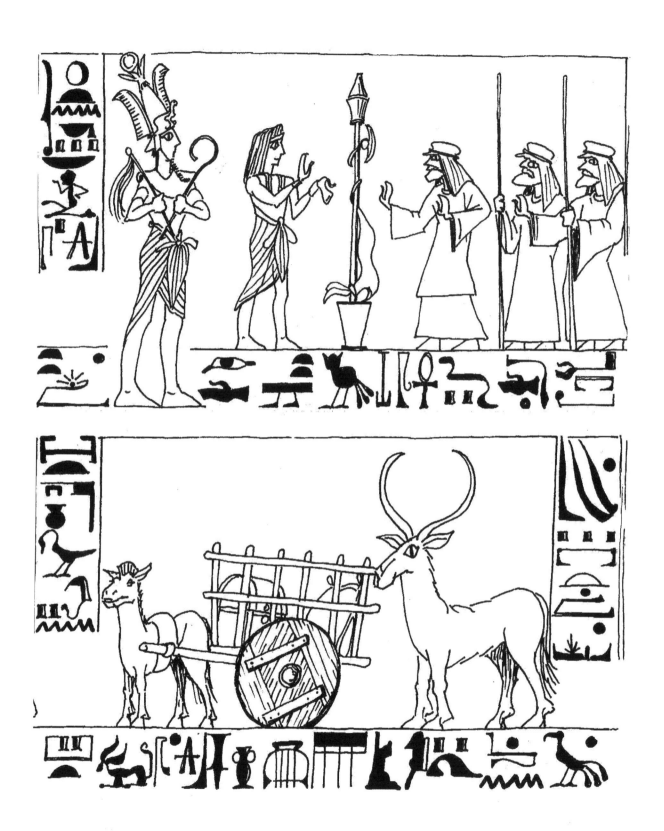

158

us there...And we told him, and he interpreted our dreams for us...And...just as he interpreted for us, so it happened."

Then Pharaoh sent and called Joseph, and they brought him quickly out of the dungeon; and he shaved, changed his clothing, and came to Pharaoh.

And Pharaoh said to Joseph, "I have had a dream, and there is no one who can interpret it. But I have heard it said of you that you can understand a dream, to interpret it."

So Joseph answered Pharaoh, saying, "It is not in me; God will give Pharaoh an answer of peace." Genesis 41:9-16

Joseph did not trust in his own wisdom; he trusted in God. Joseph knew that only God could tell him the meaning of Pharaoh's dream.

Then Joseph said to Pharaoh, "...The seven good cows...and the seven good heads are seven years...And the seven thin and ugly cows...and the seven empty heads blighted by the east wind are seven years...God has shown Pharaoh what He is about to do. Indeed seven years of great plenty will come throughout all the land of Egypt; but after them seven years of famine will arise, and all the plenty will be forgotten...the famine will...be very severe. And the dream was repeated to Pharaoh twice because the thing is established by God, and God will shortly bring it to pass." Genesis 41:25-32

Even though the Egyptians worshiped false gods, God cared about them. Now that Pharaoh knew what was going to happen, the Egyptians would be able to prepare for the coming food shortage.

"Now therefore, let Pharaoh select a discerning and wise man, and set him over the land of Egypt...let him appoint officers over the land...And let them gather all the food of those good years that are coming, and store up grain...Then that food shall be as a reserve for...the seven years of famine...that the land may not perish during the famine." Genesis 41:33-36

God gave Joseph wisdom so he could tell the Pharaoh what to do.

159

So the advice was good in the eyes of Pharaoh and in the eyes of all his servants...

Then Pharaoh said to Joseph, "Inasmuch as God has shown you all this, there is no one as discerning and wise as you. You shall be over my house, and all my people shall be ruled according to your word; only in regard to the throne will I be greater than you." And Pharaoh said to Joseph, "See, I have set you over all the land of Egypt."

Then Pharaoh took his signet ring off his hand and put it on Joseph's hand; and he clothed him in garments of fine linen and put a gold chain around his neck. And he had him ride in the second chariot which he had; and they cried out before him, "Bow the knee!" So he set him over all the land of Egypt. Genesis 41:37-43

This was a huge change for Joseph! In one afternoon he went from being a prisoner in the king's dungeon to being governor over the entire land of Egypt.

Who made this happen? God did. God is in charge of everything that happens in this world. God was working everything out according to His plan.

Joseph was thirty years old when he stood before Pharaoh king of Egypt. And Joseph went out from the presence of Pharaoh, and went throughout all the land of Egypt. Now in the seven plentiful years the ground brought forth abundantly. So he gathered up all the food...and laid up the food in the cities; he laid up in every city the food of the fields which surrounded them. Joseph gathered very much grain, as the sand of the sea, until he stopped counting, for it was immeasurable.

Then the seven years of plenty which were in the land of Egypt ended, and the seven years of famine began to come, as Joseph had said... Then Pharaoh said to all the Egyptians, ""Go to Joseph; whatever he says to you, do." ...and Joseph opened all the storehouses and sold to the Egyptians...all countries came to Joseph in Egypt to buy grain, because the famine was severe in all lands. Genesis 41:46-57

For seven years there was lots of food in Egypt. Joseph collected and stored as much grain as possible. Then, in the eighth year, the time of hunger began. No food grew anywhere. So

Pharaoh sent the hungry Egyptians to Joseph, and he sold them the grain he had collected during the good years.

But the famine was not just in Egypt. Even in Canaan, where Joseph's family lived, people started running out of food. When Joseph's father heard there was grain in Egypt, he sent his sons to buy some.

When Jacob saw that there was grain in Egypt, Jacob said to his sons …"Indeed I have heard that there is grain in Egypt; go down to that place and buy for us there, that we may live and not die."

So Joseph's ten brothers went down to buy grain in Egypt.

Now Joseph was governor over the land; and it was he who sold to all the people of the land. And Joseph's brothers came and bowed down before him with their faces to the earth. Joseph saw his brothers and recognized them, but he acted as a stranger to them and spoke roughly to them. Then he said to them, "Where do you come from?"

And they said, "From the land of Canaan to buy food."

So Joseph recognized his brothers, but they did not recognize him. Then Joseph remembered the dreams which he had dreamed about them… Genesis 42:1-9a

When Joseph's brothers arrived in Egypt to buy food, they did not recognize Joseph. They did not guess that the Egyptian governor was their brother. They did not realize they were bowing to Joseph!

But God knew all along that someday Joseph would be a great ruler; God knew all along that someday Joseph's brothers would bow down before him.

Remember

God knows everything. He knew the meaning of Pharaoh's dreams. He knew about the coming food shortage and what Pharaoh should do to get ready. God knew that someday Joseph would be a great ruler in Egypt and that his brothers would bow down to him. There is nothing God does not know!

Questions

1. What did the king of Egypt dream? *The king of Egypt dreamed about seven skinny cows eating seven fat cows and about seven thin heads of grain swallowing seven healthy heads of grain.*

2. What did Pharaoh's dreams mean? *Pharaoh's dreams meant there would be seven years with lots of food, but afterwards there would be seven years of great hunger.*

3. Who showed Joseph the meaning of Pharaoh's dreams? *God did.*

4. Who protected Joseph from being killed by his brothers? *God protected Joseph.*

5. Who protected Joseph while he was in prison? *God did.*

6. Who caused the pharaoh to bring Joseph out of prison and make him the governor of Egypt? *God did; He is the highest authority.*

7. Did the dreams God gave Joseph about his brothers bowing down to him come true? *Yes, when Joseph's brothers came to Egypt they bowed down to Joseph.*

8. How much does God know? *God knows everything.*

Biblical Worldviews

- God is a personal being; He communicates with people.
- God is a God of love; He loves everyone.
- God knows everything; He knows what is going to happen in the future.
- God is greater than false gods and magicians.
- God works everything out according to His plan; He is the highest authority.

Activity: Pharaoh's Dream Skit

Supplies:

- Five or more student volunteers

Instructions:

- Students act out Pharaoh's dream and Joseph's interpretation of it. There are five parts: Pharaoh, Pharaoh's butler, Pharaoh's messenger (goes to prison to get Joseph), prison guard (releases Joseph), and members of Pharaoh's court.
- If there are more than five students who want to act out the skit, divide them into groups and let each group act it out while the other students watch.
- Discuss skit, emphasizing key points from the lesson.

Extra Bible References

1 Chronicles 29:11-12; Psalms 105:16-23, 115:3, 145:9, Isaiah 42:9, 46:10; Lamentations 3:22-23; Daniel 4:17, 2:27-28, 10:34; Romans 2:11; Hebrews 11:1-2, 6, 13-16, 22

24
Suffering in Egypt
Joseph Part III

Memory Verse

For the LORD Most High is awesome; He is a great King over all the earth. Psalm 47:2

Lesson

Joseph's brothers took the grain they bought in Egypt back to Canaan. But before long, they ran out of food again.

Now the famine was severe in the land. And it came to pass, when they had eaten up the grain which they had brought from Egypt, that their father said to them, "Go back, buy us a little food."
Genesis 3:1-2

Jacob sent his sons back to Egypt to buy more food. This time when Joseph saw his brothers, he told them who he was.

And Joseph said to his brothers, "...I am Joseph your brother, whom you sold into Egypt. But now, do not...be...angry with yourselves because you sold me here; for...God sent me before you to...save your lives by a great deliverance. So now it was not you who sent me here, but God; and He has made me...a ruler throughout all the land of Egypt.

"Hurry and go up to my father, and say to him, 'Thus says your son Joseph: "God has made me lord of all Egypt; come down to me, do not tarry. You shall dwell in the land of Goshen, and you shall be near to me, you and your children, your children's children, your flocks and your herds, and all that you have. There I will provide for you, lest you and your household, and all that you have, come to poverty; for there are still five years of famine."' Genesis 45:4-11

Joseph was a powerful man; only the king of Egypt was more powerful than him. It would have been easy for Joseph to put his brothers in prison, or even have them killed, but he did not do that. Instead of being angry with his brothers, Joseph trusted God. Joseph knew God was in control of all that happened to him. God's plan was for Joseph to provide food for his family during the time of hunger.

God protected Jacob and his sons because they were Abraham's descendants. God had promised to take care of Abraham's descendants and make them into a great nation. God promised that someday the Savior would come from this nation. Everything was going to happen just the way God planned.

When Jacob's sons told him Joseph was alive, he could hardly believe it.

Then they…came to the land of Canaan to Jacob their father. And they told him, saying, "Joseph is still alive, and he is governor over all the land of Egypt." And Jacob's heart stood still, because he did not believe them.

But when they told him all the words which Joseph had said to them, and when he saw the carts which Joseph had sent to carry him…Israel said, "It is enough. Joseph my son is still alive. I will go and see him before I die." Genesis 45:25-28

Jacob's (or Israel's) entire family moved to Egypt. In Egypt, many children and grandchildren were born to him. But after a few years, Jacob died. In time, his sons died too. Even the good pharaoh died.

And Joseph died, all his brothers, and all that generation. But the children of Israel were fruitful and increased abundantly…and the land was filled with them. Now there arose a new king over Egypt, who did not know Joseph. And he said to his people, "Look, the people…of Israel are more and mightier than we; come, let us deal shrewdly with them, lest they multiply, and it happen, in the event of war, that they …join our enemies and fight against us, and so go up out of the land."

Therefore they set taskmasters over them to afflict them with their burdens…But the more they afflicted them, the more they multiplied and grew…So the Egyptians made the children of Israel serve with rigor. And they made their lives bitter with hard bondage—in mortar, in brick, and in all manner of service in the field… Exodus 1:6-14a

The new pharaoh did not know Joseph. He was afraid of the children of Israel because there were so many of them. The new pharaoh was afraid the nation of Israel would become more powerful than the nation of Egypt.

To stop the Israelites from becoming too powerful, the pharaoh forced them to work hard without pay. The Egyptians were cruel and hateful to the Israelites. But no matter what they did, the Israelites just kept increasing in number!

Finally, the king ordered all Israelite baby boys to be drowned in the river. What a horrible thing to do!

So Pharaoh commanded all his people, saying, "Every son who is born you shall cast into the river, and every daughter you shall save alive." Exodus 1:22

Who was causing the pharaoh to be so mean to the Israelites? It was Satan. Satan knew God planned for the Savior to come from the nation of Israel. He did not want the Savior to rescue people from his dominion, so he tried to stop God's plans.

But God was not surprised by what was happening. Long ago He had told Abraham that his descendants would be slaves in another country.

Then He said to Abram: "Know certainly that your descendants will be strangers in a land that is not theirs, and will serve them, and they will afflict them four hundred years...But in the fourth generation they shall return here..." Genesis 15:13, 16a

God is always right; He always tells the truth. He told Abraham that after four hundred years the Israelites would be freed from slavery and return to Canaan to receive the land He had promised to give them. And that is exactly what was going to happen.

Remember

Satan hates God and people. He tries to stop God's plans. Satan did not want the Savior to be born because he wants people to be separated from God forever in the terrible place of suffering.

But neither Satan nor the king of Egypt could stop God from accomplishing His plans. God always does everything He plans to do.

The counsel of the LORD stands forever, the plans of His heart to all generations. Psalm 33:11

God was going to make Israel into a great nation and give them the land of Canaan. Someday the Savior, who would bring God's kindness and help to all people on Earth, was going to be born into this nation. The Savior would rescue people from Satan and death.

Questions

1. Why was Joseph not angry with his brothers? *Joseph was not angry with his brothers because he knew that even though they meant to hurt him, God was really the One who sent him to Egypt to keep his family alive.*

2. Why did God take special care of Jacob's family? *God protected Jacob and his children because they were Abraham's descendants. God had promised to take care of Abraham's descendants and make them into a great nation.*

3. What was Jacob's other name? *Jacob was also called Israel.*

4. Why was the new king of Egypt afraid of the Israelites? *He was afraid they would become a strong nation and fight against Egypt. The king did not want to lose his slave workers.*

5. What did the king do to stop the Israelites from increasing in number? *He made them work hard and treated them cruelly. He tried to kill all the baby boys born to the Israelites.*

6. Who was leading the king of Egypt? *Satan was leading the pharaoh.*

7. Why did Satan want to destroy the nation of Israel? *Satan knew the Savior was going to come from the nation of Israel. God had told Satan in the Garden of Eden that the Savior would bruise his head. That is why Satan wanted to stop the Savior from being born; he did not want the Savior to destroy his power over people.*

8. Could Satan or the pharaoh ruin God's plan to send the Savior? *No, no one can stop God from doing what He plans to do. God had promised to send the Savior. He promised the Savior would come from Abraham's family. Everything was going to happen just the way God planned for it to happen.*

Biblical Worldviews

- The only way to please God is to believe Him.
- God always does what He says He will do; He works everything out according to His plans.
- Even though Satan fights against God, Satan cannot win. God is stronger than Satan.
- All people are sinners.
- God planned to send the Savior to rescue people from Satan and death.

THE MOST AMAZING STORY – Lesson 24

Activity: Bible Hangman

Supplies:
- Chalkboard or dry erase board
- Chalk or dry erase markers

Instructions:
- Draw a large hangman tree on the board.
- Draw lines and spaces under the tree to correspond to the letters and spaces of the key phrase.
- **Key phrase**: No one, not even Pharaoh or Satan, could stop God's plans.
- **Key phrase for younger students**: No one can stop God's plans.
- Ask the lesson review questions, one at a time. Call on one student or one team to answer each question.
- If answer is correct, the student or team gets to pick a letter, i.e., the letter b.
- If the letter picked is in the key phrase, the teacher fills it in on the board each time it occurs.
- If the letter picked is not in the key phrase, the teacher draws one part of a stick figure on the hangman tree, i.e., a head, an arm, a stick body, etc.
- When a student (or team) thinks he knows the key phrase, he may try to solve the puzzle on his turn. The game is over when a student or team solves the puzzle or the teacher draws all the parts of the stick man, whichever comes first.

Extra Bible References

Deuteronomy 10:14; Psalm 33:11; Isaiah 14:27; Zechariah 3:2; Matthew 4:10; Luke 10:18

25
Rescued by a Princess
Moses Part I

Memory Verse

For the LORD Most High is awesome; He is a great King over all the earth. Psalm 47:2

Lesson

One day a little boy was born to an Israelite family in Egypt. The mom did not want her baby to be thrown into the river, so she kept him quiet as long as possible. But after three months, she could not hide him any longer. She made a tiny boat for him and placed it in the water at the edge of the river. This is what the Bible says:

...the woman...bore a son. And...hid him three months. But when she could no longer hide him, she took an ark of bulrushes for him, daubed it with asphalt and pitch, put the child in it, and laid it in the reeds by the river's bank. And his sister stood afar off, to know what would be done to him.

Then the daughter of Pharaoh came down to bathe at the river...and when she saw the ark among the reeds, she sent her maid to get it. And when she opened it, she saw the child, and behold, the baby wept. So she had compassion on him, and said, "This is one of the Hebrews' children."

Then his sister said to Pharaoh's daughter, "Shall I go and call a nurse for you from the Hebrew women, that she may nurse the child for you?"

Hebrews = Israelites

And Pharaoh's daughter said to her, "Go." So the maiden went and called the child's mother. Then Pharaoh's daughter said to her, "Take this child away and nurse him for me, and I will give you your wages."

So the woman took the child and nursed him. And the child grew, and she brought him to Pharaoh's daughter, and he became her son. So she called his name Moses, saying, "Because I drew him out of the water." Exodus 2:2-10

God wanted Pharaoh's daughter to find baby Moses and adopt him. But in His wonderful love and kindness, He let the baby's mom keep him till he grew a little older. God even made it so she got paid for taking care of her own baby!

God had an important plan for this little Israelite boy, and He knew that the best place for him was in the king's palace. If the king's daughter adopted him, Moses would be safe and get a good education. God was in control of everything. He was preparing Moses for a special job.

But even though Moses grew up as the grandson of the king of Egypt, he knew he was not Egyptian. Moses knew he was an Israelite, and he loved his people. He did not like the way the Egyptians treated them.

One day Moses saw an Egyptian beating up an Israelite. It made him so angry he killed the Egyptian. When Pharaoh found out, he tried to kill Moses.

Now it came to pass in those days, when Moses was grown, that he went out to his brethren and looked at their burdens. And he saw an Egyptian beating a Hebrew, one of his brethren. So he looked this way and that way, and when he saw no one, he killed the Egyptian and hid him in the sand...When Pharaoh heard of this matter, he sought to kill Moses. But Moses fled from the face of Pharaoh and dwelt in the land of Midian... Exodus 2:11-12, 15

Moses ran away to the land of Midian. There he met a man named Jethro. Jethro gave Moses a job taking care of his sheep. After a time, Moses married Jethro's daughter.

One day, Moses took the sheep to a mountain where there was grass for them to eat. While Moses was watching the sheep, he saw a strange sight. He saw a bush on fire, but the bush did not burn up.

Now Moses was tending the flock of Jethro his father-in-law...And he led the flock to Horeb, the mountain of God. And the Angel of the LORD appeared to him in a flame of fire from the midst of a bush. So he looked, and behold, the bush was burning with fire, but the bush was not consumed. Then Moses said, "I will now turn aside and see this great sight, why the bush does not burn." Exodus 3:1-3

The bush was a lot like the Israelites in Egypt. Just like the bush kept burning and burning but not disappearing, the Israelites were suffering and suffering, but they were not destroyed.

When Moses stopped to take a closer look, God spoke to him from inside the bush.

So when the LORD saw that he turned aside to look, God called to him from the midst of the bush and said, "Moses, Moses!"

And he said, "Here I am."

Then He said, "Do not draw near this place. Take your sandals off your feet, for the place where you stand is holy ground." Moreover He said, "I am the God of your father—the God of Abraham, the God of Isaac, and the God of Jacob." And Moses hid his face, for he was afraid to look upon God. Exodus 3:4-6

God told Moses to take off his sandals and not come any closer.

In the land where Moses lived, people showed respect to someone important by taking off their shoes in that person's presence. Since God is the only true and living God, and the Creator of the world and everything in it, He is the greatest and most important person ever! That is why God told Moses to take off his shoes and not come near.

From inside the bush, God told Moses what He planned to do.

"I have surely seen the oppression of My people who are in Egypt, and have heard their cry because of their taskmasters, for I know their sorrows. So I have come down to deliver them out of the hand of the Egyptians, and to bring them...to a good and large land...to the place of the Canaanites...Come...I will send you to Pharaoh that you may bring My people, the children of Israel, out of Egypt." Exodus 3:7-10

God had promised Abraham that after four hundred years He would free his descendants from slavery and take them back to Canaan. Four hundred years had passed, and now it was time for God to do what He had promised.

God loved the Israelites and saw how much they were suffering. He planned to use Moses to free the Israelites.

Since God was the One who formed Moses and gave him life, it was fine for Him to do with Moses whatever He decided. But Moses could choose whether he would believe God and do what God wanted or not. What do you think Moses decided? Would he be too afraid to go back to Egypt and speak to the pharaoh? We'll soon find out.

Remember

God is a God of love. Just like He cared for the Israelites and kept His promise to free them from slavery, He was going to keep His promise to send the Savior to free you from Satan's dominion.

God loves and cares for all people, but just like Moses could not go near the bush where God was, sinful people cannot live with God.

For You are not a God who takes pleasure in wickedness, nor shall evil dwell with You. Psalm 5:4

Only God can make us acceptable to Him so that we can come near to Him. Even though God is perfect and hates sin, He loves us so much He promised to send the Savior to free us from Satan, sin, and death and make it possible for us to be able to live with Him forever!

Questions

1. Why did God take special care to protect baby Moses? *God protected baby Moses because He had a special plan for him.*

2. What did Moses see the day he was on the mountain taking care of his father-in-law's sheep? *Moses saw a bush that was on fire, but it did not burn up.*

3. In what way was this bush not burning up a picture of what was happening to the Israelites? *Just like the bush kept burning and burning but did not burn up, the Israelites were not destroyed even though they had been suffering for a long time.*

4. Why did God tell Moses to stay back and to take off his sandals? *In the land where Moses lived, taking off shoes was a way to show respect to someone powerful and important. Since God is the only true and living God and the Creator of the world, Moses needed to respect God by staying at a distance and taking off his shoes.*

5. Why was God going to free the Israelites from slavery? *God loved the Israelites. He cared about their suffering, and He had promised Abraham that after four hundred years of slavery He would free his descendants and take them back to the land of Canaan. The time had come for God to fulfill His promise.*

6. Did God clearly communicate with Moses? Did Moses know what God wanted him to do? *Yes, God told Moses He wanted him to go to Pharaoh and tell him to let the Israelites go.*

7. Can sinful people live with God in Heaven? *No, God accepts only perfectly good people to live with Him in Heaven.*

8. Because God loves you so much, who did He promise to send? *God promised to send the Savior to save you from Satan, sin, and death and make a way for you to be able to live with God forever.*

Biblical Worldviews

- God is a personal being; He communicates with people.
- God works out everything according to His plans; He always keeps His promises.
- God is completely perfect; sinful people cannot live with God.
- God is a God of love. God planned to send a Savior.

Activity: Baby Moses Art Project

Supplies:

- "Nile River" printouts (if possible, copy onto stock paper), one per student (see appendix page 577)
- "Grass and Basket" printouts, one per student (see appendix page 578)
- Crayons or colored pencils; scissors
- Glue or double-sided tape

Instructions:

- Students cut out the "Nile River" printout and color it.
- Students color the grass and the basket on the "Grass and Basket" printout.
- Students cut out the basket and foliage. Note: the foliage needs to remain the full width of the frame.
- Next, students glue the basket on the river in the center of the paper.
- Students lay the foliage cut-out over top of the Nile River cut-out and tape or glue the edges to the "Nile River" printout.
- Students cut the foliage down the middle on the dotted line - so that it can be opened to reveal the river and the basket.
- Students draw baby Moses on a scrap of paper, cut him out, and put him in the basket.
- At the bottom or top of the page, students write: God had a special plan for baby Moses.

Extra Bible References

Joshua 5:15; Job 42:1-2; Psalms 5:4, 47:2, 71:19, 72:11, 76:4-9, 99:3, 135:6; Proverbs 19:21; Isaiah 6:2-4; John 3:16, 15:13; Acts 7:17-35; Romans 5:6, 8; 2 Corinthians 5:18; Colossians 1:21; Hebrews 11:24-27; Revelation 4:8

26
I AM
Moses Part II

Memory Verse

The king's heart is in the hand of the LORD, like the rivers of water; He turns it wherever He wishes. Proverbs 21:1

Lesson

Remember what happened to Moses when he killed the Egyptian who was beating up the Israelite? Moses had to run for his life, because when the pharaoh found out what he did, he tried to kill Moses.

Well, when God asked Moses to go back to Egypt to speak to the pharaoh, Moses did not want to go. He had already tried to help his people once; he was not willing to try again. What if the pharaoh tried once more to kill him? What if the Israelites did not believe him?

...Moses said to God, "Who am I that I should go to Pharaoh, and that I should bring the children of Israel out of Egypt?"

So He said, "I will certainly be with you. And this shall be a sign to you that I have sent you: When you have brought the people out of Egypt, you shall serve God on this mountain." Exodus 3:11-12

God promised to go with Moses and show Moses that He really was going to free the Israelites.

God promised Moses He would bring them to the very mountain where Moses now stood in front of the burning bush.

Then Moses said to God, "Indeed, when I come to the children of Israel and say to them, 'The God of your fathers has sent me to you,' and they say to me, 'What is His name?' what shall I say to them?"

And God said to Moses, "I AM WHO I AM." And He said, "Thus you shall say to the children of Israel, 'I AM has sent me to you.'"
Exodus 3:13-14

After four hundred years in Egypt, the Israelites knew more about the Egyptian gods than they did about the God of Abraham, Isaac, and Jacob. The Egyptian gods had names. The Israelites would surely want to know the name of the God who sent Moses.

God told Moses to tell the Israelites **"I AM"** sent him.

The Bible uses many names for the one true God. Each name describes God in a different way. The name I AM means that God is the only one who does not need anything, or anyone, to keep Him alive. God has always existed in the past and will continue to exist forever into the future. God is greater than all.

God told Moses to tell the Israelites that the God of Abraham, Isaac, and Jacob knew about their terrible suffering and was going to free them and take them to Canaan. God promised Moses that the leaders of Israel would listen to him.

Moreover God said to Moses, "Thus you shall say to the children of Israel: '...The LORD God of your fathers, the God of Abraham, of Isaac, and of Jacob, appeared to me, saying, "I have surely visited you and seen what is done to you in Egypt; and I have said I will bring you up out of the affliction of Egypt to the land of the Canaanites...'"

"Then they will heed your voice; and you shall come, you and the elders of Israel, to the king of Egypt; and you shall say to him, 'The LORD God of the Hebrews has met with us; and now, please, let us go...'

"But I am sure that the king of Egypt will not let you go, no, not even by a mighty hand. So I will stretch out My hand and strike Egypt with all My wonders which I will do in its midst; and after that he will let you go... and it shall be, when you go, that you shall not go empty-handed. But every woman shall ask of her neighbor...articles of silver, articles of gold, and clothing...So you shall plunder the Egyptians."
Exodus 3:15-22

God knew the pharaoh would be stubborn; He knew He would have to bring terrible suffering on Egypt before the pharaoh would be willing to free the Israelites. But, of course, no one can stop God's plans. In the end, Pharaoh would let the Israelites go, and they would leave Egypt with great riches.

But even after God promised Moses He would go with him and that the Israelites would certainly be freed and come back to the very mountain where Moses was now standing, Moses was unwilling to speak to Pharaoh.

Then Moses...said, "But suppose they will not believe me or listen to my voice; suppose they say, 'The LORD has not appeared to you.'"

So the LORD said to him, "What is that in your hand?"

He said, "A rod."

And He said, "Cast it on the ground." So he cast it on the ground, and it became a serpent; and Moses fled from it. Then the LORD said to Moses, "Reach out your hand and take it by the tail" (and he reached out his hand and caught it, and it became a rod in his hand)...

Furthermore the LORD said to him, "Now put your hand in your bosom." And he put his hand in his bosom, and when he took it out, behold, his hand was leprous, like snow. And He said, "Put your hand in your bosom again." So he put his hand in his bosom again, and drew it out of his bosom, and behold, it was restored like his other flesh...

"...And...if they do not believe...these two signs, or listen to your voice... take water from the river and pour it on the dry land. The water which you take from the river will become blood on the dry land."

Then Moses said to the LORD, "O my Lord, I am not eloquent...but I am slow of speech..."

So the LORD said to him, "Who has made man's mouth? ...Have not I, the LORD? Now therefore, go, and I will be with your mouth and teach you what you shall say."

But he said, "O my Lord, please send by the hand of whomever else You may send."

So the anger of the LORD was kindled against Moses, and He said: "Is not Aaron...your brother? I know that he can speak well...he shall be your spokesman to the people..."

"Go, return to Egypt; for all the men who sought your life are dead."
Exodus 4:1-16a, 19

God was patient with Moses and gave him three signs to show that nothing is too hard for Him, but still Moses was unwilling to believe God.

It was wrong for Moses to doubt God. God always speaks the truth. God always does everything He says He will do. Instead of being fearful, Moses should have been excited that God was getting ready to free the Israelites from slavery and give them the land He had promised to Abraham!

God was angry with Moses for his unbelief, but God is not sinful like you and I. He doesn't get mad because He can't have His way. God was displeased because Moses did not trust in the only true, living, and powerful God.

Even still, God loved Moses and sent Moses' brother Aaron to help him. With Aaron by his side, Moses was finally willing to go and speak to Pharaoh and the people of Israel.

Then Moses and Aaron went and gathered together all the elders of the children of Israel. And Aaron spoke all the words which the LORD had spoken to Moses. Then he did the signs in the sight of the people. So the people believed; and when they heard that the LORD had visited the children of Israel and that He had looked on their affliction, then they bowed their heads and worshiped.
Exodus 4:29-31

Just like God had said, the leaders of Israel believed Moses and Aaron. They believed the God of Abraham had sent Moses. They believed God would free them from the cruel pharaoh and take them to the land of Canaan. They were thankful God cared about them.

Remember

You can depend on God. God is all-powerful. He has the power to do whatever He says He will do. And God always tells the truth; He will do what He says He will do. Not only does God have all power, and not only does He always tell the truth, but God loves you more than you can imagine and wants what is best for you.

And those who know Your name will put their trust in You; For You, Lord, have not forsaken those who seek You. Psalm 9:10

179

Satan tried to make Adam and Eve think that God was keeping something good from them, but that was not true. God told Adam and Eve not to eat from The Tree of the Knowledge of Good and Evil because He loved them. He did not want them to die. It is always best to believe God.

The Bible says that the only way to please God is to believe Him. God wants you to trust in Him because He is trustworthy. God loves you and He always tells the truth.

But without faith it is impossible to please Him... Hebrews 11:6

Questions

1. To which mountain did God tell Moses He would bring the Israelites after He freed them from slavery in Egypt? *God promised Moses He would bring them to the mountain where He appeared to Moses in the burning bush.*

2. What does the name I AM tell us about God? *The name "I AM" is God's way of saying, "I exist by My own power." God is the only One who does not need anything or anyone to keep Him alive. God has always existed and will continue to exist forever into the future.*

3. Did God know Pharaoh would be stubborn about letting the Israelites go? *Yes, God knows everything. He knew Pharaoh would be stubborn. God knew He would have to bring a lot of suffering on the Egyptians before Pharaoh would let the people go.*

4. What signs did God give Moses to show Moses He was powerful enough to rescue the Israelites from Egypt? *God turned Moses' rod into a snake and then back into a rod again; He made Moses' hand sick with leprosy and then healed it again; and lastly God turned water into blood.*

5. After these three signs, did Moses finally believe God? *No, he came up with another excuse for not doing what God asked him to do. Moses said he did not want to talk to Pharaoh because he was not a good speaker.*

6. Why did God become angry with Moses? *God was angry with Moses because Moses did not believe Him, even after He showed Moses His great power and promised to go with Him.*

7. How did God show mercy to Moses? *God sent Aaron to speak for him.*

8. Does God have all power to do whatever He says He will do? *Yes, God is able do whatever He says He will do.*

9. Does God always tell the truth? *Yes, God always tells the truth.*

10. Does God love you? *Yes, God loves you more than you can imagine! That is why He tells you the truth; He wants the best for you.*

11. What is the only way to please God? *The only way to please God is to believe Him.*

Biblical Worldviews

- God is alive by His own power; He does not need anything, or anyone.
- God is a personal being; He communicates with people.
- God always does what He says He will do; God always tells the truth.
- God can do anything; He is the greatest and strongest of all.
- God knows everything; He knows what is going to happen in the future.
- All people are sinners.
- God is a God of love.
- The only way to please God is to believe Him.
- God gets angry; but God is never selfish.

Activity: Believe God Art Project

Supplies:
- Half a sheet of cardstock per student
- Crayons, assorted colors
- Stickers
- Glitter
- Glue
- Hole-punch
- Yarn

Instructions:
- Students write the words "Believe God" in large letters on the cardstock.
- Students color and/or decorate the words and the background.
- Optional: Students can cover letters with glue and sprinkle glitter on them.
- Punch two holes at the top of the cardstock.
- Students thread yarn through the holes so the pictures can be hung on the wall.

Extra Bible References

Psalms 20:1, 22:22, 27:1, 33:4, 34:8, 105:8, 119:160, 145:8-9; Proverbs 18:10, 29:25; Jeremiah 10:1-16, 17:5-8; Micah 4:5; John 5:26; 17:6, 26; Philippians 2:3-8, 4:13; Titus 1:2; Hebrews 11:6

27
Let My People Go
Plagues

Memory Verse

The king's heart is in the hand of the LORD, like the rivers of water; He turns it wherever He wishes. Proverbs 21:1

Lesson

After Moses and Aaron told the Israelites the wonderful news that God was going to free them from their misery and give them a land of their own, Moses and Aaron went to see Pharaoh.

Afterward Moses and Aaron went in and told Pharaoh, "Thus says the LORD God of Israel: 'Let My people go....'" And Pharaoh said, "Who is the LORD, that I should obey His voice to let Israel go? I do not know the LORD, nor will I let Israel go." Exodus 5:1-2

It was true that Pharaoh did not know the God of Israel. The Egyptians worshiped many false gods. They worshiped the sun and the Nile River. One of their gods had the head of a cow and another had the head of a frog. The Egyptians even worshiped the pharaoh, but they knew nothing about the one true and living God.

Pharaoh was not about to obey this God! After all, He obviously must not be very powerful since He had not saved the Israelites from slavery.

Moses' request only made Pharaoh angry. Instead of letting the Israelites go, he made them work even harder. Instead of providing straw for them like he had done before, he made them find their own straw. And he demanded that they still make the same number of bricks.

So the same day Pharaoh commanded the taskmasters of the people and their officers, saying, "You shall no longer give the people straw to make brick as before. Let them go and gather straw for themselves...For they are idle..." Exodus 5:6-8

It was Satan who was leading the pharaoh to be mean to the people of Israel. He wanted to destroy the nation of Israel so the Savior would not be born into the world.

Then the LORD said to Moses, "Now you shall see what I will do to Pharaoh…"

And God spoke to Moses and said to him: "..say to the children of Israel: '…I will rescue you…and I will redeem you with an outstretched arm and with great judgments…Then you shall know that I am the LORD your God who brings you out from under the burdens of the Egyptians. '" Exodus 6:1-7

Both the Israelites and the Egyptians were about to learn just how great and powerful the God of Israel really was.

"And the Egyptians shall know that I am the LORD, when I stretch out My hand on Egypt and bring out the children of Israel from among them." Exodus 7:5

God was going to use Pharaoh's hard heart to show the world that He is the only true and living God.

Then the LORD spoke to Moses, "Say to Aaron, 'Take your rod and stretch out your hand over the waters of Egypt, over their streams, over their rivers, over their ponds, and over all their pools of water, that they may become blood…'"

And Moses and Aaron did so, just as the LORD commanded…And all the waters that were in the river were turned to blood. The fish that were in the river died, the river stank, and the Egyptians could not drink the water of the river. So there was blood throughout all the land of Egypt.

Then the magicians of Egypt did so with their enchantments; and
Pharaoh's heart grew hard, and he did not heed them, as the LORD
had said. And Pharaoh turned and went into his house. Neither was his
heart moved by this. Exodus 7:19-23

Pharaoh's magicians were led by Satan. When they also turned water into blood, Pharaoh
would not listen to God.

And the LORD spoke to Moses, "Go to Pharaoh and say to him,
'Thus says the LORD: "Let My people go, that they may serve Me. But
if you refuse to let them go, behold, I will smite all your territory
with frogs. So the river shall bring forth frogs abundantly, which shall
go up and come into your house, into your bedroom, on your bed, into
the houses of your servants, on your people, into your ovens, and into
your kneading bowls..."'"

...So Aaron stretched out his hand over the waters of Egypt, and the
frogs came up and covered the land of Egypt. And the magicians did so
with their enchantments, and brought up frogs on the land of Egypt.
Then Pharaoh called for Moses and Aaron, and said, "Entreat the
LORD that He may take away the frogs from me and from my people;
and I will let the people go..." Exodus 8:1-8

This time, even though the magicians copied what Moses did, Pharaoh became afraid. He
promised to let the people go.

Then Moses and Aaron went out from Pharaoh. And Moses cried
out to the LORD...So the LORD did according to the word of Moses.
And the frogs died out of the houses, out of the courtyards, and out
of the fields. They gathered them together in heaps, and the land
stank. But when Pharaoh saw that there was relief, he hardened his
heart and did not heed them, as the LORD had said. Exodus 8:12-15

When the frogs were gone, Pharaoh decided not to let the people go after all. This did not
surprise God; He knew all along what Pharaoh would do.

So God sent another plague.

So the LORD said to Moses, "Say to Aaron, 'Stretch out your rod, and strike the dust of the land, so that it may become lice throughout all the land of Egypt.'" And they did so...and...All the dust of the land became lice throughout all the land of Egypt. Exodus 8:12-17

This time Pharaoh's magicians could not copy what God did. Even though Satan is powerful, he is not nearly as powerful as God.

Still Pharaoh refused to let the people go, so God sent yet another plague on Egypt. This is what God told Moses to say to Pharaoh:

"... if you will not let My people go...I will send swarms of flies on you and your servants, on your people and into your houses... And in that day I will set apart the land of Goshen, in which My people dwell, that no swarms of flies shall be there, in order that you may know that I am the LORD...I will make a difference between My people and your people." Exodus 8;21-23a

This time God protected the people of Israel to show the Egyptians that the God of Israel is the only true and powerful God.

Once again Pharaoh promised to let the Israelites go, but when God took the flies away, he changed his mind again.

Next, God destroyed all the Egyptians' farm animals.

...all the livestock of Egypt died; but of the livestock of the children of Israel, not one died. Exodus 9:6

When Pharaoh still refused to let the Israelites go, God made the Egyptians sick with boils.

Then they took ashes from the furnace and stood before Pharaoh, and Moses scattered them toward heaven. And they caused boils that break out in sores on man and beast. And the magicians could not stand before Moses because of the boils, for the boils were on the magicians and on all the Egyptians. Exodus 9:10-11

Even the magicians were covered with the terrible boils, but still Pharaoh refused to let the Israelites go. So God sent the seventh plague.

And the LORD rained hail on the land of Egypt. So there was hail, and fire mingled with the hail, so very heavy that there was none like it in all the land of Egypt since it became a nation. And the hail struck throughout the whole land of Egypt, all that was in the field, both man and beast; and the hail struck every herb of the field and broke every tree of the field. Only in the land of Goshen, where the children of Israel were, there was no hail.

And Pharaoh sent and called for Moses and Aaron, and said to them, "I have sinned this time. The LORD is righteous, and my people and I are wicked. Entreat the LORD, that there may be no more mighty thundering and hail, for it is enough. I will let you go, and you shall stay no longer." Exodus 9:23b-28

Then God stopped the hail, but...

...when Pharaoh saw that the rain, the hail, and the thunder had ceased, he sinned yet more; and he hardened his heart...neither would he let the children of Israel go, as the LORD had spoken by Moses. Exodus 9:34-35

This time when Pharaoh changed his mind, God sent locusts to eat up all the crops of food that had not been destroyed by the hail.

And the locusts...were very severe...they covered the face of the whole earth, so that the land was darkened; and they ate every herb of the land and all the fruit of the trees which the hail had left. So there remained nothing green on the trees or on the plants of the field throughout all the land of Egypt. Exodus 10:14-15

There was nothing left for the Egyptians to eat. Pharaoh begged Moses to ask God to take away the locusts. But when God did, Pharaoh still refused to do what God said. Then God sent terrible darkness over the land of Egypt.

...there was thick darkness in all the land of Egypt three days. They did not see one another; nor did anyone rise from his place for three days. But all the children of Israel had light in their dwellings. Exodus 10:22b, 23

For three days the sun did not come up in Egypt. Both inside and outside there was black darkness. No one could see anything; no one moved. But Pharaoh would not give in; he would not let God's people go. Finally, God sent one last terrible plague on Egypt. We'll soon find out what it was.

Remember

No one can defeat God. God is more powerful than Satan and his demons. God is more powerful than all the kings and governments of the world put together. God always does what He plans to do. No one can stop Him.

For the LORD Most High is awesome; He is a great King over all the earth. Psalm 47:2

Questions

1. Did Pharaoh and the Egyptians worship the one true and living God? *No, they worshiped false gods. They even worshiped Pharaoh.*

2. Could Pharaoh and Satan stop God from freeing the Israelites? *No, Pharaoh and Satan could not stop God's plans.*

3. Did God know Pharaoh would be stubborn and not let the Israelites go? *Yes, God knew how Pharaoh would respond. God knows everything.*

4. Can you name some of the plagues God sent on Egypt? *God turned the water into blood, sent hordes of frogs, turned the dust into gnats, sent swarms of flies, sent boils on the people and on the animals, killed all the Egyptians' livestock, sent a terrible hailstorm, sent locusts to destroy all the Egyptians' crops of food, and finally He sent a terrible darkness over the land.*

5. What did the plagues show about the God of Israel? *They showed that the God of Israel was the only true and powerful God.*

6. Can anyone defeat God's plans? *No, God is the Creator of the world and all people. He is the highest in command. God does whatever He decides, and no one can stop Him.*

Biblical Worldviews

- God is a personal being; He communicates with people.
- The God of the Bible is the only true and living God; all other gods are false.
- Satan is God's enemy; he tries to stop God's plans.
- Magicians are led by Satan; they are not as powerful as God.
- God knows everything. God has all power to do whatever He decides.
- God is the Creator of the world; He is the highest in command.
- God has a plan for the world; no one can or will stop Him from completing it.

Activity: Let My People Go Skits

Supplies:

- Student volunteers
- A chair for Pharaoh and a rod for Aaron (optional)

Instructions:

- One student plays Pharaoh for all the skits.
- Divide the rest of the students into 9 groups, with at least two students in each group. (If there are not enough students, each group can act out two plagues instead of one.)
- Assign each group one plague. Give them the Bible passage to read for that plague and then let them act it out for the group.
- In each skit, Pharaoh agrees to let the Hebrews go if Moses and Aaron will ask God to take away the plague. Each skit ends with Pharaoh hardening his heart and deciding NOT to let the Hebrew people go.
- Remind students that God is more powerful than any king or ruler and that God always accomplishes His plans. Remind them that next week they will learn about the final plague God sent on Egypt.
- Here are the first nine plagues and their Scripture references:
- **blood** - Exodus 7:19-23
- **frogs** - Exodus 8:1-8
- **lice** - Exodus 8:12-17
- **flies** - Exodus 8:21-33a
- **livestock** - Exodus 9:6
- **boils** - Exodus 9:10-11
- **hail** - Exodus 9:23b-28
- **locust** - Exodus 10:14-15
- **darkness** - Exodus 10:22b-23

Extra Bible References

Numbers 33:4b; Deuteronomy 4:32-40, 7:6-10; Psalms 2:1-4, 47:2, 78:43-50; Psalms 86:8-10; 96:4; 114:7; 115:3; 135:5-6, 15-18; 145:3-7; Jeremiah 10:10; 2 Thessalonians 2:9-10

28
When I See the Blood
The Passover

Memory Verse

Now the blood shall be a sign for you on the houses where you are. And when I see the blood, I will pass over you... Exodus 12:13a

Lesson

God said He would send one more terrible plague. This time He promised that Pharaoh would let the Israelites go.

And the LORD said to Moses, "I will bring one more plague on Pharaoh and on Egypt. Afterward he will let you go from here..." Exodus 11:1a

God told Moses that...

About midnight...all the firstborn in the land of Egypt shall die... Then there shall be a great cry throughout all the land of Egypt, such as was not like it before, nor shall be like it again. Exodus 11:4-6

Every firstborn son of the Egyptians was going to die. Even Pharaoh, whom the Egyptians worshiped as a god, would not be able to save his firstborn son.

But God made a way for the firstborn sons of Israel to be rescued. He explained to Moses exactly what the Israelites needed to do.

On the tenth of this month every man shall take...a lamb...Your lamb shall be without blemish, a male of the first year. Exodus 12:3-5

On the tenth day of the month, every Israelite dad was to pick out a perfect boy lamb. The lamb could not have any sores or cuts on its body. The family was to keep the lamb at its home for four days.

📖 Now you shall keep it until the fourteenth day of the same month. Then the whole assembly of the congregation of Israel shall kill it at twilight. Exodus 12:6

On the evening of the fourteenth day, the Israelites were to kill the lambs and sprinkle the blood on the tops and sides of the doorframes of their homes. Then they were to stay inside their homes until morning.

📖 And you shall take a bunch of hyssop, dip it in the blood that is in the basin, and strike the lintel and the two doorposts with the blood that is in the basin. And none of you shall go out of the door of his house until morning. Exodus 12:22

Hyssop - a plant that grew in Israel in Bible times

Do you remember what God did for Adam and Eve so they could have acceptable clothes? He killed an animal and made clothes for them out of the animal's skin. Later, in order for Cain and Abel to be accepted by God, they were to kill a lamb and offer it to God as a sacrifice. Then, when God asked Abraham to sacrifice Isaac, He provided a perfect, boy lamb to die in Isaac's place.

And now, God promised to save the lives of the firstborn sons of Israel if they killed a perfect, boy lamb and sprinkled its blood on the doorframes of their homes. The last instruction God gave the Israelites was that they were not to break any of the lamb's bones.

📖 ...nor shall you break one of its bones. Exodus 12:46

Because the Passover lamb was a picture of the coming Savior, it was important for the Israelites to follow God's instructions. On the evening of the fourteenth day, God said He would send a destroying angel through the land to kill all firstborn sons. But He promised not to enter any house where He saw the blood of the lamb on the doorframe.

Once again, the Egyptians and the Israelites were going to see that the God of Israel was the only true, living, and powerful God!

📖 For the Lord will pass through to strike the Egyptians; and when He sees the blood on the lintel and on the two doorposts, the Lord will pass over the door and not allow the destroyer to come into your houses to strike you...and against all the gods of Egypt I will execute judgment: I am the LORD. Exodus 12:23, 12b

Just like Noah built the ark exactly the way God said because he believed only God could make a way for him to be saved from the flood, the Israelites did exactly as God said because they believed He was the only One who could save their firstborn sons from death.

Then the children of Israel went away and did so; just as the LORD had commanded Moses and Aaron, so they did. Exodus 12:28

And God kept His promise. He passed over every home where He saw the blood on the doorframe. None of the Israelites died. But among the Egyptians there was great sadness.

And it came to pass at midnight that the LORD struck all the firstborn in the land of Egypt, from the firstborn of Pharaoh who sat on his throne to the firstborn of the captive who was in the dungeon...So Pharaoh rose in the night, he, all his servants, and all the Egyptians; and there was a great cry in Egypt, for there was not a house where there was not one dead. Exodus 12:29-30

Finally, Pharaoh realized he could not fight against God and win. He could see that the gods of the Egyptians were powerless against the God of Israel. And so, he called for Moses and Aaron.

Then he called for Moses and Aaron by night, and said, "Rise, go out from among my people..."And the Egyptians urged the people, that they might send them out of the land in haste. For they said, "We shall all be dead."...

Now the children of Israel...had asked from the Egyptians articles of silver, articles of gold, and clothing...And...they granted them what they requested. Thus they plundered the Egyptians. Exodus 12:31-36

Long ago God told Abraham that when the time came for Him to free his descendants He would send them on their way with great riches. Everything happened just the way God said it would.

Then He said to Abram: "Know certainly that your descendants will be strangers in a land that is not theirs, and will serve them, and they will afflict them four hundred years. And also the nation whom they serve I will judge; afterward they shall come out with great possessions." Genesis 15:13-14

After four hundred years of slavery, the Israelites were finally free! On their way out of Egypt, they asked the Egyptians for gold, silver, and clothes. By now the Egyptians were so afraid of the God of Israel that whatever the Israelites asked for the Egyptians gladly gave them.

God told Moses that He wanted the Israelites always to remember this day; He wanted them always to remember how their firstborn sons were saved from death by the blood of the lamb.

...this day shall be to you a memorial; and you shall keep it as a feast to the LORD throughout your generations. Exodus 12:14a

Every year God wanted the people of Israel to celebrate the Passover Feast. At this feast, He wanted them to remember the night He *passed over* every home where the blood of the lamb had been sprinkled on the doorframe.

Remember

God was the only One who could make a way for the firstborn sons of the Israelites to be saved from death. God said that the way they could be saved was by killing a lamb and sprinkling its blood on the doorframes of their homes. The Israelites believed God and did what He said.

Abel, Noah, Abraham and Sarah, Isaac, Jacob, Joseph, and Moses all believed God too. They knew God was the only One who could save them from the death penalty they deserved for their sin. That is why they came to God by sacrificing a lamb. Because they believed God, God accepted the death of the lamb in their place.

By faith Abel offered to God a more excellent sacrifice than Cain, through which he obtained witness that he was righteous...

Noah...Abraham...Sarah...Isaac... Jacob... Joseph...Moses...all these...obtained a good testimony through faith... Hebrews 11:4-39

In the same way, God is the only One who can make a way for you to be saved from the death penalty you deserve for your sin. But nowadays you do not need to sacrifice a lamb the way the people did long ago, because God has sent the Savior to save you from death.

Questions

1. What was the last plague God sent on Egypt? *The last plague was the death of the Egyptians' firstborn sons.*

2. What did God tell the Israelites to do in order to save their sons from death? *He told them to kill a perfect lamb and sprinkle the blood on the doorframes of their homes.*

3. If an Israelite would have sacrificed a lamb that had sores or was sick, would God have saved the firstborn son in that family? *No, God only accepted perfect lambs to take the place of the firstborn sons of the Israelites.*

4. Why were the Israelites not to break any of the lamb's bones? *The Israelites were not to break any of the lamb's bones because the lamb was a picture of the coming Savior.*

5. After they sprinkled the blood on the doorframes, where were the Israelites to go? *They were to go inside their houses and stay there till morning.*

6. Would God enter any home where the blood of the lamb had been sprinkled on the doorframe? *No, God promised to pass over every home where He saw the blood of a perfect lamb on the doorframe. No one inside that house would die.*

7. Why did the Israelites carefully follow God's instructions? *The Israelites did exactly what God told them to do because they believed God was the only One who could save their firstborn sons from death.*

8. Why was the night the Israelites were to remember each year called the Passover Feast? *It was called the Passover Feast because on that night God passed over every home where the blood of the lamb was sprinkled on the top and sides of the doorframe.*

Biblical Worldviews

- God communicates with people about what He wants them to do.
- God saves only those who believe Him.
- Only God can provide a way to be saved from death.
- God is perfect; He only accepted the death of a perfect lamb.
- The God of the Bible is the only true and living God; all other gods are false and powerless.
- God knows the future; He works everything out according to His plan.

Activity 1: Popsicle Stick Passover Picture

Supplies:

- White card stock or paper, one sheet per student
- Crayons or colored pencils
- Red crayon, marker, or paint
- Glue or glue stick
- Two full-size Popsicle sticks and one mini-size Popsicle stick per student (if you don't have a mini-size Popsicle stick, you can cut a regular Popsicle stick into two equal pieces)

Instructions:

- Students draw the outline of an ancient Israelite house. It needs to be large enough to put in a door made of Popsicle sticks.
- Students use crayons to color the house and the background scene.
- Students glue the full-size Popsicle sticks to the front of the house to create the two sides of a door.
- Students complete the doorframe by gluing the mini Popsicle stick across the top of the side posts.
- Students use red marker, crayon, or paint to put red on the door posts to symbolize the blood on the doorframes.
- Optional: Students write the following verse on their pictures: "Now the blood shall be a sign for you on the houses where you are. And when I see the blood, I will pass over you..." Exodus 12:13a

Activity 2: Passover Skit

Supplies:

- Four or more student volunteers. The following are the parts: Narrator #1 , Narrator #2, mother, and children (one child should be a boy)

Instructions:

- Students act out the skit.
- Afterwards discuss the skit as a class.

Passover Skit (by Nancy Hughes)

Narrator #1: Let's look at a very special example in the Old Testament in which God provided for the Israelites' firstborn sons to be saved from death and that at the same time pointed toward the coming of the Savior. The year was around 1450 B.C. and God's chosen people, the Israelites, were prisoners in captivity in the land of Egypt. Although the Israelites were enslaved by a powerful and wicked pharaoh, God was about to show the Israelites they needed to depend on Him and He would deliver them.

Narrator #2: Was this when God sent all those horrible plagues on the Egyptians but protected the Israelites from each one? I remember the story. Each time, Pharaoh promised to let the Israelites go, and each time, after the plague was removed, Pharaoh failed to keep his promise.

Narrator #1: Yes, that's it. Let's travel back in time and see for ourselves.

Child #1 (a boy): Mommy, mommy, what is going on around here? Everyone is busy getting ready for a feast and Daddy is getting ready to kill our best lamb tonight.

Child #2: Mommy, Daddy said to remind you to clean the basin for the lamb's blood tonight. What is going on, Mommy?

Mother: Gather around children, and I'll explain it to you. You see, God is about to show us another one of His miracles. Do you remember all the plagues He has sent on Egypt the last few weeks?

Child #2 or 3: Oh yes, the frogs, the flies, and the water turning into blood.

Mother: That's right. But Pharaoh is not listening to God, so now God is going to send a real terrible plague to Egypt. Every firstborn son in Egypt is going to die tonight unless his parents are trusting God.

Child #1: How can we trust God Momma? I am the firstborn son in our house and I don't want to die tonight!

Mother: Do not fear, my child. God will take care of you and all of us. He has made a way for you to be rescued. Daddy has chosen a lamb without any spots or sores. Tonight he will kill the lamb and catch its blood in this basin here. Then he will place the blood on both doorposts of our house and above the door as well.

Child #3: What will happen then Mommy?

Mother: God said that if our doorposts are sprinkled with the blood of the lamb, He will pass over our house and not harm our firstborn son. He will know where we live and know that we trust Him because of the lamb's blood on our door.

Child #1: So God will pass over our house tonight Mommy and deliver me from death?

Mother: Yes, child. I know He will. See our door? Do not be afraid. We are covered by the blood of the lamb.

Narrator #1: So you see, the Passover celebration was a beautiful picture of what the Savior would do for all of us someday.

Extra Bible References

Genesis 15:13-16; Exodus 18:8-11; Leviticus 17:11; Numbers 8:17, 33:3-4; Deuteronomy 7:6-10, 15:19-21; Job 19:23-26; Psalm 33:10-11; 78:51; 135:5-9, 15-18; Hebrews 11:28

29
Trapped
Red Sea Crossing

Memory Verse

Now the blood shall be a sign for you on the houses where you are. And when I see the blood, I will pass over you... Exodus 12:13a

Lesson

Long ago when Jacob moved to Egypt, there were seventy people in his family. Four hundred years later when the Israelites left Egypt, there were over two million! In Egypt, Jacob's family had truly become a great nation.

Your fathers went down to Egypt with seventy persons, and now the LORD your God has made you as the stars of heaven in multitude. Deuteronomy 10:22

God told Abraham He would give him countless descendants, and that is just what He did. And now He was going to give them the land He had promised to give them – the land of Canaan.

So God led the people around by way of the wilderness of the Red Sea. And the children of Israel went up in orderly ranks out of the land of Egypt. Exodus 13:18

And the LORD went before them by day in a pillar of cloud to lead the way, and by night in a pillar of fire to give them light... Exodus 13:21a

To get to Canaan, God led the Israelites through "the wilderness."

Who led us through the wilderness, through a land of deserts and pits, through a land of drought and the shadow of death, through land that no one crossed and where no one dwelt?' Jeremiah 2:6b

The wilderness was a dangerous place where no one lived. It was a desert without food or water. There were no roads or signs to show the Israelites where to go. They did not have a map or GPS. Without God to guide them, they would surely have gotten lost and died. But God kindly went ahead of the Israelites in a pillar of cloud to lead the way. At night a pillar of fire gave them light.

It did not take long for Pharaoh to wish he had not let his slaves go free.

...Pharaoh...said, "Why have we...let Israel go from serving us?" So he made ready his chariot and took his people with him...he took...all the chariots of Egypt with captains over every one of them.
Exodus 14:5-7

Even after God had completely destroyed the land of Egypt and killed all their firstborn sons, Pharaoh tried one more time to fight against God. His army soon caught up with the Israelites who were camped on the shores of the Red Sea.

...when Pharaoh drew near, the children of Israel lifted their eyes, and behold, the Egyptians marched after them. So they were very afraid, and the children of Israel cried out to the LORD...they said to Moses, "Because there were no graves in Egypt, have you taken us away to die in the wilderness?...it would have been better for us to serve the Egyptians than that we should die in the wilderness."
Exodus 14:10-12

The Israelites had just seen all the terrible plagues God sent on Egypt to free them from slavery. They had seen God's great power. They should have trusted God to save them. After all, God had promised to take them to Canaan.

Moses told the Israelites not to be afraid. He told them to watch and see what God was going to do.

And Moses said to the people, "Do not be afraid. Stand still, and see the salvation of the LORD, which He will accomplish for you today. For the Egyptians whom you see today, you shall see again no more forever. The LORD will fight for you, and you shall hold your peace."
Exodus 14:13-14

The Israelites were trapped. The Red Sea was in front of them and Pharaoh's army was behind them. There was no bridge across the water and they did not have any boats or a ship to get to the other side. They did not even have an army to fight against Pharaoh. There was no way of escape. Only God could rescue the Israelites from this impossible situation.

God told Moses what to do.

> ...lift up your rod, and stretch out your hand over the sea and divide it. And the children of Israel shall go on dry ground through the midst of the sea. And I indeed will harden the hearts of the Egyptians, and they shall follow them. So I will gain honor over Pharaoh and over all his army, his chariots, and his horsemen. Then the Egyptians shall know that I am the LORD, when I have gained honor for Myself over Pharaoh, his chariots, and his horsemen. Exodus 14:16-18

One more time both the Egyptians and the Israelites were going to see God's power; they were going to see that the God of Israel is the only true and living God.

God caused the pillar of cloud to move between the Israelites and the Egyptians. The cloud gave light to the Israelites, but on the Egyptian side it was dark.

> And the Angel of God, who went before the camp of Israel, moved and went behind them; and the pillar of cloud went from before them and stood behind them. So it came between the camp of the Egyptians and the camp of Israel. Thus it was a cloud and darkness to the one, and it gave light by night to the other, so that the one did not come near the other all that night. Exodus 14:19-20

Moses believed God and did what God said. He stretched his rod over the sea.

> Then Moses stretched out his hand over the sea; and the LORD caused the sea to go back by a strong east wind all that night, and made the sea into dry land, and the waters were divided. So the children of Israel went into the midst of the sea on the dry ground, and the waters were a wall to them on their right hand and on their left. And the Egyptians pursued and went after them into the midst of the sea, all Pharaoh's horses, his chariots, and his horsemen.

> Now it came to pass...that the LORD...troubled the army of the Egyptians. And He took off their chariot wheels, so that they drove them with difficulty; and the Egyptians said, "Let us flee from the face of Israel, for the LORD fights for them against the Egyptians."

Then the LORD said to Moses, "Stretch out your hand over the sea, that the waters may come back upon the Egyptians, on their chariots, and on their horsemen." And Moses stretched out his hand over the sea…Then the waters returned and covered the chariots, the horsemen, and all the army of Pharaoh that came into the sea after them. Not so much as one of them remained…

So the LORD saved Israel that day out of the hand of the Egyptians, and Israel saw the Egyptians dead on the seashore. Thus Israel saw the great work which the LORD had done in Egypt; so the people feared the LORD… Exodus 14:21-31a

What a great God! It was not hard for Him to move the water. After all, He was the One who created the water and the wind in the beginning. He was the One who separated the water above the sky from the water below the sky and gathered the water on the earth into seas so that dry land appeared. He was the One who sent the flood to destroy the earth in Noah's day.

For I know that the Lord is great, and our Lord is above all gods. Whatever the Lord pleases He does, in heaven and in earth, in the seas and in all deep places. He causes the vapors to ascend from the ends of the earth; He makes lightning for the rain; He brings the wind out of His treasuries.

He destroyed the firstborn of Egypt, both of man and beast. He sent signs and wonders into the midst of you, O Egypt, upon Pharaoh and all his servants. Psalm 135:5-9

Even though the Israelites were in a hopeless situation, God could save them.

Remember

Just like the Israelites were hopelessly trapped between the Egyptian army and the sea, you are hopelessly trapped by your sin. Nothing you can do will save you. But just as God made a way for the Israelites to be saved, God promised to send the Savior to make a way for you to be saved.

Nor is there salvation in any other, for there is no other name under heaven given among men by which we must be saved. Acts 4:12

Trust in God to save you from the death penalty you deserve because of your sin.

Questions

1. Did God give Abraham countless descendants like He promised? *Yes, He did. By the time the Israelites left Egypt there were over two million of them. Since that time, countless more Israelites have been born.*

2. How did God lead the Israelites through the wilderness? *During the day He led them with a pillar of cloud and at night He provided a pillar of fire to give them light.*

3. When the Israelites left Egypt, where were they going? *God was taking the Israelites to the land He had promised to Abraham – the land of Canaan.*

4. When the Israelites saw the Egyptian army coming after them, did they trust God to take care of them? *No, they did not. Even though they had just seen God's great power and even though God had promised to take them to Canaan, they did not trust Him to take care of them.*

5. Was there any way for the Israelites to save themselves from the Egyptians? *No, they were trapped between the Egyptian army and the Red Sea. They did not have an army or a way to cross the sea. There was no way for them to save themselves from the Egyptians.*

6. Who was the only One who could save the Israelites from the Egyptian army? *Only God could save them.*

7. What did God do to save the Israelites? *He caused the pillar of cloud to go between the Egyptian army and the Israelites. The cloud gave light to the Israelites, but on the Egyptian side it was dark. Then God made a dry path through the sea for the Israelites to cross over. When the Egyptian army went after them, God caused the water to return to its place and drown the Egyptians.*

8. How could God make a dry path through the sea? *Nothing is too hard for God. He made the wind and water in the beginning. He has the power to make the wind and water do whatever He wants.*

9. Is there anything you can do to save yourself from sin and death? *No, there is nothing you can do to save yourself. You are hopelessly trapped by your sin.*

10. Who is the only One who can save you? *Only God can save you.*

11. Who did God promise to send to make a way for all people to be saved from sin and death? *God promised to send the Savior to save people from sin and death.*

Biblical Worldviews

- God always does what He says He will do; He keeps His word.
- God can do anything; nothing is too hard for Him.
- All people are sinners.
- We cannot save ourselves from eternal death.
- God is a God of love.

- Only God can save us.
- God saves those who trust in Him.

Activity: Disappearing Memory Verse Game

Supplies:

- Chalkboard or white board
- Chalk or white board marker

Instructions:

- Write memory verse and reference in large letters on chalkboard or white board.
- Students repeat memory verse and reference in unison two times.
- Ask for a student volunteer to pick two words he would like for you to erase. Erase those two words (or have the student erase them).
- Students repeat the memory verse in unison again, including the two words that have been erased.
- Ask for a different student volunteer to pick two more words to erase. Erase the words as before.
- Once more students repeat the memory verse in unison.
- Repeat this process until all the words have been erased.
- See if the group can recite the verse in unison without any words on the board.
- Optional: Ask for individual volunteers to recite the verse from memory.

Extra Bible References

Exodus 13:17-22; Deuteronomy 26:5-8; Psalms 24:1-2, 33:8-9, 95:5, 104:5-9, 106:7-9; Isaiah 41:8-10; Jeremiah 32:17; Hebrews 11:29

30
Hungry and Thirsty
To Canaan through the Wilderness

Memory Verse

But to him who does not work but believes on Him who justifies the ungodly, his faith is accounted for righteousness, Romans 4:5

Lesson

Once they were on the other side of the Red Sea, the Israelites continued their journey to the land of Canaan. Day after day they trudged on - moms and dads, boys and girls, and animals. Carrying their babies and belongings, the Israelites followed the pillar of cloud...

...through all that great and terrible wilderness...
Deuteronomy 1:19a

After a while the Israelites needed water.

And they went three days in the wilderness and found no water. Now when they came to Marah, they could not drink the waters...for they were bitter...And the people complained against Moses, saying, "What shall we drink?"

So he cried out to the LORD, and the LORD showed him a tree. When he cast it into the waters, the waters were made sweet...
Exodus 15:22-25

Then they came to Elim, where there were twelve springs and seventy palm trees, and they camped there near the water. Exodus 15:27

Since the Israelites were born into Adam's family, they were sinners. That is why they complained. They forgot how God had freed them from slavery and delivered them from Pharaoh's army at the Red Sea. They forgot God's promise to take them safely to Canaan.

But even though the Israelites grumbled, God still loved them. In His mercy, He did not get angry with them. Instead, He graciously showed Moses what to do to make the water pure so the Israelites could drink. Afterwards, God led them to a place where they could rest.

Soon they moved on again and arrived at the Wilderness of Sin.

And they journeyed...and...came to the Wilderness of Sin...Then the whole congregation of the children of Israel complained against Moses and Aaron in the wilderness. And...said to them, "Oh, that we had died by the hand of the LORD in the land of Egypt, when we sat by the pots of meat and when we ate bread to the full! For you have brought us out into this wilderness to kill this whole assembly with hunger." Exodus 16:1-3

Again, instead of trusting God, the Israelites grumbled. And once more, God kindly took care of them.

And the LORD spoke to Moses, saying,"I have heard the complaints of the children of Israel. Speak to them, saying, 'At twilight you shall eat meat, and in the morning you shall be filled with bread. And you shall know that I am the LORD your God.'" Exodus 16:11-12

There were no gardens or grain fields in the wilderness. There were no grocery stores. The Israelites had no way of getting food. Only God could provide food for them.

So it was that quails came up at evening and covered the camp, and in the morning the dew lay all around the camp. And when the layer of dew lifted, there, on the surface of the wilderness, was a small round substance, as fine as frost on the ground. So when the children of Israel saw it, they said to one another, "What is it?" For they did not know what it was.

And Moses said to them, "This is the bread which the LORD has given you to eat." Exodus 16:13-15

What a great miracle God did for the people of Israel! He sent birds into their camp so they could eat meat. In the morning, He covered the ground with flakes of sweet bread called manna. For the rest of their journey, God continued to provide the Israelites with this manna.

And the children of Israel ate manna...until they came to the border of the land of Canaan. Exodus 16:35

After they left the Wilderness of Sin, the Israelites came to a place called Rephidim.

Then all the congregation of the children of Israel set out on their journey from the Wilderness of Sin...and camped in Rephidim...

And the people thirsted there for water, and the people complained against Moses, and said, "Why is it you have brought us up out of Egypt, to kill us and our children and our livestock with thirst?"

So Moses cried out to the LORD, saying, "What shall I do with this people? They are almost ready to stone me!" Exodus 17:1-4

God could have become impatient with the Israelites. Even though He had taken care of them in so many wonderful ways, they still did not trust Him. God could have told them to find their own water, but He didn't do that. Instead, He did another great miracle for them.

God told Moses what to do so the Israelites and their animals could drink.

...the LORD said to Moses, "Go on before the people...take in your hand your rod with which you struck the river, and go. Behold, I will stand before you there on the rock in Horeb; and you shall strike the rock, and water will come out of it, that the people may drink."

And Moses did so in the sight of the elders of Israel. Exodus 17:5-6

Moses believed God and did what God said. Then God...

...opened the rock, and water gushed out; it ran in the dry places like a river. Psalm 105:41

Only God could provide enough water in the middle of the desert for that many people and animals. God is the Creator; He could easily make water come out of a rock. Nothing is too hard for Him!

Whatever the Lord pleases He does, in heaven and in earth, in the seas and in all deep places. He causes the vapors to ascend from the ends of the earth; He makes lightning for the rain; He brings the wind out of His treasuries. Psalm 135:6-7

Because God loved them, and because of the promise He had made to Abraham, Isaac, and Jacob, God protected and cared for the Israelites. God had told Abraham He would bless his descendants and give them the land of Canaan, and that is just what He was doing.

Remember

God was merciful and gracious to the Israelites. He knew He was the only One who could give them what they needed. So instead of getting angry with Israelites, God freely supplied their needs. The Israelites did not have to work or pay for the food and water God gave them. He did not even make them promise to stop complaining.

God has not changed; He is still merciful and loving. God knows you cannot save yourself from Satan and death. He knows He is the only One who can save you. Even though you do not deserve His kindness, God has made a way for you to be rescued from eternal death through the promised Savior.

God does not ask you to do any work in order to be saved. He does not ask you to give money or promise to be good. All God wants you to do is trust in Him to save you. God promises that every person who has faith in Him will receive the gift of His righteousness and be accepted by Him.

But to him who does not work but believes on Him who justifies the ungodly, his faith is accounted for righteousness. Romans 4:5

> **Justify - to legally declare righteous**

Questions

1. When the Israelites were hungry and thirsty in the wilderness, did they trust God to provide for them? *No, instead of trusting God, they complained.*

2. What had God done for the Israelites to free them from slavery in Egypt? *He sent many terrible plagues on Egypt and killed all their firstborn sons.*

3. What did God do for the Israelites when they were trapped between Pharaoh's army and the Red Sea? *God powerfully parted the sea so the Israelites could cross on dry ground. Then He drowned the whole Egyptian army.*

4. What land did God promise to give to Abraham's descendants? *God promised Abraham He would give the land of Canaan to his descendants.*

5. Since the Israelites knew God had promised to give them the land of Canaan, and since they had seen how powerful God is, should they have worried and complained? *No, they should have believed God would keep His promise to take them safely to Canaan.*

6. Who was the only One who could provide food and water for over two million Israelites and all their animals in the middle of that endless and empty wilderness? *Only the all-powerful God could provide enough food and water for the Israelites and their animals in the wilderness.*

7. Did God get angry with the Israelites for not trusting Him? *No, God was merciful to them.*

8. What did God do for the Israelites when they grumbled about not having food and water? *He graciously provided them with food and water.*

9. Did God make the Israelites promise never to complain again before He would give them food and water? *No, He gave it to them freely.*

10. Who is the only One who can give you what you need so that you can live and not die and be separated from God forever? *Only God can save you from death and make you acceptable to Him so that you can live with Him forever.*

11. What does God ask you to do so you can be saved from eternal death? *God does not ask you to do anything; He does not ask you to pay, or do good works, or to promise to be good in order for Him to save you. God wants you simply to believe Him because He is the only One who can save you from death and make you acceptable to Him.*

Biblical Worldviews

- All people are sinners.
- God is merciful, gracious, and loving.
- God can do anything; He is all-powerful.
- God is the Creator; He controls all of nature.
- God always keeps His promises.
- We cannot save ourselves; good works, money, or a promise to be good cannot save a person.
- Only God can save us.
- God saves only those who believe Him.

Activity: Bible Tic-Tac-Toe

Supplies:
- Chalkboard or dry erase board
- Chalk or dry erase markers

Instructions:
- Draw a large tic-tac-toe on the board.
- Divide students into two teams.
- Ask review questions and let each team take turns trying to answer a question. If the team answers the question correctly, they get to put an "X" or an "O" on the board. The first team to get three in a row, horizontally, vertically, or diagonally, wins.
- Play several times until you have used all the review questions.

Extra Bible References

Genesis 12:1-3; Psalms 78:12-55, 95:8, 105:40-45, 106:6-15; John 6:31

31
A New Agreement
At Mount Sinai

Memory Verse

But to him who does not work but believes on Him who justifies the ungodly, his faith is accounted for righteousness, Romans 4:5

Lesson

Three months after leaving Egypt, the Israelites arrived at Mount Sinai (also known as Mount Horeb).

In the third month after the children of Israel had gone out of the land of Egypt...they came to the Wilderness of Sinai...So Israel camped there before the mountain. Exodus 19:1-2

This was the mountain where Moses saw the burning bush. Do you remember the promise God made to Moses at that time?

...He said, "...this shall be a sign to you that I have sent you: When you have brought the people out of Egypt, you shall serve God on this mountain." Exodus 3:12

Even though the Israelites had faced many difficulties, God had kept His promise. By His great power He had freed them from Pharaoh, made a dry path for them through the Red Sea, and provided food and water for them in the wilderness. Finally they arrived at the mountain where God had appeared to Moses.

From the mountain, God again spoke to Moses.

And Moses went up to God, and the LORD called to him from the mountain, saying,"...tell the children of Israel: 'You have seen what I did to the Egyptians, and how I bore you on eagles' wings and brought you to Myself. Now therefore, if you will indeed obey My voice and keep My covenant, then you shall be a special treasure to Me above all people; for all the earth is Mine.'" Exodus 19:3-5

Up until now, no matter how they acted, God had always lovingly cared for His chosen people, the Israelites. Even though they complained and did not believe God, God had always provided whatever they needed free of charge.

However, God now offered a new agreement. Instead of freely caring for the Israelites, God said He would give them rules to obey. If they obeyed, He would treat them really well and take good care of them. But if they did not follow God and obey His rules, they would not get this special treatment.

> **The Agreement**
>
> If the Israelites kept God's rules, God would continue to protect them and care for them.
>
> **But**, if the Israelites did not keep God's rules, He would stop showing them special favor.

Moses told the leaders of Israel what God said. The Israelites liked this new agreement. They thought they could keep God's rules, no problem!

So Moses...called for the elders of the people, and laid before them all these words which the LORD commanded him. Then all the people answered together and said, "All that the LORD has spoken we will do."

So Moses brought back the words of the people to the LORD.
Exodus 19:7-8

The Israelites must have forgotten all their complaining in the wilderness. They did not understand that they were born into Adam's family and that they were sinners who could not please God.

When the Israelites agreed to keep God's rules, God told Moses to get them ready to meet with Him.

Then the LORD said to Moses, "Go to the people and...let them wash their clothes. And let them be ready for the third day. For on the third day the LORD will come down upon Mount Sinai in the sight of all the people. You shall set bounds for the people all around, saying, 'Take heed...that you do not go up to the mountain or touch its base. Whoever touches the mountain shall surely be put to death.'"
Exodus 19:10-12

The Israelites were supposed to get ready by washing their clothes. They needed to be clean when God came down. God also told Moses to set a boundary around the mountain so that no one would touch it. If anyone touched the mountain where God was, that person would die.

This was God's way of showing the Israelites how pure and perfect He is and that only perfect people – those who have been cleaned from all sin – can live with Him.

Finally on the third day, God came down on Mount Sinai.

Then it came to pass on the third day, in the morning, that there were thunderings and lightnings, and a thick cloud on the mountain; and the sound of the trumpet was very loud, so that all the people who were in the camp trembled. And Moses brought the people out of the camp to meet with God, and they stood at the foot of the mountain. Now Mount Sinai was completely in smoke, because the LORD descended upon it in fire. Its smoke ascended like the smoke of a furnace, and the whole mountain quaked greatly. Exodus 19:16-18

Can you imagine? Smoke surrounded the mountain and billowed up into the sky as God came down in fire. There was thunder and lightning and a trumpet sound so loud it made the people tremble. Along with the terrible noise, the whole mountain was shaking really hard. Even Moses was afraid.

And so terrifying was the sight that Moses said, "I am exceedingly afraid and trembling." Hebrews 12:21

God is the One who sent the terrible flood in Noah's day when torrents of rain poured down from the sky and huge fountains of water burst up out of the ground. God is the One who rained burning sulfur on the wicked cities of Sodom and Gomorrah. God is the One who sent terrible plagues on Egypt and killed all their firstborn sons. God is the One who parted the Red Sea for the Israelites and drowned the entire Egyptian army. No one is greater or more powerful than God!

On the mountain, God wanted the Israelites to see His great majesty so they would be sure to keep His rules.

And Moses said to the people, "Do not fear; for God has come to test you, and that His fear may be before you, so that you may not sin." Exodus 20:20

Remember

God is completely pure and sinless. The Israelites were told to wash themselves before standing before God. This is a reminder that people who are dirty with sin are not acceptable to God.

📖 For You are not a God who takes pleasure in wickedness, nor shall evil dwell with You. Psalm 5:4

Sinful people must be separated from a perfect God. Only those who have been cleaned from sin can live with God in Heaven. There is nothing you can do to make yourself clean. Only God can make a way. That is why He promised to send the Savior. God planned for the Savior to make a way for you to be cleaned from your sin and made acceptable to Him.

Questions

1. Did God keep His promise to free the Israelites from slavery and bring them to the mountain where Moses saw the burning bush? *Yes, about three months after the Israelites left Egypt they arrived at Mount Sinai.*

2. Explain the agreement God made with the Israelites. *The agreement God made with the Israelites was that He would care for them and protect them only if they obeyed His commands.*

3. Did the Israelites think they could obey God's commands? *Yes, the Israelites thought they could easily keep all God's rules.*

4. Why did God say for the Israelites to wash their clothes? *This was God's way of showing that sinful (unclean) people are not acceptable to Him; in order to live with God a person must be cleaned from his or her sin.*

5. What did God say would happen to anyone who touched the mountain where He was? *Whoever touched the mountain where God was would die.*

6. Why were Moses and the people so afraid when God came down? *They were afraid because the loud trumpet sound, the thunder and lightning, the smoke and fire, and the shaking mountain were very scary.*

7. Is anyone more powerful and majestic than God? *No, God is the most powerful and greatest of all. He is more awesome and majestic that anyone else. He is the highest authority.*

8. Can anyone please God by being good? *No, we are all born sinners, and it is impossible for us to be good, no matter how hard we try. No one in Adam's family can please God.*

9. Who is the only One who can clean you from your sin and make you acceptable to God so you can live with Him forever? *Only God can make you acceptable to Him. He promised to send the Savior who would make a way for you to be cleaned from your sin and rescued from death.*

Biblical Worldviews

- God always does what He says; He keeps His promises.
- God is a personal being; He communicates with people.
- God is the greatest and most powerful of all.
- God is perfect and sinless; sinful people are not acceptable to God.
- All people are sinners, unable to please God.
- The penalty for sin is death.
- Only God can rescue people from sin and death and make them acceptable to Him.

Activity: Bible Bingo

Supplies:

- Bingo cards and game tokens (Any set will do. You can buy an inexpensive set at the dollar store.)

Instructions:

- Give each student a bingo card and some tokens.
- Ask a question from the lesson review and call on a student to answer it. If the student answers it correctly, she calls the bingo square she wants to cover. Everyone else who has that square covers it as well.
- Continue to ask questions, calling on a different student each time. Allow everyone to answer at least one question and pick at least one bingo square.
- The game is over when the first student shouts BINGO because she has covered a complete row with tokens, either vertically, horizontally, or diagonally.
- Play the game several times until everyone has had a turn answering a question and/or all the questions from the review have been asked and answered.

Extra Bible References

Leviticus 26:3-9, 14-34; Deuteronomy 7:6; 28:1-2, 15, 45; Psalms 5:4, 92:15, 97:4-6; Jeremiah 17:9; 1 Timothy 6:16; Hebrews 12:18-21; Revelation 1:17

32
Ten Rules
The Ten Commandments

Memory Verse

For whoever shall keep the whole law, and yet stumble in one point, he is guilty of all.
James 2:10

Lesson

The Israelites had made an agreement with God; they had agreed that in order to receive God's special treatment they would have to obey His rules. If they did not obey God's rules, God would not treat them as His "special treasure."

When the Israelites agreed to obey God, God gave them His rules. The most important rules God gave them are called the Ten Commandments. The Ten Commandments are still for today because they show just how perfect a person must be to be acceptable to God.

The <u>first</u> rule God gave was not to worship other gods.

You shall have no other gods before Me. Exodus 20:3

God is the only true and living God. He is the Creator of the world. He is the greatest and most powerful. All other gods are false and powerless.

But when God said not to have other gods besides Him, He was not just talking about the false gods of Egypt. If anything - clothes, sports, friends, money, movies, video games, or anything at all – is more important to you than God, you have broken this command.

You are to love God more than you love anything else. Only the God of the Bible deserves to be worshiped.

The <u>second</u> command was not to make or worship idols.

You shall not make for yourself a carved image—any likeness of anything that is in heaven above, or that is in the earth beneath, or that is in the water under the earth; you shall not bow down to them nor serve them. Exodus 20:4-5a

It is wrong to worship a man-made image, or idol. To bow down to an idol is wrong. To pray to an idol is wrong. Idols cannot see, hear, talk, or think. They are lifeless; they have no power. Since God is the only true and living God, He is the only One to whom you should pray.

The third command God gave to the Israelites was to respect God's name.

You shall not take the name of the LORD your God in vain… Exodus 20:7a

It is sin to use God's name as a swear word.

The fourth command was to rest on the seventh day of the week.

Remember the Sabbath day, to keep it holy. Six days you shall…work, but the seventh day is the Sabbath of the LORD your God. In it you shall do no work…For in six days the LORD made the heavens and the earth, the sea, and all that is in them, and rested the seventh day. Therefore the LORD blessed the Sabbath day and hallowed it. Exodus 20:8-11

Because God created the world in six days and rested on the seventh day, He set the seventh day apart as a holiday for remembering Him as the Creator of the world. The seventh day of the week is Saturday. The Israelites called it "the Sabbath day." God told the Israelites they were not to work on the Sabbath day.

Of all the Ten Commandments, this is the only one that was just for the Israelites. Nowadays God does not say for us to rest on Saturday, but He does want us always to remember that He is the Creator.*

The fifth command God gave was to honor your parents.

Honor your father and your mother… Exodus 20:12

All children are to honor their moms and dads. This means you are to respect both your mom and your dad. Anytime you disrespect, disobey, grumble, argue, or ignore either one of your parents, you have broken this rule.

If you are disrespectful or disobedient even one time, you are guilty and deserve to be separated from God forever. If you obey on the outside, but have an ugly attitude on the inside, you are guilty of breaking this rule.

God wants you to respect your parents even after you grow up and leave home.

Rule number <u>six</u> was not to murder.

You shall not murder. Exodus 20:13

To kill another person out of anger is wrong. God is the One who gives life to people. He is the only One with the right to say when someone should die.

The <u>seventh</u> command God gave was not to "commit adultery."

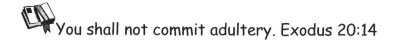You shall not commit adultery. Exodus 20:14

God wants a husband to live only with his wife, and a wife to live only with her husband. It is wrong to live with someone as though you are married to him or her, when you are not.

The <u>eighth</u> command was not to steal.

You shall not steal. Exodus 20:15

God is the One who gives people what they have.

...He gives to all life, breath, and all things. Acts 17:25b

It is wrong to take something from someone when God gave it to them. When you copy someone's answers on a test, you are stealing. Even if you apologize or give back what you took, you are still guilty of having broken this rule.

The <u>ninth</u> command God gave was not to lie.

You shall not bear false witness against your neighbor. Exodus 20:16

God does not want you to tell lies or make up stories about people; gossiping and spreading rumors is wrong.

Some people think it is okay to lie if it helps the next person or makes things turn out better in the end. But telling a lie is never right. Satan is a liar. When you lie you are acting like him.

The <u>tenth</u> and last command God gave was not to covet.

> You shall not covet...anything that is your neighbor's.
> Exodus 20:17

Coveting is being unhappy with what you have and wanting what somebody else has. God wants you to be happy with the toys, home, friends, and family He has given you; He wants you to be thankful for what you have.

When people are jealous and want what belongs to someone else, they easily become mean and hateful.

Do you think the Israelites would be able to keep all these rules? Would they be able to keep their agreement with God? We will soon see!

Remember
Breaking God's rules is sin.

> ...sin is lawlessness. 1 John 3:4b

The penalty for sin is separation from God forever in the terrible place of suffering.

> The soul who sins shall die. Ezekiel 18:4b

Even if you only ever break one of God's rules, you are guilty and deserve to die.

> For whoever shall keep the whole law, and yet stumble in one
> point, he is guilty of all. James 2:10

Let's say you were trapped in a deep pit. In order to make a rope long enough to reach you and pull you out, ten ropes had to be knotted together. What if, as you were slowly being pulled out of the pit, one of the knots broke – just one?

If one knot broke, it would be as bad as if all the knots broke, wouldn't it? If only one knot broke, you would fall to your death.

That is how it is with God's commands. Even if you break just one rule, you have to die and be separated from God forever.

Remember, God knows your thoughts. If you break a rule in your heart or mind, you are guilty. If you are angry with someone in your heart, even if you did not actually murder that person, in God's eyes it is as though you have committed murder, and for that you deserve to die. Your thoughts matter to God as much as your actions.

Man looks at the outward appearance, but the Lord looks at the heart." 1 Samuel 16:7b

God knows everything you have ever done and all the thoughts you've ever had. You cannot hide from God.

O Lord, You have searched me and known me...You understand my thought afar off. You...are acquainted with all my ways. Psalm 139:1-3

God's commands are like a mirror. Without a mirror you can't see the dirt on your face. But when you look in the mirror, you can see the dirt. It's the same with God's commands. If you did not know the Ten Commandments, you might think you were a good person. But when you learn what God's rules are, you can see that your heart is not clean. You can see that you have done and thought things that are displeasing to God.

The Bible says that no person is good, or righteous, in God's eyes; no person is good enough to be able to live with God.

For in Your sight no one living is righteous. Psalm 143:2b

That is why God promised to send the Savior. Only the Savior would be able to make people acceptable to God.

Questions

1. What did the Israelites have to do so God would keep treating them as His special treasure? *They had to obey His commands.*

2. Why is it wrong to worship other gods? *It is wrong because the God of the Bible is the only true and living God. He is the Creator of the world and the most powerful. All other gods are false and powerless.*

3. What do the Ten Commandments show us? *The Ten Commandments show us how good a person would have to be in order to be acceptable to God.*

4. Is it right to use God's name as a swear word? *No, it is not right to use God's name as a swear word. We should respect God's name.*

5. What did God mean when He said to honor your father and your mother? *He meant that you are never to disobey, grumble, argue, or ignore your parents. It is wrong to be disrespectful to your parents in any way.*

6. Is it wrong to be angry with someone? *Yes, it is. Although you may not have committed murder, if you are angry with someone you are still guilty before God. God cares as much about your thoughts as He does about your actions.*

7. What was the last command God gave? *It was not to covet. You should be thankful and happy for what you have and not want what belongs to someone else.*

8. How are God's commands like a mirror? *Just like a mirror shows you the dirt on your face, God's commands show you the sin in your heart.*

9. What is the penalty for breaking God's commands? *It is death; it is separation from God forever in the terrible place of suffering.*

10. What happens if you only break one command? *The penalty for breaking one rule is the same as for breaking many rules. Even if you break only one command one time, you are a sinner and deserve to die.*

11. Who is the only One who can make you acceptable to God and save you from the death penalty you deserve? *Only God can; He promised to send the Savior to make a way for you to be cleaned from your sin and saved from eternal death.*

Biblical Worldviews

- God is a personal being; He communicates with people.
- The God of the Bible is the only true and living God; all other gods are false.
- God is the One who gives life.
- God is the Creator of the world.
- No one is greater than God; He is the highest authority. He sets the rules we must obey.
- God is perfect and sinless.
- All people are sinners and unacceptable to God.
- God knows everything; He knows our thoughts.
- The penalty for any and all sin is death; it is separation from God forever in the terrible place of suffering.

Activity: Ten Commandments Tablet Drawing

Supplies:

- Light-colored cardstock or construction paper
- Copies of "Ten Commandment" printout, one per student (see appendix page 579)
- Scissors
- Glue or double-sided tape
- Pencil, black crayon, marker, or pen
- Chalkboard or dry erase board
- Dry erase markers or chalk

Instructions:

- Give each student a piece of cardstock or construction paper and a copy of the "Ten Commandment" printout.
- On the board, draw a large outline of the stone tablets used for the Ten Commandments.
- Students copy this outline onto the cardstock or construction paper.
- Students cut out the commandments and glue them onto the stone tablets they just drew.
- Discuss the Ten Commandments. In what ways have students broken these commands? What is the penalty for breaking God's commands? What if you break only one command one time? What if you do not murder, but are angry with someone in your mind? Is there any way you can be good enough to live with God in Heaven? Who is the only One who can make you acceptable to God?

Extra Bible References

Job 33:4; Psalm 5:4, 53:1-3; Proverbs 27:4; Ecclesiastes 7:20; Isaiah 42:8, 59:2; Habakkuk 1:13; Matthew 5:21-48, 12:36; Mark 7:21-23; John 8:44; Romans 3:9-20; Romans 14:5; 1 Corinthians 4:5; Galatians 3:10, 23-24; Ephesians 6:1-4; Colossians 3:9; Titus 1:2; Hebrews 4:12-13; James 1:22-25; 1 John 3:15; Revelation 21:8, 27

*Sabbath day command not for today – Romans 14:5; Galatians 4:9-11; Colossians 2:16

33
A Broken Agreement
The Golden Calf

Memory Verse

For whoever shall keep the whole law, and yet stumble in one point, he is guilty of all.
James 2:10

Lesson

After God gave the Israelites His rules, He called Moses to come up on the mountain.

Then the LORD said to Moses, "Come up to Me on the mountain...and I will give you tablets of stone, and the law and commandments which I have written, that you may teach them."

So...Moses went up to the mountain of God...And Moses was on the mountain forty days and forty nights. Exodus 24:12-13, 15, 18

God had written His commands on stone tablets so they would not wear out. He wanted the Israelites always to have a written copy of how He expected them to act. God gave Moses the stone tablets and said for Moses to teach these rules to the people.

But while Moses was up on the mountain with God, something terrible happened in the Israelite camp.

Now when the people saw that Moses delayed coming down from the mountain, the people gathered together to Aaron, and said to him, "Come, make us gods that shall go before us; for as for this Moses, the man who brought us up out of the land of Egypt, we do not know what has become of him."

And Aaron said to them, "Break off the golden earrings which are in the ears of your wives, your sons, and your daughters, and bring them to me." So all the people broke off the golden earrings which were in their ears, and brought them to Aaron. And he...made a molded calf.

> Then they said, "This is your god, O Israel, that brought you out of the land of Egypt!" Exodus 32:1-4

Remember the first rule God gave the Israelites? God told the Israelites not to worship other gods.

📖 You shall have no other gods before Me. Exodus 20:3

God is the only true and living God. He is the Creator of the world and everything in it. All other gods are false and powerless.

📖 For the Lord is the great God, and the great King above all gods. Psalm 95:3

And what was the second rule? God told the Israelites not to make idols.

📖 You shall not make for yourself a carved image...you shall not bow down to them nor serve them. Exodus 20:4-5a

The Israelites were not to worship or pray to idols.

📖 The idols of the nations are silver and gold, the work of men's hands. They have mouths, but they do not speak; eyes they have, but they do not see; they have ears, but they do not hear; nor is there any breath in their mouths. Psalm 135:15-17

Even though the Israelites had promised to keep all God's commands, it did not take long for them to break their agreement with God. While Moses was up on the mountain getting a written copy of God's rules, the Israelites broke His first two commands.

Why were the Israelites so foolish? Had God not saved them from slavery by ruining the land of Egypt with one terrible plague after another? Had God not made a dry path for them through the middle of the Red Sea and then drowned Pharaoh's army? Had God not provided water and food for them and kept them safe the whole time they were in the wilderness?

And what about when God just recently came down on Mount Sinai to give them His commands? The shaking mountain, the fire, smoke, thunder, lightning, and trumpet blast had been a very fearful sight.

Over and over again, God had shown the Israelites His greatness and power; they had no excuse for their actions. They knew the God of Israel was the only true and living God.

But the Israelites were born into Adam's family. That is why they so quickly turned away from God. They were sinners and could not please God. They could not keep His commands!

God knew what the Israelites and Aaron were doing at the foot of the mountain. He knows everything. Nothing is hidden from God.

This is what God told Moses to do:

And the LORD said to Moses, "Go, get down! For your people whom you brought out of the land of Egypt have corrupted themselves. They have turned aside quickly out of the way which I commanded them. They have made themselves a molded calf, and worshiped it and sacrificed to it, and said, 'This is your god, O Israel, that brought you out of the land of Egypt!'"

...And Moses turned and went down from the mountain, and the two tablets of the Testimony were in his hand. Exodus 32:7-8, 15a

Taking the two stone tablets with him, Moses went down to see for himself what was going on.

...as soon as he came near the camp...he saw the calf and the dancing. So Moses' anger became hot, and he cast the tablets out of his hands and broke them at the foot of the mountain. Then he took the calf which they had made, burned it in the fire, and ground it to powder; and he scattered it on the water and made the children of Israel drink it. And Moses said to Aaron, "What did this people do to you that you have brought so great a sin upon them?"

...then Moses stood in the entrance of the camp...And he said to them, "Thus says the LORD God of Israel: 'Let every man put his sword on his side, and go...throughout the camp...'" So... about three thousand men of the people fell that day...

So the LORD plagued the people because of what they did with the calf which Aaron made. Exodus 32:19-21, 26-28, 35

229

The penalty for breaking God's rules is death. Because the Israelites broke God's law, three thousand people died.

But God had mercy on the Israelites. Instead of completely destroying them, He gave them another chance. God told Moses to cut two more stone tablets. Then He kindly wrote His rules on the new tablets. If the Israelites would keep these rules, God would still treat them as His special people.

And the LORD said to Moses, "Cut two tablets of stone like the first ones, and I will write on these tablets the words that were on the first tablets which you broke. Exodus 34:1

Remember

The Israelites could not keep God's rules after all. Before Moses even came down from the mountain, they had already broken the first two commandments!

You and I cannot keep God's rules, either. Just like the Israelites, we were born into Adam's family. We were born sinners separated from God. It is impossible for us to please God. The Bible says no one is good; no one keeps God's commands.

There is none righteous, no, not one...there is none who does good, no, not one. Romans 3:10, 12b

Because you have broken God's commands, you deserve to be separated from God forever in the terrible place of suffering. But God is merciful and gracious. Even though you should die for your sin, He promised to send the Savior to make a way for you to be saved from death.

Only God can save you. Trust in Him!

Questions

1. What was the first command God gave the Israelites? *He said they were not to have any other gods.*

2. What was the second command? *They were not to make idols or worship them.*

3. Why did God write His rules on tablets of stone? *He wrote them on stone tablets so they would not wear out. God wanted the Israelites always to know how He expected them to act.*

4. While Moses was up on the mountain getting the stone tablets, what did the Israelites ask Aaron to do? *They asked Aaron to make idols for them to worship instead of worshiping the one true God.*

5. Do man-made gods have any power? *No! They are dead and useless. They cannot see, hear, talk, or think.*

6. Did Aaron do what the people asked? *Yes, he made a golden calf for them out of their gold jewelry.*

7. What did the people say about the calf? *They said: "This is your god, O Israel, that brought you out of the land of Egypt."*

8. Did God know what the people were doing? *Yes, God sees and knows everything.*

9. What happened to the Israelites because of this sin? *Three thousand of the men were killed.*

10. In what way are you like the Israelites? *Just like the Israelites, you were born into Adam's family. You are a sinner and no matter how hard you try, you cannot keep God's rules.*

11. Who is the only One who can save you from eternal separation from God? *God is the only One who can save you. In His grace, He promised to send the Savior who would make a way for you to be saved from death.*

Biblical Worldviews

- God is a personal being; He communicates with people.
- The God of the Bible is the only true and living God.
- God is the Creator of the world and everything in it.
- God can do anything; no one is stronger than God.
- False gods and idols are powerless.
- All people are sinners.
- God is the highest authority who declares that the penalty for sin is death.
- God is a God of love and mercy.
- God is everywhere at all times and knows everything.
- Only God can make a way for us to be saved from death.

Activity: Memory Verse Ball

Supplies:

- Several mid-size balls
- Copy of memory verse: "For whoever shall keep the whole law, and yet stumble in one point, he is guilty of all." James 2:10

Instructions:

- Depending on the number of students, students either divide into teams or form one large circle.

- Students then practice the memory verse while throwing the ball to each other and catching it.

- For example: The teacher says the first part of the verse to be memorized. Then she throws the ball to one of the students, who repeats word for word what she just said and throws the ball to another student. Go around until everyone has had a chance to catch the ball and say the first part of the verse. Now add the second part of the verse and do the same thing. Then add the third part and so on until each student has memorized the entire verse, including the reference.

- If students have been working in small groups, they now come together to form a large circle and each one recites the verse and reference in front of the entire class with or without the balls.

Extra Bible References

Psalm 95:3; 96:4-5; 97:7; 135:15-18; 147:8-9, 15-18; Jeremiah 10:1-16, 14:22; Acts 7:37-41

34
A Beautiful Tent
Tabernacle Construction

Memory Verse

The LORD is great in Zion, and He is high above all the peoples. Let them praise Your great and awesome name—He is holy. Psalm 99:2-3

Lesson

God was not surprised when the Israelites broke His commands. But they had made an agreement with Him that He would only give them special treatment if they kept His commands. When the Israelites broke God's rules, they deserved to die and be separated from Him forever.

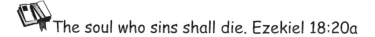The soul who sins shall die. Ezekiel 18:20a

Even still, God had mercy on the Israelites and did not destroy them. In His love and grace He made a way for them to have their sins forgiven.

Then the LORD spoke to Moses, saying: "Speak to the children of Israel, that they bring Me an offering…this is the offering which you shall take from them: gold, silver, and bronze; blue, purple, and scarlet thread, fine linen, and goats' hair; ram skins dyed red, badger skins, and acacia wood; oil for the light, and spices for the anointing oil and for the sweet incense; onyx stones, and stones to be set in the ephod and in the breastplate. And let them make Me a sanctuary, that I may dwell among them." Exodus 25:1-8

God told Moses to tell the Israelites to construct a beautiful house for Him.

God was going to come live with the Israelites in their camp. That way, whenever a person broke one of His commands, he could come to God for forgiveness.

Since the Israelites were always moving from place to place, this special house for God needed to be portable. That is why God told them to make it out of animal skins and cloth. It was going to be a tent that could be set up and taken down again. It would be called the tabernacle.

In the same way God gave Noah careful instructions for how to build the ark, God told Moses exactly how He wanted the Israelites to make the tabernacle.

God said to put a fence all around the outside of the tabernacle. The fence was to have only one entrance located right in front of the doorway of the tabernacle.

Within the fence was an open area called the courtyard of the tabernacle.

You shall also make the court of the tabernacle. Exodus 27:9a

God said to put a big altar and a bowl for washing in front of the doorway of the tabernacle. Whenever anyone came through the entrance in the fence, the first thing they would see was the big altar.

The altar was to be made of acacia wood and covered in bronze. It was to have a horn at each corner.

You shall make an altar of acacia wood...You shall make its horns on its four corners...And you shall overlay it with bronze.
Exodus 27:1-2

The bowl for washing was to be made of bronze. It stood between the altar and the door of the tabernacle.

You shall...make a laver of bronze...for washing. You shall put it between the tabernacle of meeting and the altar. Exodus 30:18

Holy - set apart for a special purpose.

Inside the tabernacle God said to make two rooms: the Holy Place and the Most Holy Place. Holy means "set apart." The Holy Place and the Most Holy Place were set apart for God's use only.

The doorway of the tabernacle would open into the Holy Place. Inside the Holy Place God said to put three pieces of furniture: A table with twelve loaves of bread on it, a lampstand, and an incense altar. God gave Moses specific instructions on how to make each of these pieces of furniture.

God said to hang a curtain between the Holy Place and the Most Holy Place.

You shall make a veil woven of blue, purple, and scarlet thread, and fine woven linen. It shall be woven with an artistic design of cherubim…The veil shall be a divider for you between the holy place and the Most Holy. Exodus 26:31, 33b

Behind the curtain, inside the Most Holy Place, God told Moses to put a special box called "the Ark of the Testimony." The ark was to be covered with pure gold.

God also told Moses to make a lid for the Ark of the Testimony. The lid was called the "mercy seat."

You shall make a mercy seat of pure gold…And you shall make two cherubim of gold…at the two ends of the mercy seat…the cherubim shall stretch out their wings above, covering the mercy seat with their wings, and they shall face one another; the faces of the cherubim shall be toward the mercy seat.

You shall put the mercy seat on top of the ark, and in the ark you shall put the Testimony that I will give you. And there I will meet with you, and I will speak with you from above the mercy seat, from between the two cherubim which are on the ark of the Testimony…
Exodus 25:17-22a

The mercy seat was going to be the place where God would live.

God said to make two gold cherubim (angels), one on each end of the mercy seat. The cherubim were to stand facing each other with their wings touching.

Inside the gold box, underneath the mercy seat, Moses was to place the stone tablets with God's commands written on them.

The Israelites carefully followed all God's instructions. Because they trusted in God, they built every part of the tabernacle exactly the way He told them to.

Thus all the work of the tabernacle of the tent of meeting was finished. And the children of Israel did according to all that the LORD had commanded Moses; so they did. Exodus 39:32

When all the parts of the tabernacle were ready, God told Moses to assemble the tabernacle and put all the pieces of furniture where they belonged.

So Moses raised up the tabernacle...he brought the ark into the tabernacle, hung up the veil of the covering, and partitioned off the ark of the Testimony, as the LORD had commanded Moses.

He put the table in the tabernacle of meeting, on the north side of the tabernacle, outside the veil; and he set the bread in order upon it before the LORD, as the LORD had commanded Moses. He put the lampstand in the tabernacle of meeting, across from the table, on the south side of the tabernacle; and he lit the lamps before the LORD, as the LORD had commanded Moses. He put the gold altar in the tabernacle of meeting in front of the veil; and he burned sweet incense on it, as the LORD had commanded Moses.

He hung up the screen at the door of the tabernacle. And he put the altar of burnt offering before the door of the tabernacle of the tent of meeting...He set the laver between the tabernacle of meeting and the altar, and put water there for washing...And he raised up the court all around the tabernacle and the altar, and hung up the screen of the court gate.

So Moses finished the work. Then the cloud covered the tabernacle of meeting, and the glory of the LORD filled the tabernacle.
Exodus 40:18-34

Since the Israelites believed God and carefully followed His instructions, God could come to live inside the tabernacle. Now, whenever any Israelite broke one of God's commands, he could go to the tabernacle to be forgiven.

Remember

God always tells people what He expects them to do. He always communicates with people about how they can be accepted by Him and saved from death. In the same way God gave Noah exact plans for building the boat, God gave Moses detailed instructions for making the tabernacle. Moses and the Israelites believed God and were careful to do everything exactly like He said.

Remember Cain? He did not believe God. Even though God had shown Cain and Abel how to come to Him, Cain thought he could come to God according to his own ideas. But God did not accept Cain or his offering, and in the end, Cain became separated from God forever.

The same holds true for you and me. God has made a way for your sins to be forgiven so that He can accept you and you can be saved from death.

Being kind, going to church, getting baptized, or trying to keep God's rules will not make you acceptable to God. It is impossible for you to be good enough for God to accept you.

There is only one way for you to come to God. God wants you to admit you are a sinner and to trust in Him to save you. God's way for you to be forgiven and made acceptable to Him is by trusting in Him and in the Savior He promised to send.

Questions

1. Did the Israelites keep their agreement with God to obey all His rules? *No, the Israelites did not keep their agreement with God; they broke God's rules right away.*

2. What is the penalty for breaking God's rules? *The penalty for breaking God's rules is death; it is eternal separation from God in the terrible place of suffering.*

3. What did God tell the Israelites to build so He could come live in their camp? *He told them to make a tent that would be called the tabernacle.*

4. Did God tell the Israelites how to build the tabernacle? *Yes, He gave them clear instructions.*

5. What two rooms did God tell Moses to put inside the tabernacle? *The two rooms in the tabernacle were the Holy Place and the Most Holy Place.*

6. Where did God tell Moses to put the Ark of the Testimony? *God told Moses to put the Ark of the Testimony behind the curtain in the Most Holy Place.*

7. When God came to live in the tabernacle, where was He going to live? *He was going to live on the lid of the Ark of the Testimony. The lid was called the mercy seat.*

8. Why were the Israelites careful to build everything exactly the way God told them to? *The reason the Israelites carefully followed God's instructions was because they believed God.*

9. What would have happened if the Israelites would not have built the tabernacle exactly as God said? *If the Israelites would not have made every part exactly like God said, God would not have come to live among them.*

10. Is there anything you can do to make God accept you? *No, there is nothing you can do. It is impossible for you to be good enough to please God. Being baptized or going to church do not make you acceptable to God either.*

11. How does God want you to come to Him to be forgiven of your sin? *God wants you to admit you are a sinner and trust in Him to save you from the death penalty you deserve.*

Biblical Worldviews

- God is a personal God; He communicates with people.
- God is perfect.
- All people are sinners.
- The penalty for sin is death.
- God is a God of mercy, grace, and love.
- Only God can make a way for people to be forgiven.
- The only way to please God is to believe Him.

Activity: Tabernacle Diagram

Supplies:

- Chalkboard or dry erase board
- Chalk or dry erase markers
- Pencil and crayons
- White paper, one piece per student

Instructions:

- The teacher draws a diagram of the tabernacle on the board.
- Students copy the diagram onto their papers.
- Students label and color their diagrams.
- At the top of the page, above the tabernacle, students write: "...the glory of the LORD filled the tabernacle." Exodus 40:34
- Discuss: What would have happened if Israelites would not have believed God and built the tabernacle exactly like He said? What if they would have followed their own ideas like Cain did?

Extra Bible References

Exodus 35-40, Lamentations 3:22-23

35
Forgiveness
Sacrifices at the Tabernacle

Memory Verse

> *The LORD is great in Zion, and He is high above all the peoples. Let them praise Your great and awesome name—He is holy. Psalm 99:2-3*

Lesson

Even though God was now living in the Israelite camp, the Israelites could not just go visit Him any time they wanted. No, if the Israelites wanted to come near to God, they had to come in the way God said.

Remember how God showed Cain and Abel the way He wanted them to come to Him? The only way for Cain and Abel to be accepted by God was for them to kill an animal and bring it to Him as an offering. For many years, those who believed God came to Him in this way. Abel, Noah, Abraham, Isaac, and Jacob all came to God by killing an animal and offering it to Him. That is how God wanted the Israelites to come to Him too.

If an Israelite broke one of God's rules, he was to bring a sacrifice to the tabernacle where God lived. God told Moses exactly how He wanted the Israelites to offer these sacrifices.

If his offering is a burnt sacrifice of the herd, let him offer a male without blemish; he shall offer it...at the door of the tabernacle of meeting before the Lord. Then he shall put his hand on the head of the burnt offering, and it will be accepted on his behalf to make atonement for him.

He shall kill the bull before the Lord; and the priests, Aaron's sons, shall bring the blood and sprinkle the blood all around on the altar...Then the priests, Aaron's sons, shall lay the parts...on the wood that is on the fire upon the altar...And the priest shall burn all on the altar as a burnt sacrifice, an offering made by fire, a sweet aroma to the Lord.. Leviticus 1:3-5, 8-9

Whenever an Israelite sinned, he was to bring a sheep or goat to the big bronze altar outside the tabernacle. The sheep or goat had to be perfect; it could not have any defects. Then the sinner was to lay his hand on the head of the animal while he cut its throat. By putting his hand on the head of the sheep while he killed it, the person showed that the animal was taking his place. In this way, the Israelite did not have to die for his own sin.

Whenever an Israelite broke a command and came to God in this way, God forgave his sin. Even though the person who sinned deserved to die, God accepted the animal's death in his place.

The Bible says that God accepted the animal sacrifice as *atonement* for the sinner. This meant that God accepted the death of the animal as a covering for the person's sin. Since the person's sin was now covered, God could forgive him.

Atonement- a covering for sin

God chose Moses' brother, Aaron, along with Aaron's sons, to be priests.

Now take Aaron your brother, and his sons with him, from among the children of Israel, that he may minister to Me as priest...
Exodus 28:1a

The priests' job was to help with the sacrifices and to work in the tabernacle. But before the priests could go into the tabernacle or near the big bronze altar, they always had to wash their hands and feet in the big bronze bowl that stood between the altar and the tabernacle.

Of course, washing their hands and feet did not make the priests clean on the inside, but it was God's way of reminding them that only those who have been cleaned from sin are acceptable to Him.

He set the laver between the tabernacle of meeting and the altar, and put water there for washing; and Moses, Aaron, and his sons would wash their hands and their feet with water from it. Whenever they went into the tabernacle of meeting, and when they came near the altar, they washed, as the LORD had commanded Moses.
Exodus 40:30-32

Sometimes an Israelite did not realize he had broken a command and didn't bring a sacrifice to God. But because God is merciful, He made a way for even these unnoticed sins to be forgiven.

God said that once a year the high priest was to go into the Most Holy Place with the blood of a special sacrifice.

But into the second part the high priest went alone once a year, not without blood, which he offered for himself and for the people's sins committed in ignorance; Hebrews 9:7

The high priest was to sprinkle the blood of this special sacrifice on the mercy seat where God lived.

Then he shall kill the goat of the sin offering, which is for the people, bring its blood inside the veil... and sprinkle it on the mercy seat and before the mercy seat. Leviticus 16:15

Every year the high priest had to sprinkle the blood of this special sacrifice on the mercy seat inside the Most Holy Place.

For on that day the priest shall make atonement for you, to cleanse you, that you may be clean from all your sins before the Lord. Leviticus 16:30

In this way the high priest made sure that all the Israelite's sins for the past year, including those committed unknowingly, were covered. If the priest would not have sprinkled the blood of this sacrifice on the mercy seat, God would not have been able to forgive the Israelites for all their sins.

Since the tabernacle was located right in the middle of the Israelite camp, the Israelites always saw the smoke rising from the sacrifices. Every day the smoke reminded them that the penalty for breaking God's rules is death.

Remember

God is completely perfect in every way. He is so pure that He cannot stand sin of any kind.

You hate all workers of iniquity. Psalm 5:5b

Your sin makes you God's enemy; because of your sin you must be separated from God.

And you, who once were alienated and enemies in your mind by wicked works... Colossians 1:21a

The Bible says that sinful people will be separated from God forever in the terrible place of suffering.

And anyone not found written in the Book of Life was cast into the lake of fire. Revelation 20:15

But even though God hates sin, God is a God of love. Just like He made a way for the sinful Israelites to be forgiven, He has made a way for you to be forgiven.

...we shall be saved from wrath through Him. Romans 5:9b

Through the promised Savior, God has made a way for you not to have to be separated from Him. You will see that because of what the Savior did for you, you can be God's friend instead of His enemy.

Questions

1. Why did God want the priests to wash before serving Him in the tabernacle? *This was God's way of reminding them that only those who have been cleaned from sin are acceptable to Him.*

2. Where in the tabernacle did God live? *God lived on the mercy seat in the Most Holy Place.*

3. Whenever an Israelite broke one of God's rules, what did he have to do? *Whenever an Israelite sinned he was to bring a perfect sheep or goat to the altar that was in front of the tabernacle where God lived. He was to lay his hand on the sheep or goat and kill it there in front of God's presence.*

4. What did God mean when He said the offering would make atonement for the person? *He meant that the sacrifice covered the person's sin so that God could forgive him.*

5. Why did the high priest take the blood of a special sacrifice into the Most Holy Place once a year? *God told the high priest to do this so He could forgive all the sins the Israelites had committed unknowingly over the past year.*

6. In what way were the Israelites reminded every day that the payment for sin is death? *The smoke rising from the bronze altar in the middle of their camp was a continual reminder to them that all sin must be paid for with death.*

7. What happens to sinful people when they die? *They must be separated from God forever in the terrible place of suffering.*

8. Is there any way to escape this terrible penalty? *Yes, through the Savior God has made a way for us sinners to be forgiven.*

Biblical Worldviews

- God communicates with people: He clearly tells people what He expects them to do.
- All people are sinners.
- God is perfect; sinful people cannot live in His presence.
- The penalty for sin is death; it is eternal separation from God in the terrible place of suffering.
- Only God can make a way for sinners to be forgiven.
- God is a God of love.
- God accepted a perfect substitute to die in place of the sinner.
- God planned to send the Savior to rescue you and me from Satan, sin, and death.

Activity: Bible Bingo

Supplies:

- Bingo cards and game tokens (Any set will do. You can buy an inexpensive set at the dollar store.)

Instructions:

- Give each student a bingo card and some tokens.
- Ask a question from the lesson review and call on a student to answer it. If the student answers it correctly, she calls the bingo square she wants to cover. Everyone else who has that square covers it as well.
- Continue to ask questions, calling on a different student each time. Allow everyone to answer at least one question and pick at least one bingo square.
- The game is over when the first student shouts BINGO because she has covered a complete row with tokens, either vertically, horizontally, or diagonally.
- Play the game several times until everyone has had a turn answering a question and/or all the questions from the review have been asked and answered.

Extra Bible References

Leviticus 4:1-35, 16:1-34, 17:11; Numbers 5:8; Lamentations 3:22-23; Malachi 1:13-14; Acts 2:23; Romans 5:9-11; Colossians 2:13; Titus 3:3-5; Hebrews 9:6-10, 22; 10:1-14; 1 Peter 1:20

36
Spies
Moses Sends Spies into Canaan

Memory Verse

So we see that they could not enter in because of unbelief. Hebrews 3:19

Lesson

Sometime after the Israelites finished building the tabernacle, the pillar of cloud started to rise. It was time for the Israelites to pack up their belongings and continue on their journey to the land God had promised to give them.

Remember long ago when God told Abraham to leave his home in Mesopotamia and move to a land he didn't know? At that time, God took Abraham to Canaan. The people in Canaan worshiped false gods and were very wicked. God promised Abraham that someday He would give their land to his descendants.

Abraham, Isaac, and Jacob lived in Canaan many years; but during the food shortage, Jacob moved his family to Egypt. In Egypt, Jacob's family grew into a great nation that came to be called Israel.

For four hundred years, the Israelites lived as slaves in Egypt, just as God had told Abraham they would. During that time, the people living in the land of Canaan became more and more wicked. The Bible says that they even sacrificed their children in the fire to false gods.

for every abomination to the LORD which He hates they have done to their gods; for they burn even their sons and daughters in the fire to their gods. Deuteronomy 12:31b

Now it was time for God to destroy these terrible nations and give their land to the people of Israel. Finally, after months of trudging through the endless wilderness, the Israelites arrived at the border of Canaan. Moses sent spies to check out the land.

And the LORD spoke to Moses, saying, "Send men to spy out the land of Canaan, which I am giving to the children of Israel..."

So Moses sent them...according to the command of the LORD...
Numbers 13:1-3

The spies found that the land of Canaan was a beautiful place.

So they went up and spied out the land...they came to the Valley of Eshcol, and there cut down a branch with one cluster of grapes; they carried it between two of them on a pole. They also brought some of the pomegranates and figs...And they returned from spying out the land...

...and came back to Moses and Aaron and all the congregation of the children of Israel...they brought back word to them...and showed them the fruit of the land...they...said: "We went to the land where you sent us. It truly flows with milk and honey, and this is its fruit. Nevertheless the people who dwell in the land are strong; the cities are fortified and very large..."

Then Caleb...said, "Let us go up at once and take possession, for we are well able to overcome it."

But the men who had gone up with him said, "We are not able to go up against the people, for they are stronger than we." And they gave the children of Israel a bad report of the land which they had spied out, saying, "...we saw the giants...and we were like grasshoppers in our own sight...." Numbers 13:21-28, 30-33

The land of Canaan was amazing. The spies reported that it flowed "with milk and honey." That meant it was a rich and fruitful land. They brought back pomegranates, figs, and grapes to show to the people. Just one bunch of grapes was so big it had to be carried on a pole between two men!

The children of Israel should have been thankful. They should have cheered and celebrated because of all God had done for them. God had rescued them from slavery in Egypt, He had brought them safely through the terrible desert, and now He was about to give them a wonderful land of their own.

Who brought us up out of the land of Egypt, who led us through the wilderness, through a land of deserts and pits, through a land of drought and the shadow of death, through a land that no one crossed and where no one dwelt?'

I [God] brought you into a bountiful country, to eat its fruit and its goodness. Jeremiah 2:6b, 7a

But even though it was a wonderful land, the spies did not think God was powerful enough to give it to Israel. They did not believe God would do what He said He would do. They told the Israelites about giants who lived there in huge, walled cities.

When the Israelites heard this bad report...

...all the congregation lifted up their voices and cried, and the people wept that night. And all the children of Israel complained against Moses and Aaron, and...said to them, "If only we had died in the land of Egypt! Or if only we had died in this wilderness! Why has the LORD brought us to this land to fall by the sword, that our wives and children should become victims? Would it not be better for us to return to Egypt?" So they said to one another, "Let us select a leader and return to Egypt."

But Joshua...and Caleb...who were among those who had spied out the land...spoke to...the children of Israel, saying: "The land we passed through to spy out is an exceedingly good land...do not rebel against the LORD, nor fear the people of the land, for...their protection has departed from them, and the LORD is with us. Do not fear them." Numbers 14:1-4, 6-9

Just like Adam and Eve had listened to Satan instead of believing God, the Israelites listened to the spies instead of believing God's word. They became afraid of what would happen to their families. They began to think it would have been better to die in Egypt, or in the wilderness, than to have to face the giant Canaanites.

The only two spies who believed God were Joshua and Caleb. Joshua and Caleb told the Israelites not to be afraid. They told them not to rebel against God. God had promised to give them this "exceedingly good land," and God always keeps His promises. Just like God destroyed the Egyptians, He would destroy the Canaanites. The Israelites had no reason to doubt or fear.

Then the LORD said: "...because all these men who have seen My glory and the signs which I did in Egypt and in the wilderness, and have put Me to the test now these ten times, and have not heeded My voice, they certainly shall not see the land of which I swore to their fathers, nor shall any of those who rejected Me see it. ...

"How long shall I bear with this evil congregation who complain against Me? ...The carcasses of you who have complained against Me shall fall in this wilderness, all of you...from twenty years old and above. Except for Caleb...and Joshua...you shall by no means enter the land which I swore I would make you dwell in.

"But your little ones, whom you said would be victims, I will bring in, and they shall know the land which you have despised. But as for you, your carcasses shall fall in this wilderness. And your sons shall be shepherds in the wilderness forty years...

"According to the number of the days in which you spied out the land, forty days, for each day you shall bear your guilt one year, namely forty years, and you shall know My rejection. I the LORD have spoken this. I will surely do so to all this evil congregation who are gathered together against Me. In this wilderness they shall be consumed, and there they shall die." Numbers 14:20, 22-23, 27a, 29-35

Because the Israelites did not trust the all-powerful God who always keeps His promises, God made them turn around and go back into the wilderness for forty more years. After forty years, when all who disbelieved God were dead, God promised to bring the Israelites' children back to possess the land. Only Joshua and Caleb would remain alive because they believed God. Joshua and Caleb would be able to return and enter the land.

Remember

What a sad story! Because the Israelites did not believe God, they did not get to have the wonderful land He had promised to give them.

So we see that they could not enter in because of unbelief.
Hebrews 3:19

The Bible says the only way to please God is to believe Him.

📖 But without faith it is impossible to please Him... Hebrews 11:6a

God warns you and me not to have an evil heart of unbelief like the Israelites did.

📖 Beware...lest there be in any of you an evil heart of unbelief in departing from the living God; Hebrews 3:12

You need to believe God. Believe what He says in the Bible. Just like God wanted to do good things for Israel, He wants to do good things for you. He wants to rescue you from Satan and the death penalty. That is why He promised to send the Savior.

Questions

1. What was the land called that God promised to give to Abraham and his descendants? *God promised to give them the land of Canaan.*

2. What were the people in Canaan like? *The Canaanites did not care at all about the true and living God. They did very evil things and worshiped false gods.*

3. What good things did the spies find in the land of Canaan? *They found pomegranates, figs, and huge grapes. They saw that it was a fruitful and fertile land.*

4. Why were the spies scared of the people of Canaan? *The Canaanites were big and strong. The spies said that compared to the Canaanites they were as small as grasshoppers.*

5. Who did most of the spies think was more powerful – God or the giant Canaanites? *The spies thought the Canaanites were too strong for God to conquer.*

6. What did the people do when they heard there were giants in Canaan? *They cried all night and said they wished they had died either in Egypt or in the wilderness instead of having to face these terrifying people. They were afraid of what would happen to their children.*

7. Which two spies believed God? *Joshua and Caleb believed God.*

8. Why should the Israelites have believed God? *The Israelites should have believed God because He had already proven to them that He is all-powerful and always does what He says He will do. God had freed them from the mighty Egyptians and by His great power had fed them and kept them safe during their travels through the dangerous wilderness.*

9. What did God do when the people did not believe Him? *God sent them back to the wilderness to wander around for 40 more years until everyone twenty years old and above was dead, except for Joshua and Caleb.*

10. What is the only way to please God? *The only way to please God is to believe Him. God is all-powerful and He always does what He says He will do. You need to trust in Him because He is the only One who can rescue you from Satan and make you acceptable to Him.*

Biblical Worldviews

- God always keeps His promises.
- The only way to please God is to believe Him.
- God is all-powerful; nothing is too hard for Him.
- God is the highest authority; He decides what will happen to the nations.
- The payment for sin is death.

Activity: Spies Skit

Supplies:

- Five or more student volunteers

Instructions:

- Student volunteers act out the scene in which the spies report their findings about the land of Canaan. The key parts are: 1) Joshua 2) Caleb 3) three or more unbelieving spies 4) a crowd of unbelieving Israelites. (If you have a small group, the audience can be the crowd and you can prompt them to participate at the appropriate times.)
- Make sure students act out the difference between those who believed God (Joshua and Caleb) and those who didn't.
- If you have more than five students who want to act, divide them into more than one group and let each group act it out while the other students watch.
- Discuss skit, emphasizing key points from the lesson.

Extra Bible References

Genesis 12:1-3, 15:12-21; Numbers 10:11-13; Deuteronomy 1:19-25; Jeremiah 27:5; 1 Timothy 2:4; Hebrews 3:7-19, 11:6; Jude 1:5

37
Snakes
The Bronze Snake on the Pole

Memory Verse

So we see that they could not enter in because of unbelief. Hebrews 3:19

Lesson

It must have been sad for the Israelites to return to the wilderness. I am sure they wished they had believed God! They should have trusted Him, but they did not. And now they found themselves out in the desert again without water to drink.

Then the children of Israel, the whole congregation, came into the Wilderness of Zin in the first month...

Now there was no water for the congregation; so they gathered together against Moses and Aaron. And the people contended with Moses and spoke, saying: "...Why have you brought up the assembly of the Lord into this wilderness, that we and our animals should die here? And why have you made us come up out of Egypt, to bring us to this evil place?" Numbers 20:1-5a

Unfortunately, even after losing their chance to enter the land of Canaan, the Israelites had not learned to trust God to take care of them. In spite of this, God was incredibly patient. He told Moses what to do.

Then the LORD spoke to Moses, saying, "...Speak to the rock...and it will yield...water; thus you shall bring water...out of the rock, and give drink to the congregation and their animals." Numbers 20:7-8

At Rephidim when the Israelites ran out of water, God told Moses to hit the rock with his rod, but this time God told Moses to speak to the rock.

So Moses...and Aaron gathered the assembly together before the rock; and he said to them, "Hear now, you rebels! Must we bring water for you out of this rock?" Then Moses lifted his hand and struck the rock twice with his rod; and water came out abundantly, and the congregation and their animals drank. Numbers 20:9-11

Moses was tired of the Israelites' complaining and spoke angrily to them. Then, instead of speaking to the rock like God said, he hit the rock two times. In His mercy and kindness, God caused water to pour out of the rock, but He was displeased with Moses and Aaron.

Then the LORD spoke to Moses and Aaron, "Because you did not believe Me, to hallow Me in the eyes of the children of Israel, therefore you shall not bring this assembly into the land which I have given them." Numbers 20:12

God had chosen Moses and Aaron to be Israel's leaders; they were to teach the people to believe God. But instead, they dishonored God before the Israelites. Instead of believing God and speaking to the rock as God said, Moses angrily hit the rock.

When Moses and Aaron failed to respect God before the Israelites, they were disqualified from being able to lead the people of Israel into the land of Canaan.

As the Israelites continued to wander about in the empty wilderness day after day, they began to feel more and more hopeless and they started complaining again.

...they journeyed...and the soul of the people became very discouraged on the way. And the people spoke against God and against Moses: "Why have you brought us up out of Egypt to die in the wilderness? For there is no food and no water, and our soul loathes this worthless bread." Numbers 21:4-5

It was not God's fault the Israelites were back in the wilderness. If they had believed God instead of believing the spies, they would have been in Canaan by now.

God was displeased with their attitude.

So the LORD sent fiery serpents among the people, and they bit the people; and many of the people of Israel died.

> Therefore the people came to Moses, and said, "We have sinned, for we have spoken against the LORD and against you; pray to the LORD that He take away the serpents from us." So Moses prayed for the people. Numbers 21:6-7

After many of the people died, the Israelites finally admitted they were wrong for complaining against God and against God's leader, Moses. They asked Moses to pray that God would take away the snakes. They knew God was the only One who could save them.

> Then the LORD said to Moses, "Make a fiery serpent, and set it on a pole; and it shall be that everyone who is bitten, when he looks at it, shall live." Numbers 21:8

God could have let the people die for their sin. He could have told the Israelites to find their own way of escape from the snakes. After all, they did not deserve His kindness. But when they admitted they were wrong and called out to Him, God was merciful and showed Moses what to do so the Israelites could be saved.

> So Moses made a bronze serpent, and put it on a pole; and so it was, if a serpent had bitten anyone, when he looked at the bronze serpent, he lived. Numbers 21:9

This time Moses trusted God and did what He said.

God promised that whoever looked at the snake on the pole would live. Of course, it was not the snake that healed the people. The snake had no power. God was the One who healed the Israelites.

All God asked them to do was look at the snake on the pole. He did not ask them to promise never to complain again, or to say a prayer, or to give Him money or a gift. Those who believed God did as He said and were saved. Every Israelite who simply looked up at the snake lived.

Remember

Just like the Israelites died because they grumbled, you too deserve to die for your sin.

> The soul who sins shall die. Ezekiel 18:20

And, in the same way God was the only One who could make a way for the Israelites to be saved, God is the only One who can save you from death.

In order to be saved from death, the Israelites were simply to look at the snake on the pole, nothing else.

It is the same for you. In order for you to be saved from eternal death, God says for you to believe Him, nothing else. To try to save yourself by doing anything else – like going to church, being kind to others, being baptized or praying – would show you do not believe God. It would show that you think you need to help God out. God will not save those who trust both in Him and in themselves.

But those who trust only in God will most certainly be saved from death because God always keeps His promises. None of those who trust in God will be condemned to death.

And none of those who trust in Him shall be condemned.
Psalm 34:22b

Questions

1. What did God tell Moses to do to the rock so the Israelites could have water? *God told Moses to speak to the rock.*

2. Did Moses do what God said? *No, instead of speaking to the rock, he hit it two times.*

3. Why did God tell Moses and Aaron they could not lead the Israelites into the land of Canaan? *Moses and Aaron were not allowed to lead Israel into the land of Canaan because they did not believe God. By not believing God and doing what He said, they dishonored God in front of the Israelites.*

4. What is the end result of sin? *Sin always leads to death.*

5. Why did God send poisonous snakes to bite the Israelites? *God sent snakes to bite the Israelites because they complained against Him.*

6. What did the Israelites do when many of them died from the snake bites? *They admitted they were wrong and asked Moses to pray that God would save them.*

7. Who was the only One who could save the Israelites from death? *Only God could.*

8. Did the snake on the pole have special power to save the Israelites? *No, it was God's power that saved the Israelites when they believed Him and did what He said.*

9. Besides looking up at the snake on the pole, what else did God ask the Israelites to do in order to be saved? *All God asked the Israelites to do was to look up at the snake, nothing else.*

10. Who is the only One who can save you from the death you deserve for your sin? *Only God can save you.*

11. Is there anything you can do to help God save you? *No, you cannot do anything to save yourself. If you try to help God out, He will not save you. God saves only those who trust in Him alone.*

Biblical Worldviews

- God is a personal being; He communicates with people.
- God can do anything; nothing is too hard for Him.
- God is the Creator; He rules over nature.
- All people are sinners.
- God is patient, loving, merciful, and gracious.
- The payment for sin is death.
- Only God can save us from death.
- We cannot save ourselves.
- God saves only those who believe Him.

Activity: Disappearing Memory Verse Game

Supplies:
- Chalkboard or dry erase board
- Chalk or dry erase marker

Instructions:
- Write memory verse and reference in large letters on chalkboard or white board.
- Students repeat memory verse and reference in unison two times
- Student volunteer picks two words for you to erase. Erase those two words (or student can come up and erase them).
- Students repeat the memory verse in unison again, including the two words that have been erased.
- A different student volunteer picks two more words to erase. Erase the words as before.
- Students repeat the memory verse again in unison.
- Repeat this process until all the words have been erased.
- Finally, students try to recite the verse in unison without any words on the board.
- Individual volunteers may try to recite the verse from memory.

Extra Bible References

Numbers 27:14; 2 Kings 18:4; Nehemiah 9:19-21; Psalms 106:32-33; 145:18-19; Psalm 147:8-9, 15-18; John 3:14, 6:40, 8:28, 12:32; 1 Corinthians 1:21

38
Canaan at Last
Crossing the Jordan and Conquering Jericho

Memory Verse

Great is our Lord, and mighty in power; His understanding is infinite. Psalm 147:5

Lesson

For forty long years the Israelites wandered in the wilderness. Finally, when no one was left of those who had disbelieved God, God brought them back to the border of Canaan.

Before the Israelites entered the land, Moses encouraged them. He told them not to be afraid. Even though the Canaanites were much stronger than the Israelites, God promised to fight for them.

...You are to cross over the Jordan today, and go in to dispossess nations greater and mightier than yourself, cities great and fortified up to heaven, a people great and tall...Therefore understand today that the LORD your God is He who goes over before you...He will destroy them and bring them down before you... Deuteronomy 9:1-2

Moses also wanted the Israelites to understand that...

It is not because of your righteousness...that you go in to possess their land, but because of the wickedness of these nations that the LORD your God drives them out from before you, and that He may fulfill the word which the LORD swore to your fathers, to Abraham, Isaac, and Jacob. Deuteronomy 9:5

All land belongs to God. He could give the land of Canaan to whomever He decided. God wanted the Israelites to know that it was not because of their good behavior that He was giving this land to them. It was because of the great wickedness of the Canaanites and because of His promise to give the land to Abraham's descendants, that God was now going to give the land to the Israelites.

Moses, however, could not go with the Israelites because he had dishonored God in front of them when he struck the rock instead of speaking to it in the Wilderness of Zin. Even still, God was kind to Moses and let him look at the land from a distance.

> Then Moses went up...to Mount Nebo...which is across from Jericho. And the LORD showed him all the land...
>
> So Moses the servant of the LORD died there...according to the word of the LORD. And He buried him in a valley in the land of Moab...but no one knows his grave to this day. Moses was one hundred and twenty years old when he died...And the children of Israel wept for Moses in the plains of Moab thirty days. Deuteronomy 34:1, 4-8

After Moses died, God chose Joshua to be Israel's new leader. Joshua would be the one to lead the Israelites into the land of Canaan.

> After the death of Moses the servant of the LORD, it came to pass that the LORD spoke to Joshua the son of Nun, Moses' assistant, saying: "Moses My servant is dead. Now therefore, arise, go over this Jordan, you and all this people, to the land which I am giving to them... Joshua 1:1-2

In order to get into Canaan, the Israelites would have to cross the Jordan River. But the river was flooded. It was overflowing its banks and the water was very deep. There was no bridge across the river and the Israelites did not have boats. There was no way for them to get to the other side.

So God told Joshua what to do. God said for the priests who were carrying the Ark of the Testimony to go in front of everyone else.

> And the LORD said to Joshua, "This day I will begin to exalt you in the sight of all Israel, that they may know that, as I was with Moses, so I will be with you. You shall command the priests who bear the ark of the covenant, saying, 'When you have come to the edge of the water of the Jordan, you shall stand in the Jordan.'"

So Joshua said to the children of Israel, "Come here, and hear the words of the LORD your God." And Joshua said, "By this you shall know that the living God is among you, and that He will without fail drive out from before you the Canaanites...Behold, the ark of the covenant of the Lord of all the earth is crossing over before you into the Jordan...And it shall come to pass, as soon as the soles of the feet of the priests who bear the ark of the LORD, the Lord of all the earth, shall rest in the waters of the Jordan, that the waters of the Jordan shall be cut off, the waters that come down from upstream, and they shall stand as a heap."

So it was...as...the feet of the priests who bore the ark dipped in the edge of the water (for the Jordan overflows all its banks during the whole time of harvest), that the waters which came down from upstream stood still, and rose in a heap very far away...and the people crossed over opposite Jericho.

Then the priests who bore the ark of the covenant of the LORD stood firm on dry ground in the midst of the Jordan; and all Israel crossed over on dry ground, until all the people had crossed completely over the Jordan. Joshua 3:7-17

Once again, God exercised authority over nature. Even though the river was flooded, as soon as the priests stepped in, the water stopped flowing. It was like God created an invisible dam to hold the water back so the Israelites could cross over on dry ground.

Absolutely no one is as powerful as God! If He had the power to make a dry path through the middle of the raging Jordan River, He certainly was strong enough to defeat the fierce and frightening Canaanites. The Israelites had no reason to fear.

On the other side of the river was the Canaanite city of Jericho. The people in Jericho had heard about all God had done for His people. They were afraid of the God of Israel.

Now Jericho was securely shut up because of the children of Israel; none went out, and none came in. And the LORD said to Joshua: "See! I have given Jericho into your hand, its king, and the mighty men of valor. You shall march around the city, all you men of war; you shall go all around the city once. This you shall do six days.

And seven priests shall bear seven trumpets of rams' horns before the ark. But the seventh day you shall march around the city seven times, and the priests shall blow the trumpets. It shall come to pass, when they make a long blast with the ram's horn, and when you hear the sound of the trumpet, that all the people shall shout with a great shout; then the wall of the city will fall down flat. And the people shall go up every man straight before him."

So they did six days. But…on the seventh day…they…marched around the city seven times in the same manner…And the seventh time it happened, when the priests blew the trumpets, that Joshua said to the people: "Shout, for the LORD has given you the city!

…And it happened when the people heard the sound of the trumpet, and…shouted with a great shout, that the wall fell down flat. Then the people went up into the city…And they utterly destroyed all that was in the city… Joshua 6:1-5, 14b-16, 20-21

Every day for six days the men of Israel marched around Jericho one time in this order: first the armed men, then the priests who carried the trumpets, then the priests who carried the Ark of the Testimony, and finally the rear guard. On the seventh day, they marched around the city seven times. Then the priests blew their trumpets and the people of Israel shouted. Suddenly, the enormous walls of Jericho "fell down flat"!

Because the Israelites trusted God and followed His instructions, God fought for them. It was almighty God who crumbled the huge walls of Jericho so that the Israelites could go in and take the city.

Over and over again God defeated the Canaanites, until finally the land belonged to Israel.

So Joshua took the whole land, according to all that the LORD had said to Moses; and Joshua gave it as an inheritance to Israel…Then the land rested from war. Joshua 11:23

As always, God kept His promise. He had promised to give the land of Canaan to Abraham's descendants, and that is just what He did!

Remember

The Canaanites were too strong for the Israelites. Only God had the power to destroy them.

In much the same way, you also have enemies that are too strong for you. Your enemies are Satan, your own sin, and death. You cannot conquer these enemies. Only God is able to conquer them for you.

God promised that if the Israelites would trust Him, He would fight for them. God wants you to trust Him too. If you will trust in Him, and not in yourself, He will fight for you. Only God has the power to rescue you from Satan, sin, and death.

Questions

1. Did God give the land of Canaan to the Israelites because of how good they were? *No, the Israelites were sinners like everyone else.*

2. Since God did not give Canaan to the Israelites because of their good behavior, why did He give the land to Israel? *God gave them the land because of the wickedness of the Canaanites and because He had promised Abraham He would give this land to his descendants.*

3. How did God show His love to Moses before Moses died? *Before Moses died, God let him go up on a mountain and see the land of Canaan from a distance.*

4. After Moses died, who did God choose to be the next leader of Israel? *God chose Joshua.*

5. Were the Israelites strong enough to defeat the Canaanites? *No, the Canaanites were huge compared to the Israelites. They lived in massive walled cities and were well armed.*

6. Who was the only One who could defeat the Canaanites and give their land to the people of Israel? *Only God had the power to defeat the Canaanites.*

7. What did God tell the Israelites to do at Jericho? *God told them to march around the city one time every day for six days. On the seventh day, they were to march around the city seven times and then blow their trumpets and shout.*

8. Because the Israelites believed God and followed His commands, what happened to the city of Jericho? *God made the walls fall down flat so the people could go in and take the city.*

9. Did God keep His promise to Abraham to give the land of Canaan to his descendants? *Yes, the land of Canaan finally belonged to the people of Israel.*

10. Who is the only One who can rescue you from your sin, Satan, and the death penalty? *Only God can rescue you from the death penalty, from sin, and from Satan.*

Biblical Worldviews

- God always keeps His promises.
- God is merciful and gracious.
- The only way to please God is to believe Him.
- We cannot save ourselves; only God can save us.
- God can do anything; nothing is too hard for Him.
- God is the owner of everything; He is in charge of the world; He is the highest authority.
- The penalty for sin is death.

Activity: Jericho Skit

Supplies:

- Student volunteers - everyone

Instructions:

- Students act out the scene from this lesson. These are the key parts: Joshua, one or more priests (with pretend trumpets), Israelites.

- Following the biblical account, Joshua pretends to lead everyone around an imaginary Jericho once a day for six days.

- On the seventh day on the seventh time around, Joshua shouts, "Shout, for the Lord has given you the city!"

- Students imagine the walls of Jericho tumbling down and run into the city.

- Discuss: God can do anything. God fought for the Israelites because they trusted in Him. Only He had the power to defeat the city of Jericho. Only God can save us; God saves those who trust in Him and not in themselves.

Extra Bible References

Genesis 12:1-3, 15:18-20; Exodus 23:23-24, 32:13; Leviticus 18:3, 24-28;
Numbers 33:51-56; Deuteronomy 9:1-2, 31:1-8; Joshua 1:1-2, 11:23, 21:45, 23:9-16;
Joshua 24:21; Judges 1:1, 19, 21, 27-33; 2:1-6, 21-23; Psalm 95:1-5, 105:8, 135:5-12;
Jeremiah 25:5, 27:5; Acts 10:34, 13:19; 1 Timothy 2:4

39
False Gods
Judges of Israel – Deborah

Memory Verse

Great is our Lord, and mighty in power; His understanding is infinite. Psalm 147:5

Lesson

At Mount Sinai the Israelites had agreed that in order to get God's special treatment, they would have to keep all His commands. God had promised that as long as they followed Him and obeyed His rules, He would take good care of them and make them into a very great nation. On the other hand, if they turned away from Him and stopped doing what He said, He would let their enemies conquer them and they would become scattered across the earth.

Moses had told them that…

...if you diligently obey the voice of the LORD your God, to observe carefully all His commandments…the LORD your God will set you high above all nations of the earth. And all these blessings shall come upon you…

But…if you do not obey the voice of the LORD your God…all these curses will come upon you…the LORD will scatter you among all peoples, from one end of the earth to the other…there the LORD will give you a trembling heart, failing eyes, and anguish of soul. Deuteronomy 28: 1-2, 15, 64-65

Before Joshua died, he reminded the Israelites of all God had done for them. God had saved them from slavery in Egypt and from Pharaoh's mighty army. He had taken them across the Red Sea on dry land and brought them safely through the terrible wilderness. He had parted the waters of the flooded Jordan River and conquered the mighty Canaanite nations for them. God had kept all His promises, and now they were living peacefully in their own land.

Now it came to pass, a long time after the LORD had given rest to Israel from all their enemies round about, that Joshua was old, advanced in age. And Joshua called for all Israel…and said to them:

"I am old, advanced in age. You have seen all that the LORD your God
has done to all these nations because of you, for the LORD your God is
He who has fought for you. Joshua 23:1-3

"...not one thing has failed of all the good things which the LORD your
God spoke concerning you. All have come to pass for you; not one word
of them has failed." Joshua 23:14

But Joshua warned the Israelites that if they broke their agreement with the true and living
God, He would destroy them, even after all He had done for them.

If you forsake the LORD and serve foreign gods, then He will
turn and do you harm and consume you, after He has done you good.
Joshua 24:20

As long as Joshua lived, the Israelites followed God.

So the people served the LORD all the days of Joshua...
Judges 2:7a

But after Joshua died, the people broke their agreement with God. Instead of destroying the
rest of the Canaanites who were left in the land, they let them live.

They did not destroy the peoples, concerning whom the LORD had
commanded them, but they mingled with the Gentiles and learned
their works; they served their idols, which became a snare to them.
Psalms 106:34-36

Before long, the Israelites began to follow the evil ways of the godless people around them.

Then the children of Israel...forsook the LORD God of their
fathers, who had brought them out of the land of Egypt; and they
followed other gods from among the gods of the people who were all
around them, and they bowed down to them; and they provoked the
LORD to anger. Judges 2:11-12

The Israelites should not have allowed any of the Canaanite people to stay in the land. When
the Israelites broke their agreement with God and followed after false gods, God did just what
He said He would do: He allowed the Canaanites to conquer them and treat them cruelly.

And the anger of the LORD was hot against Israel. So He delivered them into the hands of plunderers who despoiled them; and He sold them into the hands of their enemies all around, so that they could no longer stand before their enemies. Wherever they went out, the hand of the LORD was against them for calamity, as the LORD had said, and as the LORD had sworn to them. And they were greatly distressed. Judges 2:14-15

In their suffering, the Israelites called out to God to save them. And God lovingly did. But then the Israelites turned away from God again. Once more God allowed the nations, whose gods the Israelites were worshiping, to defeat them. Again, they called out to God to save them, and once more God rescued them.

This happened over and over again. Every time the Israelites called out to God for help, God had mercy on them and sent a special rescuer, called a judge, to save them from their suffering. As long as the judge ruled over Israel, the people followed the true and living God, but as soon as the judge died, the Israelites went back to worshiping false gods.

And...the LORD raised up judges for them...and delivered them out of the hand of their enemies all the days of the judge; for the LORD was moved to pity by their groaning because of those who oppressed them and harassed them. And it came to pass, when the judge was dead, that they reverted and behaved more corruptly...by following other gods, to serve them and bow down to them. Judges 2:18-19a

One of the judges who helped save the Israelites was Deborah. Deborah helped free the Israelites from a powerful Canaanite king named Jabin.

...the children of Israel again did evil in the sight of the LORD. So the LORD sold them into the hand of Jabin king of Canaan...The commander of his army was Sisera...And the children of Israel cried out to the LORD; for Jabin had nine hundred chariots of iron, and for twenty years he had harshly oppressed the children of Israel.

Now Deborah, a prophetess, the wife of Lapidoth, was judging Israel at that time...Then she sent and called for Barak...and said to him, "Has not the LORD God of Israel commanded, 'Go and deploy troops at

269

Mount Tabor; take with you ten thousand men...and against you I will deploy Sisera, the commander of Jabin's army...and I will deliver him into your hand'?"

And Barak said to her, "If you will go with me, then I will go; but if you will not go with me, I will not go!"

...Then Deborah arose and went with Barak...

So Sisera gathered together all his chariots, nine hundred chariots of iron, and all the people who were with him...

Then Deborah said to Barak, "Up! For this is the day in which the LORD has delivered Sisera into your hand. Has not the LORD gone out before you?" So Barak went down from Mount Tabor with ten thousand men following him.

And the LORD routed Sisera and all his chariots and all his army with the edge of the sword before Barak; ...and all the army of Sisera fell by the edge of the sword; not a man was left.

So on that day God subdued Jabin king of Canaan in the presence of the children of Israel. Judges 4:1-16, 23

Under Deborah's leadership, the Israelites defeated Jabin. For forty years there was peace in the land. But then the Israelites began once more to worship false gods!

Remember

When the Israelites broke their agreement with God, they deserved to suffer; they deserved to be destroyed. But every time they called out to God, He mercifully sent a judge to deliver them.

Just like the Israelites, you are guilty of breaking God's commands

271

📖 For all have sinned and fall short of the glory of God…
Romans 3:23

Because of your sin, you deserve to suffer.

📖 The soul who sins shall die. Ezekiel 18:20

But just like God sent judges to deliver the Israelites from their enemies, He promised to send the Savior to deliver you from Satan, sin, and death. Even though you deserve to die for your sin, God is merciful and loving. He rescues all who trust in Him.

📖 …that whoever believes in Him should not perish but have everlasting life. John 3:16b

Questions

1. Did God always take care of the Israelites? *Yes, God always took care of them.*

2. What did God warn the Israelites would happen if they broke their agreement with Him? *God said they would be conquered by their enemies and scattered across the earth.*

3. What did the people do after Joshua died? *They began to follow the evil ways of the Canaanites who remained in the land.*

4. Does God always do what He says He will do? *Yes, God always keeps His word. If the Israelites kept their agreement with God, He would make them great; but if they broke their agreement, they would be conquered by their enemies.*

5. Whenever the Israelites called out to God to save them, what did He do? *He had mercy on them and sent a judge to rescue them from their enemies.*

6. What happened every time the judge died? *The people stopped following the one true God and went back to worshiping false gods again.*

7. Who was the woman God used to deliver the Israelites from the Canaanite king, Jabin? *God used Deborah to rescue the Israelites from Jabin.*

8. What does the word mercy mean? *It means you do not get the punishment you should.*

9. What do you deserve for breaking God's rules? *You deserve to be separated from God forever in the terrible place of suffering.*

10. Who did God promise to send to rescue you from the death penalty you deserve? *God promised to send the Savior to rescue you.*

Biblical Worldviews

- God is a personal being; He communicates with people.
- God tells the truth; He means what He says.
- The God of the Bible is the only true and living God; all other gods are false.
- All people are sinners.
- The penalty for sin is death.
- God is merciful and gracious.
- God promised to send the Savior to save us from death.

Activity: Bible Hangman

Supplies:

- Chalkboard or dry erase board
- Chalk or dry erase markers

Instructions:

- Draw a large hangman tree on the board
- Draw lines and spaces under the tree to correspond to the letters and spaces in the key phrase
- **Key phrase**: God gave the Israelites over to their enemies when they followed false gods, but He showed mercy when they cried out to him.
- **Key phrase for younger students**: God showed mercy on the Israelites.
- Ask the lesson review questions, one at a time. Call on one student or one team to answer each question.
- If answer is correct, the student or team gets to pick a letter, i.e., the letter b.
- If the letter picked is in the key phrase, the teacher fills it in on the board each time it occurs.
- If the letter picked is not in the key phrase, the teacher draws one part of a stick figure on the hangman tree, i.e., a head, an arm, a stick body, etc.
- When a student (or team) thinks he knows the key phrase, he may try to solve the puzzle on his turn. The game is over when a student or team solves the puzzle or the teacher draws all the parts of the stick man, whichever comes first.

Extra Bible References

Numbers 23:19; Deuteronomy 4:25-26; 7:2, 16; 8:19; Joshua 21:43-45, 24:19-20; Judges 1:21, 27; 2:7-19; 5:1-31; Jeremiah 10:1-16, 32:21-23; Psalms 106, 135:15-18; Acts 13:20; Titus 1:2; Hebrews 6:18

273

40
A Trumpet and a Pitcher
Judges of Israel – Gideon

Memory Verse

Oh, give thanks to the LORD, for He is good! For His mercy endures forever. Psalm 118:29

Lesson

Forty years after they defeated Jabin, the Israelites turned away from God again. This time God let them be conquered by the Midianite people.

Then the children of Israel did evil in the sight of the LORD. So the LORD delivered them into the hand of Midian for seven years...Because of the Midianites, the children of Israel made for themselves the dens, the caves, and the strongholds which are in the mountains.

So it was, whenever Israel had sown, Midianites would come up; also Amalekites and the people of the East would come up against them. Then they would encamp against them and destroy the produce of the earth as far as Gaza, and leave no sustenance for Israel, neither sheep nor ox nor donkey.

For they would come up with their livestock and their tents, coming in as numerous as locusts; both they and their camels were without number; and they would enter the land to destroy it. So Israel was greatly impoverished because of the Midianites, and the children of Israel cried out to the LORD. Judges 6:1-6

The Midianites were cruel and hateful. They came in hordes and destroyed all the Israelites' food and all their animals. In fear, the Israelites hid in caves in the mountains. Finally when there was nothing left to eat, the Israelites cried out to God to save them.

This time God used a man by the name of Gideon to help deliver Israel from the Midianites. Gideon was also afraid of the Midianites, but God wanted Gideon to trust Him.

Now the Angel of the LORD came...while...Gideon threshed wheat in the winepress, in order to hide it from the Midianites...Then the LORD...said, "...you shall save Israel from the hand of the Midianites..."

So he said to Him, "O my Lord, how can I save Israel?..."

And the LORD said to him, "Surely I will be with you, and you shall defeat the Midianites..." Judges 6:11, 14-16

Gideon gathered together an army of thirty-two thousand Israelites to fight against the Midianites.

And the LORD said to Gideon, "The people who are with you are too many...lest Israel claim glory...saying, 'My own hand has saved me.' Now therefore, proclaim in the hearing of the people, saying, 'Whoever is fearful and afraid, let him turn and depart at once from Mount Gilead.'"

And twenty-two thousand of the people returned, and ten thousand remained. Judges 7:1-3

God did not want the Israelites to trust in their own strength; He wanted them to trust in Him. That is why God told Gideon to get rid of all the soldiers who were afraid. Twenty-two thousand men went home. This left Gideon with only ten thousand soldiers.

But God said there were still too many. He told Gideon to take the ten thousand men who were left down to the water to get a drink.

But the LORD said to Gideon, "The people are still too many; bring them down to the water...So he brought the people down to the water. And the LORD said to Gideon, "Everyone who laps from the water with his tongue, as a dog laps, you shall set apart by himself; likewise everyone who gets down on his knees to drink."

And the number of those who lapped, putting their hand to their mouth, was three hundred men; but all the rest of the people got down on their knees to drink water. Then the LORD said to Gideon, "By the three hundred men who lapped I will save you, and deliver the

Midianites into your hand. Let all the other people go, every man to his place." Judges 7:4-7

God told Gideon to send home everyone who got down on his knees to drink. Only those who "lapped, putting their hand to their mouth" were allowed to stay. This made Gideon's army very, very small. He had only three hundred men to fight against the massive Midianite army that spread across the land like sand on the seashore.

But God encouraged Gideon. He told him to go down to the Midianite camp and listen to what was being said.

It happened on the same night that the LORD said to him, "Arise, go down against the camp, for I have delivered it into your hand. But if you are afraid to go down, go down to the camp with Purah your servant, and you shall hear what they say; and afterward your hands shall be strengthened to go down against the camp." Then he went down with Purah his servant to the outpost of the armed men who were in the camp. Now the Midianites and Amalekites, all the people of the East, were lying in the valley as numerous as locusts; and their camels were without number, as the sand by the seashore in multitude.

And when Gideon had come, there was a man telling a dream to his companion. He said, "I have had a dream: To my surprise, a loaf of barley bread tumbled into the camp of Midian; it came to a tent and struck it so that it fell and overturned, and the tent collapsed."

Then his companion answered and said, "This is nothing else but the sword of Gideon the son of Joash, a man of Israel! Into his hand God has delivered Midian and the whole camp." Judges 7:9-14

Gideon heard one of the Midianite soldiers tell his dream to a friend. The soldier said that in his dream a loaf of bread rolled into the camp and knocked down a tent. His friend knew immediately what the dream meant. It meant that just like the little loaf of bread knocked down a big tent, the tiny Israelite army was going to overthrow the huge Midianite army.

When Gideon heard this he was no longer fearful. Now he was certain the Israelites would win. Gideon returned to the Israelite camp to prepare for battle.

Then he divided the three hundred men into three companies, and he put a trumpet into every man's hand, with empty pitchers, and torches inside the pitchers. And he said to them, "Look at me and do likewise; watch, and when I come to the edge of the camp you shall do as I do: When I blow the trumpet, I and all who are with me, then you also blow the trumpets on every side of the whole camp, and say, 'The sword of the LORD and of Gideon!'"

So Gideon and the hundred men who were with him came to the outpost of the camp at the beginning of the middle watch, just as they had posted the watch; and they blew the trumpets and broke the pitchers that were in their hands. Then the three companies blew the trumpets and broke the pitchers—they held the torches in their left hands and the trumpets in their right hands for blowing—and they cried, "The sword of the LORD and of Gideon!"

And every man stood in his place all around the camp; and the whole army ran and cried out and fled. When the three hundred blew the trumpets, the LORD set every man's sword against his companion throughout the whole camp; and the army fled... Judges 7:16-22a

Gideon divided his men into three groups and positioned them around the Midianite camp. The soldiers carried trumpets, clay pitchers, and torches. In the middle of the night, at Gideon's command, every Israelite soldier blew his trumpet and smashed the pitcher he was holding.

The Midianites jumped out of their sleep. The sound of the trumpets and the explosions of light from the torches on every side made them terrified. They thought they were surrounded by a great army! In their confusion, the Midianite soldiers panicked and began killing each other. Many of the soldiers ran off in fear. Once again, God won a mighty battle for Israel.

After the Midianites were defeated, Israel was at peace again for another forty years, but...

...as soon as Gideon was dead...the children of Israel...made Baal-Berith their god. Thus the children of Israel did not remember the LORD their God, who had delivered them from the hands of all their enemies on every side; Judges 8:28

Remember

God did not want the Israelites to trust in their own strength to save them; He wanted them to trust in Him. God was the only One who could save the Israelites from the enormous Midianite army.

God does not want you to trust in yourself either. Just like the Israelites could not save themselves from the Midianites, you cannot save yourself from Satan, sin, and death. You cannot please God or make yourself acceptable to Him.

God is the only One who can save you. Trust in Him!

Thus says the LORD: "Cursed is the man who trusts in man...whose heart departs from the LORD. Blessed is the man who trusts in the LORD, and whose hope is the LORD. Jeremiah 17:5, 7

Questions

1. What were the Midianites doing to the Israelites to make them suffer? *They were destroying all their food and animals. The fearful Israelites were forced to hide in caves in the mountains.*

2. How many Midianite people were there? *There were more than could be counted; they were like sand on the seashore.*

3. Were the Israelites powerful enough to defeat the Midianites? *No, they were not.*

4. Even though the Israelites kept turning away from God, did God have mercy on them whenever they cried out to Him because of their suffering? *Yes, He did. God always sent a judge to deliver them from their enemies. This time He chose Gideon to help deliver the Israelites from the Midianites.*

5. At first, how many Israelite soldiers did Gideon gather to help him fight the Midianites? *He gathered thirty-two thousand.*

6. What did God say to Gideon about his large army? *He said there were too many men.*

7. Why did twenty-two thousand of Gideon's men leave? *They left because they were afraid. God had told Gideon to tell everyone who was afraid to go home.*

8. What did God tell Gideon to do next to make even more soldiers leave? *He told Gideon to take the soldiers down to the water to drink. Only those who lapped water like a dog were allowed to stay.*

9. Why did God want Gideon's army to be so small? *God did not want the Israelites to trust in their own strength to save them. God wanted the Israelites to trust in Him to fight for them.*

10. Who is the only One who can rescue you from Satan, sin, and death? *Only God can save you. No matter how good you try to be, you cannot make yourself acceptable to God. You cannot free yourself from Satan's control. You cannot pay for your sin. Only God can save you from the death penalty and make you acceptable to Him.*

Biblical Worldviews

- God is a personal being; He communicates with people.
- All people are sinners.
- God is merciful; God is a God of love.
- We cannot save ourselves. Only God can save us.
- To please God we must trust in Him alone.
- God is the greatest; He can do anything.

Activity: The Story of Gideon Puppet Show or Skit

Supplies:

- Puppets and/or student volunteers

Instructions:

- Use the attached script to perform a puppet show or skit.

The Story of Gideon (by Casey Hughes)

Mark: Hey Lucy, watcha doing?

(Lucy is reading her Bible and appears to be very interested in it.)

Mark: Lucy!

Lucy: Oh, I'm sorry Mark! I was just reading in my Bible about how God used Gideon to command an army and fight against the Midianites. It is even more exciting than any of my adventure books.

Mark: Oh wow! That sounds exciting. Will you tell me about it?

Lucy: Sure Mark, I'd love to.

Mark: Oh good! Please start right away.

Lucy: Well, you know all about the Israelites, don't you?

Mark: Oh yes!

Lucy: Well, Israel started to forget about God. They started to worship idols.

<u>Mark</u>: Oh no!

<u>Lucy</u>: So God allowed another nation called the Midianites to come into Israel. The Midianites stole the Israelites' crops and animals; the Israelites were so scared of them they hid in the hills.

<u>Mark</u>: Oh wow, what happened then?

<u>Lucy</u>: Well, the Israelites finally remembered God and asked Him to deliver them. At this time, there lived a man named Gideon. One day an angel visited Gideon and told him that the Lord was with him. When Gideon asked the angel why all this bad stuff was happening to his country, the angel told him that God was going to use him to save Israel. Gideon had doubts, but by the time the angel left, he knew he had seen an angel of the Lord!

<u>Mark</u>: Wow, that's neat!

<u>Lucy</u>: Gideon sent messengers to call all of Israel's soldiers together, but he still doubted. One evening Gideon put out a fleece (that is the wool coat of a sheep). He wanted to make sure God really was going to be with him. He wanted God to prove He was going to help him by causing the fleece to get wet with dew, but the ground around it to stay dry. In the morning, guess what happened?

<u>Mark</u>: I bet God made the fleece wet and left the ground dry.

<u>Lucy</u>: You guessed right! He did. The next morning Gideon squeezed a whole bowlful of water out of the fleece. But Gideon still had doubts, so he asked God for another sign. This time he asked that the fleece be dry and the ground wet. In the morning, that's just what happened. Finally, Gideon believed God would help him fight the Midianites.

<u>Mark</u>: Wow! What happened? Did the Israelites win?

<u>Lucy</u>: Well, Gideon had 32,000 soldiers in his army.

<u>Mark</u>: Really?

<u>Lucy</u>: Yes… and guess what? God told Gideon he had too many. God didn't want the Israelites to think they won the battle by themselves; He wanted them to know His power. So God said to let all the men who were scared leave the camp.

<u>Mark</u>: Really? That doesn't make sense, but I'm sure God knew what he was doing.

Lucy: Yes, Mark. You're right – God did know what He was doing. Twenty-two thousand soldiers left camp. But still God thought Gideon's army was too big. He said to take the men down to the water to get a drink. According to God's instructions, only the men who brought water up to their mouths with their hands were to stay with Gideon. The rest of the men who got down on their knees to drink were to go home. Now Gideon's army was down to 300 men.

Mark: That sounds unbelievable.

Lucy: I know, but it's true. I can't wait to tell you what happened next!

Mark: Oh please, please tell me!

Lucy: OK… that night God told Gideon to go fight the Midianites. Gideon divided his small army into 3 groups. Each man had a trumpet, a pitcher, and a burning torch. They crept into the camp and each group went to a different side. At midnight, Gideon gave a command and the soldiers blew their trumpets and shouted, "The sword of the Lord and of Gideon!" Then the soldiers broke their pitchers. I'm sure it made a lot of noise. Imagine the loud shattering and the bursts of light! The Midianites woke up and thought a huge army had attacked them.

Mark: Oh this is getting exciting! You were right, this story is better than an adventure novel.

Lucy: It sure is! The Midianites were so afraid and confused they began killing each other. Some of them ran for their lives. The Midianites lost a lot of men and the Israelites won the battle.

Mark: That is an amazing story. Gideon sure was a good leader.

Lucy: This story is pretty amazing, but we should always remember that the Israelites didn't win the battle because of Gideon; God was the one who made them win.

Mark: You're right, Lucy. Thank you so much for telling me that story. I didn't know the Bible could be so exciting and that God is so powerful. I am going to start reading the Bible myself!

41
Tricked

Judges of Israel – Samson

Memory Verse

Oh, give thanks to the LORD, for He is good! For His mercy endures forever.
Psalm 118:29

Lesson

Sometime after God saved the Israelites from the Midianites, the Philistines began to torment them. Once more God raised up a judge to save Israel from its enemies.

One day, God appeared to an Israelite man named Manoah and his wife. He told them they would have a son who would deliver Israel from the Philistines.

Again the children of Israel did evil in the sight of the LORD, and the LORD delivered them into the hand of the Philistines for forty years.

Now there was a certain man...whose name was Manoah; and his wife was barren and had no children. And the Angel of the LORD appeared to the woman and said to her, "...you shall conceive and bear a son. And no razor shall come upon his head, for the child shall be a Nazirite to God from the womb; and he shall begin to deliver Israel out of the hand of the Philistines." Judges 13:1-5

Although Manoah's wife had never been able to have children, God was going to give her a baby. God could do that because He is the One who gives life.

Manoah and his wife named their baby Samson. God planned for Samson to be a Nazirite. A Nazirite was someone who was dedicated to God. A Nazirite was never allowed to have a haircut; he had to let his hair grow long.

God gave Samson incredible strength, so that by himself Samson was able to fight the Philistines. One time Samson burned down the Philistines' fields of grain by setting on fire the tails of three hundred foxes.

...Samson...caught three hundred foxes; and he took torches, turned the foxes tail to tail, and put a torch between each pair of tails. When he had set the torches on fire, he let the foxes go into the standing grain of the Philistines, and burned up...the...grain, as well as the vineyards and olive groves. Judges 15:4-5

Another time Samson killed one thousand men with the jawbone of a donkey.

He found a fresh jawbone of a donkey...and killed a thousand men with it. Judges 15:15

But even though Samson was set apart for God, he was still a sinner. Some of his actions displeased God, like the time he fell in love with a Philistine woman. The woman tricked Samson and caused him to lose his strength.

...it happened that he loved a woman...whose name was Delilah. And the lords of the Philistines came up to her and said to her, "Entice him, and find out where his great strength lies, and by what means we may overpower him, that we may bind him...and every one of us will give you eleven hundred pieces of silver." Judges 16:4-5

The rulers (lords) of the Philistines promised to pay Delilah a lot of money if she could discover what made Samson so strong.

So Delilah said to Samson, "Please tell me where your great strength lies..."

And Samson said to her, "If they bind me with seven fresh bowstrings, not yet dried, then I shall become weak, and be like any other man." Judges 16:6-7

Samson told her that if he were tied with seven brand-new bowstrings, he would become as weak as any other man.

So the lords of the Philistines brought up to her seven fresh bowstrings, not yet dried, and she bound him with them. Now men were lying in wait, staying with her in the room. And she said to him, "The Philistines are upon you, Samson!" But he broke the bowstrings as a strand of yarn breaks when it touches fire. So the secret of his strength was not known. Judges 16:8-9

While Samson slept, Delilah tied him with the bowstrings. Then she yelled that the Philistines were coming, but he broke the strong bowstrings easily.

Then Delilah said to Samson, "Look, you...told me lies. Now, please tell me what you may be bound with."

So he said to her, "If they bind me securely with new ropes that have never been used, then I shall become weak, and be like any other man."

Therefore Delilah took new ropes and bound him with them, and said to him, "The Philistines are upon you, Samson!" And men were lying in wait, staying in the room.

But he broke them off his arms like a thread. Judges 16:10-12

Delilah did not give up. This time she tied Samson up with strong ropes, but he broke the ropes as though they were threads.

Delilah said to Samson, "Until now you have...told me lies. Tell me what you may be bound with."

And he said to her, "If you weave the seven locks of my head into the web of the loom"—

So she wove it tightly with the batten of the loom, and said to him, "The Philistines are upon you, Samson!" But he awoke from his sleep, and pulled out the batten and the web from the loom. Judges 16:13-14

Samson told Delilah that if she wove his hair into a loom - the way thread is woven into a loom to make cloth - he would not be able to free himself. So Delilah wove his hair into a loom, but when she yelled that the Philistines were coming, Samson effortlessly pulled his hair out of the loom.

Delilah became upset. She accused Samson of not loving her.

Then she said to him, "How can you say, 'I love you,' when your heart is not with me? You have mocked me these three times, and have not told me where your great strength lies."

And it came to pass, when she pestered him daily with her words...that he told her..., "No razor has ever come upon my head, for I have been a Nazirite...If I am shaven, then my strength will leave me, and I shall become weak, and be like any other man."

When Delilah saw that he had told her all his heart, she sent and called for the lords of the Philistines, saying, "Come up once more, for he has told me all his heart."

So the lords of the Philistines came up to her and brought the money in their hand. Then she lulled him to sleep on her knees, and called for a man and had him shave off the seven locks of his head...and his strength left him.

And she said, "The Philistines are upon you, Samson!" So he awoke from his sleep...But he did not know that the LORD had departed from him.

Then the Philistines took him and put out his eyes, and brought him down to Gaza. They bound him with bronze fetters, and he became a grinder in the prison. However, the hair of his head began to grow again after it had been shaven. Judges 16:15-22

Finally, Samson gave away his secret and the Philistines overpowered him. They gouged out his eyes, chained him up, and put him in prison where he was forced to work like an animal. But as Samson's hair began to grow, his strength slowly returned.

One day a great crowd of Philistines gathered at the temple of their false god.

Now...the Philistines gathered together to offer a great sacrifice to Dagon their god...And they said: "Our god has delivered into our hands Samson our enemy!" So they called for Samson from the prison...And they stationed him between the pillars.

Then Samson said to the lad who held him by the hand, "Let me feel the pillars which support the temple, so that I can lean on them." Now the temple was full of men and women...about three thousand men and women on the roof watching...

Then Samson called to the LORD, saying, "O Lord GOD...Strengthen me, I pray, just this once..."

And Samson took hold of the two middle pillars which supported the temple, and he braced himself against them, one on his right and the other on his left. Then Samson said, "Let me die with the Philistines!" And he pushed with all his might, and the temple fell on the lords and all the people who were in it.

So the dead that he killed at his death were more than he had killed in his life. Judges 16:15-30

One last time God gave Samson strength so that he was able to topple the temple of the Philistines' false god, Dagon. Samson killed more Philistines in his death than he did in his entire life.

For twenty years, God had used Samson to save Israel from the Philistines.

And he judged Israel twenty years in the days of the Philistines. Judges 15:2

Remember

God does whatever He wants; nothing is too hard for Him. Even though Manoah and his wife had never been able to have a baby, God gave them a baby. When Samson grew to be a man, God gave him super-human strength to defeat Israel's enemies.

The God of the Bible is the only true, living, and powerful God. The Bible says that God is...

...the Most High over all the earth. Psalm 83:18b

Questions

1. How could God give Manoah's wife a baby when she had never been able to have children before? *God is the One who gives life. He is all-powerful. Even though Manoah's wife had never been able to have a baby, God could easily give her a child.*

2. What was God's plan for this baby named Samson? *God planned for the baby to help deliver Israel from the Philistines.*

3. What was a Nazirite? *A Nazirite was someone who was set apart for God's use.*

4. As a Nazirite, what was Samson not allowed to do? *God said Samson was never to have his hair cut.*

5. Who gave Samson his incredible strength? *God did.*

6. How did Samson use his God-given strength to defeat the Philistines? *One time Samson burned up the Philistines' fields by setting on fire torches tied to foxes' tails. Another time he killed a thousand men all by himself with the jawbone of a donkey.*

7. Was Samson a sinner? *Yes, even though Samson was dedicated to God, he was a sinner.*

8. What did Samson do that caused him to get caught by the Philistines? *He fell in love with a Philistine woman and let her trick him into telling her the secret of his strength.*

9. How did Samson kill more Philistines in his death than he did during his life? *When a great crowd of Philistines was gathered at the temple of their false god, Samson pushed down the main pillars of the temple so that it collapsed, killing all the Philistines who were in the temple and on the roof.*

10. Who is the only true, living, and powerful God? *The God of the Bible is the only true and powerful God. All other gods are false and powerless.*

Biblical Worldviews

- God is the One who gives life.
- God is all-powerful; nothing is too hard for Him.
- God is "the Most High over all the earth."
- God is the only true God; all other gods are false and powerless.
- All people are sinners.

Activity: Samson Skit

Supplies:

- Three puppets or student volunteers
- A crowd
- Skit script

Instructions:

- Students either act out the skit themselves or act it out using the puppets.

Samson and Delilah Skit (by Nancy Hughes)

<u>Narrator</u>: Again the Israelites did evil in the eyes of the Lord, so the Lord delivered them into the hand of the Philistines for 40 years. One day, an angel came to a lady. The angel said, "You are going to have a son." The angel told the lady her son should never get his hair cut as a sign that he belonged to God.

Years later…

Once Samson caught 300 foxes and tied them together by their tails. He set their tails on fire and let them loose to burn the Philistines' fields. The Philistines were very angry. But even though Samson knew the Philistines hated him, he fell in love with a Philistine woman whose name was Delilah.

Some of the Philistine leaders heard that Samson was in love with Delilah, so they asked Delilah to get Samson to tell her why he was so strong. If she did this, each Philistine leader agreed to give Delilah 1,100 pieces of silver.

Delilah must have thought of the many things she could buy with that money. And, she loved her own people more than she loved Samson. So she agreed to cooperate with the Philistines and find out Samson's secret.

The next time Samson came to visit her, Delilah asked Samson a question.

<u>Delilah</u>: Samson, oh Samson, tell me the secret of your great strength.

<u>Samson</u>: If I were tied with seven brand-new bowstrings, my strength would be the same as any other man.

(Samson falls asleep.) (Delilah goes over to crowd.)

<u>Delilah</u>: Hey everyone. I know Samson's secret. If you tie seven new bow-strings around him, his strength will be the same as that of any other man! Does anyone have any bow string?

(Someone in the crowd holds up a thin rope that looks like a bow string.)

<u>Delilah</u>: Great, give it to me.

(Delilah goes back to Samson and ties him up with the rope.)

<u>Delilah</u>: Samson, oh Samson, wake up! The Philistines are after you!

(Samson wakes up and breaks the cords.)

Delilah: Samson, I can't believe you. You were just making fun of me. That wasn't the secret of your strength. Now tell me the truth.

Narrator: At this point, Samson should have realized he could not trust Delilah, but he had not yet learned his lesson.

Delilah: Samson, oh Samson, tell me the secret of your strength.

Samson: If you were to tie me with strong ropes, I would be the same as any man.

(Samson falls asleep.) (Delilah goes over to crowd.)

Delilah: Hey you guys, I know Samson's secret this time. The bow string wasn't strong enough. If you tie him up with stronger ropes, his strength will be the same as any man! Does anyone have some strong rope?

(Someone hands her a thicker rope.)

Delilah: Great, give it to me!

(Delilah goes back to Samson and ties him up with the rope.)

Delilah: Samson, oh Samson, wake up! The Philistines are after you!

(Samson wakes up and breaks the strong rope.) (Delilah gasps and leaves.)

Narrator: You would think Samson would have been wise by now, but see what happened the next time he visited her.

(Delilah enters first. Samson knocks at her door. They sit down together.)

Delilah: Samson, oh Samson, tell me the secret of your great strength.

Samson: If you were to weave the braids of my head into the loom and tighten it, I could not free myself and my strength would be the same as any other man.

Delilah: Really?

Samson: Really.

(Samson falls asleep.) (Delilah goes over to crowd.)

Delilah: Okay... I'm sure this is it. Now I know Samson's secret. If his hair is woven into the loom, then he cannot free himself and his strength will be the same as any man! Does anyone have a loom?

(Someone pretends to hand Delilah a loom.)

Yes! I need it!

(Delilah goes back to Samson and weaves his hair into the loom.)

Delilah: Samson, oh Samson, wake up! The Philistines are after you!

(Samson wakes up and easily loosens his hair.)

Narrator: Delilah wondered if she would ever get the money the rulers had offered. The more she thought about it the unhappier she became. Day after day, she pleaded with Samson to tell her the secret of his strength.

Delilah: (Very dramatic) How can you say you love me when you won't even tell me your secret?

Narrator: Samson became so tired of Delilah's coaxing and pleading you won't believe what he said.

Delilah: Samson, oh Samson, tell me the secret of your great strength.

Samson: Okay, Delilah. You want to know the secret of my strength? (Sighs deeply) Because I am a Nazarite, my hair has never been cut. (Silence) If my hair was cut, the strength of the Lord would leave me and my strength would be the same as any other man.

(Samson falls asleep.)

Narrator: This time Delilah knew that Samson spoke the truth.

(Delilah goes over to crowd.)

Delilah: Wow, I know he spoke the truth this time. Anyone have any scissors? Come help me now. Quick, before he wakes up.

(Delilah and person from crowd go back to Samson, and person from crowd cuts his hair.)

Delilah: Samson, oh Samson, wake up... the Philistines are after you!

(Samson wakes up and realizes his strength is gone. The guy and some others from the crowd rush towards him and capture him.)

Narrator: The Philistines were so glad they had finally captured Samson. They tied him and took him to Gaza. In prison, they put out his eyes and made him grind grain. Poor Samson! He should never have told the secret of his strength to Delilah, because she wasn't his friend.

Day after day he worked in prison, but while he was working, his hair was also growing back. Around this time, the Philistines gave a great feast in honor of their false god, Dagon. They wanted to thank Dagon for giving them power over Samson. All the Philistines rejoiced and celebrated. During the feast, the Philistines said, "Bring Samson so he can perform for us."

A boy brought Samson in. When the people saw him blinded and in chains, they made fun of him. Samson knew the temple was crowded with people. Samson told the boy to lead him to where he could lean against the pillars of the building.

As the people were making fun of him, Samson prayed, "Oh Lord God, remember me and strengthen me this once, for the Philistines have put out my eyes."

Samson stood between the pillars of the temple and pushed against them with all his might so that the whole building fell down and everyone was killed.

Extra Bible References

Numbers 6:1-21; Psalm 135:15; Jeremiah 10:3-16

42
A Giant
The Last Judge, the First King, and David and Goliath

Memory Verse

But I have trusted in Your mercy; my heart shall rejoice in Your salvation. Psalm 13:5

Lesson

Israel's last judge was Samuel.

Samuel's parents were Hannah and Elkanah. Just like Samson's mom, Samuel's mom was unable to have children. But one day she promised God that if He would give her a son, she would give him back to Him. God answered Hannah's prayer and gave her a baby boy. Hannah named her baby Samuel.

Hannah kept her promise. When Samuel was a young boy, she took him to the temple to stay with Eli, the priest.

Every year when Hannah and Elkanah went to the temple to worship God, Hannah brought little Samuel a new robe.

Moreover his mother used to make him a little robe, and bring it to him year by year when she came up with her husband to offer the yearly sacrifice. 1 Samuel 2:19

As Samuel grew up, he helped Eli in the temple. Later, he became a judge of Israel. For many years Samuel led Israel, but when Samuel got old the Israelites asked for a king to rule over them.

Now it came to pass when Samuel was old that... all the elders of Israel gathered together and came to Samuel...and said to him, "Look, you are old...Now make us a king to judge us like all the nations."

But the thing displeased Samuel...So Samuel prayed to the LORD...And the LORD said to Samuel, "Heed the voice of the people...for they have not rejected you, but they have rejected Me, that I should not reign over them." I Samuel 8:1, 4-7

Even though God used the judges to lead Israel and deliver them from their enemies, God was Israel's true leader. God was the One who rescued the Israelites from Egypt and conquered their enemies for them. But the Israelites did not want God to be their king anymore; they wanted a human king like the nations around them.

So God gave the Israelites their request.

Then Samuel...said to the children of Israel, "Thus says the LORD God of Israel: 'I...delivered you from the hand of the Egyptians and from the hand of all kingdoms and from those who oppressed you.' But you have today rejected your God, who...saved you from all your adversities...and you have said to Him, 'No, set a king over us!' Now therefore, present yourselves before the LORD..."

And when Samuel had caused all...of Israel to come near...Saul the son of Kish was chosen.

So all the people shouted and said, "Long live the king!"
1 Samuel 10:17-21a, 24b

God chose Saul to be king. During Saul's reign, the Philistines gathered their armies together to fight against Israel.

The Philistines stood on a mountain on one side, and Israel stood on a mountain on the other side, with a valley between them.

And a champion went out from the camp of the Philistines, named Goliath...whose height was six cubits and a span.

...he stood and cried out to the armies of Israel, and said to them, "...Choose a man for yourselves, and let him come down to me. If he is able to fight with me and kill me, then we will be your servants. But if I...kill him, then you shall be our servants and serve us."

...When Saul and all Israel heard these words of the Philistine, they were dismayed and greatly afraid. 1 Samuel 17:3-4, 8-9, 11

Goliath was a giant; he was over nine feet tall. That's more than two of you stacked on top of each other! The Bible says that Goliath "came out of the Philistine camp with a bronze helmet on his head and a coat of bronze armor that weighed about one hundred twenty-five pounds." (1 Samuel 17:4b-5 NCV) He carried a sword, a spear, and a javelin.

All the Israelite soldiers were terrified! But one day a young shepherd boy came to the Israelite camp to bring food to his brothers who were serving in Saul's army. The shepherd's name was David. David saw how scared the soldiers were, so he went to the king and offered to fight the giant himself!

Then David said to Saul, "...your servant will...fight with this Philistine."

And Saul said to David, "You are not able to go against this Philistine to fight with him; for you are a youth..."

But David said to Saul, "Your servant used to keep his father's sheep, and when a lion or a bear came and took a lamb out of the flock, I went out after it and struck it, and delivered the lamb from its mouth; and when it arose against me, I caught it by its beard, and struck and killed it. Your servant has killed both lion and bear; and this...will be like one of them...The LORD, who delivered me from the paw of the lion and from the paw of the bear, He will deliver me from the hand of this Philistine."

And Saul said to David, "Go, and the LORD be with you!"

Then he took his staff in his hand; and he chose for himself five smooth stones from the brook, and put them in a shepherd's bag...and his sling was in his hand...

And...the Philistine...saw David...was only a youth...So the Philistine said to David, "Am I a dog, that you come to me with sticks?...Come to me, and I will give your flesh to the birds of the air and the beasts of the field!"

Then David said to the Philistine, "You come to me with a sword, with a spear, and with a javelin. But I come to you in the name of the LORD...the God of the armies of Israel...This day the LORD will deliver you into my hand, and I will strike you and take your head from you.

"And this day I will give the carcasses of...the Philistines to the birds of the air and the wild beasts of the earth, that all the earth may know that there is a God in Israel. Then all this assembly shall know that the LORD does not save with sword and spear; for the battle is the LORD's, and He will give you into our hands."

So it was, when the Philistine arose and came...near to meet David, that David hurried and ran...to meet the Philistine. Then David put his hand in his bag and took out a stone; and he slung it and struck the Philistine in his forehead, so that the stone sank into his forehead, and he fell on his face to the earth...But there was no sword in the hand of David.

Therefore David ran and stood over the Philistine, took his sword and drew it out of its sheath and killed him, and cut off his head with it. And when the Philistines saw that their champion was dead, they fled. 1 Samuel 17:32-51

David was only a youth. He did not even own a sword or a spear. But he remembered how God had saved him from the lion and the bear while he was watching his dad's sheep. He knew that the God of Israel was way more powerful than this bragging giant. David believed God could do anything. Because David trusted in God, God used him to kill Goliath.

David was a sinner like everyone else, yet in the same way Abel, Noah, Abraham, Isaac, Jacob, Moses, and Joshua believed God, David believed God too. He believed God was the only One who could save him from the death penalty he deserved for his sin.

Many years after David killed Goliath, he became one of the prophets who wrote part of the Bible. A lot of the book of Psalms is written by David. In the book of Psalms, David wrote about how he trusted in God to save him.

But I have trusted in Your mercy; my heart shall rejoice in Your salvation. Psalm 13:5

God chose David to be king of Israel after King Saul. During David's reign, Israel defeated all their enemies so that finally they lived in peace again. David led the Israelites to follow God.

Remember

Even though David was young, he trusted in God. David trusted in God to help him kill the lion and the bear that attacked his father's sheep, and he trusted in God to help him kill the giant Goliath with only a stone and a sling.

God called David "a man after [His] own heart."

...He raised up for them David as king...and said, "I have found David the son of Jesse, a man after My own heart, who will do all My will." Acts 13:22

The only way to please God is to believe Him.

But without faith it is impossible to please Him... Hebrews 11:6a

You need to believe God the way David did. God is the only One who can save you from the death penalty and make you acceptable to Him. God saves all who trust in Him.

Questions

1. For what did Hannah pray? *She asked God to give her a baby boy.*

2. What was the promise Hannah made to God? *She promised that if God gave her a son, she would give him back to God.*

3. In what way did Israel reject God? *They asked for a king. They did not want God to be their king anymore. They wanted a human king.*

4. Who did God choose to be Israel's first king? *God chose Saul.*

5. While Saul was king, who came against the Israelites in battle? *The Philistines came against the Israelites.*

6. Why were all the Israelite soldiers afraid? *They were afraid of the Philistine giant, Goliath.*

7. Why was the young shepherd boy David not afraid to fight Goliath? *David trusted in God. God had helped him fight the lion and the bear, and he knew God would deliver him from this giant.*

8. When David became king of Israel, did he lead the Israelites to follow God? *Yes, he led them to follow God and defeat their enemies.*

9. Who did David believe was the only One who could save him from the death penalty he deserved for his sin? *He believed God was the only One who could save him from the death penalty.*

Biblical Worldviews

- God is the One who gives life.
- God can do anything; nothing is too hard for Him.
- All people are sinners.
- The only way to please God is to believe Him.
- Only God can save us from the death penalty and make us acceptable to Him.

Activity: David and Goliath Skit

Supplies:

- Student volunteers. These are the key parts: David, David's brothers, Saul, Goliath, the Philistine army, the Israelite army, and narrator, optional
- Sling shot, shield, sword, etc., optional

Instructions:

- Students act out the story of David and Goliath.
- Discuss how David trusted in the Lord even though he was a youth.

Extra Bible References

1 Samuel 1-9, 17; 2 Samuel 2:1-7, 5:1-5, 7:1, 8:15; Psalm 32:1-2; Acts 2:30, 13:20-22; Romans 4:5-8; Hebrews 11:32

43
An Awesome Temple
King Solomon Builds the Temple

Memory Verse

But I have trusted in Your mercy; my heart shall rejoice in Your salvation. Psalm 13:5

Lesson

Remember the tabernacle the Israelites made in the wilderness? God told the Israelites to make it like a tent so they could carry it with them wherever they went. But now that the Israelites were peacefully living in their own land, King David wanted to build a permanent house for God.

Now it came to pass when the king was dwelling in his house, and the LORD had given him rest from all his enemies all around, that the king said to Nathan the prophet, "See now, I dwell in a house of cedar, but the ark of God dwells inside tent curtains." 2 Samuel 7:1-2

But God did not want King David to be the one to build Him a permanent house. Instead, God chose King David's son to build Him a house. This is what God said to David:

When your days are fulfilled and you rest with your fathers, I will set up your seed after you, who will come from your body, and I will establish his kingdom. He shall build a house for My name…

And your house and your kingdom shall be established forever before you. Your throne shall be established forever. 2 Samuel 7:12-13a, 16

Even though King David would not be the one to build a house for God, God made an amazing promise to King David. God told him that Someone from his family line would reign as king of Israel forever.

And God said that this king from King David's family line would be none other than the Christ, the promised Savior!

📖 ...God had sworn with an oath to him that...He would raise up the Christ to sit on his throne...Acts 2:30b

King David ruled Israel for forty years. When he died, his son Solomon took his place as the king of Israel.

📖 Thus David the son of Jesse reigned...over Israel...forty years...he died in a good old age, full of days and riches and honor; and Solomon his son reigned in his place. 1 Chronicles 29:26-28

> The country of Israel and the city of Jerusalem still exist today. Many people visit Israel to see the places talked about in the Bible. Often we hear about Israel and Jerusalem in the news.

King Solomon built the house for God that King David had wanted to build.

📖 Now Solomon began to build the house of the LORD at Jerusalem... 2 Chronicles 3:1a

Jerusalem was the capital city of Israel. It was where the king's palace was located.

The house Solomon built for God was called the temple. The temple replaced the tabernacle the Israelites constructed long ago at Mt. Sinai. The temple had two rooms just like the tabernacle - the Holy Place and the Most Holy Place. The rooms were separated by a heavy curtain.

The Bible says that King Solomon...

📖 ...overlaid the inside with pure gold...decorated the house with precious stones for beauty...and he carved cherubim on the walls. 2 Chronicles 3:4b-7

What a magnificent house! Can you imagine? The walls were decorated with expensive jewels and covered with pure gold that had angels carved into it.

Solomon also had a bronze altar and a huge bowl for washing made for the outside of the temple.

📖 ...he made a bronze altar...

Then he made the Sea of cast bronze...It stood on twelve oxen: three looking toward the north, three looking toward the west, three looking toward the south, and three looking toward the east...

Solomon had all the furnishings made for the house of God...of pure gold. 2 Chronicles 4:1-4, 19-22

Finally, when every piece of furniture was in place, King Solomon ordered the priests to bring the Ark of the Testimony from the tabernacle and set it behind the curtain.

Then the priests brought in the ark of the covenant of the LORD to its place, into the inner sanctuary of the temple, to the Most Holy Place, under the wings of the cherubim.

And it came to pass...that the house...of the LORD, was filled with a cloud, so that the priests could not continue ministering because of the cloud; for the glory of the LORD filled the house of God. 2 Chronicles 5:7, 11-14

Once the Ark of the Testimony was safely behind the curtain, the brilliant light of God's presence filled the temple.

But do you know what's really sad? When Solomon became an old man he turned away from God. Even after he built such a beautiful house for God, he stopped following God and began to worship false gods.

For it was so, when Solomon was old, that his wives turned his heart after other gods; and his heart was not loyal to the LORD his God, as was the heart of his father David.

So the LORD became angry with Solomon, because his heart had turned from the LORD God of Israel, who had...commanded him...that he should not go after other gods...

Therefore the LORD said to Solomon, "Because you have done this...I will surely tear the kingdom away from you...Nevertheless I will not do it in your days...I will tear it out of the hand of your son.

However I will not tear away the whole kingdom; I will give one tribe to your son for the sake of My servant David, and for the sake of Jerusalem which I have chosen." 1 Kings 11:4, 9-13

When King Solomon turned away from God, God divided Israel into two kingdoms: a northern kingdom and a southern kingdom. The northern kingdom was called Israel, and the southern kingdom, where the city of Jerusalem was located, was called Judah.

Because of His promise to King David, God let King David's family continue to live in Jerusalem and rule over the southern kingdom of Judah, but other kings from other family lines ruled over the northern kingdom.

Remember

Before the world began, God planned to send the Savior to save people from Satan, sin, and death.

He indeed was foreordained before the foundation of the world… 1 Peter 1:20a

After Adam and Eve joined Satan's side in the Garden of Eden, God told Satan He would send the Child of a woman to bruise his head. Someday the Child of a woman would give Satan a fatal injury that would destroy his power over mankind.

After many years, God chose Abraham to be the father of the nation of Israel. God planned for the Savior to come from this nation.

Long after Abraham died, God promised King David that the Savior would come from his family line and be king forever.

God never forgot His promise. All through the ages of history He was working out His plan to rescue people from Satan and death and make a way for them to be His friends again like Adam and Eve were in the beginning.

Questions

1. Now that the Israelites were at peace with the other nations, what did King David want to do for God? *He wanted to build God a permanent house to replace the tabernacle.*

2. Who did God choose to build a permanent house for Him instead of King David? *He chose David's son, King Solomon.*

3. What promise did God make to King David? *He promised him that the **Savior** would come from his family line and **be king forever**.*

4. What was the house called that King Solomon built for God? *It was called the temple.*

5. What was the capital city of Israel where King Solomon built the temple? *It was Jerusalem.*

6. In what way was the temple like the tabernacle? *It had two rooms called the Holy Place and the Most Holy Place. These two rooms were separated by a heavy curtain. Behind the curtain in the Most Holy Place was the Ark of the Testimony that had been in the tabernacle.*

7. Who lived behind the heavy curtain in the Most Holy Place of the temple? *God lived there above the mercy seat in the form of a bright light.*

8. When King Solomon turned away from God, what happened to the nation of Israel? *God divided it into two kingdoms: the northern kingdom of Israel, and the southern kingdom of Judah.*

9. Over which kingdom did King David's family rule? *King David's family ruled over the southern kingdom of Judah.*

Biblical Worldviews

- God is a personal being; He communicates with people.
- God is the highest authority; He is the One in charge.
- No matter what happens God always accomplishes His plans; He always does what He says He will do.
- All people are sinners.
- God is a God of love; He planned to send the Savior to rescue us from Satan, sin, and death.

Activity 1: Temple Drawing

Supplies:

- Colored pencils, pencils, and crayons
- Paper, one sheet per student
- Gold glitter
- Glue
- Jewel stickers, optional

Instructions:

- Students draw the beautiful temple built by Solomon.
- Students decorate the temple with crayons, stickers, and gold glitter.

Activity 2: Memory Verse Ball

Supplies:

- One or more mid-size balls

- Copy of memory verse: "But I have trusted in Your mercy; my heart shall rejoice in Your salvation." Psalm 13:5

Instructions:

- Depending on the number of students, students either divide into teams or form one large circle.

- Students then practice the memory verse while throwing the ball to each other and catching it.

- For example: The teacher says the first part of the verse to be memorized. Then she throws the ball to one of the students, who repeats word for word what she just said and throws the ball to another student. Go around until everyone has had a chance to catch the ball and say the first part of the verse. Now add the second part of the verse and do the same thing. Then add the third part and so on until each student has memorized the entire verse, including the reference.

- If students have been working in small groups, they now come together to form a large circle and each one recites the verse and reference in front of the entire class with or without the balls.

Extra Bible References

1 Kings 2:1-4, 10; 7:13-51; 8:1-6; 1 Chronicles 22:5-6; Psalm 132:11-18; Isaiah 9:6-7; Isaiah 41:8-10; Jeremiah 23:3-8; John 17:24; Acts 2:29-36, 13:22-23; Romans 1:3; Ephesians 1:4; 2 Timothy 2:7; 1 Peter 1:20

God's Promise to King David: 2 Samuel 23:1-7; 1 Chronicles 17:11-27, 28:4; Psalm 89; Jeremiah 33:14-22; Ezekiel 37:24-25; Luke 1:32-33

44
Cry Louder!
The Prophet Elijah and the Prophets of Baal

Memory Verse

...for this is good and acceptable in the sight of God our Savior, who desires all men to be saved and to come to the knowledge of the truth... 1Timothy 2:3-4

Lesson

Although some of the kings of Judah followed God, all the kings of Israel and many of the kings of Judah led the people to be very evil and to follow false gods. God sent his prophets to warn the people in both kingdoms that if they did not turn back to Him, He would destroy them.

> **Prophet - someone who speaks God's words to the people**

Many of the prophets wrote down the words God told them to speak to the Israelites. What they wrote can be found in the Old Testament part of the Bible. The books written by the prophets are named after them. For example, the prophet Ezekiel wrote the book of Ezekiel, and the prophet Isaiah wrote the book of Isaiah.

In the book of Ezekiel, Ezekiel the prophet wrote the following words of God to Israel:

"Therefore I will judge you, O house of Israel, every one according to his ways," says the Lord God. "Repent, and turn from all your transgressions, so that iniquity will not be your ruin."

"For I have no pleasure in the death of one who dies," says the Lord God. "Therefore turn and live!" Ezekiel 18:30, 32

The words transgressions and iniquity mean sin. Ezekiel told the people that if they did not turn from their sin they would die. Sin always leads to death. God did not want the Israelites to die; He wanted them to live!

One of Israel's worst kings was King Ahab who...

...served Baal and worshiped him...he set up an altar for Baal in the temple of Baal, which he had built in Samaria...Ahab did more to provoke the LORD God of Israel to anger than all the kings of Israel who were before him. 1 Kings 16:31b-33

God sent the prophet Elijah to speak to King Ahab. Elijah told the king that because of his evil ways, there would be no rain in Israel for three years.

And Elijah...said to Ahab, "As the LORD God of Israel lives...there shall not be dew nor rain these years..." 1 Kings 17:1

Although Elijah lived in Israel, God protected him from the famine.

Then the word of the LORD came to him, saying, "Get away from here...and hide by the Brook Cherith, which flows into the Jordan...you shall drink from the brook, and I have commanded the ravens to feed you there."

So he went and...The ravens brought him bread and meat in the morning, and bread and meat in the evening; and he drank from the brook. 1 Kings 17:2-6

God sent Elijah to a stream where he could get water to drink. He commanded birds to bring Elijah bread and meat every morning and evening.

God is the Creator of the world and everything in it. He can stop the rain if He decides to do so. And He can send birds to feed people. Nothing is too hard for God.

But since there was no rain, the stream finally dried up.

...after a while...the brook dried up, because there had been no rain in the land. 1 Kings 17:7

Then God sent Elijah to the home of a widow (a widow is a lady whose husband has died).

Then the word of the LORD came to him, saying, "Arise, go to Zarephath...I have commanded a widow there to provide for you."

So he...went to Zarephath...indeed a widow was there gathering sticks. And he called to her and said, "Please bring me a little water in a cup, that I may drink." And as she was going to get it, he called to her and said, "Please bring me a morsel of bread in your hand."

...she said, "...I do not have bread, only a handful of flour in a bin, and a little oil in a jar; and see, I am gathering a couple of sticks that I may go in and prepare it for myself and my son, that we may eat it, and die." 1 Kings 17:8-12

All the widow had was a handful of flour and a tiny bit of oil, just enough to make one last meal for her son and herself. But Elijah assured her that if she would make him some bread first, God would provide for her.

And Elijah said to her, "Do not fear...make me a small cake...first...afterward make some for yourself and your son.

"For thus says the LORD God of Israel: 'The bin of flour shall not be used up, nor shall the jar of oil run dry, until the day the LORD sends rain on the earth.'"

So she went away and did according to the word of Elijah; and she and he and her household ate for many days... 1 Kings 17:13-15

Because the widow trusted God and did what Elijah asked, God took care of her and her son. Every day she made another loaf of bread, but the flour and oil never ran out!

After some time, God sent Elijah back to King Ahab. This is what Elijah said:

...you have forsaken the commandments of the LORD and have followed the Baals. Now therefore, send and gather all Israel to me on Mount Carmel, the four hundred and fifty prophets of Baal, and the four hundred prophets of Asherah...

So Ahab sent for all the children of Israel, and gathered the prophets together on Mount Carmel. And Elijah came...and said, "How long will you falter between two opinions? If the LORD is God, follow Him; but if Baal, follow him."

...Then Elijah said to the people, "...give us two bulls...choose one bull...cut it in pieces, and lay it on the wood, but put no fire under it; and I will prepare the other bull, and lay it on the wood, but put no fire under it. Then you call on the name of your gods, and I will call on the name of the LORD; and the God who answers by fire, He is God." 1 Kings 18:18-24

So the prophets of Baal cut up a bull and placed it on their altar. Then they prayed to Baal to send down fire.

So they...called on the name of Baal from morning even till noon, saying, "O Baal, hear us!" But there was no voice; no one answered. Then they leaped about the altar which they had made.

...Elijah mocked them and said, "Cry aloud, for he is a god; either he is meditating, or he is busy, or he is on a journey, or perhaps he is sleeping and must be awakened." So they cried aloud, and cut themselves...But there was no voice; no one answered, no one paid attention.

Then Elijah said to all the people, "Come near to me." ...he built an altar...and he made a trench around the altar...And he put the wood in order, cut the bull in pieces, and laid it on the wood, and said, "Fill four waterpots with water, and pour it on the burnt sacrifice and on the wood." Then he said, "Do it a second time," and they did it a second time; and he said, "Do it a third time," and they did it a third time. So the water ran all around the altar; and he also filled the trench with water.

And...Elijah the prophet came near and said, "LORD God of Abraham, Isaac, and Israel, let it be known this day that You are God in Israel...Hear me, O LORD, hear me, that this people may know that You are the LORD God, and that You have turned their hearts back to You again."

Then the fire of the LORD fell and consumed the burnt sacrifice, and the wood and the stones and the dust, and it licked up the water that was in the trench. Now when all the people saw it, they fell on their faces; and they said, "The LORD, He is God! The LORD, He is God!"

313

And Elijah said to them, "Seize the prophets of Baal! Do not let one of them escape!" So they seized them; and Elijah brought them down to the Brook Kishon and executed them there. 1 Kings 18:26-40

When Israel saw that the gods they were worshiping were powerless, they turned back to the one and only true and living God: the God of Abraham, Isaac, and Jacob; the God of the Bible. Then God sent rain on the land again.

Remember

Remember how God warned Adam and Eve what would happen if they ate from The Tree of the Knowledge of Good and Evil? God said that if they ate from that tree, they would die. Did God want them to die? No! He wanted them to live. That is why He warned them not to eat the fruit from that tree.

God did not want the people in Noah's day to die either. For many years Noah warned the people about the coming flood. God wanted them to turn to Him so they could be saved.

And God did not want the Israelites to die. Through the words of the prophets He warned them of what would happen if they kept on in their evil ways. God wanted them to turn to Him and live.

God tells people the truth because He wants them to be saved. In the Bible God warns us that the penalty for sin is death. God warns us so that we will trust in Him to save us. God warns people because He wants them to live and not die.

"For I have no pleasure in the death of one who dies," says the Lord GOD. "Therefore turn and live!" Ezekiel 18:32

God wants everyone to know the truth so they can be saved.

who desires all men to be saved and to come to the knowledge of the truth. 1 Timothy 2:4

God saves all who trust in Him.

Questions

1. Did most of the kings of Israel and Judah follow God? *No, most of the kings of Judah and all the kings of Israel followed false gods.*

2. What were the men called whom God sent to warn the Israelites about the consequences of their sin? *The men God sent to warn the Israelites were called prophets. The prophets spoke God's words to the people.*

3. What warning did the prophets give to the Israelites and their kings? *They told them that if they did not turn to God they would be destroyed by their enemies.*

4. Did God want the Israelites to die? *No, He wanted them to live. That is why He sent His prophets to warn them.*

5. Does God have the power to control nature? *Yes, God made the rain. He made the birds. He made the whole world. All creation is under His control.*

6. How did God take care of the widow who helped the prophet Elijah? *God caused her not to run out of flour or oil.*

7. What happened when the prophets of Baal called on their god to send down fire? *No matter how much they prayed, nothing happened, because Baal was not real. Baal could not see, hear, talk, or move. He had no power.*

8. What happened when Elijah called on God to send down fire? *Immediately fire came down and burned up everything - the bull, the stones of the altar, and even the dust and water around the outside of the altar.*

9. How does God speak to us today? *He speaks to us through the words of the Bible.*

10. What does the Bible say is the penalty for sin? *The Bible says the penalty for sin is death.*

11. How can you be saved from death? *You cannot save yourself. No one else can save you. A religion cannot save you. The only way for you to be saved is to trust in God to save you.*

Biblical Worldviews

- God is a personal being; He communicates with people.
- God is a God of love; He is patient and warns people so they will live and not die.
- God is the Creator.
- God can do anything; nothing is too hard for Him.
- False gods have no power; they cannot see, hear, talk, or move.
- There is only one true God, and He is the God of the Bible.
- All people are sinners.
- The penalty for sin is death.
- The only way to please God is to believe Him.

Activity 1: Bible Hangman

Supplies:
- Chalkboard or dry erase board
- Chalk or dry erase markers

Instructions:

- Draw a large hangman tree on the board.
- Draw lines and spaces under the tree to correspond with the words and spaces of the key phrase.
- **Key phrase**: God is perfect. People are sinners. The penalty for sin is death.
- **Key phrase for younger students**: "The Lord, He is God!"
- Ask the lesson review questions, one at a time. Call on one student or one team to answer each question.
- If answer is correct, the student or team gets to pick a letter, i.e., the letter b.
- If the letter picked is in the key phrase, the teacher fills it in on the board each time it occurs.
- If the letter picked is not in the key phrase, the teacher draws one part of a stick figure on the hangman tree, i.e., a head, an arm, a stick body, etc.
- When a student (or team) thinks he knows the key phrase, he may try to solve the puzzle on his turn. The game is over when a student or team solves the puzzle or the teacher draws all the parts of the stick man, whichever comes first.

Activity 2: Elijah Skit

Supplies:

- Volunteers for King Ahab, Elijah, and the prophets of Baal
- Tables for altars, optional

Instructions:

- Students act out the story of Elijah and the prophets of Baal

Extra Bible References

Deuteronomy 9:24; Psalm 135:15-18; Ezekiel 18:30-32; Romans 3:23; 2 Peter 3:8-9

45
Swallowed by a Fish
The Prophet Jonah

Memory Verse

The Lord is...longsuffering toward us, not willing that any should perish but that all should come to repentance. 2 Peter 3:9

Lesson

Long ago at Mount Sinai the Israelites had made an agreement with God. The agreement was that they would only receive God's special treatment if they obeyed His commands. If they did not obey His commands, He would destroy them by letting other nations conquer them.

Even though the Israelites broke their agreement with God, God continued to love them. He gave them many chances to change their minds and turn back to Him. God patiently sent prophet after prophet to warn the Israelites about what would happen if they continued in their evil ways.

But the people of Israel and Judah ignored God's prophets. No matter what God said, they just kept worshiping false gods and following the evil ways of the nations around them. They even sacrificed their children to idols!

...the LORD testified against Israel and against Judah, by all of His prophets...saying, "Turn from your evil ways, and keep My commandments...which I commanded your fathers, and which I sent to you by My servants the prophets."

Nevertheless they would not hear, but stiffened their necks, like...their fathers, who did not believe in the LORD their God. And they rejected His statutes and His covenant that He had made with their fathers...they followed idols...and went after the nations who were all around them.

So they left all the commandments of the LORD their God, made for themselves a molded image and two calves, made a wooden image and worshiped all the host of heaven, and served Baal. And they caused their sons and daughters to pass through the fire, practiced witchcraft and soothsaying, and sold themselves to do evil in the sight of the LORD, to provoke Him to anger. 2 Kings 17:13-17

When God's prophets warned the Israelites about what was going to happen if they did not turn to God, the Israelites got angry. They did not want to hear this bad news.

Not only were there prophets sent by God, but there were also men who claimed to be sent from God but were really telling the people lies. These men were false prophets. The false prophets told the Israelites what they wanted to hear.

God's prophet Jeremiah wrote this about the false prophets:

...the LORD said to me, "The prophets prophesy lies in My name. I have not sent them..." Jeremiah 14:14a

"They speak a vision of their own heart, not from the mouth of the LORD. They continually say to those who despise Me, 'The LORD has said, "You shall have peace"'; and to everyone who walks according to the dictates of his own heart, they say, 'No evil shall come upon you.'" Jeremiah 23:16b, 17

The false prophets said God sent them to say there would be peace and that everything would be fine. Of course, this was not true. The false prophets were led by Satan. Just like Satan lied when he told Adam and Eve they would not die if they ate the fruit, it was a lie that the Israelites would not be destroyed for their sinful behavior.

The truth was that Satan wanted the Israelites to do evil so that God would destroy them. If the nation of Israel disappeared, the Savior would not be born into the world and Satan could continue to be in charge.

Of course, the prophets who were truly sent by God told the truth. When Isaiah the prophet predicted that the Assyrians would conquer the northern kingdom, he was telling the truth.

Woe to Assyria, the rod of My anger...I will send him against an ungodly nation, and against the people of My wrath...to tread them down like the mire of the streets. Isaiah 10:5-6

The Assyrians were cruel. They tortured their captives in terrible ways. But God gave even the evil Assyrians a chance to turn to Him. He sent a prophet from the northern kingdom of Israel to Nineveh, the capital city of Assyria, with a warning just for them.

Now the word of the LORD came to Jonah...saying, "Arise, go to Nineveh, that great city, and cry out against it; for their wickedness has come up before Me." Jonah 1:1-2

Jonah did not want God to give the evil Assyrians a chance to turn to Him. So he got on a ship going the opposite direction.

...Jonah arose to flee...from the presence of the LORD. He went down to Joppa, and found a ship going to Tarshish...

But the LORD sent out a great wind on the sea, and there was a mighty tempest on the sea, so that the ship was about to be broken up...

But Jonah had gone down into the lowest parts of the ship...and was fast asleep.

So the captain came to him, and said to him, "What do you mean, sleeper? Arise, call on your God..."

So he said to them, "I am a Hebrew; and I fear the LORD, the God of heaven, who made the sea and the dry land."

Then the men were exceedingly afraid, and said to him, "Why have you done this?" For the men knew that he fled from the presence of the LORD, because he had told them. Then they said to him, "What shall we do to you that the sea may be calm for us?"—for the sea was growing more tempestuous.

And he said to them, "Pick me up and throw me into the sea; then the sea will become calm for you. For I know that this great tempest is because of me."

Nevertheless the men rowed hard to return to land, but they could not, for the sea continued to grow more tempestuous against them...So they picked up Jonah and threw him into the sea, and the sea ceased from its raging.

Now the LORD had prepared a great fish to swallow Jonah. And Jonah was in the belly of the fish three days and three nights.

Then Jonah prayed to the LORD his God from the fish's belly.

So the LORD spoke to the fish, and it vomited Jonah onto dry land.

So Jonah arose and went to Nineveh, according to the word of the LORD.

...the people of Nineveh believed God...

God saw...that they turned from their evil way; and God relented from the disaster that He had said He would bring upon them, and He did not do it. Jonah 1:1-17; 2:1, 10; 3:3, 5, 10

Jonah could not hide from God! God sent a terrible storm to Jonah's ship and a big fish to swallow him. After three days in the fish's belly, Jonah was finally ready to do what God asked. So the fish vomited Jonah onto the shore near Nineveh.

When Jonah gave God's message to the people of Nineveh, they believed God and changed their ways just as Jonah was afraid they would.

But with the passing of time, the people of Nineveh went back to their old ways and Isaiah's prediction came true.

...the king of Assyria...carried Israel away to Assyria...

For...the children of Israel had sinned against the LORD their God, who had brought them up out of the land of Egypt, from under the hand of Pharaoh king of Egypt; and they had feared other gods...

Therefore the LORD was very angry with Israel, and removed them from His sight; there was none left but the tribe of Judah alone. 2 Kings 17:6-7, 18

The Assyrians conquered the northern kingdom of Israel, wiping it out forever. Only a few Israelites were left in the land. The rest of the people were either killed or scattered across the Assyrian empire.

The Assyrians brought people from other lands to live in Israel. These people married the Israelites who had been left behind. From this came a new group of people called Samaritans, who were part Israelite and part another race.

Though the Assyrians were powerful, after some time, they were conquered by the Babylonian Empire.

Remember

Satan is a liar and a murderer. He tries to get people to believe His lies so that they will die and be separated from God forever.

Satan wants you to believe that God does not exist, or at least that God does not care what you do. Satan wants you to think you can do whatever you want because there is no penalty for sin.

...the devil...was a murderer from the beginning, and does not stand in the truth, because there is no truth in him...for he is a liar and the father of it. John 8:44

But God speaks the truth when He says you deserve to die for your sin.

The soul who sins shall die. Ezekiel 18:4b

If Adam and Eve and the Israelites would have believed God, they would not have died. In the same way, you need to believe God and not Satan. Believe God when He says you deserve to die for your sin. Then trust in Him to save you.

Remember God's promise to send the Savior to save you from Satan and death? The Bible says that whoever believes in Him will not die, but will live forever.

...whoever believes in Him should not perish but have everlasting life. John 3:16

Don't let Satan trick you. Believe God and live!

Questions

1. What did God's prophets warn the Israelites would happen if they continued to sin? *They told the Israelites that if they did not turn back to God He would send their enemies to destroy them.*

2. What did the false prophets tell the Israelites? *They said there would be peace in Israel, and Israel would not be destroyed.*

3. Who sent the false prophets? *Satan did.*

4. Did God love the Assyrians even though they were not His special people and even though they were wicked and hateful? *Yes, God loves all people. God wants everyone to believe in Him and be saved.*

5. Why was Jonah unwilling to go to Nineveh? *Jonah knew that if the people of Nineveh believed God, God would have mercy on them. Jonah wanted God to destroy the cruel Assyrians, not be merciful to them*!

6. Could Jonah hide from God? *No, God is everywhere. No one can hide from God.*

7. Who finally conquered the northern kingdom of Israel? *The Assyrians did.*

8. Is everything God says in the Bible true? *Yes, it is.*

9. Is it true that the penalty for sin is separation from God forever in the terrible place of suffering? *Yes, it is.*

10. Why does Satan try to trick you with lies like, "There is no God," and "There is no terrible place of suffering"? *Satan wants you to think that there is no penalty for sin. He does not want you to believe the truth because he does not want you to trust in the Savior and be saved from sin and death.*

Biblical Worldviews

- All people are sinners.
- The penalty for sin is death.
- God communicates with people; He warns people they will die if they do not believe Him.
- God is patient and merciful; He is a God of love.
- Satan is a liar and a murderer.
- God is not partial; He loves *all* people and wants everyone to be saved.
- God is everywhere and knows everything; you cannot hide from God.
- God always does what He says He will do; He keeps His word.
- There is a place of eternal suffering.

Activity 1: Bible Tic-Tac-Toe

Supplies:
- Chalkboard or dry erase board
- Chalk or dry erase markers

Instructions:
- Draw a large tic-tac-toe on the board.
- Divide students into two teams.
- Ask review questions and let each team take turns trying to answer a question. If the team answers the question correctly, that team gets to put an "X" or an "O" on the board. The first team to get three in a row, horizontally, vertically, or diagonally, wins.
- Play several times until you have used all the review questions.

Activity 2: Jonah Skit

Supplies:

- Volunteers for Jonah, the ship crew, and the people of Nineveh
- No props are needed

Instructions:

- Students act out the story of Jonah.

Extra Bible References

1 Kings 9:7-8; 2 Chronicles 28:1-4; Psalm 106; Isaiah 10:5-6, 29:13, 64:6; Jeremiah 5:31; Jeremiah 23:9-40, 27:9, 35:15; Nahum 3:1-4; 1 Timothy 2:4; 2 Peter 2:1; 1 John 4:1

46
A Burning Fiery Furnace
Three Captives: Shadrach, Meshach, and Abed-Nego

Memory Verse

Look to Me, and be saved, all you ends of the earth! For I am God, and there is no other. Isaiah 45:22

Lesson

In time, the Israelites in the southern kingdom of Judah became just as evil as the people in the northern kingdom.

Also Judah did not keep the commandments of the LORD their God, but walked in the statutes of Israel... 2 Kings 17:19

The prophet Jeremiah warned the people of Judah that if they did not turn to God, He would send the nation of Babylon to conquer them and take them captive just like the Assyrians had done to the southern kingdom of Israel.

I will give all Judah into the hand of the king of Babylon, and he shall carry them captive to Babylon and slay them with the sword. Jeremiah 20:4b

> Jews - another
> name for Israelites

And that is just what happened.

...on the seventh day of the month (which was the nineteenth year of King Nebuchadnezzar king of Babylon), Nebuzaradan the captain of the guard...came to Jerusalem. He burned the house of the LORD and the king's house; all the houses of Jerusalem...And...broke down the walls of Jerusalem all around.

Then Nebuzaradan...carried away captive the rest of the people who remained in the city...with the rest of the multitude. But the captain of the guard left some of the poor of the land as vinedressers and farmers. 2 Kings 25:8-12

The Babylonians demolished the city of Jerusalem. They broke down the walls around the city and burned King Solomon's magnificent temple. The people who were not killed in the attack were taken to Babylon as captives. Only the poorest Israelites were allowed to remain in Judah.

Among the captives taken to Babylon were four extraordinary young men named Daniel, Hananiah, Mishael, and Azariah. Even though Daniel and his friends grew up in the godless land of Judah, they still believed in the true and living God. The king of Babylon chose these four men to serve in his palace.

Then the king instructed Ashpenaz...to bring some of the children of Israel... who had ability to serve in the king's palace...

...from among those of...Judah were Daniel, Hananiah, Mishael, and Azariah...he gave Daniel the name Belteshazzar; to Hananiah, Shadrach; to Mishael, Meshach; and to Azariah, Abed-Nego.

Then the king interviewed them, and among them all none was found like Daniel, Hananiah, Mishael, and Azariah; therefore they served before the king. And in all matters of wisdom and understanding about which the king examined them, he found them ten times better than all the magicians and astrologers who were in all his realm.
Daniel 1:3-4, 6-7, 19-20

When the king interviewed Daniel, Shadrach, Meshach, and Abed-Nego, he found they were ten times more intelligent than all the magicians and astrologers in his entire kingdom! Of course, it was God who gave these young men wisdom and understanding.

After a time, King Nebuchadnezzar decided to make a gigantic gold statue. He ordered everyone in his kingdom to bow down to the image of gold he had made.

Nebuchadnezzar the king made an image of gold...

So...all the officials of the provinces gathered together for the dedication of the image that King Nebuchadnezzar had set up...

Then a herald cried aloud: "To you it is commanded, O peoples, nations, and languages, that at the time you hear the sound of...all kinds of music, you shall fall down and worship the gold image that King Nebuchadnezzar has set up; and whoever does not fall down and worship shall be cast immediately into the midst of a burning fiery furnace."

So...when all the people heard the sound of...all kinds of music, all the people...fell down and worshiped the gold image which King Nebuchadnezzar had set up.

...at that time certain Chaldeans came forward and accused the Jews. They...said to King Nebuchadnezzar, "O king, live forever! ...There are certain Jews whom you have set over the affairs of the province of Babylon: Shadrach, Meshach, and Abed-Nego; these men, O king, have not paid due regard to you. They do not serve your gods or worship the gold image which you have set up."

Then Nebuchadnezzar, in rage and fury, gave the command to bring Shadrach, Meshach, and Abed-Nego. So they brought these men before the king. Nebuchadnezzar spoke, saying to them, "Is it true, Shadrach, Meshach, and Abed-Nego, that you do not serve my gods or worship the gold image which I have set up? Now if you are ready at the time you hear the sound of...all kinds of music, and you fall down and worship the image which I have made, good! But if you do not worship, you shall be cast immediately into the midst of a burning fiery furnace. And who is the god who will deliver you from my hands?"

Shadrach, Meshach, and Abed-Nego answered and said to the king, "O Nebuchadnezzar...our God whom we serve is able to deliver us from the burning fiery furnace, and He will deliver us from your hand, O king. But if not, let it be known to you, O king, that we do not serve your gods, nor will we worship the gold image which you have set up."

Then Nebuchadnezzar...commanded that they heat the furnace seven times more than it was usually heated. And he commanded certain mighty men...who were in his army to bind Shadrach, Meshach, and Abed-Nego, and cast them into the burning fiery furnace. Then these men were bound in their coats, their trousers, their turbans, and their other garments, and were cast into the midst of the burning fiery furnace. Therefore, because the...furnace [was] exceedingly hot, the flame of the fire killed those men who took up Shadrach, Meshach,

and Abed-Nego. And these three men, Shadrach, Meshach, and Abed-Nego, fell down bound into the midst of the burning fiery furnace.

Then King Nebuchadnezzar was astonished; and he...spoke...to his counselors, "Did we not cast three men bound into the midst of the fire?"

They answered and said to the king, "True, O king."

"Look!" he answered, "I see four men loose, walking in the midst of the fire; and they are not hurt, and the form of the fourth is like the Son of God."

Then Nebuchadnezzar went near the mouth of the burning fiery furnace and spoke, saying, "Shadrach, Meshach, and Abed-Nego, servants of the Most High God, come out, and come here." Then Shadrach, Meshach, and Abed-Nego came from the midst of the fire. And...they saw these men on whose bodies the fire had no power; the hair of their head was not singed nor were their garments affected, and the smell of fire was not on them.

Nebuchadnezzar spoke, saying, "Blessed be the God of Shadrach, Meshach, and Abed-Nego, who sent His Angel and delivered His servants who trusted in Him, and they have frustrated the king's word, and yielded their bodies, that they should not serve nor worship any god except their own God! Therefore I make a decree that any people, nation, or language which speaks anything...against the God of Shadrach, Meshach, and Abed-Nego shall be cut in pieces, and their houses shall be made an ash heap; because there is no other God who can deliver like this."

Then the king promoted Shadrach, Meshach, and Abed-Nego in the province of Babylon. Daniel 3:1-30

When Shadrach, Meshach, and Abed-Nego lived in Judah, they did not worship false gods like most of the other people living there, and now they also refused to bow to King Nebuchadnezzar's golden image.

Because these three young men refused to deny God, the great and mighty king of Babylon came to believe in the only true and living God. Isn't that incredible? King Nebuchadnezzar even made it illegal for the people in his kingdom to speak against God! Then he promoted Shadrach, Meshach, and Abed-Nego to a higher-rank in his service.

Remember

Do you remember King David? Before he became king, he was a shepherd boy. While watching his father's sheep, God helped him kill both a lion and a bear. Later when he went to see his brothers on the battlefield, he saw that everyone was afraid of the giant Goliath. Even though David was young, he trusted God to help him kill the scary giant.

Daniel, Shadrach, Meshach, and Abed-Nego were also young when they were captured. The people around them did not believe in the true and living God. They practiced evil customs and worshiped idols.

Many people today do not believe in God either. They do not believe God is the Creator of the world. Some people do not even believe there is a God.

You should take courage and be like David, Daniel, Shadrach, Meshach and Abed-Nego. Even though you are young and many of the people around you do not believe in God, you can still trust in God because no matter what people say, the Bible is true. God does exist. He is the Creator of the world and the Most High over all the earth!

That they may know that You, whose name alone is the Lord, are the Most High over all the earth. Psalm 83:18

Questions

1. Why did God allow the nation of Babylon to conquer Judah and destroy the city of Jerusalem? *Because the people and kings of Judah refused to listen to the prophets and turn to God.*

2. Who gave Daniel, Shadrach, Meshach, and Abed-Nego wisdom and understanding? *God did. God knows everything. Only He could make these young men so wise.*

3. What was King Nebuchadnezzar's command that Shadrach, Meshach, and Abed-Nego refused to follow? *He commanded everyone in his kingdom to bow down to the gold image he made.*

4. What did the king say would happen to anyone who did not bow down to his image? *Whoever did not bow down to the image would be thrown into a burning furnace.*

5. What did Shadrach, Meshach, and Abed-Nego say to King Nebuchadnezzar? *They said they would not worship his false gods or bow to his gold image. They told him that their God was strong enough to rescue them, but even if He did not, they would still trust in Him.*

6. What happened to the men who threw the three Israelites into the fire? *The fire was so hot they were killed by the flames.*

7. Who did the king see in the fire with the three Israelites? *He saw a fourth person who looked like the Son of God.*

8. Were the three men who were thrown into the fire burned at all? *No, their clothes did not even smell like fire!*

9. What did the king learn about the God of Israel? *He learned that the God of Israel is the only true God who is more powerful than anyone else.*

10. Why should you believe God? *You should believe God because God tells the truth and He truly is the Most High in all the earth.*

Biblical Worldviews

- God is a personal being; He communicates with people.
- God is a God of love; He warns people of coming judgment.
- God always does what He says He will do.
- The God of the Bible is the only true and living God.
- God can do anything; nothing is too hard for Him.
- The only way to please God is to believe Him.

Activity 1: Bible Bingo

Supplies:

- Bingo cards and game tokens. (Any set will do. You can buy an inexpensive set at the dollar store.)

Instructions:

- Give each student a bingo card and some tokens.
- Ask a question from the lesson review and call on a student to answer it. If the student answers it correctly, she calls the bingo square she wants to cover. Everyone else who has that square covers it as well.
- Continue to ask questions, calling on a different student each time. Allow everyone to answer at least one question and pick at least one bingo square.
- The game is over when the first student shouts BINGO because she has covered a complete row with tokens, either vertically, horizontally, or diagonally.

- Play the game several times until everyone has had a turn answering a question and/or all the questions from the review have been asked and answered.

Activity 2: Shadrach, Meshach, and Abed-Nego Skit

Supplies:

- Volunteers to play the parts of Nebuchadnezzar, Shadrach, Meshach, Abed-Nego, and the men who threw them into the fire
- No props are needed

Instructions:

- Students act out the story.
- Discuss how these young men believed God even when most of the people in Judah did not and even though they would be thrown into the burning furnace.
- Discuss how their trust in God changed the king.

Extra Bible References

2 Chronicles 36:15-21; Jeremiah 20:5, 21:1-14, 25:8-11, 50:17, 52:1-30; Luke 6:26

47
In the Lions' Den
The Prophet Daniel

Memory Verse

Look to Me, and be saved, all you ends of the earth! For I am God, and there is no other. Isaiah 45:22

Lesson

Daniel was one of the captives from Judah who was taken to Babylon along with Shadrach, Meshach, and Abed-nego. Daniel became a prophet and wrote the book of Daniel in the Bible. The book of Daniel is where we find the story of King Nebuchadnezzar.

Remember how King Nebuchadnezzar came to believe in God? Part of the book of Daniel is written in King Nebuchadnezzar's own words!

Now I, Nebuchadnezzar, praise and extol and honor the King of heaven, all of whose works are truth, and His ways justice. And those who walk in pride He is able to put down. Daniel 4:37

After Nebuchadnezzar died, Belshazzar became king of Babylon. During the reign of Belshazzar, the Medes and Persians conquered Babylon. The king of the Medes and Persians was Darius.

That very night Belshazzar...was slain. And Darius the Mede received the kingdom... Daniel 5:30-31

King Darius liked Daniel because he was honest and responsible; he considered making Daniel the highest official in the land. This special treatment made the other officials jealous.

It pleased Darius to set over the kingdom one hundred and twenty satraps, to be over the whole kingdom; and over these, three governors, of whom Daniel was one...Then this Daniel distinguished himself above the governors and satraps, because an excellent spirit was in him; and the king gave thought to setting him over the whole realm.

So the governors and satraps sought to find some charge against Daniel concerning the kingdom; but they could find no charge or fault, because he was faithful; nor was there any error or fault found in him.

Then these men said, "We shall not find any charge against this Daniel unless we find it against him concerning the law of his God."

So these governors and satraps thronged before the king, and said thus to him: "King Darius, live forever! All the governors of the kingdom, the administrators and satraps, the counselors and advisors, have consulted together to establish a royal statute and to make a firm decree, that whoever petitions any god or man for thirty days, except you, O king, shall be cast into the den of lions. Now, O king, establish the decree and sign the writing, so that it cannot be changed, according to the law of the Medes and Persians, which does not alter."

Therefore King Darius signed the written decree. Daniel 6:1-9

The officials knew they couldn't find anything to accuse Daniel of, so they decided to make a law against worshiping God. The law said that for the next thirty days no one was allowed to pray to any god or man except to the king himself. If anyone broke this law, he or she would be thrown into a den of hungry lions.

The king liked the thought of everyone praying to him. He did not think about how this might affect Daniel. And the worst thing was that according to the law of the Medes and Persians, no one, not even the king, could change a law once it was signed. But even though Daniel knew when the law was signed, he continued to pray to God, as the governors and officials of the king knew he would.

Now when Daniel knew that the writing was signed, he went home. And in his upper room, with his windows open toward Jerusalem, he knelt down on his knees three times that day, and prayed and gave thanks before his God, as was his custom since early days.

Then these men...found Daniel praying...before his God. And they went before the king, and spoke concerning the king's decree: "Have you not signed a decree that every man who petitions any god or man within thirty days, except you, O king, shall be cast into the den of lions?"

The king answered and said, "The thing is true, according to the law of the Medes and Persians, which does not alter."

So they answered and said before the king, "That Daniel, who is one of the captives from Judah, does not show due regard for you, O king, or for the decree that you have signed, but makes his petition three times a day."

And the king, when he heard these words, was greatly displeased with himself, and...he labored till the going down of the sun to deliver him. Daniel 6:10-14

No matter how hard King Darius looked for a way to change the law, he could find none. So Daniel was cast into the den of lions.

...and they brought Daniel and cast him into the den of lions. But the king spoke...to Daniel, "Your God, whom you serve continually, He will deliver you."

Then a stone was brought and laid on the mouth of the den, and the king sealed it with his own signet ring... Daniel 6:16-17a

That night the king could not sleep. Would Daniel's God save him from the hungry lions? In the morning, he rushed to see if Daniel was still alive.

Now the king went to his palace and spent the night fasting...Also his sleep went from him. Then the king arose very early in the morning and went in haste to the den of lions. And when he came to the den, he cried out..., "Daniel, servant of the living God, has your God, whom you serve continually, been able to deliver you from the lions?"

Then Daniel said to the king, "O king, live forever! My God sent His angel and shut the lions' mouths, so that they have not hurt me..."

Now the king was exceedingly glad for him, and commanded that they should take Daniel up out of the den. So Daniel was taken up out of the den, and no injury whatever was found on him, because he believed in his God.

And the king gave the command, and they brought those men who had accused Daniel, and they cast them into the den of lions…

Then King Darius wrote: To all peoples, nations, and languages that dwell in all the earth: …I make a decree that in every dominion of my kingdom men must tremble and fear before the God of Daniel. For He is the living God…His kingdom is the one which shall not be destroyed, and His dominion shall endure to the end. He delivers and rescues, and He works signs and wonders in heaven and on earth, who has delivered Daniel from the power of the lions.

So…Daniel prospered in the reign of Darius and in the reign of Cyrus the Persian. Daniel 6:18-28

Just like Shadrach, Meshach, and Abed-Nego, Daniel trusted in God even though he knew he would be thrown into a den of hungry lions. When King Darius saw the faith of Daniel and the great power of God, he also came to believe in God just like King Nebuchadnezzar had.

Remember

God is stronger than a den full of lions. Nothing is too hard for God!

Ah, Lord GOD! Behold, You have made the heavens and the earth by Your great power and outstretched arm. There is nothing too hard for You. Jeremiah 32:17

God is the Creator of the world and everything in it; He is highest authority. No one is greater than God!

Questions

1. Who were the four young captives from Judah who believed God? *Shadrach, Meshach, Abed-Nego, and Daniel were the four captives who believed God.*

2. Which of God's prophets wrote the book of Daniel? *Daniel wrote the book of Daniel.*

3. Did Nebuchadnezzar, king of the great Babylonian empire, believe in God? *Yes, at the end of his life King Nebuchadnezzar worshiped the one true God.*

4. Who conquered Babylon? *The Medes and Persians conquered Babylon.*

5. Who was the king of the Medes and Persians when Babylon was conquered? *King Darius was king of the Medes and Persians.*

6. Could a law of the Medes and Persians be changed? *No, once a law was signed it could not be changed; not even the king could change the law.*

7. Why were the governors and officials jealous of Daniel? *They were jealous of Daniel because the king was thinking of making Daniel the highest official in the land.*

8. How did the governors, princes, and supervisors trick the king? *They persuaded the king to pass a law saying no one could pray to anyone but him for thirty days. The king liked this law and did not think about how it would affect Daniel.*

9. Did Daniel pray to God even though he knew he would be thrown into the den of lions? *Yes, Daniel still prayed to God like he always had.*

10. Did God have the power to save Daniel from the lions? *Since God is the Creator of lions, He has the power to stop hungry lions from eating people. Nothing is too hard for God!*

11. Who is the highest authority in the whole world? *God is the Most High over all the earth!*

Biblical Worldviews

- The God of the Bible is the only true and living God.
- All people are sinners.
- The only way to please God is to believe Him.
- God can do anything; nothing is too hard for Him.
- God is the Creator of the world; He is the highest authority.

Activity: Daniel Skit

Supplies:

- Volunteers for Daniel, King Darius, and the king's officials
- No props are needed

Instructions:

- Students act out the story.

48
God's Plans
The Years before the Savior

Memory Verse

> *I, even I, am the LORD, and besides Me there is no savior. Isaiah 43:11*

Lesson

When Cyrus became king of Persia, he let some of the captives from Judah go back to Jerusalem to rebuild the ruined temple.

Thus says Cyrus king of Persia: ...the LORD God...has commanded me to build Him a house at Jerusalem which is in Judah. Who is among you of all His people? May his God be with him, and let him go up to Jerusalem which is in Judah, and build the house of the LORD God of Israel (He is God), which is in Jerusalem. Ezra 1:2-3

Although the people of Judah were Israelites, they came to be called Jews.

When the Jews arrived in Jerusalem, they rebuilt the temple and started offering sacrifices. Once again, they tried to keep the laws God had given Moses on Mount Sinai.

...the people gathered together...to Jerusalem...and built the altar of the God of Israel, to offer burnt offerings on it, as it is written in the Law of Moses the man of God. Ezra 3:1-2

The Jews who stayed behind built meeting places called synagogues wherever they were scattered throughout the known world. Every Sabbath (or Saturday) they gathered in these synagogues to hear the religious leaders read from the Old Testament, which is the writings of Moses and the prophets.

The religious leaders tried to explain God's words to the people, but they themselves did not understand the true meaning of what Moses and the prophets had written. Since most of the Jews who stayed behind, as well as those who went to Jerusalem, did not know what the Bible was really all about, they just went to the synagogue or to the temple and kept God's laws as a way of doing good works to make God happy.

The Jews thought God was pleased with them because they came from Abraham and tried to keep the commandments God gave them on Mt. Sinai.

If the Jews would have understood the true meaning of the Old Testament, they would have realized they were not at all acceptable to God.

In his writings, Moses told about how Adam and Eve believed Satan instead of God and of God's promise to send the Child of a woman to rescue people from Satan. Moses wrote about Cain and Abel. God accepted Abel because Abel trusted in Him, but God did not accept Cain because Cain thought he could come to God in his own way by giving God a gift. Moses wrote about God's promise to Abraham that the Savior would come from his nation.

In your seed all the nations of the earth shall be blessed...
Genesis 22:18

The Israelites should have understood from the writings of Moses that they were sinners separated from God, that there was nothing they could do to please God, and that only God could save them by sending the promised Savior.

Moses also wrote about how God gave His laws to the Israelites and how they broke them immediately. He wrote about how God accepted the death of a perfect lamb in the place of the person who broke His command.

The Israelites should have understood that the penalty for sin is death and that they needed a substitute to pay this penalty for them. They should have been waiting for God to send the promised Savior to save them from death.

Not only was the Savior foretold in the books of the Bible written by Moses, but the prophets who came after Moses also wrote about the Savior.

The prophet Micah said that the Savior would be born in Bethlehem.

But you, Bethlehem...out of you shall come forth...The One to be Ruler in Israel, whose goings forth are from of old, from everlasting.
Micah 5:2

The prophet Hosea wrote that the Savior would spend some time in Egypt.

...And out of Egypt I called My son. Hosea 11:1

The prophet Isaiah prophesied that a man in the wilderness would prepare the Jews for the coming of the Savior and that the Savior would be the Lord.

> The voice of one crying in the wilderness: "Prepare the way of the LORD..." Isaiah 40:3

The prophet Isaiah also foretold that the Savior would be born of a woman who had never been married.

> Therefore the Lord Himself will give you a sign: Behold, the virgin shall conceive and bear a Son, and shall call His name Immanuel. Isaiah 7:14

King David prophesied that the Savior would be betrayed by a close friend and that His hands and feet would be pierced.

> Even my own familiar friend in whom I trusted...has lifted up his heel against me. Psalm 41:9
>
> ...They pierced My hands and My feet; Psalm 22:16

King David also wrote about God's promise that the Savior would come from his family line and rule as king forever.

> I have made a covenant with My chosen, I have sworn to My servant David: "Your seed I will establish forever, and build up your throne to all generations." Psalm 89:3-4

The Jews should have been waiting eagerly for this promised Savior, but they were not. Only a few of them understood the true meaning of what Moses and the prophets wrote. Only a few were waiting for the Savior to come rescue them from sin and death and make them acceptable to God.

After some time, the Greeks conquered the Persians, and as a result almost everyone in the known world learned to speak the Greek language.

Then the Romans came to power. All across their vast empire, the Romans built roads for their armies.

Caesar Augustus, the emperor of Rome at that time, allowed the Jews to continue worshiping God at the temple in Jerusalem. He even allowed them to have a Jewish king, although the king had to do whatever he said. Mostly, though, the emperor was cruel and hateful. Under his direction many Jews were killed by the sword and many were crucified by having their hands and feet nailed to a tree and hanging there until they suffocated.

But God was using the Greeks and Romans to prepare the world for the coming of the Savior. Because most people now spoke the same language and because of the roads that crossed the Roman empire, news about the Savior could easily spread to everyone. Even the synagogues would be used by God to make known the message of the Savior.

Although the Jews were not waiting for the Savior and the Greeks and Romans did not care about God, God was working out His plan.

No matter what the governments and leaders of the world did, God's plan was going to be completed just the way He decided long ago. The Savior was coming, and just as predicted, He would come from the nation of Israel and be born into King David's family line!

The LORD brings the counsel of the nations to nothing; He makes the plans of the peoples of no effect. The counsel of the LORD stands forever, the plans of His heart to all generations. Psalm 33:10-11

Remember

Even when people stop caring about God, He still cares about them. God loves everyone, even the worst of sinners. He wants all people to know the truth so they can be rescued from death and be made acceptable to Him. That is why He promised to send the Savior.

For this is good and acceptable in the sight of God our Savior, who desires all men to be saved and to come to the knowledge of the truth. 1 Timothy 2:3-4

Questions

1. What did Cyrus, king of Persia, allow some of the Jews do? *He allowed them go back to Jerusalem to rebuild the temple.*

2. What were the buildings called where the Jews outside of Jerusalem met to hear God's Word? *They were called synagogues.*

3. Did the Jewish religious leaders understand the true meaning of what Moses and the prophets wrote in the Old Testament? *No, even though they were religious leaders, they did not understand the true meaning of God's words in the Bible.*

4. Why did the Jews think God accepted them? *The Jews thought they were acceptable to God because they came from Abraham and because they tried to keep God's commands.*

5. Why were the Jews not acceptable to God? *They were not acceptable to God because they were sinners separated from God.*

6. Who was the only One who could save the Jews from sin and death and make them acceptable to God? *Only the coming Savior could save them from sin and death and make them acceptable to God.*

7. Into what nation was the Savior going to be born? *The Savior would be born into the nation of Israel.*

8. From whose family line would the Savior come? *The Savior was going to come from King David's family line.*

9. Where did the prophet Micah say the Savior would be born? *The prophet Micah said the Savior would be born in Bethlehem.*

10. What language did almost everyone in the known world speak? *Almost everyone spoke Greek.*

11. What did the Romans build that would help the news about the Savior spread to all people? *They built roads all across their empire.*

12. Was the Roman emperor kind to the Jews? *Not really. Even though he let the Jews worship at the temple, he had many of them killed, either by the sword or by crucifixion.*

13. Can anyone stop God from doing what He plans to do? *No, no one can stop God, not even great nations and important leaders. God always does what He plans to do.*

Biblical Worldviews

- All people are sinners separated from God.
- There is nothing we can do to save ourselves from death or make ourselves acceptable to God.
- God is a personal being; He communicates with people.
- God knows what is going to happen in the future.
- God works out everything according to His plan.
- Only the Savior can save us from Satan, sin, and death and make us acceptable to God.

Activity 1: Timeline

Supplies:

- Chalkboard or dry erase board
- Chalk or dry erase marker

- Paper, one sheet per student
- Pencils and crayons

Instructions:

- The teacher writes the following events on the dry erase board.

  First: The Jews were scattered across Babylon.

  Second: Wherever the Jews went they built synagogues.

  Third: The Greeks took over the world and made everyone learn their language.

  Fourth: The Romans took over the Greeks, built roads all across their empire, and practiced crucifixion.

- Option #1: Students draw a timeline and write the above-mentioned events on the timeline in the order in which they occurred.
- Option #2: Students draw a picture of each event and then number the events in the order in which they occurred.

Activity 2: Prophecies

Supplies:

- Paper, one sheet per student
- Pencils, markers, crayons

Instructions:

- Review the prophecies made about the Savior in the Old Testament.
- Then students write out, or illustrate, one or more of the prophecies on their papers.

  The Savior would be born in Bethlehem.

  The Savior would escape from Egypt

  Someone in the wilderness would prepare the way for the Savior ("the Lord").

  The Savior would be born to a woman who had never been married.

  The Savior would be betrayed by a close friend.

  The hands and feet of the Savior would be pierced.

- Optional: Students roll up their papers like a scroll as a reminder that the prophecies were written on scrolls by the prophets hundreds of years before the Savior arrived.

Extra Bible References

1 Chronicles 29:11; Ezra 1; Isaiah 1:11-13, 44:28; Luke 4:16-21, 24:44-45; John 8:37-47; Acts 2: 29-31, 3:17-26, 9:20, 10:43, 15:21; Hebrews 1:1; 1 Peter 1:10-12; 2 Peter 3:1-2

The Most Amazing Story

New Testament

49
A Special Baby
An Angel Appears to Zacharias

Memory Verse

> Behold, I send My messenger, and he will prepare the way before Me… Malachi 3:1a

Lesson

Remember how the prophets told the people of Israel and Judah that they would be conquered by Assyria and Babylon? When everything happened just as the prophets said it would, the people knew the prophets had truly been sent by God.

These same prophets wrote about the coming of the Savior hundreds of years before He arrived. They also wrote about other events that would take place thousands of years from then.

Of course, the prophets were always careful to write exactly what God told them to write. And do you know what? Every detail the prophets wrote about the Savior came true. For this reason, you can be sure that everything the prophets foretold about events that are still in the future will most certainly happen, just like the Bible says.

Everything the prophets wrote before the Savior came to Earth is found in the Old Testament part of the Bible. The last prophet who wrote about the Savior's coming was Malachi. Malachi is the last book in the Old Testament.

Malachi was quoting God's words when he wrote the following verse:

Behold, I send My messenger, and he will prepare the way before Me… Malachi 3:1a

God said He was sending a messenger to prepare the way for *Him*. This meant that God Himself was coming to Earth to be the promised Savior!

After God spoke to Malachi, He did not speak to another prophet for four hundred years. It was not until after the arrival of the Savior that God once again chose prophets to write for Him.

The books the prophets wrote after the Savior came to Earth are found in the New Testament part of the Bible.

The third book in the New Testament is called Luke and was written by a doctor named Luke. Doctor Luke wrote about the messenger Malachi predicted would come to prepare the way for God. This is what Dr. Luke wrote:

> There was in the days of Herod, the king of Judea, a certain priest named Zacharias...His wife was...Elizabeth...they were both righteous before God...But they had no child...and they were both well advanced in years.
>
> So it was, that while he was serving as priest...he went into the temple of the Lord...Then an angel of the Lord appeared to him...And when Zacharias saw him, he was troubled....
>
> But the angel said to him, "Do not be afraid, Zacharias, for your prayer is heard; and your wife Elizabeth will bear you a son, and you shall call his name John...he will turn many of the children of Israel to the Lord their God. He will also go before Him...to make ready a people prepared for the Lord."
>
> And Zacharias said to the angel, "How shall I know this? For I am an old man, and my wife is well advanced in years."
>
> And the angel answered and said to him, "I am Gabriel, who stands in the presence of God, and was sent to speak to you and bring you these glad tidings. ...behold, you will be mute and not able to speak until the day these things take place, because you did not believe my words which will be fulfilled in their own time." Luke 1:5-20

Zacharias was a priest who worked at the temple. The Bible says that Zacharias and Elizabeth were "both righteous before God." Zacharias and Elizabeth were sinners just like everyone else, but God made them acceptable to Him because they believed in Him. Zacharias and Elizabeth had trusted in God to save them from the death penalty they deserved for their sin. That is why God called them "righteous."

Zacharias and Elizabeth were like Abraham and Sarah; they had never been able to have a baby, and now they were old.

Then one day while Zacharias was working as a priest in the temple, an angel appeared to him. The angel's name was Gabriel. Gabriel told Zacharias that God was going to give him and Elizabeth a son.

God is the One who gives life, isn't He? God made Adam out of the dust of the ground. He made Eve out of Adam's rib. He gave Abraham and Sarah a baby when Abraham was 100 years old and Sarah 90. Nothing is too hard for God. He could easily give Zacharias and Elizabeth a baby.

But Zacharias did not believe the angel's message; he did not believe God could give Elizabeth and him a baby in their old age. Because Zacharias did not believe God, the angel said he would not be able to speak until after the baby was born.

And even though the custom in those days was to name the oldest boy in the family after his dad, the angel told Zacharias that when the baby was born, they were to name him John.

God had a special plan for John; John was going to "make ready a people prepared for the Lord." John was the messenger the prophet Malachi had written about four hundred years earlier; he was the messenger who would get the Israelites ready for God's coming.

Remember

Zacharias should have believed God. The only way to please God is to believe Him.

But without faith it is impossible to please Him…Hebrews 11:6

God can do anything. Nothing is too hard for Him! And God always tells the truth. No matter what happens, God always does what He says He will.

You can always depend on God!

Questions

1. Did the prophets tell the truth when they said Israel and Judah would be taken captive by their enemies? *Yes, they did.*

2. Who told the prophets what would happen in the future? *God did. God knows what will happen in the future.*

3. Were the prophets careful to write down exactly what God said, or did they write some of their own ideas in the Bible? *The prophets were careful to write exactly what God told them to write.*

4. Did everything the prophets wrote in the Old Testament about the Savior come true? *Yes, everything God told the prophets to write about the coming Savior came true.*

5. Who did the prophet Malachi say was coming to Earth? *He said God was coming to Earth!*

6. Who did Zacharias and Elizabeth believe was the only One who could save them from the death penalty they deserved for their sin? *They believed only God could save them from the death penalty they deserved.*

7. What did the angel Gabriel say to Zacharias? *He told Zacharias God was going to give Elizabeth and him a baby boy.*

8. Why should Zacharias have believed God? *Zacharias should have believed God because first of all, God never tells a lie; and secondly, nothing is too hard for God. He can do anything*!

9. What did God tell Zacharias and Elizabeth to name their baby? *He said to name him John.*

10. What was God's plan for John? *God planned for John to be the messenger who would prepare the Israelites for God's coming.*

Biblical Worldviews

- God is a personal being; He communicates with people.
- God knows the future.
- God will do everything He says He will do.
- God is a God of love; He Himself was coming to Earth as the Savior!
- Angels are God's messengers; they do whatever God sends them to do.
- God is the One who gives life.
- God is all-powerful; He can do anything.
- All people are sinners.
- The only way to please God is to believe Him.

Activity 1: Memory Verse Ball

Supplies:

- One or more mid-size balls
- Copy of memory verse: "Behold, I send My messenger, and he will prepare the way before Me…" Malachi 3:1a

Instructions:

- Depending on the number of students, students either divide into teams or form one large circle.
- Students then practice the memory verse while throwing the ball to each other and catching it.
- For example: The teacher says the first part of the verse to be memorized. Then she throws the ball to one of the students, who repeats word for word what she just said and throws the ball to another student. Go around until everyone has had a chance to catch the ball

and say the first part of the verse. Now add the second part of the verse and do the same thing. Then add the third part and so on until each student has memorized the entire verse, including the reference.

-   If students have been working in small groups, they now come together to form a large circle and each one recites the verse and reference in front of the entire class with or without the balls.

Activity 2: Zacharias Skit

Supplies:

-   Two volunteers to play the part of Zacharias and the angel

Instructions:

-   Divide the class into groups of two.
-   Groups take turns acting out the interaction between Zacharias and the angel.

Extra Bible References

Psalm 115:3; Isaiah 40:3; Matthew 25:34; Ephesians 1:4; 1 Peter 1:20

50
Immanuel: God with Us
Gabriel Appears to Mary

Memory Verse

"Behold, the virgin shall be with child, and bear a Son, and they shall call His name Immanuel," which is translated, "God with us." Matthew 1:23

Lesson

After Elizabeth became pregnant, the angel Gabriel appeared to Mary, Elizabeth's relative. Mary was engaged to be married to Joseph. Gabriel told Mary that she also was going to have a baby.

Now in the sixth month the angel Gabriel was sent by God to a city of Galilee named Nazareth, to a virgin betrothed to a man whose name was Joseph, of the house of David. The virgin's name was Mary...

Then the angel said to her, "Do not be afraid, Mary...behold, you will conceive in your womb and bring forth a Son, and shall call His name JESUS. He will be great, and will be called the Son of the Highest; and the Lord God will give Him the throne of His father David. And He will reign over the house of Jacob forever, and of His kingdom there will be no end."

Then Mary said to the angel, "How can this be, since I do not know a man?"

And the angel answered and said to her, "The Holy Spirit will come upon you, and the power of the Highest will overshadow you; therefore, also, that Holy One who is to be born will be called the Son of God. Now indeed, Elizabeth your relative has also conceived a son in her old age; and this is now the sixth month for her...For with God nothing will be impossible."

Then Mary said, "Behold the maidservant of the Lord! Let it be to me according to your word." And the angel departed from her.
Luke 1:26-38

353

Mary was a virgin; she had never lived with a man. How could she possibly have a baby? The angel said God the Holy Spirit would place this baby inside her. The baby would be called "the Son of God." How incredible! God the Son was going to become a tiny baby and be born into the world in the same way all human babies are born.

Remember what the prophet Malachi wrote? He said God was coming to Earth. The prophet Isaiah said the same thing.

...Behold, the virgin shall conceive and bear a Son, and shall call His name Immanuel. Isaiah 7:14b

Hundreds of years before the angel appeared to Mary, Isaiah the prophet foretold that a virgin would have a Son who would be called Immanuel. Immanuel means **God with us**.

"Behold, the virgin shall be with child, and bear a Son, and they shall call His name Immanuel," which is translated, "God with us." Matthew 1:23

The angel said for Mary to name her Son Jesus. The name Jesus means **Savior**. Not only would Mary's Son be "God with us," He would also be the Savior. What wonderful news! God Himself was coming to Earth to rescue mankind from Satan and death.

Mary's Son Jesus would be completely God and completely human at the same time. Jesus was going to be like you and me in every way except that He would never do, or even think, anything wrong. Jesus would be completely perfect.

When Adam joined Satan's side in the Garden of Eden, he became sinful on the inside and was no longer able to please God. Since Cain and Abel were born into Adam's family, they were born with a sinful nature, too, just like their dad.

Ever since Adam passed his sinful nature on to Cain and Abel, every dad has passed that same sinful nature on to his children. That is why everyone is a sinner. Even Mary, the mother of Jesus, was born a sinner.

Therefore, just as through one man sin entered the world... Romans 5:12a

But Jesus would be different. Since God the Holy Spirit was going to place Jesus inside Mary before she and Joseph were married, Joseph's sinful nature would not be passed on to Jesus.

Jesus is the only Person ever who would *not* be born into Adam's family. Jesus would not be born a sinner like everyone else.

This was God's plan. Jesus, the Savior, had to be sinless because only a perfect Savior could save mankind from the death penalty and make us acceptable to God.

Jesus would also be the Christ, or Messiah, meaning He would be God's **Chosen One**.

> ...but these are written that you may believe that Jesus is the Christ, the Son of God... John 20:31a

From the beginning, God chose Jesus for three special jobs.

> The baby God was going to give to Mary would have many names.
>
> He would be called Jesus. Jesus means Savior.
>
> He would be called Immanuel. Immanuel means God with us.
>
> He would also be the Christ, or the Messiah. Christ and Messiah mean the same thing. Messiah is the Hebrew word used in the Old Testament. Christ is the Greek word used in the New Testament. Both names mean Chosen One.

First of all, Jesus would be God's **prophet**. Just like the prophets of old, Jesus would explain God's words to people; He would be God's messenger to people on Earth.

> I will raise up for them a Prophet...and will put My words in His mouth, and He shall speak to them all that I command Him. Deuteronomy 18:18

Secondly, Jesus would be a **priest**. Remember how once a year the High Priest went into God's presence behind the veil in the tabernacle with the blood of an animal sacrifice so that God could forgive the sins of the Israelites? Well, Jesus was going to be the last High Priest ever to offer the blood of a sacrifice to God.

> ...even Jesus, having become High Priest forever... Hebrews 6:20

Lastly, Jesus Christ was going to be a **king** from King David's family line and rule over Israel and the over the world forever.

> ...and the Lord God will give Him the throne of His father David. And He will reign over the house of Jacob forever, and of His kingdom there will be no end. Luke 1:32b, 33

After Jesus was born, Mary and Joseph were married and Joseph became Jesus' earthly dad.

📖 Jesus of Nazareth, the son of Joseph. John 1:45b

Since Joseph and Mary were both from King David's family line, their Son Jesus was also going to be from King David's family line.

📖 Joseph...was of the house and lineage of David, Luke 2:4

Remember

Before Adam and Eve sinned in the Garden of Eden, God had already chosen His Son to be the Savior who would rescue mankind from Satan, sin, and death. God always does everything He plans to do; He always completes what He starts.

All through the years, God was working out His plan. He chose Abraham to become the father of the nation of Israel. God said the Savior would come from this nation. Later God promised King David that the Savior would come from his family line and rule as king forever.

The Old Testament prophets foretold many more details about the coming Savior.

Now the angel Gabriel appeared to Mary to tell her that she was the woman who would give birth to the Child who would bruise Satan's head.

📖 He indeed was foreordained before the foundation of the world, but was manifest in these last times for you... 1 Peter 1:20

Questions

1. Who did the angel Gabriel appear to this time? *He appeared to Elizabeth's relative, Mary.*

2. What did Gabriel tell Mary? *He told her she would have a baby who would be called the Son of God.*

3. What does the name Jesus mean? *It means Savior.*

4. What had the prophet Isaiah predicted about the virgin hundreds of years earlier? *He predicted that a virgin (a woman who had never been married) would have a Son whose name would be Immanuel.*

5. What does the name Immanuel mean? *It means God with us.*

6. How would the baby Jesus be different from every other person born into the world? *Since Jesus was not going to have a human father, He would not be born into Adam's family. Jesus would not have a sin nature; He would be completely perfect.*

7. Could an imperfect Savior rescue you and me from Satan's dominion and from the death penalty we deserve for our sin? *No! Only a perfect Savior could save us.*

8. What does the name Christ (or Messiah) mean? *It means Jesus would be God's Chosen One.*

9. What were the three special jobs God planned for the Messiah, Jesus, to do? *Jesus was going to be a prophet, a priest, and a king.*

10. From the very beginning, who did God plan to send to Earth to rescue us from Satan and make us acceptable to Him? *From the beginning, God planned that He Himself would come to Earth as the Savior.*

Biblical Worldviews

- God is a personal being; He communicates with people.
- Angels are God's messengers; they do what God sends them to do.
- There is only one God who exists as God the Father, God the Holy Spirit, and God the Son.
- God is the One in charge of the world; no one is greater than God.
- God works everything out according to His plan.
- God can do anything; nothing is too hard for Him.
- God is a God of love; He Himself was coming to Earth as the Savior.
- Jesus Christ is God; Jesus is perfect.
- Jesus Christ is a human being.
- All people are sinners.
- Only Jesus Christ the Savior can save us.

Activity: Jesus Christ, the Chosen One of God

Supplies:

- Paper, one sheet per student
- Pencils, crayons, markers

Instructions:

- Students title their papers: Jesus Christ the Messiah.
- Students divide their papers into three parts.
- Label one part **Prophet**, one part **Priest**, and one part **King.**
- Under the heading **Prophet**, students draw a man telling people the words of God.
- Under the heading **Priest**, they draw a picture of a priest making a sacrifice.
- And under the title **King**, they draw a king.
- Discuss: The coming Savior was going to be all three: a prophet, a priest, and a king.

Extra Bible References

Genesis 3:15, 12:3; Deuteronomy 18:15, 18; 1 Chronicles 17:11-14; Psalm 33:11;
Psalm 89:3-4; Isaiah 9:7; 43:10, 11; 45:21-22; Matthew 1:1-18, 2:2, 16:16, 27:37;
Mark 1:1; Luke 3:23-38, 4:16-21; John 1:1-16, 41; 3:16; 4:25-26; Acts 2:30; 3:22-23;
Acts 4:12, 7:37; Romans 1:3, 5:12-19; 1 Corinthians 2:7; Galatians 4:4;
Colossians 2:9; 1 Timothy 2:5; 2 Timothy 2:7; Hebrews 1:1-4, 6:19-20, 7:20-28;
1 Peter 1:20; Revelation 19:16

51
A Preacher in the Desert
John the Baptist

Memory Verse

For there is born to you this day in the city of David a Savior, who is Christ the Lord.
Luke 2:11

Lesson

Remember how God told Zacharias that he and Elizabeth would have a baby? Zacharias did not believe God; he thought he and Elizabeth were too old to have a baby. But God always does what He says. Nothing is too hard for Him. Zacharias and Elizabeth did have a baby just like God said they would.

Now Elizabeth's full time came...and she brought forth a son. When her neighbors and relatives heard how the Lord had shown great mercy to her, they rejoiced with her.

...and they would have called him by the name of his father, Zacharias. His mother answered and said, "No; he shall be called John."

But they said to her, "There is no one among your relatives who is called by this name." So they made signs to his father—what he would have him called.

And he asked for a writing tablet, and wrote, saying, "His name is John." ...Immediately his mouth was opened and his tongue loosed, and he spoke, praising God...And all those who heard...kept...saying,"What kind of child will this be?"...

Now his father Zacharias was filled with the Holy Spirit, and prophesied, saying: "Blessed is the Lord God of Israel, for He has... raised up a horn of salvation for us in the house of His servant David, as He spoke by the mouth of His holy prophets...to remember...the oath which He swore to our father Abraham...

"And you, child, will be called the prophet of the Highest..."
Luke 1:57-64, 67-76

After baby John was born, God allowed Zacharias to speak again. Zacharias praised God and prophesied.

Zacharias was speaking God's words when he announced that the Savior the prophets wrote about would soon be born into King David's family. God's promise to Abraham was about to be fulfilled. In just a short while, the One who would bring God's kindness and help to all the families of the world would arrive.

Zacharias said that the child born to them would be "the prophet of the Highest." John was going to be God's prophet - he was going to speak God's words to the Jews so they could get ready for the Savior's coming. Baby John was the messenger the Old Testament prophets said would prepare the way for God.

"Behold, I send My messenger, and he will prepare the way before Me..." Malachi 3:1a

When John grew up, he lived in a desert place outside Jerusalem. The people called him "John the Baptist." Out in the desert, John the Baptist preached God's message. Many people in Israel came to hear him.

In those days John the Baptist came, preaching in the wilderness of Judea, and saying, "Repent, for the kingdom of heaven is at hand!" For this is he who was spoken of by the prophet Isaiah, saying: "The voice of one crying in the wilderness: Prepare the way of the Lord; make His paths straight.'" Matthew 3:1-3

> **Repent** – to have a change of mind, or to begin to think differently

Hundreds of years earlier, the prophet Isaiah foretold that God's messenger would live in the wilderness, where he would preach to the people and prepare them for the Savior's coming.

> The voice of one crying in the wilderness: "Prepare the way of the LORD..." Isaiah 40:3

Remember that most of the Jews were *not* waiting expectantly for the promised Savior. All through the Old Testament, Moses and the prophets wrote about the coming Savior and King, but the Jews were not interested. It was as though they were asleep. They needed John to wake them up.

Most of the Jews did not think they needed a Savior. They thought they were acceptable to God because they came from Abraham and tried to keep God's commands. The Israelites thought they were God's friends and would most certainly go to Heaven when they died.

John warned the Jews to repent; they needed to change their thinking. They needed to understand that they were not acceptable to God. They needed to see that they were sinners separated from God and that only the Savior could save them from their sin and make them acceptable to God.

If the Jews did not have a change of thinking, they would not be ready to trust in Jesus Christ to save them, and they would not be able to enter God's kingdom.

Some of the Jews listened to John and admitted they were sinners.

The Jews who agreed with John about their sinful condition and their need for a Savior were baptized by him in the Jordan River. When they were baptized they were dipped under water and then raised up again. Being baptized did not wash away people's sin or make them pleasing to God; it was simply a way for the Jews to show they agreed with John's teaching.

Now John himself was clothed in camel's hair, with a leather belt around his waist; and his food was locusts and wild honey.

Then Jerusalem, all Judea, and all the region around the Jordan went out to him and were baptized by him in the Jordan, confessing their sins. Matthew 3:4-6

Not all the Jews admitted they were sinners. Most of the religious leaders disagreed with John.

But when he saw many of the Pharisees and Sadducees coming to his baptism, he said to them: "Brood of vipers! Who warned you to flee from the wrath to come?" Matthew 3:7

There were three groups of religious leaders in Israel: the Pharisees, the Scribes, and the Sadducees.

The **Pharisees** added rules to the ones God gave Moses. This gave them a lot of rules to follow. They thought that having so many rules made them better than other people.

The **Scribes** were called the teachers of the law. They were the ones who made copies of the Old Testament - the writings of Moses and the prophets. The scribes knew what was written in the Bible, but they did not understand it.

The **Sadducees** did not care a lot about God; they did not believe all of the Bible was true. Mostly, the Sadducees were interested in keeping their positions of leadership in Israel. They tried hard to please the Roman government.

The Pharisees, Sadducees, and Scribes all worshiped at the temple. They acted religious, but in their hearts they disagreed with God. They thought that being part of Abraham's family made them acceptable to God. They thought they were especially important because they were the religious leaders of Israel.

When the religious leaders came to John, he asked them, "Who warned you to flee from the coming wrath?" Wrath is anger. God is angry about sin; He says the penalty for sin is death.

For the wrath of God is revealed from heaven against all ungodliness and unrighteousness of men… Romans 1:18a

John knew the religious leaders did not believe they were separated from God. They did not believe God was angry about their sin. So then why did they come to hear him speak?

John called the religious leaders a "brood of vipers" because they were like snakes, poisoning the people of Israel with lies. They taught the Jews they were already acceptable to God. This made the people think they did not need a Savior.

Of course, Satan was behind it all. Just like he led Adam and Eve to believe they would not die if they went against what God said, he was leading the Jews to believe they would not die for their sin either.

Satan is a liar and a murderer. He did not want the Jews to believe the truth because he did not want them to trust in the Savior to save them. Satan wanted the Jews to remain separated from God forever.

Remember

Just like God wanted the Jews to change their thinking (repent), God wants you to change the way you think. God does not want you to try to make yourself acceptable to Him by doing good works, going to church, or being baptized. God does not want you to try to pay for your own sin.

No, God wants you simply to trust in Him to save you. You need to understand that God is perfect and pure and that your sin separates you from Him. There is nothing you can do to make yourself acceptable to God, nor is there anything you can do to pay for your sin. Only the Savior can save you from death and make you acceptable to God.

Believe in Him!

The Lord is…not willing that any should perish but that all should come to repentance. 2 Peter 3:9

Questions

1. Did God give Zacharias and Elizabeth a baby like the angel said He would? *Yes, God always does what He says He will do. Nothing is too hard for Him.*

2. What happened to Zacharias when he wrote the baby's name on the tablet of paper? *He was able to speak again.*

3. What did John tell the people of Israel to do in order to get ready for the coming of the Savior? *He told them to change their minds and believe the truth. The Jews needed to believe they were sinners separated from God so that they would be ready to trust in the Savior when He came.*

4. Did getting baptized in water make the Jews acceptable to God? *No, being baptized was simply a way for them to show they agreed with John's message.*

5. Who were the three groups of religious leaders in Israel? *They were the Pharisees, the Sadducees, and the Scribes.*

6. Why did John call the religious leaders a "brood of vipers"? *John called the religious leaders a bunch of snakes because of their poisonous teaching. If the Jews believed what the religious leaders told them, they would end up being separated from God forever in the terrible place of suffering.*

7. How does God feel about sin? *God hates sin; sin makes God angry. The penalty for sin is separation from God forever in the terrible place of suffering.*

8. What does God want you to change your mind about? *God wants you to believe you are a sinner separated from Him and that there is nothing you can do to save yourself. God wants you to believe that He is the only One who can rescue you from death and make you acceptable to Him.*

9. What will happen to those who do not trust in the Savior to save them? *Those who do not trust in the Savior to save them will be separated from God forever.*

Biblical Worldviews

- God is a personal being; He communicates with people.
- God can do anything; nothing is too hard for Him.
- God is the One who gives life.
- God always does what He says He will do; He completes His plans and keeps His promises.
- All people are sinners separated from God and unable to please God.
- God is perfect and pure; sin makes God angry.

- The penalty for sin is death.
- We cannot save ourselves. Only God can save us.
- God is a God of love; He does not want anyone to be separated from Him.
- God sent His Son Jesus to be the Savior.
- God saves only those who believe Him.
- Those who do not believe God will be separated from Him forever in the terrible place of suffering.
- Satan is a liar and a murderer.

Activity: Meaning of Repent

Supplies:

- Paper, one sheet per student
- Pencils, crayons, markers
- Stickers, etc.

Instructions:

- Students write" repent = change your mind" on their papers and decorate them in any way they like.
- Discuss: About what does God want people to change their minds? What did the Israelites need to change their minds about so that they would be ready to trust in the Savior when He came?

Extra Bible References

Psalm 5:4-5; Matthew 11:8; John 1:6-28, 8:44, 16:5-11; Acts 19:3-4; Romans 2:5; Ephesians 2:1-3; Colossians 1:15-17; 1 Timothy 2:4

52
Good News for Everyone
The Birth of Jesus

Memory Verse

For there is born to you this day in the city of David a Savior, who is Christ the Lord.
Luke 2:11

Lesson

Not long after baby John was born to Elizabeth and Zacharias, baby Jesus was born in Bethlehem.

Before Mary gave birth, the emperor of Rome made a law that everyone in the land had to be registered. Being registered meant having your name recorded on a list. The emperor wanted a list of everyone in his empire.

In order to be registered, the Israelites were required to return to the city of their ancestors. Since Joseph was from King David's family line, he and Mary went to the city of David, which was Bethlehem, to be registered there.

And it came to pass in those days that a decree went out from Caesar Augustus that all the world should be registered...So all went to be registered, everyone to his own city.

Joseph also went up from Galilee, out of the city of Nazareth, into Judea, to the city of David, which is called Bethlehem, because he was of the house and lineage of David, to be registered with Mary, his betrothed wife, who was with child. So it was, that while they were there, the days were completed for her to be delivered. And she brought forth her firstborn Son, and wrapped Him in swaddling cloths, and laid Him in a manger, because there was no room for them in the inn. Luke 2:1-7

While they were in Bethlehem, the time came for Mary to give birth. Since all the motels were full because of the registration, the only place for Mary and Joseph to spend the night was in a barn. That night, in a lonely, dirty barn, God the Son, the Creator of the world, was born into the world He had created! But no one, except Mary and Joseph, were there to celebrate.

Since no one in Israel realized what a wonderful event had just taken place, God sent an angel to make the announcement to some shepherds who were watching their sheep in the fields near Bethlehem.

Now there were in the same country shepherds living out in the fields, keeping watch over their flock by night. And behold, an angel of the Lord stood before them, and the glory of the Lord shone around them, and they were greatly afraid.

Then the angel said to them, "Do not be afraid, for behold, I bring you good tidings of great joy which will be to all people. For there is born to you this day in the city of David a Savior, who is Christ the Lord. And this will be the sign to you: You will find a Babe wrapped in swaddling cloths, lying in a manger."

And suddenly there was with the angel a multitude of the heavenly host praising God and saying: "Glory to God in the highest, and on earth peace, goodwill toward men!" Luke 2:8-14

When the night sky suddenly lit up with the dazzling light of God's glory, the shepherds were afraid. But the angel brought good news; there was nothing to be afraid of. That very day, in the city of Bethlehem, the Savior, who would bring God's kindness and help to all people, had been born! The shepherds would find Him wrapped in cloths, lying in a feeding-box in a barn.

Suddenly, a great multitude of angels appeared. They praised God for His wonderful kindness to mankind. Then the angels returned to Heaven, and the shepherds hurried to find the newborn baby.

So it was, when the angels had gone away from them into heaven, that the shepherds said to one another, "Let us now go to Bethlehem and see this thing that has come to pass, which the Lord has made known to us." And they came with haste and found Mary and Joseph, and the Babe lying in a manger. Luke 2:15-16

Meanwhile, in a far-off eastern land, some wise men became aware of an unusual star. Somehow they understood that this star meant that the King of the Jews had been born, so they set off on a long journey to find Him.

Now after Jesus was born in Bethlehem of Judea in the days of Herod the king, behold, wise men from the East came to Jerusalem, saying, "Where is He who has been born King of the Jews? For we have seen His star in the East and have come to worship Him."

When Herod the king heard this, he was troubled...And when he had gathered all the chief priests and scribes of the people together, he inquired of them where the Christ was to be born.

So they said to him, "In Bethlehem of Judea, for thus it is written by the prophet: 'But you, Bethlehem, in the land of Judah, are not the least among the rulers of Judah; for out of you shall come a Ruler who will shepherd My people Israel.'" Matthew 2:1-6

The "king of the Jews" was Jesus, the promised Savior the prophets foretold in the Old Testament. Herod was upset by what the wise men said. He did not want another king to replace him. He called for the scribes so they could explain to him what the prophets had foretold about where this king would be born.

The scribes were the ones who made copies of the Old Testament; they knew what the Bible said. They knew the Savior and King of Israel would be born in Bethlehem.

Then Herod, when he had secretly called the wise men, determined from them what time the star appeared. And he sent them to Bethlehem and said, "Go and search carefully for the young Child, and when you have found Him, bring back word to me, that I may come and worship Him also."

When they heard the king, they departed; and behold, the star which they had seen in the East went before them, till it came and stood over where the young Child was. When they saw the star, they rejoiced with exceedingly great joy. And when they had come into the house, they saw the young Child with Mary His mother, and fell down and worshiped Him. And when they had opened their treasures, they presented gifts to Him: gold, frankincense, and myrrh.

Then, being divinely warned in a dream that they should not return to Herod, they departed for their own country another way.

Now when they had departed, behold, an angel of the Lord appeared to Joseph in a dream, saying, "Arise, take the young Child and His mother, flee to Egypt, and stay there until I bring you word; for Herod will seek the young Child to destroy Him."

When he arose, he took the young Child and His mother by night and departed for Egypt, and was there until the death of Herod, that it might be fulfilled which was spoken by the Lord through the prophet, saying, "Out of Egypt I called My Son."

Then Herod, when he saw that he was deceived by the wise men, was exceedingly angry; and he sent forth and put to death all the male children who were in Bethlehem and in all its districts, from two years old and under, according to the time which he had determined from the wise men. Matthew 2:7-16

King Herod might have tricked the wise men, but he could not trick God. God knew King Herod planned to kill baby Jesus, so He warned the wise men not to return to Jerusalem.

When Herod finally realized that the wise men were not coming back, he sent soldiers to Bethlehem to kill all baby boys two years old and younger. Of course, by the time the soldiers arrived, Mary, Joseph, and Jesus had fled to Egypt.

King Herod was led by Satan. In the Garden of Eden God had said that someday Satan would try to destroy the Savior.

Satan did not want the Savior to rescue people from his dominion. But Satan could not stop God's plan. God is a lot more powerful than Satan.

Hundreds of years earlier, God foretold through the prophets many details of Jesus' life on Earth. The prophet Micah prophesied that Israel's king would be the everlasting God and that He would be born in Bethlehem.

What the prophet Micah prophesied:

But you, Bethlehem Ephrathah, though you are little among the thousands of Judah, yet out of you shall come forth to Me the One to be Ruler in Israel, whose goings forth are from of old, from everlasting. Micah 5:2

What the prophet Hosea wrote:

"...And out of Egypt I called My son." Hosea 11:1

What the prophet Jeremiah wrote:

Thus says the LORD: "A voice was heard in Ramah, lamentation and bitter weeping, Rachel weeping for her children, refusing to be comforted for her children, because they are no more." Jeremiah 31:15

The prophet Hosea prophesied that God's Son would go to Egypt; and the prophet Jeremiah foretold that at Jesus' birth many baby boys would be killed.

God was in control of Jesus' life. Everything the prophets said would happen came to pass exactly as the prophets had said it would. Nothing happened to Jesus that God the Father did not know about or allow.

After King Herod died, God told Joseph to take Jesus back to Israel.

Now when Herod was dead, behold, an angel of the Lord appeared in a dream to Joseph in Egypt, saying, "Arise, take the young Child and His mother, and go to the land of Israel, for those who sought the young Child's life are dead." Then he arose, took the young Child and His mother, and came into the land of Israel. Matthew 2:19-21

When Mary and Joseph returned to Israel, they moved back to their hometown of Nazareth. Here Joseph worked as a carpenter, and more children were added to their family.

So...they returned to Galilee, to their own city, Nazareth. And the Child grew and became strong in spirit, filled with wisdom; and the grace of God was upon Him. Luke 2:39-40

Jesus grew up in Nazareth and became a carpenter like his dad.

Is this not the carpenter, the Son of Mary, and brother of James, Joses, Judas, and Simon? And are not His sisters here with us? Mark 6:3a

The Bible says Jesus was a kind and wise child. Of course, since Jesus is God, He never did anything wrong. He was never mean to other kids, nor did He ever tell a lie. Jesus always happily did whatever His parents asked him to do. Even as a young man, He was perfect and good in all His ways!

Questions

1. Why did Joseph and Mary go to Bethlehem? *They went to Bethlehem because of the new law that required everyone to be registered in the town of his or her family line.*

2. Whose family line was Joseph from? *He was from King David's family line.*

3. What important event happened while Joseph and Mary were in Bethlehem? *The most important event in all of history: Jesus Christ, God the Son, was born into the world.*

4. Were the people of Israel waiting for the Savior to be born? *No, they were not. They thought they were already accepted by God. They did not think they needed the Savior to save them from sin and death and make them acceptable to God.*

5. Who told the shepherds about the Savior's birth? *An angel announced Jesus' birth to the shepherds.*

6. Was baby Jesus, God the Son, born in a hospital? *No, He was born in a barn. His bed was an animal feeding box.*

7. How did the scribes know where the King of the Jews was to be born? *They knew what the Old Testament said. The prophet Micah foretold that the Christ would be born in Bethlehem.*

8. Was King Herod happy that a king was born in Bethlehem? *No, he did not want another king to replace him.*

9. What did King Herod do to all the babies around Bethlehem? *He had all the babies, two years old and under, killed.*

10. How did baby Jesus escape being killed by Herod's soldiers? *God warned the wise men in a dream not to go back to King Herod. God also warned Joseph. He told him to take the baby and escape to Egypt.*

11. Did God know Satan would try to hurt Jesus? *Yes, in the Garden of Eden God had said that Satan would bruise the heel of the woman's Child. In the same way a snake strikes its prey to cause its death Satan would try to kill Jesus.*

12. Did everything the prophets predicted about Jesus come to pass? *Yes, everything happened just the way the prophets said it would.*

13. Who was in control of Jesus' life? *God was. Nothing happened to Jesus that God did not know about or allow.*

14. Where did Jesus grow up? *Jesus grew up in a town called Nazareth in Israel.*

15. Did Jesus ever do anything wrong when He was growing up? *No, He never did anything bad. He was always good.*

Biblical Worldviews

- God is a personal being; He communicates with people.
- God has a plan for the world; He works everything out according to His plan.
- God is a God of love; He Himself came to rescue us from sin and death and make us acceptable to God.
- God knows everything; He knows what people are thinking and He knows what will happen in the future.
- God is the highest authority; He is in control of everything that happens.

- Satan is a murderer; He did not want the Savior to rescue mankind from death.
- Satan cannot defeat God.
- Jesus Christ is perfect.
- Jesus Christ was completely God and completely human at the same time.
- All people are sinners.

Activity: Manger Scene Drawing

Supplies:

- Pencil, colored pencils, and crayons
- Paper, one sheet per student
- Star stickers, optional

Instructions:

- Students draw and color a picture of the manger scene.
- Or, they can draw a picture of the home in Bethlehem where Jesus lived as a baby and place a star (or draw one) above the home.
- Students write the memory verse on their pictures.

Extra Bible References

Genesis 3:15; Matthew 13:55; Luke 1:39-56; Hebrews 1:6

53
God's Lamb
Jesus Baptized by John

Memory Verse

The next day John saw Jesus coming toward him, and said, "Behold! The Lamb of God who takes away the sin of the world!" John 1:29

Lesson

When Jesus was about thirty years old, He left His home in Nazareth, Galilee to begin the work God sent Him to do.

Now Jesus Himself began His ministry at about thirty years of age... Luke 3:23a

The first thing Jesus did was go to the wilderness of Judea where John the Baptist was teaching and baptizing.

Then Jesus came from Galilee to John at the Jordan to be baptized by him... When He had been baptized, Jesus came up immediately from the water; and behold, the heavens were opened to Him, and He saw the Spirit of God descending like a dove and alighting upon Him. And suddenly a voice came from heaven, saying, "This is My beloved Son, in whom I am well pleased." Matthew 3:13, 16-17

Jesus wanted John to baptize Him because He wanted the people of Israel to see that He agreed with John's teaching.

When Jesus came up out of the water, God the Holy Spirit came to be with Him. Even though Jesus was God, He was also totally human. As a human being, Jesus chose to depend on the Holy Spirit. God the Holy Spirit was going to give God the Son the power and wisdom He needed to do the work God the Father had planned for Him to do on Earth.

As God the Holy Spirit came down on Jesus, God the Father spoke from Heaven announcing that Jesus was His Son. God the Father said He loved Jesus and was pleased with Him.

You and I are born sinners. We are not born pleasing to God, but Jesus was completely perfect; He did not have any sin. That is why God the Father was pleased with Him. Jesus was acceptable to God.

As a human being, Jesus looked just like any other man. But when John saw God the Holy Spirit come down from Heaven and remain on Him, John knew Jesus was the promised Savior and announced to the Jews that Jesus was, "The Lamb of God who takes away the sin of the world!"

...John saw Jesus coming toward him, and said, "Behold! The Lamb of God who takes away the sin of the world!"

And John bore witness, saying, "I saw the Spirit descending from heaven like a dove, and He remained upon Him. I did not know Him, but He who sent me to baptize with water said to me, 'Upon whom you see the Spirit descending, and remaining on Him, this is He...' And I have seen and testified that this is the Son of God." John 1:29, 32-34

The Jews knew all about lambs. They knew that throughout history, all the way from Cain and Abel till the present, the only way for a person to approach God was through the sacrifice of a perfect lamb. They remembered how their forefathers had sprinkled the blood of the lamb on the doorframes of their homes to save their firstborn sons from death in Egypt. Everyone knew about Abraham and Isaac and how God had provided a perfect ram (male sheep) to die in Isaac's place.

Then Abraham lifted his eyes and looked, and there behind him was a ram caught in a thicket by its horns. So Abraham went and took the ram, and offered it up for a burnt offering instead of his son. Genesis 22:13

The Jews knew about the tabernacle and God's instructions to Moses. God had said that if an Israelite broke one of His commands, he was to bring a perfect lamb to the bronze altar in front of the tabernacle, put his hand on its head, and then cut its throat. In this way, the person who sinned showed that the lamb was taking his death for him. God accepted the death of the lamb in the place of the one who had broken God's law.

In fact, the Jews were still sacrificing lambs on the bronze altar at the temple when Jesus was born. They all understood that the penalty for sin is death and that God accepted the death of the lambs in their place.

The people must have wondered why John called Jesus "the Lamb of God, who takes away the sin of the world." How was Jesus a lamb? And how would He take away the sins of the world?

Remember

Jesus was the Savior the prophets had said would come. Jesus, God the Son, came to Earth to make a way for people to be saved from the death penalty they deserved for their sin.

> For there is not a just man on earth who does good and does not sin. Ecclesiastes 7:20

All people are sinners. No one is pleasing to God. The payment for sin is to be separated from God forever in the terrible place of suffering.

> The soul who sins shall die. Ezekiel 18:4b

But in His very great love, God sent Jesus Christ, the Son of God, to Earth to be your Savior. Jesus came as God's perfect Lamb. He came to take away your sin and rescue you from the death penalty.

Questions

1. Why did Jesus want John the Baptist to baptize Him? *Jesus wanted John to baptize Him to show the Jews that He agreed with John the Baptist's message.*

2. Who came to be with Jesus to give Him strength and wisdom to accomplish God's work on Earth? *God the Holy Spirit came to be with Jesus.*

3. What did God the Father say about Jesus when He came out of the water after John baptized Him? *God the Father said Jesus was His Son whom He loved and that He was pleased with Jesus.*

4. Has any other person ever been pleasing to God like Jesus was? *No, all of us are born separated from God. We are all sinners. The only Person who ever lived a perfect life is Jesus. The only One who has ever been acceptable to God is Jesus.*

5. How did John recognize Jesus as the promised Savior? *John recognized Jesus because God the Father told John that when he saw the Holy Spirit descend and remain on a man, that man would be God the Son, the promised Savior.*

6. Up until now, how could an Israelite who broke God's command be saved from death? *If an Israelite who broke one of God's commands offered a perfect lamb to God as a sacrifice, God would forgive that person's sin. God would accept the death of the lamb in the place of the person who sinned.*

7. What did John the Baptist say about Jesus? *He said Jesus was "the Lamb of God who takes away the sin of the world."*

8. Who did God provide to rescue you from the death penalty you deserve? *God provided the Savior, who is Jesus Christ, God the Son. Jesus Christ is the perfect Lamb of God. He is the only One who can save you from death and make you acceptable to God.*

Biblical Worldviews

- God is a personal God; He communicates with people.
- Jesus Christ is God; Jesus Christ is perfect. Jesus Christ is the only Savior.
- There is only one God who exists as God the Father, God the Son, and God the Holy Spirit.
- All people are born into Adam's family and are sinners separated from God.
- The penalty for sin is death.

Activity: Wall Hanging

Supplies:

- Cardstock or paper, one sheet per student
- Pencils, crayons, markers, hole-punch, yarn or string

Instructions:

- Students write: "Behold! The Lamb of God who takes away the sin of the world!" on a piece of paper, or draw a picture to illustrate this verse.
- Students decorate their papers any way they like.
- Next, punch holes in the pictures and pull yarn through the holes so pictures can by hung.
- Optional: make tassels for hanging the pictures.

Activity 2: Tassel

Supplies:

- Three one-yard long strands of yarn of different colors per student

Instructions:

- Students put all three strands together.
- Then two students work together to help each other make their tassels.
- One student holds one end of the strands and the other holds the other end, taking a few steps back so the strands are taut.
- One of the students twists the strands till they cannot be twisted any more.
- To finish the tassel, students tie off the ends.

Extra Bible References

Isaiah 11:2; John 1:12, 5:18; Acts 16:31

54
Satan Tries to Trick Jesus
Jesus Tempted in the Wilderness

Memory Verse

The next day John saw Jesus coming toward him, and said, "Behold! The Lamb of God who takes away the sin of the world!" John 1:29

Lesson

After Jesus was baptized, God the Holy Spirit led Him into the desert.

Then Jesus, being filled with the Holy Spirit, returned from the Jordan and was led by the Spirit into the wilderness, Luke 4:1

Remember how in the beginning the beautiful angel Lucifer rebelled against God? Lucifer wanted to take God's place so that he could be the one in charge. Many angels followed Lucifer in his rebellion, but of course God would not allow anyone to take His place. God threw Lucifer and his angel followers out of Heaven.

When God threw Lucifer down to Earth, Lucifer's name changed to Satan and his angel followers became demons. Ever since that time, Satan has been God's great enemy. He and his demons always seek to ruin everything God does. The Bible calls Satan a liar and a murderer.

When God first made Adam and Eve, Satan was right there to cause trouble. It seemed like he won a victory against God when Adam and Eve joined his side by believing him instead of God. But God already had a plan. God told Satan that one day the Child of a woman would bruise his head.

That Child was Jesus, God the Son. Jesus came to Earth to rescue people from Satan's dominion. Of course, Satan did everything he could to stop Jesus.

When Satan realized Jesus had been in the wilderness for forty days without food, he saw his chance to ruin God's plan. Just like he persuaded Adam and Eve to believe him instead of God, Satan tried to get Jesus to do what he said instead of what God said.

And when He had fasted forty days and forty nights, afterward He was hungry. Matthew 4:2

Jesus was human. After forty days of not eating, He was very hungry.

Now when the tempter came to Him, he said, "If You are the Son of God, command that these stones become bread." Matthew 4:3

Since Jesus is God, He could easily have turned the stones into bread. But Jesus would not do what Satan told Him to do.

Jesus told Satan that there is something much more important than food, and that is God's Word. Food keeps a person alive for a while, but God's words give everlasting life to all who believe them.

But He answered and said, "It is written, 'Man shall not live by bread alone, but by every word that proceeds from the mouth of God.'" Matthew 4:4

Satan tried once more to get Jesus to obey him.

Then the devil took Him up into the holy city, set Him on the pinnacle of the temple, and said to Him, "If You are the Son of God, throw Yourself down. For it is written: 'He shall give His angels charge over you,' and, 'In their hands they shall bear you up, lest you dash your foot against a stone.'" Matthew 4:5-6

Satan knows what the Bible says. He knew that in the book of Psalms God the Father had promised to send His angels to watch over Jesus during His life on Earth.

> For He shall give His angels charge over you, to keep you in all your ways. In their hands they shall bear you up, lest you dash your foot against a stone. Psalm 91:11-12

Satan dared Jesus to jump down from the roof of the temple. After all, God had promised to send His angels to protect Him. But Jesus would not do what Satan said. He did not need to jump off the temple to prove that God would keep His promise; He believed what God said.

Jesus told Satan that the Bible says not to tempt God.

Jesus said to him, "It is written again, 'You shall not tempt the LORD your God.'" Matthew 4:7

To tempt God means to test God to see if what He says is true. It is wrong to test God. It is wrong to say, "I will only believe God if He does a miracle."

God always tells the truth. He wants people simply to believe what He says without demanding proof. When you believe God, you honor Him; when you doubt what God says, you call Him a liar.

But without faith it is impossible to please Him... Hebrews 11:6

Satan tried for the third time to get Jesus to obey him.

Again, the devil took Him up on an exceedingly high mountain, and showed Him all the kingdoms of the world and their glory. And he said to Him, "All these things I will give You if You will fall down and worship me." Matthew 4:8-9

Although all the kingdoms of the world belong to God, Satan is the ruler of the world right now. When Adam and Eve believed Satan instead of God, they joined Satan's side. Because everyone in the world is born into Adam's family, everyone is born on Satan's side. That makes Satan the one in charge of all people and all kingdoms of the world.

Satan promised to give Jesus all the kingdoms of the world if Jesus would just worship him, but, of course, Jesus would never worship Satan!

Jesus came to bruise Satan's head. God had sent Him to destroy Satan's power. Jesus knew that He would be the king of the world forever. At the right time, God the Father would give the nations to Jesus; He did not need to bow to Satan to get the kingdoms of the world.

...I will give You the nations for Your inheritance, and the ends of the earth for Your possession. Psalm 2:8b

Once again, Jesus told Satan what the Bible says: God is the only One you should worship and obey.

Then Jesus said to him, "Away with you, Satan! For it is written, 'You shall worship the LORD your God, and Him only you shall serve.'" Matthew 4:10

Jesus could tell Satan what to do because Jesus, God the Son, created Lucifer in the beginning. Jesus is the One who threw Lucifer and his followers out of Heaven. And one day Jesus will throw Satan and his demons into the Lake of Fire where they will suffer forever and ever.

The devil, who deceived them, was cast into the lake of fire and brimstone...And...will be tormented day and night forever and ever. Revelation 20:10

Finally Satan left Jesus alone, but only for a time.

Now when the devil had ended every temptation, he departed from Him until an opportune time. Luke 4:13

During Jesus' life on Earth, Satan tried many times to get Him to go against God, but Jesus never obeyed Satan.

...because Christ...committed no sin... 1 Peter 2:21-22

Satan could not tell Jesus what to do; Jesus only ever did what God the Father told Him to do.

And He who sent Me is with Me. The Father has not left Me alone, for I always do those things that please Him." John 8:29

Jesus is the only perfect human being who has ever lived on Earth; He is the only human being who has ever been acceptable to God.

Remember

Satan is a liar and a murderer.

...the devil...was a murderer from the beginning, and does not stand in the truth, because there is no truth in him...for he is a liar and the father of it. John 8:44

Satan only acts like he cares about people so that he can trick them. Satan does not want people to believe God and be saved from his power. He wants to keep his control over people; he wants people to be separated from God forever.

Every time Satan tried to tell Jesus what to do, Jesus told Satan what the Bible says. You need to know what God says in the Bible so that you won't be tricked by Satan. God loves you and always tells the truth! Don't believe Satan's lies.

Your word I have hidden in my heart, that I might not sin against You. Psalm 119:11

Questions

1. Why did Jesus not turn the stones into bread like Satan asked him to do? *Even though Jesus was hungry and had the power to turn the stones into bread, He would never do what Satan told Him to do.*

2. What did Jesus say is more important than food? *Jesus said that the words of God are more important than food.*

3. Why is the Bible more important than food? *The food we eat every day keeps our bodies alive for a time, but through knowing God's Word we can have life that lasts forever.*

4. Why did Satan want Jesus to jump off the roof of the temple? *Long ago in the book of Psalms, God promised to send His angels to protect Jesus. Satan wanted Jesus to prove that God would do what He had said.*

5. Why is it wrong to test God to see if He is telling the truth? *God always tells the truth; He wants you simply to believe Him. If you have to have proof that what God says is true, it shows that you really do not believe God.*

6. Why do the kingdoms of the world belong to Satan? *When Adam and Eve sinned, they joined Satan's side. Since all people come from Adam and Eve, all people are born on Satan's side and are under his dominion.*

7. Who was the Child of a woman who would bruise Satan's head? *Jesus, God the Son, was going to fatally injure Satan so that Satan would lose his control over this world.*

8. Every time Satan tried to get Jesus to do what he said, what did Jesus tell Satan? *He told Satan what God says in the Bible.*

9. Did Jesus ever do what Satan told Him to do? *No, Jesus only ever obeyed God the Father. Jesus never sinned. He was perfect in every way.*

Biblical Worldviews

- God created Lucifer and all the angels; God is greater than Satan.
- Satan is God's enemy; he is a liar and a murderer; he hates people.
- All people are born into Adam's family, and are therefore under Satan's dominion.
- Jesus Christ is God.
- Jesus Christ is a human being.
- Only God gives eternal life.

- God always tells the truth; everything written in the Bible is true.
- The only way to please God is to believe Him.
- Jesus Christ is perfect. He never sinned. He never obeyed Satan.
- Jesus Christ is the only Savior; He came to Earth to rescue mankind from Satan's dominion.
- Someday God will completely defeat Satan, and Jesus will be king of the world forever.

Activity 1: Memory Verse Ball

Supplies:

- One or more mid-size balls
- Copy of memory verse: "The next day John saw Jesus coming toward him, and said, 'Behold! The Lamb of God who takes away the sin of the world!'" John 1:29

Instructions:

- Depending on the number of students, students either divide into teams or form one large circle.
- Students then practice the memory verse while throwing the ball to each other and catching it.
- For example: The teacher says the first part of the verse to be memorized. Then she throws the ball to one of the students, who repeats word for word what she just said and throws the ball to another student. Go around until everyone has had a chance to catch the ball and say the first part of the verse. Now add the second part of the verse and do the same thing. Then add the third part and so on until each student has memorized the entire verse, including the reference.
- If students have been working in small groups, they now come together to form a large circle and each one recites the verse and reference in front of the entire class with or without the balls.

Activity 2: Temptation Skit or Puppet Show

Supplies:

- Two volunteers to play Jesus and Satan
- One volunteer to be the narrator
- Three copies of the script, or three puppets and three puppeteers

Instructions:

- Three students either act out the skit, following the script, or three students do a puppet show, using the script.

Temptation Script (by Nancy Hughes)

Narrator: After Jesus was baptized by John the Baptist, He went into the wilderness. After having nothing to eat for forty days, Satan came to Him.

Satan: "If You are the Son of God, command that these stones become bread." Matthew 4:3

Jesus: The Bible says, "Man shall not live by bread alone, but by every word that proceeds from the mouth of God." God's Word is more important than food!

Narrator: Since Jesus would not turn the stones into bread, Satan tried another trick. He took Jesus to the rooftop of the temple in Jerusalem.

Satan: "If You are the Son of God, throw Yourself down." After all, the Bible says God will send His angels to take care of You so that You won't hurt yourself.

Jesus: The Bible says not to tempt God.

Narrator: To tempt God means to test Him to see if He is telling the truth. Jesus did not need to test God; He believed what God said. Jesus would not jump off the temple. So, Satan tried one more trick: He took Jesus to the top of a high mountain to show Him all the kingdoms of the world. After all, didn't Jesus want to be king of the world?

Satan: I will let You be king of the whole world if "You will fall down and worship me."

Narrator: Jesus refused to worship Satan.

Jesus: "Away with you, Satan! For it is written, 'You shall worship the LORD your God, and Him only you shall serve.'" Matthew 4:10

Narrator: Finally Satan left, but later he tried to get Jesus to sin again. Jesus never ever did what Satan said. He always obeyed God.

Extra Bible References

Genesis 3:1-8; Leviticus 22:21; Psalm 2:1-12, 12:6; Isaiah 14:13-14; 53:9;
Ezekiel 28:15, 28:17; 25:41; Luke 22:42; John 5:30; 6:38; 8:28-29, 44; 12:31;
2 Corinthians 4:4, 5:21; Ephesians 2:1-3; Philippians 2:9-11; Colossians 1:16, 2:13-15;
Hebrews 4:15, 10:7; Revelation 1:18, 20:10

55
Jesus Teaches and Heals
Jesus Begins His Ministry and Chooses Disciples

Memory Verse

Nor is there salvation in any other, for there is no other name under heaven given among men by which we must be saved. Acts 4:12

Lesson

One day, King Herod put John the Baptist in prison because John told him his actions were wrong. This King Herod was the son of the king who killed all the baby boys in Bethlehem after Jesus was born, and he was just evil as his dad. In the end, Herod had John beheaded.

But, God was in control. God did not allow John to die before John had completed the work God had given him to do.

John's teaching had helped prepare the Jews for the Savior's arrival. Many of them now understood they were sinners separated from God and that they needed the Savior to save them from sin and death. Of course, many others, like the Pharisees and other religious leaders, never believed what John said. They did not believe they were sinners who deserved eternal death; they thought they were acceptable to God just the way they were.

Now after John was put in prison, Jesus came to Galilee, preaching the gospel of the kingdom of God, and saying, "The time is fulfilled, and the kingdom of God is at hand. Repent, and believe in the gospel." Mark 1:14-15

Remember that Jesus Christ was God's Chosen One. Jesus came to Earth as a prophet, a priest, and a king. After John was put in prison, Jesus started doing the work of a prophet: He started teaching God's words to the people.

Gospel means good news. The good news was that God was ready to set up His kingdom on Earth. Jesus the Messiah had come to Earth to be the Savior and to be king. The Jews needed to change their minds and trust in the Savior to save them from sin and make them acceptable to God so that they could be part of God's kingdom.

Jesus chose twelve men to be His special students. These men were called Jesus' disciples. Jesus' twelve disciples followed Jesus wherever He went. Day after day as they walked with Jesus along the dusty roads of Israel, Jesus taught them.

By watching Jesus work and listening to Him explain God's words to the people, the disciples learned how to be workers for God. Someday Jesus planned for these twelve disciples to become His representatives to the world.

...He appointed twelve, that they might be with Him and that He might send them out to preach...: Simon, to whom He gave the name Peter; James the son of Zebedee and John the brother of James... Andrew, Philip, Bartholomew, Matthew, Thomas, James the son of Alphaeus, Thaddaeus, Simon the Cananite; and Judas Iscariot, who also betrayed Him. Mark 3:14-19a

> The twelve disciples later came to be known as the twelve apostles.

The men Jesus chose to be His disciples were not rich or educated; they were just ordinary people. In fact, four of Jesus' disciples were fishermen.

And as He walked by the Sea of Galilee, He saw Simon and Andrew his brother casting a net into the sea; for they were fishermen. Then Jesus said to them, "Follow Me, and I will make you become fishers of men." They immediately left their nets and followed Him.

When He had gone a little farther from there, He saw James the son of Zebedee, and John his brother, who also were in the boat mending their nets. And immediately He called them, and they left their father Zebedee in the boat with the hired servants, and went after Him. Mark 1:16-20

Jesus told these fishermen He would teach them to fish for people instead of fish. Instead of pulling fish out of the sea, He wanted to use them to pull people out of Satan's dominion.

One day Jesus and His disciples came to a town called Capernaum.

Then they went into Capernaum, and immediately on the Sabbath He entered the synagogue and taught. Mark 1:21

There were synagogues in every important town in Israel. Many of the Jews went to the synagogue on the Sabbath (Saturday) to listen to the teachers of the law read the Old Testament books of the Bible written by Moses and the prophets.

In Capernaum, Jesus and His disciples joined the other Jews at the synagogue. After a while, Jesus stood up and began to teach.

And they were astonished at His teaching, for He taught them as one having authority, and not as the scribes. Mark 1:22

The people were amazed by what Jesus taught. Jesus' teaching was different from the teaching of the scribes.

The scribes, who made copies of the Old Testament, knew what was written in the Bible, but because they did not believe God, they did not understand the true meaning of God's words.

Jesus obviously understood the true meaning of the Bible. Even though the people did not realize it, Jesus was God, the author of the Bible.

In the synagogue where Jesus was teaching there was a man who had a demon inside him.

Now there was a man in their synagogue with an unclean spirit. And he cried out, saying, "Let us alone! What have we to do with You, Jesus of Nazareth? Did You come to destroy us? I know who You are—the Holy One of God!" Mark 1:23-24

The "unclean spirit" inside the man recognized Jesus. He knew Jesus was the One who created him as an angel in the beginning. When he and the other angels rebelled, Jesus threw them out of Heaven. The demon knew Jesus had the power to throw him into the Lake of Fire at any time.

...Jesus rebuked him, saying, "Be quiet, and come out of him!" And when the unclean spirit had convulsed him and cried out with a loud voice, he came out of him. Mark 1:25-26

As their Creator, Jesus had authority over evil spirits. The unclean spirit obeyed Jesus' command.

Then they were all amazed, so that they questioned among themselves, saying, "What is this? What new doctrine is this? For with authority He commands even the unclean spirits, and they obey Him." And immediately His fame spread throughout all the region around Galilee. Mark 1:27-28

The people could see Jesus was no ordinary man. They could see He had great power.

Jesus went throughout the region of Galilee healing the sick and teaching in the synagogues.

He healed many who were sick with various diseases, and cast out many demons; and He did not allow the demons to speak, because they knew Him...

And He was preaching in their synagogues throughout all Galilee, and casting out demons. Mark 1:34-39

Evil spirits are God's enemies. They are liars just like their master, Satan. Jesus did not trust the evil spirits. That is why He did not want them to announce who He was.

One day a man with leprosy came to Jesus, begging for Jesus to heal him.

Now a leper came to Him, imploring Him, kneeling down to Him and saying to Him, "If You are willing, You can make me clean." Mark 1:40

Leprosy is a terrible disease that deforms the body. In Jesus' day, leprosy was incurable. It was also thought to be very contagious. People did not go near lepers because they did not want to get their sickness; they called lepers "unclean."

The man who came to Jesus knew Jesus was the only One who could help him.

Then Jesus, moved with compassion, stretched out His hand and touched him, and said to him, "I am willing; be cleansed." As soon as He had spoken, immediately the leprosy left him, and he was cleansed. Mark 1:41-42

Jesus loved the leper; He did not reject him like everyone else did. Jesus was not afraid to touch him. When Jesus spoke, the man was healed!

From the beginning of His work on Earth, Jesus showed in many ways that He was indeed God. He was the only One who clearly understood the meaning of the Old Testament writings. He was the only One who had power over demons and who could heal incurable diseases.

Remember

Because of your sin you are a lot like the leper in this true story. Just like the leprosy made the leper unclean, your sin makes you unclean. Your sin makes you dirty on the inside and unacceptable to God so that you cannot live near God.

For You are not a God who takes pleasure in wickedness, nor shall evil dwell with You. Psalm 5:4

No person can cure you of your sin or save you from death. You cannot save yourself. Jesus is the only One who can cure you.

Even though you are dirty with sin, Jesus loves you just like He loved the unclean leper. If you trust in Him like the leper did, He will make you clean and acceptable to God, and He will save you from death.

Questions

1. What did King Herod do to John the Baptist? *King Herod put John the Baptist in prison and had him killed.*

2. What was the good news for the Israelites? *The good news was that God was ready to set up His kingdom; Jesus Christ, the Messiah, had come to Earth to be Savior and king.*

3. The name Christ, or Messiah, means Chosen One. Why was Jesus called God's Chosen One? What was He chosen to do? *Jesus was chosen to be a prophet, a priest, and a king.*

4. What did Jesus mean when He said He would make the disciples fishers of men? *He meant that instead of pulling fish out of the sea, He was going to teach them to pull people out of Satan's dominion and bring them to God.*

5. Did the scribes know what was written in God's Word? *Yes, they knew what was written in God's Word, but they did not believe it.*

6. Why were the people in the synagogue amazed at Jesus' teaching? *The people were amazed because they could tell His teaching was different from the way the scribes taught. They could tell Jesus understood God's Word.*

7. Why could Jesus explain God's Word so well? *Jesus is God. He is the One who told Moses and the prophets what to write in the Bible.*

8. Why did Jesus have the power to make demons leave out of people? *Jesus is God. He created the angels in the beginning. Even though the demons no longer lived in Heaven, Jesus still had the power to tell them what to do.*

9. Who was the only One who could heal the man with leprosy? *Only Jesus had the power to heal him.*

10. Did Jesus stay away from the man with leprosy like everyone else did? *No, Jesus loved the man. He got close to him, touched him, and healed him.*

11. In what way are you like the man who had leprosy? *Just like the leper was unclean, you are unclean because of your sin. Your sickness – your sin – is also going to end in death. You cannot save yourself. No one else can help you either. In the same way Jesus was the only One who could make the leper clean and save him from death, Jesus is the only One who can make you acceptable to God and save you from death.*

Biblical Worldviews

- God is in control of all that happens.
- Jesus Christ is God's Chosen One; He was chosen to be a prophet, a priest, and a king.
- Demons are Satan's followers; they hate people just like Satan does.
- God created the angels; He has power over Satan and the demons.
- Jesus is God; Jesus has all power.
- Jesus is God; Jesus knows everything.
- All people are sinners.
- The penalty for sin is death.
- We cannot save ourselves; only God can save us.
- God is a God of love.
- Jesus Christ is the only Savior.

Activity: Bible Hangman

Supplies:

- Chalkboard or dry erase board
- Chalk or dry erase markers

Instructions:

- Draw a large hangman tree on the board.
- Draw lines and spaces under the tree to correspond to the letters and spaces of the key phrase.
- **Key phrase**: Jesus explained the Bible, had authority over demons, and healed the sick.
- **Key phrase for younger students**: Jesus is God and can do anything.
- Ask the lesson review questions, one at a time. Call on one student or one team to answer each question.
- If answer is correct, the student or team gets to pick a letter, i.e., the letter b.

- If the letter picked is in the key phrase, the teacher fills it in on the board each time it occurs.

- If the letter picked is not in the key phrase, the teacher draws one part of a stick figure on the hangman tree, i.e., a head, an arm, a stick body, etc.

- When a student (or team) thinks he knows the key phrase, he may try to solve the puzzle on his turn. The game is over when a student or team solves the puzzle or the teacher draws all the parts of the stick man, whichever comes first.

Extra Bible References

Psalm 145:8; Isaiah 61:1; Matthew 14:1-12; Luke 8:28; John 12:31; Colossians 1:16

56
A Visitor at Night
Nicodemus

Memory Verse

Nor is there salvation in any other, for there is no other name under heaven given among men by which we must be saved. Acts 4:12

Lesson

One night a Pharisee named Nicodemus came to Jesus secretly.

There was a man of the Pharisees named Nicodemus, a ruler of the Jews. This man came to Jesus by night and said to Him, "Rabbi, we know that You are a teacher come from God; for no one can do these signs that You do unless God is with him." John 3:1-2

The Pharisees were the ones who added their own rules to the ones God gave the Israelites on Mount Sinai. Most of the Pharisees did not like Jesus, but Nicodemus believed Jesus was sent by God. He called him "rabbi." Rabbi means teacher.

Jesus...said to him, "Most assuredly, I say to you, unless one is born again, he cannot see the kingdom of God."

Nicodemus said to Him, "How can a man be born when he is old? Can he enter a second time into his mother's womb and be born?"

Jesus answered, "Most assuredly, I say to you, unless one is born of water and the Spirit, he cannot enter the kingdom of God. That which is born of the flesh is flesh, and that which is born of the Spirit is spirit." John 3:3-6

Nicodemus did not know what Jesus was talking about, so Jesus explained it to him.

The Pharisees thought God accepted them because they were Israelites. They thought being born into Abraham's family made them acceptable to God, but that was not true. The Pharisees did not understand that all Abraham's descendants are born into Adam's family and are born sinners separated from God.

Even though Nicodemus thought he was born into the right family, he was really born into the wrong family. Jesus told Nicodemus that the only way for him to enter the kingdom of God was for him to be born a second time.

Jesus said, "That which is born of the flesh is flesh." Jesus meant that every child born of human parents is born a human being into Adam's family, and because of that his spirit is dead to God. Everyone born into Adam's family is separated from God.

Then Jesus said, "That which is born of the Spirit is spirit." Only God the Holy Spirit can give life to a person's spirit. Only God the Holy Spirit could make Nicodemus' spirit alive to God and make him be born a second time into the right family.

Remember how the Israelites were bitten by poisonous snakes in the wilderness? Because the Israelites complained against God many of them died.

> Then the LORD said to Moses, "Make a fiery serpent, and set it on a pole; and it shall be that everyone who is bitten, when he looks at it, shall live."
>
> So Moses made a bronze serpent, and put it on a pole; and so it was, if a serpent had bitten anyone, when he looked at the bronze serpent, he lived. Numbers 21:8-9

There was nothing the Israelites could do to keep from dying because of the snake bites. They did not have the right kind of medicine and there were no hospitals or doctors who could help them. But in His mercy, God made a way for the Israelites to be saved.

The Bible says that "if a serpent had bitten anyone, when he looked at the bronze serpent, he lived." In order to be healed from a snake bite, all an Israelite had to do was believe what God said and look up at the snake on the pole.

Jesus told Nicodemus that just like Moses hung the snake on the pole, He (Jesus) was going to be hung on a pole.

> And as Moses lifted up the serpent in the wilderness, even so must the Son of Man be lifted up, that whoever believes in Him should not perish but have eternal life. John 3:14-15

In the same way the Israelites who looked up at the snake on the pole were saved, whoever looks at Jesus, God the Son, and believes in Him will have everlasting life.

...everyone who looks to the Son and believes in him shall have eternal life... John 6:40

Just like the Israelites were poisoned by the snakes, all people have been poisoned by sin. There is nothing we can do to save ourselves from death. No one else can save us either. There is no cure for this poison.

Only God can save us. Jesus told Nicodemus that God loved everyone in the world so much He sent His only Son to Earth so that whoever believes in Him will not die but will have eternal life.

For God so loved the world that He gave His only begotten Son, that whoever believes in Him should not perish but have everlasting life. John 3:16

Jesus is the only Savior; He came into the world to save people from sin and death.

For God did not send His Son into the world to condemn the world, but that the world through Him might be saved.

He who believes in Him is not condemned; but he who does not believe is condemned already, because he has not believed in the name of the only begotten Son of God.

And this is the condemnation, that the light has come into the world, and men loved darkness rather than light, because their deeds were evil. John 3:17-19

Jesus said that whoever believes in Him will be rescued from Adam's family, but whoever does not believe in Him will remain in Adam's family and be separated from God forever because he has not believed in Jesus, God the Son, the Savior of the world.

Nicodemus' first birth put him into Adam's family. In Adam's family, Nicodemus' spirit was dead to God. Unless Nicodemus was born a second time into God's family, he would be separated from God forever in the terrible place of suffering. But if Nicodemus would trust in Jesus the Savior, God the Holy Spirit would give life to his spirit and place him into God's family.

Jesus is the light that came into the world, but most people did not want Jesus to shine His light on their sin. They loved their evil ways and did not want to trust in the Savior so they could have eternal life.

Remember

It does not matter to God whether you are tall or short, rich or poor, smart or not-so-smart. When God looks down on this world, He sees only two kinds of people – those who have been born only once and those who have been born twice.

When you were born into this world as a baby, you were born into Adam's family. In Adam's family your spirit was dead to God. But Jesus said that whoever believes in Him will receive eternal life. If you trust in the Savior, God the Holy Spirit will make your spirit alive to God and cause you to be born again into God's family. That's the right family to be in!

Questions

1. Why do you think Nicodemus came to Jesus at night? *Nicodemus probably came at night so the other Pharisees would not see him. The Pharisees did not like Jesus.*

2. What made the Pharisees think they were acceptable to God? *They thought God accepted them because they were born into Abraham's family.*

3. Into whose family were the Pharisees really born? *Even though the Pharisees came from Abraham, they were born into Adam's family, meaning they were born separated from God.*

4. When God looks at mankind, what two kinds of people does He see? *He sees those who have been born once, and those who have been born twice. Those who have been born once are still in Adam's family. Those who have been born twice are in God's family.*

5. If you are in Adam's family, is your spirit dead or alive to God? *Everyone in Adam's family is dead to God and separated from Him.*

6. Who is the only One who can give life to your spirit and place you into God's family? *Only God the Holy Spirit can make your spirit alive and give you new life in His family.*

7. When the Israelites were bitten by the snakes in the wilderness, was there anything they could do to be saved from death? *No, there was nothing they could do. Only God could save them from death.*

8. Who did Jesus say was going to be hung on a pole? *Jesus said that He was going to be hung on a pole.*

9. What did Jesus promise would happen to everyone who believes in Him? *Jesus said that whoever believes in Him will be saved from death and receive everlasting life.*

10. Why did the Jews not want Jesus to shine His light on their sin? *They liked their sin and wanted to continue on sinning; they did not want Jesus to tell them that what they were doing was wrong.*

Biblical Worldviews

- All people are born into Adam's family and are dead to God.
- In order to enter God's family you must be born a second time into the right family.
- You cannot save yourself. Only God can save you.
- The only way to be born again is to trust in Jesus the Savior.
- God loves everyone in the world and wants ALL people to be saved.
- Those who do not believe in the Savior will stay in Adam's family and be separated from God forever in the terrible place of suffering.

Activity: Snake on a Pole

Supplies:

- Option #1: Wooden base with hole drilled in it for a stick
- Option #2: Clay (for base)
- Sticks gathered from outdoors
- String
- Glue gun
- Toy plastic snakes
- Copies of memory verse, one per student

Instructions:

- Students gather two sticks, one a little longer than the other.
- Students tie the two sticks together to form a cross.
- Sticks can be glued with glue gun.
- Option #1: Students stand the cross in the base and hang the snake on the cross.
- Option #2: Students make a base out of clay and stick the cross into the clay.
- Glue the memory verse cut-outs to the base.
- The teacher can use a glue gun to help make the crafts sturdier.

Extra Bible References

John 12:3233; 14:6; Acts 4:12, 10:34; Romans 5:12, 6:23; 1 Corinthians 15:22, 44-55; 1 Timothy 2:4; 1 Peter 1:23

57
Two Sick Men
The Paralytic and the Tax Collector

Memory Verse

In the beginning was the Word, and the Word was with God, and the Word was God.
John 1:1

Lesson

Even though the Jews did not like Jesus to shine His light on their sin, many still followed Him. They did not want Jesus to save them from sin and death, but they did want Him to save them from the cruel Roman government, to provide food for them, and to heal them of their sicknesses.

The religious leaders followed Jesus because they were looking for a reason to accuse Him. They wanted to catch Jesus doing something wrong so they could have Him arrested. The religious leaders were jealous of Jesus because of the huge crowds that followed Him; they were jealous because Jesus was more popular than they were.

Only a few Jews followed Jesus for the right reason; only a few believed Jesus was the promised Savior who had come to rescue them from sin and death.

One day when Jesus was once again in the city of Capernaum, a big crowd gathered around Him in the house where He was teaching.

And again He entered Capernaum after some days, and it was heard that He was in the house. Immediately many gathered together, so that there was no longer room to receive them, not even near the door. And He preached the word to them. Mark 2:1-2

Since Jesus was God's chosen prophet, He taught God's Word to the people. He explained to them the meaning of what Moses and the prophets had written long ago.

While Jesus was teaching, four men brought their friend to see Jesus.

Then they came to Him, bringing a paralytic who was carried by four men. And when they could not come near Him because of the crowd, they uncovered the roof where He was. So when they had broken through, they let down the bed on which the paralytic was lying. Mark 2:3-4

The paralyzed man could not move; all he could do was lie on his bed all day long. No doctor in Israel could heal him. There was no hope for him except what his friends had heard about Jesus. They believed Jesus could heal him.

In those days most houses had flat roofs made of sticks and mud. A stairway on the outside of the house usually led up to the roof.

Since they could not get in through the front door because of the crowd, the man's friends carried him up to the roof. They dug a hole in the roof above Jesus' head and lowered the man down right in front of Jesus.

When Jesus saw their faith, He said to the paralytic, "Son, your sins are forgiven you."

And some of the scribes were sitting there and reasoning in their hearts, "Why does this Man speak blasphemies like this? Who can forgive sins but God alone?" Mark 2:5-7

> **Blaspheme** - to be disrespectful of God
>
> **If a person claims he can do what only God can do, he makes himself equal to God. The Jews called this blaspheming.**

The scribes were right about God being the only One who can forgive sins. All people, even priests and pastors, are born sinners. A sinful person cannot forgive sin. But the scribes did not understand who Jesus was. Jesus was not an ordinary man; Jesus was God. Jesus could forgive sins. He was not blaspheming when He told the paralyzed man his sin was forgiven.

Jesus knew that, more than needing his body healed, the man needed to be healed on the inside. In order to be accepted by God, the man needed His sins forgiven. The reason Jesus Christ came to Earth was to forgive people of their sin so they could be saved from death and live with Him forever. But the religious leaders did not believe Jesus was God the Savior.

Jesus knew their thoughts.

But immediately, when Jesus perceived in His spirit that they reasoned thus within themselves, He said to them, "Why do you reason about these things in your hearts? Which is easier, to say to the paralytic, 'Your sins are forgiven you,' or to say, 'Arise, take up your bed and walk'?

"But that you may know that the Son of Man has power on earth to forgive sins"—He said to the paralytic, "I say to you, arise, take up your bed, and go to your house."

Immediately he arose, took up the bed, and went out in the presence of them all, so that all were amazed and glorified God, saying, "We never saw anything like this!" Mark 2:8-12

When Jesus healed this man simply by speaking, it proved He was not blaspheming. Only God could heal a paralyzed man just by saying the words. Jesus is God! He is the Creator of the world, and He had the authority to forgive sins.

Afterwards, Jesus left to go down to the sea.

Then He went out again by the sea; and all the multitude came to Him, and He taught them. As He passed by, He saw Levi the son of Alphaeus sitting at the tax office. And He said to him, "Follow Me." So he arose and followed Him. Mark 2:13-14

The Jews disliked the tax collectors. The tax collectors were Israelites who worked for the Roman government. They were dishonest, making the people pay more taxes than what the government said. The tax collectors became rich by cheating their own people.

But Jesus loves all sinners. He came to save everyone, even tax collectors.

When Jesus called Levi, Levi left his tax booth and followed Jesus. He even invited Jesus to his home.

Now it happened, as He was dining in Levi's house, that many tax collectors and sinners also sat together with Jesus and His disciples; for there were many, and they followed Him. And when the scribes and Pharisees saw Him eating with the tax collectors and sinners, they said to His disciples, "How is it that He eats and drinks with tax collectors and sinners?" Mark 2:15-16

The Pharisees would never eat a meal with tax collectors. They did not hang around people they thought were bad, but that is just the kind of people Jesus came to save.

When Jesus heard it, He said to them, "Those who are well have no need of a physician, but those who are sick. I did not come to call the righteous, but sinners, to repentance." Mark 2:17

The Pharisees were like people who won't go to the doctor because they don't think they are sick. The Pharisees would not go to Jesus to be healed, because they did not think they needed healing. The Pharisees did not think they were going to die because of their sin.

But the tax collectors and "bad" people knew they were sick with sin. They knew they needed the Savior to save them from death.

Jesus could not heal the Pharisees because the Pharisees would not admit they were sick. Jesus can only help those who admit they are sick and come to Him for help.

Levi knew he was a sinner and that only Jesus Christ could help him. He trusted in Jesus to save him from the death penalty he deserved for his sin. Levi was also called Matthew. Matthew became one of Jesus' twelve disciples and wrote the first book of the New Testament.

Remember

The Pharisees refused to believe the truth; they did not believe they were sick with sin. They did not believe their sin would lead to death.

The heart is deceitful above all things, and desperately wicked; Who can know it? Jeremiah 17:9

The Bible says our hearts easily trick us into thinking we are not so bad after all. But God sees the inside of us; He knows our hearts are "desperately wicked." God can see we are awfully sick with sin.

Jesus Christ the Savior is the only One who can cure you of your terrible sickness so that you won't die and be separated from Him forever. Just like a sick person needs to admit she is sick and go to the doctor, you need to admit you are a sinner and go to Jesus to be saved. Trust in Jesus the way Levi did! Jesus saves all who trust in Him.

Questions

1. Why did most of the Jews not accept Jesus as their Savior? *They did not accept Jesus as their Savior because they did not think they were sinners separated from God. They thought they were acceptable to God; they did not think they needed anyone to save them.*

2. Even though most of the Jews did not want to accept Jesus as their Savior, what did they want Him to do? *They wanted Jesus to save them from the cruel Roman government, to provide them with food, and to heal them of their sicknesses.*

3. Why were the Pharisees and religious leaders jealous of Jesus? *They were jealous of the huge crowds of people who followed Jesus.*

4. What does it mean to blaspheme? *It means to speak disrespectfully about God. When Jesus said He forgave the man's sin, the Pharisees said He was blaspheming because only God can forgive sins.*

5. Were the scribes right when they said only God can forgive sins? *Yes, they were.*

6. Why was it not wrong for Jesus to tell the man his sins were forgiven? *Jesus is God; He can forgive sins.*

7. How could Jesus heal the paralyzed man just by speaking? *Jesus is God. Since He created the whole world just by speaking, He had the power to heal this man just by saying the words.*

8. What kind of people did Jesus say need a doctor? *Sick people need a doctor.*

9. Why did the Pharisees not come to Jesus to be "healed"? *The Pharisees did not come to Jesus to be saved from death because they did not think they were sick with sin.*

10. In what way does God say you are sick? *God says you are sick with sin. Because of your sin you are going to die and be separated from God forever.*

11. Who is the only One who can cure you so you won't die? *Jesus is the only One who can save you from death. He is the only Savior.*

Biblical Worldviews

- Jesus Christ is God; He can do anything.
- Jesus Christ is God; He knows everything.
- All people are sinners.
- Only God can forgive sin; Jesus Christ can forgive sin.
- We cannot save ourselves. Only Jesus the Savior can save us.
- God saves only those who admit they are sinners and trust in Him to save them.
- God is a God of love; He loves everybody.

Activity 1: Paralyzed Man Skit

Supplies:

- Volunteers to be paralyzed man, four friends, Jesus, crowd and Pharisees

Instructions:

- Four students pretend to carry a smaller student and act out the story of the paralyzed man.

Activity 2: Bible Bingo

Supplies:

- Bingo cards and game tokens (Any set will do. You can buy an inexpensive set at the dollar store.)

Instructions:

- Give each student a bingo card and some tokens.
- Ask a question from the lesson review and call on a student to answer it. If the student answers it correctly, she calls the bingo square she wants to cover. Everyone else who has that square covers it as well.
- Continue to ask questions, calling on a different student each time. Allow everyone to answer at least one question and pick at least one bingo square.
- The game is over when the first student shouts BINGO because she has covered a complete row with tokens, either vertically, horizontally, or diagonally.
- Play the game several times until everyone has had a turn answering a question and/or all the questions from the review have been asked and answered.

Extra Bible References

Matthew 23:1-39; Colossians 1:16; I Timothy 2:4

58
Hypocrites
Jesus Rebukes the Pharisees

Memory Verse

In the beginning was the Word, and the Word was with God, and the Word was God. John 1:1

Lesson

One Sabbath day when Jesus went to the synagogue, He met a man with a disabled hand.

And He entered the synagogue again, and a man was there who had a withered hand. So they watched Him closely, whether He would heal him on the Sabbath, so that they might accuse Him. Mark 3:1-2

One of the ten commands God gave Moses on Mt. Sinai was that the Israelites were to rest on the Sabbath day, which is Saturday. The Pharisees, who liked to add rules to the ones God gave, added that it was wrong to heal a person on Saturday.

Jesus obeyed God's laws, but He did not follow the made-up rules of the Pharisees. In fact, He told the crowds that the Pharisees were hypocrites. The Pharisees were like a dish that is washed on the outside, but is still dirty on the inside. Because of all their rules, the Pharisees looked religious on the outside, but Jesus knew their hearts were dirty with sin.

A hypocrite - someone who pretends to love God, but on the inside he or she does not care about God at all

Woe to you, scribes and Pharisees, hypocrites! For you cleanse the outside of the cup and dish, but inside they are full of extortion and self-indulgence. Matthew 23:25

Jesus said that on the inside the Pharisees were greedy and selfish. He warned the Jews not to be hypocrites like the Pharisees.

> And when you pray, you shall not be like the hypocrites. For they love to pray standing in the synagogues and on the corners of the streets, that they may be seen by men... Matthew 6:5a

The Pharisees loved to pray in public so everyone could see them. When Jesus shone His light on them showing what they were really like, the Pharisees got angry. They did not want everyone to know what they were really like on the inside.

Jesus asked the Pharisees if it was wrong to do a good deed on the Sabbath.

> And He said to the man who had the withered hand, "Step forward." Then He said to them, "Is it lawful on the Sabbath to do good or to do evil, to save life or to kill?"
>
> But they kept silent. Mark 3:3-4

The Pharisees did not know what to say; they knew it was never wrong to be kind.

It saddened Jesus that the Pharisees were so stubborn and refused to believe the truth.

> And when He had looked around at them with anger, being grieved by the hardness of their hearts, He said to the man, "Stretch out your hand." And he stretched it out, and his hand was restored as whole as the other. Mark 3:5

The Pharisees were leading the Jews to believe a lie; they taught that following rules makes people acceptable to God. That, of course, is not true.

All people are separated from God because of sin. You cannot make yourself acceptable to God by doing good works. Jesus the Savior is the only One who can make you acceptable to God.

If the Jewish people believed the Pharisee's lies, they would remain separated from God forever. Jesus was angry with the Pharisees for leading the people of Israel to trust in themselves and not in the Savior.

Even though Jesus knew the Pharisees were looking for a reason to arrest Him, He refused to obey their rules. Right in front of everyone, Jesus told the man to stretch out his hand. Then He healed him on the Sabbath!

Once again Jesus healed a sick person simply by speaking. Only the Creator of the world could do that! The Pharisees should have realized that Jesus is God.

The Pharisees were a lot like the pharaoh in Egypt. No matter how many terrible plagues God sent on Egypt, the pharaoh refused to listen to God. That's how the Pharisees were. No matter how many incredible things Jesus did, the Pharisees refused to believe He was God. Instead, just like Pharaoh, their hearts became harder and harder until they finally decided He must be killed.

Then the Pharisees went out and immediately plotted with the Herodians against Him, how they might destroy Him. Mark 3:6

The Pharisees hated Jesus so much they were willing to join King Herod's evil followers, the Herodians, in order to get rid of Him.

But Jesus withdrew with His disciples to the sea. And a great multitude from Galilee followed Him…So He told His disciples that a small boat should be kept ready for Him because of the multitude, lest they should crush Him. For He healed many, so that as many as had afflictions pressed about Him to touch Him. Mark 3:7-10

Because the Pharisees were ready to kill Him, Jesus left and went to the coast. A huge crowd followed Him. Everyone wanted to be healed of their sicknesses. Jesus had compassion on the people and healed them; even those who touched Jesus were healed.

Jesus was obviously God; even the demons knew that. They used to live with God in Heaven; they knew Jesus was God the Son.

And the unclean spirits, whenever they saw Him, fell down before Him and cried out, saying, "You are the Son of God." But He sternly warned them that they should not make Him known. Mark 3:11-12

But since the demons were Jesus' enemies, Jesus did not trust them. He did not want them to be the ones to announce who He was.

Remember

You cannot make yourself acceptable to God by keeping the Ten Commandments. Good deeds like going to church, reading your Bible, praying, or being kind will not make you acceptable to God.

The people around you might see your good behavior and call you a good person, but don't be tricked by that. God sees your heart. He knows what you are like on the inside and that is what matters to Him.

For the LORD does not see as man sees; for man looks at the outward appearance, but the LORD looks at the heart." 1 Samuel 16:7b

No matter how many good things you do, the penalty for the sin in your heart is death. Only Jesus the Savior can save you from death. Only Jesus can make you acceptable to God. You need to trust in Him, not in yourself!

Questions

1. What rule did the Pharisees make up about the Sabbath, or Saturday? *The Pharisees said it was wrong to heal someone on Saturday.*

2. Did Jesus obey the laws of the Pharisees? *No, He only obeyed God's rules.*

3. What is a hypocrite? *A hypocrite is someone who pretends to love God, but on the inside he or she does not care about God at all.*

4. In what way were the Pharisees like a dish that was washed on the outside, but was still dirty on the inside? *The Pharisees had many rules and acted very religious, but on the inside they were selfish and greedy. The Jews thought the Pharisees were good people, but God knew their hearts.*

5. Why were the Pharisees angry with Jesus? *The Pharisees were angry with Jesus for telling people how sinful they were on the inside. They wanted the Jews to think they were good.*

6. How could Jesus heal the man's hand just by speaking? *Jesus could heal the man's hand just by speaking because Jesus is God. In the beginning, He made the whole world and everything in it just by speaking.*

7. Why was Jesus angry with the Pharisees? *Jesus was angry with the Pharisees because they were the religious leaders of Israel, but instead of teaching the truth, they taught lies to the people of Israel. The Pharisees taught the Jews that keeping rules made them acceptable to God. This was a lie that was causing many Jews not to believe in Jesus. If the people did not trust in Jesus to save them they would be separated from God forever. This made Jesus angry.*

8. In what way were the Pharisees like the pharaoh of Egypt? *Just like the pharaoh refused to believe in God even though he saw the mighty deeds God did, the Pharisees refused to believe Jesus was God even though they saw the wonderful miracles He did.*

9. What did the Pharisees and the Herodians want to do to Jesus? *They wanted to have Jesus killed.*

10. How did the demons know who Jesus was? *They used to live with Jesus in Heaven.*

11. Can keeping the Ten Commandments, reading the Bible, or doing good deeds make you acceptable to God? *No, you cannot make yourself acceptable to God by doing good things, because even though you are good on the outside, your heart is still sinful. The payment for sin is separation from God forever.*

12. Who is the only One who can make you acceptable to God? *Only Jesus Christ the Savior can make you acceptable to God.*

Biblical Worldviews

- Only God has the authority to make the rules.
- God knows and sees everything, even our hearts.
- All people are sinful.
- The penalty for sin is death.
- There is nothing we can do to make ourselves acceptable to God.
- Jesus Christ is the only Savior; only He can save us from death and make us acceptable to God.
- Jesus Christ is God the Son.
- Jesus can do anything; nothing is too hard for Him.
- Jesus is the Creator of the world.
- Jesus created the angels who became demons.
- Jesus loves people.
- Those who believe God will live with Him in Heaven forever; those who do not believe God will be separated from Him forever in the terrible place of suffering.

Activity: Bible Tic-Tac-Toe

Supplies:
- Chalkboard or dry erase board
- Chalk or dry erase markers

Instructions:
- Draw a large tic-tac-toe on the board.
- Divide students into two teams.
- Ask review questions and let each team take turns trying to answer a question. If the team answers the question correctly, they get to put an "X" or an "O" on the board. The first team to get three in a row, horizontally, vertically, or diagonally, wins.
- Play several times until you have used all the review questions.

Extra Bible References

1 Kings 8:39; Matthew 6:2, 5, 16; 15:18-20; Luke 16:15; Colossians 1:16

59
Supernatural Power
Jesus Calms the Storm and Sends Demons into Pigs

Memory Verse

Therefore if the Son makes you free, you shall be free indeed. John 8:36

Lesson

Jesus came to Earth as God's prophet to teach the people of Israel the truth of God's Word. The Sea of Galilee was a great place for Jesus to teach since many Jews lived near the sea and many others went there to fish.

And again He began to teach by the sea. And a great multitude was gathered to Him, so that He got into a boat and sat in it on the sea; and the whole multitude was on the land facing the sea.

On the same day, when evening had come, He said to them, "Let us cross over to the other side."

Now when they had left the multitude, they took Him along in the boat as He was. And other little boats were also with Him. And a great windstorm arose, and the waves beat into the boat, so that it was already filling. But He was in the stern, asleep on a pillow. And they awoke Him and said to Him, "Teacher, do You not care that we are perishing?"

Then He arose and rebuked the wind, and said to the sea, "Peace, be still!" And the wind ceased and there was a great calm. But He said to them, "Why are you so fearful? How is it that you have no faith?"

And they feared exceedingly, and said to one another, "Who can this be, that even the wind and the sea obey Him!" Mark 4:1, 35-41

The human part of Jesus was tired after a long day of teaching. When Jesus got in the boat He fell asleep.

Suddenly the wind started to blow really hard and the waves began to fill the boat with water. The disciples got scared. They could not believe Jesus was sleeping!

417

When the disciples woke Jesus up, He calmly spoke to the raging sea. Just like that the wind died down and the sea became peaceful.

The disciples were greatly amazed at Jesus' power. They did not yet understand Jesus was God, the Creator of the world.

For by Him all things were created that are in heaven and that are on earth, visible and invisible...All things were created through Him and for Him. Colossians 1:16

If the disciples would have understood that Jesus was God, they would not have gotten afraid.

As soon as the boat landed, a crazy man came up to Jesus.

And when He had come out of the boat, immediately there met Him out of the tombs a man with an unclean spirit, who had his dwelling among the tombs; and no one could bind him, not even with chains, because he had often been bound with shackles and chains. And the chains had been pulled apart by him, and the shackles broken in pieces; neither could anyone tame him. And always, night and day, he was in the mountains and in the tombs, crying out and cutting himself with stones. Mark 5:2-5

Satan has been a murderer from the beginning. Remember how he wanted Adam and Eve to die and be separated from God forever? Satan's followers, the demons, also hated people and tried to hurt them (and they still do!).

The man who came to Jesus was controlled by Satan's demons. He was homeless and out of his mind. He lived in a graveyard. Day and night he went around screaming and cutting himself with stones. The demons were destroying him, and no one was strong enough to help him.

When he saw Jesus from afar, he ran and worshiped Him. And he cried out with a loud voice and said, "What have I to do with You, Jesus, Son of the Most High God? I implore You by God that You do not torment me."

For He said to him, "Come out of the man, unclean spirit!" Then He asked him, "What is your name?"

And he answered, saying, "My name is Legion; for we are many." Also he begged Him earnestly that He would not send them out of the country. Mark 5:6-10

Even though the demons were very strong, they were afraid of Jesus.

Jesus is God; He is the highest authority. He created the angels in the beginning. When Lucifer and his followers tried to fight against God, He threw them out of Heaven. Someday He will send them to the Lake of Fire where they will remain forever, never to escape.

The devil, who deceived them, was cast into the lake of fire and brimstone where the beast and the false prophet are. And they will be tormented day and night forever and ever. Revelation 20:10

The demons knew who Jesus was. They knew He could throw them into the Lake of Fire at any time. They knew they could not do anything without Jesus' permission. They begged Jesus to send them into the herd of pigs nearby.

Now a large herd of swine was feeding there near the mountains. So all the demons begged Him, saying, "Send us to the swine, that we may enter them." And at once Jesus gave them permission. Then the unclean spirits went out and entered the swine (there were about two thousand); and the herd ran violently down the steep place into the sea, and drowned in the sea. Mark 5:11-13

Even though the pigs died, the demons remained alive. Demons are spirits. They do not have physical bodies that die. After the pigs drowned, the demons went somewhere else to continue their evil work.

When the people saw that Jesus had authority over the demons, they were afraid.

So those who fed the swine fled, and they told it in the city and in the country. And they went out to see what it was that had happened. Then they came to Jesus, and saw the one who had been demon-possessed and had the legion, sitting and clothed and in his right mind. And they were afraid. And those who saw it told them how it happened to him who had been demon-possessed, and about the swine. Then they began to plead with Him to depart from their region. Mark 5:14-17

As long as this man was under Satan's control, he was homeless and crazy. He continually hurt himself. He could not free himself from Satan's power. No one else could free him either. The man had to do whatever the demons made him do.

Jesus was the only One powerful enough to free the man from the demons and bring him into God's family. Jesus loved the man; He made a wonderful and beautiful change in him.

The man was so happy he begged to go with Jesus.

And when He got into the boat, he who had been demon-possessed begged Him that he might be with Him. However, Jesus did not permit him, but said to him, "Go home to your friends, and tell them what great things the Lord has done for you, and how He has had compassion on you." And he departed and began to proclaim in Decapolis all that Jesus had done for him; and all marveled. Mark 5:18-20

Jesus wanted this man to stay where he was and tell his friends and family what a great change God had made in his life; He wanted him to tell others how God had rescued him from Satan's dominion. Jesus wanted this man to be His messenger to tell others about God's love.

Remember

Because all people are born into Adam's family, all people are born on Satan's side and are under his dominion. Satan leads people to hurt and destroy themselves and others.

Just like the demon-possessed man, you cannot save yourself from Satan's control. No one else can save you either. Only Jesus Christ can rescue you from Satan.

Nor is there salvation in any other, for there is no other name under heaven given among men by which we must be saved. Acts 4:12

Even though you were born on Satan's side, God loves you. That is why He sent the Savior to free you from Satan and make a way for you to enter God's family.

Questions

1. If Jesus is God, why did Jesus get tired at the end of the day? *Jesus got tired because He was also a human being.*

2. Why were the disciples surprised when the wind and the sea obeyed Jesus? *They were surprised because they did not understand that Jesus was God, the Creator of the world.*

3. Who was the only One who could rescue the demon-possessed man? *Only Jesus the Son of God could free him from the demons.*

4. How did the demons cause the man to act? *They caused him to be crazy and to hurt himself.*

5. Did the demons know who Jesus was? *Yes, they recognized Jesus. They knew He was God. They knew He was the One who threw them out of Heaven and made the Lake of Fire for them.*

6. Why did the demons have to ask permission from Jesus to go into the pigs? *They had to ask permission because Jesus is God, the Creator of the world. He is the highest authority.*

7. After Jesus freed the man from the demons, what did He want the man to do? *Jesus wanted the man to tell his friends and his family what Jesus had done for him.*

8. Who is the only One who can rescue you from Satan's dominion and place you into God's family? *Only Jesus has the power to rescue you from Satan and place you into God's family.*

Biblical Worldviews

- Jesus Christ is a human being.
- Jesus Christ is God; He is the Creator of the world.
- Satan and his demons hurt and destroy people.
- Jesus is God; He is more powerful than Satan and his demons; He has authority over them.
- God created the Lake of Fire for Satan and his demons.
- Jesus Christ loves people.
- Jesus Christ is the only Savior; He is the only One who can deliver people from Satan and bring them into God's family.

Activity: Nehemiah Worksheet

Supplies:

- One "Nehemiah 9:6" printout for each student (see appendix page 580)
- Pencil and/or crayons

Instructions:

- Option #1: Using pencil or crayon, students copy the verse into the corresponding squares. This will help enforce memorization. They can try to use their best handwriting, or vary the colors in each box to make it colorful.

- Option #2: Using pencil or crayon, students draw and/or color a scene in each box that depicts the words under the box.

- Students can share their work with others in the class and discuss Nehemiah 9:6 as they are writing and drawing.

Extra Bible References

Deuteronomy 18:18-19; Jeremiah 32:27; Job 1:12; Psalms 24:1-2, 95:1-7, 107:23-30; Psalm 148:1-5; Matthew 25:41; John 4:25, 8:44; Ephesians 6:12; Hebrews 1:2-3; Revelation 20:10

60
Bread that Gives Eternal Life
Jesus Feeds Multitude and Walks on Water

Memory Verse

"I am the living bread which came down from heaven. If anyone eats of this bread, he will live forever;" John 6:51a

Lesson

There were always huge crowds following Jesus. They came because Jesus had the power to do whatever they needed - He could create food, heal all types of sicknesses, and even make demons leave out of people.

...a great multitude followed Him, because they saw His signs which He performed on those who were diseased...

Then Jesus lifted up His eyes, and seeing a great multitude coming toward Him, He said to Philip, "Where shall we buy bread, that these may eat?" But this He said to test him, for He Himself knew what He would do.

Philip answered Him, "Two hundred denarii worth of bread is not sufficient for them, that every one of them may have a little."
John 6:2, 5-7

Philip was one of Jesus' twelve disciples, but Philip did not yet fully understand who Jesus was. If he would have understood that Jesus was God, the Creator of the world, he would not have cared about the amount of money they would need to buy food; he would have known that it was nothing for Jesus to provide all the food the world could need.

Jesus told the disciples to have the people sit down on the grass.

One of His disciples, Andrew, Simon Peter's brother, said to Him, "There is a lad here who has five barley loaves and two small fish, but what are they among so many?"

Then Jesus said, "Make the people sit down." Now there was much grass in the place. So the men sat down, in number about five thousand. And Jesus took the loaves, and when He had given thanks He distributed them to the disciples, and the disciples to those sitting down; and likewise of the fish, as much as they wanted.

So when they were filled, He said to His disciples, "Gather up the fragments that remain, so that nothing is lost." Therefore they gathered them up, and filled twelve baskets with the fragments of the five barley loaves which were left over by those who had eaten. John 6:8-13

How many people could you feed with one sandwich? Could you feed your whole family? Could you feed all the people on your street? No, one sandwich is only enough for one person, or maybe two.

But Jesus is God. He could do the impossible. He could easily feed thousands of people with one boy's lunch. After everyone ate, the disciples gathered twelve basketfuls of crumbs. Only God could do that!

When the crowd saw what Jesus did, they believed He was the Chosen One foretold by the Old Testament prophets.

Then those men, when they had seen the sign that Jesus did, said, "This is truly the Prophet who is to come into the world."

Therefore when Jesus perceived that they were about to come and take Him by force to make Him king, He departed again to the mountain by Himself alone. John 6:14-15

The Jews knew about the promised Savior from the Old Testament Scriptures. They knew God said the Savior would be a prophet and a king. When Jesus fed more than five thousand people with just five small loaves of bread and two fish, they were ready to make Him king right then and there. They wanted Jesus to keep feeding them and healing their sicknesses. They wanted Him to rescue them from the cruel Roman government.

But it was not God's plan for Jesus to become king in this way, so Jesus went up on a mountain to get away.

In the evening, Jesus' disciples left in a boat, but Jesus was not with them.

Now when evening came, His disciples went down to the sea, got into the boat, and went over the sea toward Capernaum. And it was already dark, and Jesus had not come to them. Then the sea arose because a great wind was blowing. So when they had rowed about three or four miles, they saw Jesus walking on the sea and drawing near the boat; and they were afraid. But He said to them, "It is I; do not be afraid." Then they willingly received Him into the boat, and immediately the boat was at the land where they were going. John 6:16-21

As they were trying to row across the rough sea, the disciples noticed Someone walking towards them on the waves. At first they were afraid, but then they realized it was Jesus. The instant Jesus got in the boat, it reached its destination on the other side of the sea!

Jesus did many great deeds that proved He was God. No one but God could do the things Jesus did.

Four prophets wrote about Jesus' life on Earth - Matthew, Mark, Luke, and John. These men wrote the first four books of the New Testament. Matthew and John were Jesus' disciples and later became apostles.

The apostle John said that if they had written down everything Jesus did, there would not have been enough room in the world to contain all the books! During Jesus' life on Earth He continually amazed His disciples with His great power and wisdom.

And there are also many other things that Jesus did, which if they were written one by one, I suppose that even the world itself could not contain the books that would be written. Amen. John 21:25

The next day after Jesus fed them, the crowd caught up to Him on the other side of the sea.

On the following day...they found Him on the other side of the sea, they said to Him, "Rabbi, when did You come here?"

Jesus answered them and said, "Most assuredly, I say to you, you seek Me, not because you saw the signs, but because you ate of the loaves and were filled." John 6:22-26

Since Jesus was God, He knew the true reason the crowd was looking for Him; He knew it was because they wanted more food.

But Jesus explained that there is something much more important than food.

> Do not labor for the food which perishes, but for the food which endures to everlasting life...the bread of God is He who comes down from heaven and gives life to the world... I am the bread of life..."
> John 6:27, 33, 35

Rather than desiring food that only gives temporary life, Jesus advised the Jews to seek the food that gives life that never ends. That food is Jesus; Jesus said He was the bread of life that came down from Heaven to give life to everyone in the world. The life Jesus gives goes on forever!

Remember

Remember Jacob and Esau? Remember how Esau cared more about his hungry stomach than he did about God's promises? The promise of the Savior was unimportant to Esau.

The Jews were a lot like Esau. They were only concerned about their present situation; they wanted Jesus to provide food for them, heal their diseases, and rescue them from the cruel Roman government, but they did not care about Jesus saving them from their sin. They did not care about what would happen to them after they died.

What about you? What is most important to you? Is it having fun and playing with your friends? Is it getting a new game, or toy, or phone, or computer? Do you care more about your short life on Earth than about where you will live forever and ever without end? The Bible says that the things in this life are only for a short while; they do not last.

> For the things which are seen are temporary, but the things which are not seen are eternal. 2 Corinthians 4:18b

Your soul lasts forever. What will happen to your soul after you leave this Earth? If you do not care about the Savior while you are alive, you will be separated from God forever in the terrible place of suffering. But if you trust in the Savior to save you from sin and death, then you will live with God forever and ever in Heaven.

Most assuredly, I say to you, he who hears My word and believes in Him who sent Me has everlasting life, and shall not come into judgment, but has passed from death into life. John 5:24

Believe in Jesus! That is what really matters.

Questions

1. What did the crowds want from Jesus? *The crowds saw how powerful and good Jesus was, so they wanted Him to be their leader. They wanted Him to heal their diseases, provide food for them, and save them from the cruel Roman government.*

2. Why did Jesus ask Philip how they could feed the crowd? *Jesus was testing Philip to see if Philip believed Jesus was God the Creator of the world who could do anything.*

3. In what ways did Jesus prove He was God? *Jesus turned five loaves of bread and two fish into enough food for thousands of people. He walked on water, made the boat reach the opposite shore instantly, healed all types of diseases, and ordered demons to come out of people.*

4. What did the apostle John say about the amount of great and incredible things Jesus did? *He said that if everything Jesus did were written down, the world could hardly contain all the books.*

5. When the people saw the great miracles Jesus did, who did they think Jesus was? *They thought Jesus was the Chosen One the prophets wrote about in the Old Testament; they wanted Jesus to be their king.*

6. Did the Jews want Jesus to save them from Satan's dominion and the death penalty they deserved for their sin? *No, most of the Jews did not think their sin separated them from God; they did not think they were on Satan's side. They thought they were acceptable to God and did not need to be saved from Satan, sin, and death.*

7. What kind of food did Jesus tell the Jews they should be seeking? *He said they should be seeking the food that gives eternal life.*

8. Who is the bread of life who came down from Heaven? *Jesus Christ the promised Savior is the bread of life. He is the only One who can give life that lasts forever.*

Biblical Worldviews

- Jesus Christ is God. Jesus Christ loves people; He cared for the multitudes.
- Jesus Christ can do anything; nothing is too hard for Him.
- Jesus Christ is the Creator of the world; He has power over nature.
- Jesus Christ is the only Savior; He is the only One who can give eternal life.
- After you die, you either go to Heaven or to the place of suffering.
- God saves only those who trust in Him to save them.

Activity 1: Bread of Life Drawing

Supplies:

- Paper, one sheet per student
- Pencils, crayons, markers

Instructions:

- Give each student a piece of paper.
- Students fold paper in half.
- On one side students draw a picture of a loaf of bread.
- Inside the loaf of bread students write: I give temporary life.
- On the other side students draw a picture of a man who represents Jesus Christ.
- Students draw a bubble for Jesus. Inside the bubble they write: "I give everlasting life. Believe in Me."
- Discuss: Jesus is the bread of life. He is better than the bread we eat every day. Those who believe in Jesus will live forever.

Activity 2: Memory Verse Ball

Supplies:

- One or more mid-size balls
- Copy of memory verse: And those who know Your name will put their trust in You; For You, LORD, have not forsaken those who seek You. Psalm 9:10

Instructions:

- Depending on the number of students, students either divide into teams or form one large circle.
- Students then practice the memory verse while throwing the ball to each other and catching it.
- For example: The teacher says the first part of the verse to be memorized. Then she throws the ball to one of the students, who repeats word for word what she just said and throws the ball to another student. Go around until everyone has had a chance to catch the ball and say the first part of the verse. Now add the second part of the verse and do the same thing. Then add the third part and so on until each student has memorized the entire verse, including the reference.
- If students have been working in small groups, they now come together to form a large circle and each one recites the verse and reference in front of the entire class with or without the balls.

Extra Bible References

Daniel 12:2; Matthew 25:46; Luke 12:22-23; John 5:29; Acts 7:37; Colossians 1:16

61
Dirty on the Inside

Parable of Two Prayers: The Pharisee's and the Tax Collector's

Memory Verse

So they said, "Believe on the Lord Jesus Christ, and you will be saved..." Acts16:31

Lesson

Remember how the Pharisees added their own rules to the ones God gave on Mount Sinai? The Pharisees actually began to believe that their rules and traditions were more important than God's rules.

Then the Pharisees and some of the scribes...when they saw some of His disciples eat bread with...unwashed hands, they found fault. For the Pharisees and all the Jews do not eat unless they wash their hands in a special way, holding the tradition of the elders. When they come from the marketplace, they do not eat unless they wash. And there are many other things which they...hold, like the washing of cups, pitchers, copper vessels, and couches.

Then the Pharisees and scribes asked Him, "Why do Your disciples not walk according to the tradition of the elders, but eat bread with unwashed hands?" Mark 7:1-5

The Pharisees had rules about washing their hands before eating and when returning from the market. The Pharisees also had rules about washing dishes.

When the Pharisees and scribes saw that Jesus' disciples did not wash their hands before they ate, they were upset. They thought Jesus' disciples should follow their rules.

He answered and said to them, "Well did Isaiah prophesy of you hypocrites ...'This people honors Me with their lips, but their heart is far from Me...'

"For laying aside the commandment of God, you hold the tradition of men—the washing of pitchers and cups, and many other such things you do."

433

He said to them, "All too well you reject the commandment of God, that you may keep your tradition." Mark 7:6-9

Jesus told the Pharisees they were just like Isaiah the prophet said. Even though they pretended to love God, in their hearts they did not care about Him at all. They cared more about their own traditions than they did about God's commands.

Remember the Ten Commandments God gave Israel? The first four commands are about loving God. If you love God, you will keep these commands.

You shall have no other gods before Me.

You shall not make for yourself a carved image...

You shall not take the name of the LORD your God in vain...

Remember the Sabbath day, to keep it holy. Exodus 20:3-8

If you love God you won't use His name as a swear word, you won't have idols, you will worship God alone, and you will honor Him as the Creator of the world.

The next six commands are about loving other people. If you love others, you will keep these commands.

Honor your father and your mother...

You shall not murder.

You shall not commit adultery.

You shall not steal.

You shall not bear false witness against your neighbor.

You shall not covet...anything that is your neighbor's. Exodus 20:12-17

If you love others, you'll honor them. You won't kill them, steal from them, lie about them, or want what they have.

The Pharisees did not understand that God's commands are about love - loving God and loving others.

One of the teachers of the law...asked Jesus, "Which of the commands is most important?"

Jesus answered, "The most important command is this: '...Love the Lord your God with all your heart, all your soul, all your mind, and all your strength.' The second command is this: 'Love your neighbor as you love yourself.' There are no commands more important than these."
Mark 12:28-31

The Pharisees thought God accepted them because of all the rules they followed, but they were not following God's rules. They did not love God or people! Remember how upset they were when Jesus healed a man on the Sabbath? The Pharisees cared more about keeping their own made-up rules than they did about showing love to those around them.

Jesus explained to the people of Israel that a person does not become clean on the inside by keeping rules like eating out of clean dishes or washing one's hands before a meal. It is not dirty food that makes a person unclean; it is a person's sinful heart that makes him unacceptable to God.

When He had called all the multitude to Himself, He said to them, "Hear Me, everyone, and understand: There is nothing that enters a man from outside which can defile him; but the things which come out of him, those are the things that defile a man."

"...For from within, out of the heart of men, proceed evil thoughts, adulteries, fornications, murders, thefts, covetousness, wickedness, deceit, lewdness, an evil eye, blasphemy, pride, foolishness. All these evil things come from within and defile a man." Mark 7:14-15, 21-23

To help the Jews understand that a person cannot be made acceptable to God by keeping rules, Jesus told them a parable.

Also He spoke this parable to some who trusted in themselves that they were righteous, and despised others: "Two men went up to the temple to pray, one a Pharisee and the other a tax collector. The Pharisee stood and prayed..., 'God, I thank You that I am not like other men—extortioners, unjust,

> **Parable** - a made-up story about everyday life that teaches an important lesson

adulterers, or even as this tax collector. I fast twice a week; I give tithes of all that I possess.' And the tax collector, standing afar off, would not so much as raise his eyes to heaven, but beat his breast, saying, 'God, be merciful to me a sinner!'

"I tell you, this man went down to his house justified rather than the other; for everyone who exalts himself will be humbled, and he who humbles himself will be exalted." Luke 18:9-14

> **Justified - to be legally declared righteous so that you are acceptable to God**

Tax collectors worked for the Roman government. They got rich by stealing from their own people.

In Jesus' story the tax collector realized he was a sinner who deserved to be separated from God forever. He begged God to have mercy on Him. But the Pharisee came to God with a list of his good deeds. He was thankful he was not as bad as other people, especially tax collectors.

Does that sound like Cain and Abel? Just like the Pharisees tried to make themselves acceptable to God by following their own made-up rules, Cain tried to come to God according to his own ideas.

Abel, on the other hand, was like the tax collector. He knew he was a sinner who deserved to die; therefore, he trusted in God to save him.

Jesus said the tax collector in the parable was the one justified before God, not the Pharisee. God accepted the tax collector because he admitted he was a sinner and trusted in God to save him. But God did not accept the Pharisee because the Pharisee did not trust in the Savior.

Remember

Both Cain and the Pharisees were religious. Religious people think they can make themselves acceptable to God according to their own ideas. They try to do good deeds to get to Heaven.

The Pharisees thought they were acceptable to God because of all their rules. Cain tried to gain God's acceptance by bringing God a gift.

But you cannot be made acceptable to God according to your own, or someone else's, beliefs. Religion and doing good deeds cannot save you.

The Bible says that our hearts are full of sin.

📖"For from within, out of the heart of men, proceed evil thoughts… murders, thefts, covetousness, wickedness, deceit…pride, foolishness. All these evil things come from within and defile a man." Mark 7:21-23

The penalty for the sin in your heart is death. You cannot pay for your sin by praying, getting baptized, going to church, or being kind to others. Religion and doing good deeds cannot make you clean on the inside.

Only Jesus the Savior can make you acceptable to God. If you try to make yourself right with God by being good or giving something to God like Cain and the Pharisees did, you will be separated from God forever. But if you come to God like Abel and the tax collector did, by admitting your sin and trusting in God to save you, then God will give you the gift of His righteousness.

Jesus came to save all who admit they are sinners and trust only in Him to save them from the death penalty they deserve.

Questions

1. Why were the Pharisees upset with Jesus' disciples? *The Pharisees were upset with Jesus' disciples because Jesus' disciples did not wash their hands before eating.*

2. What was more important to the Pharisees than loving God and loving people? *It was more important to the Pharisees to keep their made-up rules than it was to keep God's commands to love Him and other people.*

3. Could the Pharisees make themselves clean on the inside by washing their hands before eating? *No, they could not make themselves clean on the inside by eating only what was clean.*

4. Could the Pharisees make themselves acceptable to God by keeping rules? *No, they could not make themselves acceptable to God by keeping rules.*

5. What makes a person dirty on the inside? *Our dirty, sinful hearts make us unclean and unacceptable to God.*

6. How were the Pharisees like Cain? *Neither Cain nor the Pharisees believed they were sinners who deserved death. Cain and the Pharisees tried to get God's acceptance according to their own way, by doing good deeds.*

7. How was the tax collector who prayed in the temple like Abel? *He was humble. He knew he deserved to die for his sin, but he trusted in God to save him.*

8. Can you make yourself acceptable to God by going to church, praying, being baptized, or doing good deeds? *No, there is nothing you can do to make yourself acceptable to God.*

9. Who is the only One who can make you acceptable to God? *Jesus Christ the Savior is the only One who can make you acceptable to God.*

Biblical Worldviews

- All people are full of sin on the inside.
- There is nothing you can do to make yourself acceptable to God.
- Religion and good works will not make you acceptable to God.
- The penalty for sin is death.
- Jesus Christ is the only Savior; He is the only One who can save you from death and make you acceptable to God.
- God saves only those who admit they are sinners and trust in Him to save them.

Activity 1: Temple Prayer Skit

Supplies:

- Three volunteers to be a Pharisee, a tax collector, and the narrator

Instructions:

- Students read and act out the following script, or they can perform the skit using their own version of the story.
- Discuss: Why did God accept the tax collector and not the Pharisee?

Pharisee/Tax Collector Script (by Nancy Hughes)

Narrator: "Two men went up to the temple to pray, one a Pharisee and the other a tax collector." (Luke 18:10)

Pharisee: (Very Proud) "God, I thank You that I am not like other men…" (Luke 18:11) Name the sins you do not do and all the good deeds you do.

Tax Collector: (Stands far off, head bowed, and beating breast in anguish) "God, be merciful to me a sinner!" (Luke 18:13)

Activity 2: Bible Hangman

Supplies:

- Chalkboard or dry erase board
- Chalk or dry erase markers

Instructions:

- Draw a large hangman tree on the board.
- Draw lines and spaces under the tree to correspond to the letters and spaces of the key phrase.

439

- **Key phrase**: Praying, getting baptized, being kind to others, or being religious do not make you clean on the inside.

- **Key phrase for younger students**: Only Jesus can make you acceptable to God.

- Ask the lesson review questions, one at a time. Call on one student or one team to answer each question.

- If answer is correct, the student or team gets to pick a letter, i.e., the letter b.

- If the letter picked is in the key phrase, the teacher fills it in on the board each time it occurs.

- If the letter picked is not in the key phrase, the teacher draws one part of a stick figure on the hangman tree, i.e., a head, an arm, a stick body, etc.

- When a student (or team) thinks he knows the key phrase, he may try to solve the puzzle on his turn. The game is over when a student or team solves the puzzle or the teacher draws all the parts of the stick man, whichever comes first.

Extra Bible References

Psalm 143:2; Ecclesiastes 7:20; Isaiah 29:13; Jeremiah 9:23-24; Matthew 6:1-18; Matthew 22:36-40, 23:1-39; Romans 3:9-31, 13:9; Galatians 5:14; Hebrews 4:13

62
Who is Jesus?
The Transfiguration

Memory Verse

So they said, "Believe on the Lord Jesus Christ, and you will be saved..." Acts16:31

Lesson

Because of the incredible miracles Jesus did, some of the Jews thought Jesus was John the Baptist. They knew King Herod had killed John the Baptist, but they thought he must have come back to life as Jesus.

Other people thought Jesus was Elijah. Elijah was one of the prophets of Israel who never died because God took him to Heaven in a whirlwind. They thought Elijah had come back to Earth as Jesus.

Still others thought Jesus was one of the Old Testament prophets who rose from the dead.

Everyone knew Jesus was great. Only Someone very powerful could heal people's diseases and feed thousands of people with one boy's lunch. Only someone powerful could make demons come out of people. But even though they knew Jesus was special, most of the Jews did not believe Jesus was God the Son who came to Earth to save people from Satan and death.

Many people today are like the Jews. They think Jesus was a good man who lived long ago and did many great things. They think it is good to try to be like Jesus, but they do not believe Jesus is who He said He was; they do not believe Jesus is God the Son, the only Savior.

But thinking like this does not make sense. Jesus was not a good man if He lied about who He was. If Jesus said He was God when He was really just another human being, He would have been blaspheming. You should not try to imitate someone who tells a big lie like that!

Then there are other people who simply don't care about Jesus at all; they don't think it matters what they believe about Him.

One day Jesus asked His twelve disciples who they thought He was.

Now Jesus and His disciples went out to the towns of Caesarea Philippi; and on the road He asked His disciples..., "Who do men say that I am?"

So they answered, "John the Baptist; but some say, Elijah; and others, one of the prophets."

He said to them, "But who do you say that I am?"

Peter answered and said to Him, "You are the Christ." Mark 8:27-29

Remember that the names Christ and Messiah mean God's Chosen One. Peter believed Jesus was the Christ foretold by the Old Testament prophets. He believed Jesus was the One chosen by God to be a prophet, a priest, and a king. He believed Jesus was God the Savior.

The Bible says that when the disciples finally understood who Jesus was, Jesus...

...strictly warned them that they should tell no one about Him. Mark 8:30

Jesus did not want people to believe in Him because of what His disciples said or because someone persuaded them to believe in Him. Jesus wanted the people of Israel to decide for themselves whether or not they believed He was God the Son, the promised Messiah.

Now that the disciples understood that Jesus was the Christ, Jesus began to explain to them what was going to happen to Him. He started telling them how He was going to suffer in order to save people from Satan and the death penalty.

And He began to teach them that the Son of Man must suffer many things, and be rejected by the elders and chief priests and scribes, and be killed, and after three days rise again. Mark 8:31

Old Testament Prophecies about the Savior suffering:

He is despised and rejected by men, a Man of sorrows and acquainted with grief. And we hid, as it were, our faces from Him; He was despised, and we did not esteem Him. Isaiah 53:3

For dogs have surrounded Me; the congregation of the wicked has enclosed Me. They pierced My hands and My feet; Psalm 22:16

For You will not leave my soul in Sheol, nor will You allow Your Holy One to see corruption. Psalm 16:10

Remember what the prophets wrote about the coming Savior? Hundreds of years before Jesus came to Earth, they foretold that the Savior would be hated and falsely accused. They predicted He would die and then rise again.

Jesus knew that everything the prophets foretold would happen; He knew Satan was going to use the Jewish religious leaders to have Him killed. He also knew that after three days He would rise from the dead.

One day Jesus took Peter, James, and John up on a mountain.

Now after six days Jesus took Peter, James, and John, and led them up on a high mountain apart by themselves; and He was transfigured before them. His clothes became shining, exceedingly white, like snow, such as no launderer on earth can whiten them. Mark 9:2-3

When the Bible says Jesus was transfigured, it means Jesus' appearance changed.

Remember the tabernacle – the tent where God lived among the Israelites in the wilderness? Even though God lived inside the tabernacle, all that could be seen from the outside was the covering of animal skins. The Israelites could not see the brilliant light of God's presence that was inside.

Jesus' human body was kind of like the covering of animal skins on the tabernacle - it hid the God part of Him from view. But when Jesus took Peter, James, and John up on the mountain, they saw the God part of Jesus.

His face shone like the sun, and His clothes became as white as the light. Matthew 17:2

Jesus is the all-powerful, all-knowing Creator of the world. He is the One who holds the stars and planets in place. He is the highest king. Jesus is more majestic and amazing than you could ever imagine. On the mountain, God allowed Peter, James, and John to get a tiny glimpse of Jesus' greatness.

And behold, two men talked with Him, who were Moses and Elijah, who appeared in glory and spoke of His decease which He was about to accomplish at Jerusalem. Luke 9:30-31

Just like Abel, Abraham, Sarah, Isaac, Noah, Joshua, King David, and many others, Moses and Elijah believed in God. They believed they were sinners separated from God. While they were alive on Earth, they had believed God would someday send a Savior to make a way for them to be made acceptable to God. Because all these people had trusted in God while they lived on Earth, God took them to Heaven when they died.

While Jesus was transfigured on the mountain, Moses and Elijah came down from Heaven and talked with Jesus about what was going to happen to Him. They knew Jesus was the promised Savior they had been waiting for when they lived on Earth so long ago.

Then God the Father spoke.

And a cloud came and overshadowed them; and a voice came out of the cloud, saying, "This is My beloved Son. Hear Him!" Suddenly, when they had looked around, they saw no one anymore, but only Jesus with themselves... Mark 9:7-8

God the Father called Jesus His Son. This was proof that what Peter believed about Jesus was true. Jesus really was God the Son, the promised Savior.

Many years later, Peter talked about what he, James, and John saw.

...we...were eyewitnesses of His majesty. For He received from God the Father honor and glory when such a voice came to Him from the Excellent Glory: "This is My beloved Son, in whom I am well pleased." And we heard this voice which came from heaven when we were with Him on the holy mountain. 2 Peter 1:16-18

Besides the fact that God the Father said Jesus was His Son, there are other proofs Jesus was who He claimed to be.

Those who were with Jesus while Jesus lived on Earth saw with their own eyes all that Jesus said and did. They saw Jesus walk on water and calm the sea simply by speaking. They saw Him cast out demons and raise people back to life. Only God could do the incredible miracles they saw Jesus do. In the first four books of the New Testament, Matthew, Mark, Luke, and John tell about what they and other eye-witnesses saw and heard. These <u>eye-witnesses</u> are another proof that Jesus was (and is) God.

And lastly, <u>every detail the prophets foretold about Jesus hundreds of years before Jesus was born came to pass</u> exactly like the prophets predicted. Humanly speaking, it would be totally impossible for so many events foretold hundreds of years beforehand all to come true. Only God could make that happen. Jesus truly was God, the promised Messiah.

Remember

What you believe about Jesus is important.

The Bible says Jesus is God the Son.

And we have seen and testify that the Father has sent the Son as Savior of the world. Whoever confesses that Jesus is the Son of God, God abides in him, and he in God. I John 4:14-15

The Bible also says Jesus is the only Savior.

Nor is there salvation in any other, for there is no other name under heaven given among men by which we must be saved. Acts 4:12

The only One who can save you from eternal death is God the Son, Jesus Christ. That is why it is important what you believe about Jesus. Those who believe in Jesus will live with Him forever in Heaven. But those who do not believe Jesus is God, the only Savior, will be separated from Him forever in the terrible place of suffering.

Questions

1. The Jews knew Jesus was someone special because of the miracles He did. Who did they think Jesus was? *They thought Jesus was either John the Baptist, Elijah, or one of the Old Testament prophets who must have come back to life.*

2. Who did Peter think Jesus was? *Peter believed Jesus was God the Son, the promised Savior.*

3. What did Jesus say was going to happen to Him? *He said He was going to suffer at the hands of the Jewish religious leaders and be killed but after three days He would come back to life.*

4. Even though Jesus looked like any other man, what was different about Him? *Jesus was both human and God at the same time.*

5. What happened to Jesus on the mountain? *He was transfigured; His body was changed so that the God-part of Him showed through. His face shone like the sun and His clothes became as white as the light.*

6. Why were Moses and Elijah in Heaven with God? *They were in Heaven because while they lived on Earth they had trusted in God to save them. During their lifetime they had believed God would send a Savior who would make them acceptable to God.*

7. What were Jesus, Moses, and Elijah talking about up on the mountain? *They were talking about the fact that Jesus was soon going to die.*

8. What did God the Father say about Jesus when Jesus was transfigured? *God the Father said Jesus was His beloved Son and that the disciples should listen to Him.*

9. What proofs do we have that Jesus is who He said He was? *1. Peter, James, and John heard God the Father call Jesus His Son. 2. Jesus' followers were eye-witnesses of all that Jesus said and did. What they saw is written in the New Testament part of the Bible. 3. Everything the prophets wrote about Jesus hundreds of years before He came to Earth happened just exactly like they predicted.*

10. Is it important what you believe about Jesus? *Yes, it is very important. Jesus was not just a good man; He was (and is) God, the only Savior. The Bible says that those who do not trust in Jesus to save them from sin and death will be separated from God forever in the terrible place of suffering.*

Biblical Worldviews

- Jesus Christ was more than just a good man; Jesus is God the Son, the only Savior.
- Jesus Christ is a human being; Jesus Christ is God.
- One proof that Jesus is God the Son is that God the Father pronounced Jesus to be His Son.
- The writings of eye-witnesses – men who were with Jesus every day – testify to the fact that Jesus is who He said He was.
- Everything the prophets foretold about the coming Savior was fulfilled in Jesus, proving Him to be who He said He was.
- God knows the future; He works out everything according to His plans.
- Jesus Christ is the only Savior; He saves only those who believe in Him.

Activity: Three Proofs

Supplies:

- Paper, one piece per student
- Pencils and crayons

Instructions:

- Students label their papers: Three Proofs Jesus is God
- Then they write out the following proofs:

  God said Jesus was His Son

  Many eye-witnesses saw the great things Jesus did.

  All that the prophets predicted about Jesus came true.

- Younger students can draw a picture of a great miracle Jesus did. Some examples might be walking on the water, calming the sea, or feeding thousands of people with only a boy's lunch.

Extra Bible References

Exodus 36:14-19, 40:34-35; Deuteronomy 34:5-6; 2 Kings 2:11; Isaiah 46:10; Mark 6:14; Luke 1:1-4, 24:6-7; John 1:1, 14-18; 3:16; 4:25-26; 5:17-47; 8:58; 10:30; John 14:1-9; Colossians 1:15-18; 1 Timothy 6:16; Hebrews 11:24-28, 32-40; 1 Peter 1:10-11; 2 Peter 1:16-21; 1 John 4:1-3

63
The Good Shepherd
Jesus: The Door of the Sheepfold

Memory Verse

"I am the good shepherd. The good shepherd gives His life for the sheep." John 10:11

Lesson

In Jesus' day, all Jews knew about sheep. In fact, many of them were shepherds. Remember King David? He was a shepherd when he was young. As a young man, David killed a lion and a bear that attacked his sheep.

Sometimes the shepherds in Israel had to take their sheep far away from home to find grass and water for them. Out in these far-off places were robbers and dangerous wild animals like lions, bears, and wolves.

At night, the shepherds had to find a safe place for their sheep to sleep. Sometimes they found a cave where they could spend the night, but other times they had to build a pen for the sheep.

This pen was called a sheepfold. It was built by piling up rocks for the walls and laying thorny vines on top.

The shepherd left only one opening in the wall. After all the sheep were safely inside for the night, the shepherd lay down in this doorway. This is where he spent the night. If wild animals or robbers tried to get in, he would fight them off. A good shepherd would even die in order to protect his sheep.

Jesus compared Himself to the good shepherd who slept in the doorway of the sheepfold.

Then Jesus said to them again, "Most assuredly, I say to you, I am the door of the sheep...If anyone enters by Me, he will be saved...The thief does not come except to steal, and to kill, and to destroy. I have come that they may have life, and that they may have it more abundantly.

"I am the good shepherd. The good shepherd gives His life for the sheep." John 10:7-11

Jesus is the one and only door into God's sheepfold. God's sheepfold is the place of safety from Satan and death. Do you remember how God told Noah to make only one door in the ark? Only those who entered through this one door were saved from death in the flood. The only way to be saved from the second death is by believing in Jesus Christ.

This is what Jesus told Thomas, one of His disciples.

Jesus said to him, "I am the way, the truth, and the life. No one comes to the Father except through Me." John 14:6

People have many ideas about how to be saved from Satan and eternal death. Some people say that in order for God to save you must do good works or be baptized. Other people say you must pray a prayer, or give your life or your heart to Jesus. Some people even say you need to put Jesus on the throne of your heart, but the Bible does not say that any of these are the way to get into God's place of safety.

The Bible says that Jesus is the only **way** to God. Remember Jacob's dream in the Old Testament? Jacob dreamed about a ladder going from Earth to Heaven. The ladder in Jacob's dream pointed to Jesus. Only by believing in Jesus can sinful people from Earth go up to Heaven.

Jesus is the **truth.** He is the author of the Bible. In the Bible, Jesus tells us the truth about how we can be saved from death.

And Jesus is the **life**. All those in Adam's family are dead to God; they do not have a relationship with God and will have to be separated from Him forever. But those who trust in Jesus Christ to save them from sin and death are made alive to God.

He who believes in the Son has everlasting life; John 3:36a

Whoever believes in Jesus Christ, receives everlasting life.

Jesus tells the truth and gives life, but Satan is a liar and a murderer. Satan is the robber who comes "to steal, and to kill, and to destroy." Remember how Satan tricked Adam and Eve? Adam and Eve belonged to God, but when they believed Satan's lie they joined Satan's side and became separated from God.

The Bible says that Satan is always looking for someone to hurt. Even now Satan tries to keep people away from God; He does not want people to trust in the Savior and be saved from death. He wants to kill and destroy the sheep.

...the devil...was a murderer from the beginning, and...there is no truth in him...for he is a liar and the father of it. John 8:44

Jesus is the Good Shepherd who was going to give His life for the sheep. Jesus was going to die for us.

I am the good shepherd. The good shepherd gives His life for the sheep. John 10:11

Many hundreds of years before Jesus came, the prophet Isaiah wrote that the Savior would be wounded and bruised for our sins (our transgressions and iniquities).

> **The prophet Isaiah wrote:**
>
> But He was wounded for our transgressions, He was bruised for our iniquities; the chastisement for our peace was upon Him, and by His stripes we are healed. Isaiah 53:5

The prophet Isaiah said the Savior would receive the punishment (or chastisement) we deserve. What is the punishment we deserve? It is death, isn't it? You and I deserve death, but Jesus was coming to die for us. Like a good shepherd, Jesus was going to die so that we could live!

But God demonstrates His own love toward us, in that while we were still sinners, Christ died for us. Romans 5:8

Remember

Jesus is God. He is the Creator of the world and the highest authority. He did not have to come to Earth; He could have stayed in Heaven.

Jesus did not have to die because He never did anything to deserve death. But Jesus came to Earth for you and me. Jesus came as the promised Savior to rescue us from Satan, sin, and death.

Even though we are all sinners, Jesus loved us and planned to give His life for us. Jesus truly is the Good Shepherd! He is the only door into God's sheepfold; only by believing in Him can you enter God's place of safety from Satan and death.

Questions

1. Why did shepherds build sheepfolds? *Shepherds built sheepfolds to protect their sheep from robbers and wild animals at night.*

2. How many openings, or doorways, did the shepherd make in the sheepfold? *The shepherd put only one doorway in the sheepfold.*

3. Where did the shepherd sleep at night? *He slept in the doorway of the sheepfold.*

4. What would a good shepherd do if a robber or wild animal tried to get through the door of the sheepfold? *A good shepherd would fight off the robber or the wild animal. He would die if he needed to in order to protect the sheep in the sheepfold.*

5. How is God's sheepfold like the sheepfold the shepherds built for the sheep? *God's sheepfold is a place of safety from Satan and death.*

6. Who is the thief who comes to steal and kill and destroy? *Satan is. Satan tries to keep people from trusting in the Savior. He wants people to die and be separated from God forever in the terrible place of suffering.*

7. In what way is Jesus like the good shepherd who slept in the doorway of the sheepfold? *Jesus is like the shepherd because just like the shepherd would give his life to protect his sheep, Jesus was going to give His life to save us from Satan and death.*

8. How many doors are there into God's place of safety? *There is only one door and that is Jesus Christ the Son of God. He is the only Savior; only by believing in Him can you enter God's place of safety from Satan and eternal death.*

Biblical Worldviews

- God is a God of love.
- Jesus Christ is good; He planned to give His life for us.
- Satan is a liar and a murderer.
- All people are sinners and deserve death.
- Jesus Christ is the only Savior; He is the only way to God.
- Jesus Christ gives life.
- Jesus Christ tells the truth.
- Jesus Christ is God; He is the Creator and the highest authority.

Activity: Sheepfold Craft

Supplies:

- Cardstock
- Sticks and stones from outdoors
- Pencils, pencil crayons, crayons
- Cotton balls
- Glue

- Clay, optional

Instructions:

- Take students outside to collect small sticks and stones.
- When they come in, students draw the outline of a large sheepfold on a piece of cardstock.
- Students can make sheepfolds by gluing the sticks and stones to the outline, making sure to leave a space for the doorway.
- Students draw a shepherd in the doorway.
- Optional: Students shape a shepherd out of clay and place him in the doorway.
- Students make sheep by gluing cotton balls to the cardstock and drawing heads and feet.
- Optional: Students make the body of sheep by gluing together a number of cotton balls and forming heads and legs out of clay. Glue the head and legs to the cotton-ball body.
- When the glue is dry, students may color their pictures.
- Optional: Write the memory verse above the sheepfold.

Extra Bible References

Isaiah 43:11, 45:21-22; John 3:16, 17:3; Acts 4:12; Romans 3:12, 5:6-11;
2 Corinthians 11:13-15; Philippians 2:5-8; Colossians 1:13-22; 1 Timothy 2:5-6;
2 Timothy 1:10; Hebrews 2:14-15; 1 Peter 1:18-21, 5:8; 1 John 5:12, 20;
Revelation 20:15

64
Little Children
The Man Who Called Jesus "Good Teacher"

Memory Verse

> *Jesus answered and said to them, "This is the work of God, that you believe in Him whom He sent." John 6:29*

Lesson

One day some little children were brought to Jesus.

Then they brought little children to Him, that He might touch them; but the disciples rebuked those who brought them. But when Jesus saw it, He was greatly displeased and said to them, "Let the little children come to Me, and do not forbid them; for of such is the kingdom of God. Assuredly, I say to you, whoever does not receive the kingdom of God as a little child will by no means enter it." And He took them up in His arms, laid His hands on them, and blessed them. Mark 10:13-16

Jesus wanted the little children to come to Him; He was upset with the disciples for scolding those who brought them. Jesus loves children. He was not too busy for them.

In fact, Jesus said that unless the Jews became like little children, they could not enter His kingdom. Just like the tax collector in Jesus' parable, little children are humble.

Therefore whoever humbles himself as this little child is the greatest in the kingdom of heaven. Matthew 18:4

The Jews were proud; they did not think they were sinners separated from God. They thought they were acceptable to God because they came from Abraham and because they had God's laws. Jesus told the Jews that in order to be a part of God's kingdom, they would have to be humble - they would have to admit they were sinners and trust in Jesus to save them.

After Jesus blessed the little children, He went on His way. As He walked along, a man ran up to Him.

Now as He was going out on the road, one came running, knelt before Him, and asked Him, "Good Teacher, what shall I do that I may inherit eternal life?" Mark 10:17

This man did not believe Jesus was God the Son; he thought Jesus was just a good man. He wanted Jesus to tell him how he could be a good man too. He wanted to know what good things he needed to do to earn eternal life.

Jesus told the man that no person is good. God is the only One who is good.

So Jesus said to him, "Why do you call Me good? No one is good but One, that is, God. You know the commandments: 'Do not commit adultery,' 'Do not murder,' 'Do not steal,' 'Do not bear false witness,' 'Do not defraud,' 'Honor your father and your mother.'"

And he answered and said to Him, "Teacher, all these things I have kept from my youth." Mark 10:18-20

This man was proud; he thought he had kept all God's rules. He did not understand that the Ten Commandments are all about loving God and loving other people. In order to earn eternal life, he would have to be perfect. He would have to love God and love others.

Then Jesus, looking at him, loved him, and said to him, "One thing you lack: Go your way, sell whatever you have and give to the poor, and you will have treasure in heaven; and come, take up the cross, and follow Me." Mark 10:21

Jesus knew this man's heart; He knew he did not love God or other people. When Jesus told the man to sell his possessions, give the money to the poor, and come follow Him, the man became sad because he loved his possessions more than he loved God or other people. He did not want to sell all his things that he loved so much. He did not want to give the money to the poor, and he did not want to follow Jesus.

But he was sad at this word, and went away sorrowful, for he had great possessions. Mark 10:22

This man thought he could earn eternal life by doing good works and keeping the Ten Commandments, but Jesus showed him he could never be good enough to get to Heaven.

Remember

The Bible says all people are sinners. No one is good, not even you.

There is none who does good, no, not one. Romans 3:12

God says the good things you do are like filthy rags to Him.

But we are all like an unclean thing, and all our righteousnesses are like filthy rags; Isaiah 64:6a

In order to earn eternal life for yourself, you would have to be perfect on the inside as well as on the outside. You would have to love all people all the time and never be angry or upset. You can never be that good; you can never be good enough to earn eternal life!

The only way to get eternal life is to trust in God. God sent Jesus His Son into the world to make a way for us to have eternal life.

Do not be proud like this man who thought he could be good enough to make it to Heaven. Be humble like a little child. Admit you have broken God's rules and trust in Jesus to save you from sin and death. God saves all who trust in Him.

Questions

1. Does Jesus care about children? *Yes, Jesus loves children.*

2. In what way did the Jews need to be like little children? *In order to enter God's kingdom the Jews needed to be humble. They needed to admit they were helpless to save themselves and trust in God to save them.*

3. Is it true that some people are good and others are bad? *No, God says that we are all bad; we are all sinners. Even our good deeds are filthy rags to God.*

4. Who is the only One who is good? *God is the only One who is good.*

5. How did the rich young man who came running up to Jesus think he could earn eternal life? *He thought he could earn eternal life by keeping God's commandments.*

6. What did Jesus tell the man to do? *Jesus told the man to sell all he owned, give the money to the poor, and come follow Him.*

7. Why did this man not want to do what Jesus said? *The man did not want to do what Jesus said because he loved his riches more than he loved God or other people.*

8. How good did Jesus say the man would have to be in order to earn eternal life? *Jesus said the man would have to be perfect. In order to earn eternal life he would have to be totally good on the inside. He would have to love God and love other people.*

9. What does God want you to be humble about? *God wants you to admit you are a sinner and that you cannot be good enough to earn eternal life. Then He wants you to trust in Jesus Christ to give you eternal life.*

Biblical Worldviews

- God loves children.
- All people are sinners; only God is good.
- Only perfect people can live with God in Heaven.
- We cannot save ourselves; only God can save us.
- God saves only those who trust in Him.

Activity: Bible Bingo

Supplies:

- Bingo cards and game tokens (Any set will do. You can buy an inexpensive set at the dollar store.

Instructions:

- Give each student a bingo card and some tokens.
- Ask a question from the lesson review and call on a student to answer it. If the student answers it correctly, she calls the bingo square she wants to cover. Everyone else who has that square covers it as well.
- Continue to ask questions, calling on a different student each time. Allow everyone to answer at least one question and pick at least one bingo square.
- The game is over when the first student shouts BINGO because she has covered a complete row with tokens, either vertically, horizontally, or diagonally.
- Play the game several times until everyone has had a turn answering a question and/or all the questions from the review have been asked and answered.

Extra Bible References

1 Samuel 16:7; Jeremiah 17:9-10; Matthew 5:17-28; John 3:16; Romans 3:11-23; 4:2, 6; Romans 13:9; Galatians 5:14; Ephesians 2:8-9; 1 Timothy 2:4

65
Riches are Tricky
Lazarus and the Rich Man

Memory Verse

Jesus answered and said to them, "This is the work of God, that you believe in Him whom He sent." John 6:29

Lesson

Jesus was God's prophet. He always taught God's Word to the huge crowds that followed Him.

In the meantime, when an innumerable multitude of people had gathered together, so that they trampled one another, He began to say to His disciples first of all, "Beware of the leaven of the Pharisees, which is hypocrisy."

And..., "Take heed and beware of covetousness, for one's life does not consist in the abundance of the things he possesses." Luke 12:1a, 15

Jesus warned the Jews not to be covetous. To be covetous is to be greedy, always wanting more money and more things. The young man who loved his riches more than he loved God or other people was covetous.

Jesus told a parable to show how useless money really is.

Then He spoke a parable to them, saying: "The ground of a certain rich man yielded plentifully. And he thought within himself, saying, 'What shall I do, since I have no room to store my crops?' So he said, 'I will do this: I will pull down my barns and build greater, and there I will store all my crops and my goods. And I will say to my soul, "Soul, you have many goods laid up for many years; take your ease; eat, drink, and be merry."' Luke 12:16-19

Jesus often used stories about real life, called parables, to teach the people.

The farmer in Jesus' story was very successful. His fields produced so much food he had to pull down his old barns and build bigger ones to store it all.

If Jesus were telling the same story today, He might tell about someone who saves up so much money he never has to work again. He can buy whatever he wants without worrying about a thing. He can do everything fun he wants to do.

It is easy to be jealous of people who have that much money, but Jesus gave a warning about being greedy.

But God said to him, "Fool! This night your soul will be required of you; then whose will those things be which you have provided?" Luke 12:20

Jesus called this man foolish because his great riches had tricked him into thinking he had nothing to worry about. He did not realize that money cannot keep you from getting sick or even from dying. Right when this man thought his life was perfect, he died. Of course, when he died, the wealthy man left all his riches behind.

Jesus told the crowd that this is what happens when money is more important to people than God.

So is he who lays up treasure for himself, and is not rich toward God. Luke 12:21

The Bible says that...

...the Pharisees...were lovers of money... Luke 16:14

The Pharisees were hypocrites. They pretended to love God, when what they really loved was their money. Jesus told the crowd to "beware of the leaven of the Pharisees, which is hypocrisy."

One of the most important ingredients in bread is yeast (or leaven). When bakers put yeast into bread dough, the yeast spreads all through the dough to make it grow into a big loaf.

Jesus warned the people of Israel not to let the yeast of hypocrisy spread into their lives. He did not want the Jews to copy the ways of the Pharisees who acted like they loved God but in truth loved only their money and possessions.

Jesus talked a lot about the dangers of riches. That is because riches easily trick us. It is easy to think money is more important than a relationship with God.

One day, Jesus told a true story about a man named Lazarus.

> There was a certain rich man who was clothed in purple and fine linen and fared sumptuously every day. But there was a certain beggar named Lazarus, full of sores, who was laid at his gate, desiring to be fed with the crumbs which fell from the rich man's table. Moreover the dogs came and licked his sores. So it was that the beggar died, and was carried by the angels to Abraham's bosom. The rich man also died and was buried. And being in torments in Hades, he lifted up his eyes and saw Abraham afar off, and Lazarus in his bosom.
> Luke 16:19-23

Both the rich man and Lazarus the beggar died. The rich man, who always had nice clothes and lived every day as though it were a party, went to the terrible place of suffering.

But Lazarus went to paradise. Paradise was the place believers went before the Savior died. Abraham was in paradise because during his life on Earth he had trusted in the promised Savior.

In the place of suffering, the rich man was in terrible pain and misery. He begged Abraham to send Lazarus over to him with a drop of water to cool his tongue.

> Then he cried and said, "Father Abraham, have mercy on me, and send Lazarus that he may dip the tip of his finger in water and cool my tongue; for I am tormented in this flame."
>
> But Abraham said, "Son, remember that in your lifetime you received your good things, and likewise Lazarus evil things; but now he is comforted and you are tormented. And besides all this, between us and you there is a great gulf fixed, so that those who want to pass from here to you cannot, nor can those from there pass to us."
> Luke 16:24-26

It is important to understand that the rich man did not go to the place of suffering because he was rich; it is not bad to have money. God is the One who gives money and possessions to people.

The problem was that the rich man let his riches trick him. He thought life was all about having money. He did not realize that money cannot buy what is most important; money cannot buy eternal life. The rich man should have trusted in God instead of in his riches.

In the same way the rich man did not go to the place of suffering because he was rich, Lazarus did not go to paradise because he was poor. Lazarus went to paradise because, during the time he lived on Earth, he had trusted in God to save him from Satan and the death penalty he deserved for his sin.

The payment for sin is separation from God forever in a terrible burning place of suffering called Hell. Those who do not trust in the Savior while they are alive on Earth will end up in this place when their life is over. Day after day, forever and ever, they will suffer unimaginable agony. There is no way of escape; once a person goes to the place of suffering, he or she will be there for all time without end.

Abraham told the rich man that it was impossible to pass over from paradise to the place of suffering. No one from the place of suffering can pass over to paradise either.

When the rich man realized there was no hope for him, he begged Abraham to send Lazarus to warn his brothers who were still living on Earth, so at least they would not end up where he was.

Then he said, "I beg you therefore, father, that you would send him to my father's house, for I have five brothers, that he may testify to them, lest they also come to this place of torment."

Abraham said to him, "They have Moses and the prophets; let them hear them."

And he said, "No, father Abraham; but if one goes to them from the dead, they will repent."

But he said to him, "If they do not hear Moses and the prophets, neither will they be persuaded though one rise from the dead."
Luke 16:27-31

People in the place of suffering remember what happened during their lifetime on Earth. They remember the loved ones they left behind. The rich man did not want his five brothers to join him in his torment. He thought his brothers would listen to someone who came back from the dead.

But Abraham told the rich man that his brothers knew what Moses and the prophets had written. If they did not believe what was written in the Bible, they would not believe someone who came back from the dead either.

Remember

Do not let riches and money trick you. It is easy to imagine you would be happy if you had lots of money; after all, you could do whatever you pleased and buy whatever you wanted. But don't be tricked; God is way more important than money.

The Bible says to...

...be content with such things as you have. Hebrews 13:5

Money cannot buy long life or peace. It cannot buy a happy family, true friends, or eternal life with God in Heaven. Only God can give eternal life. Only life with God brings peace, joy, and true contentment.

Life on Earth is so short compared to life after death. Heaven and the place of suffering are forever and ever. If during your life on Earth you trust in riches rather than trusting in God, you will go to the place of suffering where you will be forevermore. But if you trust in God to save you, He will give you eternal life with Him.

Because Abel, Noah, Moses, and Abraham trusted in God while they lived on Earth, they went to paradise when they died. Later, after the Savior died and rose again, God took them to Heaven. And that is where they are right now and where they will be forever.

So you see, it is very important to trust in Jesus Christ while you are still alive on Earth. Trusting in the Savior is more important than becoming rich. What good would it do for you to be a millionaire on Earth, if you ended up being separated from God forever in the terrible place of suffering?

For what will it profit a man if he gains the whole world, and loses his own soul? Mark 8:36

Questions

1. How were the Pharisees hypocrites? *The Pharisees were hypocrites because they pretended to love God when what they really loved was their riches.*

2. What happened to the successful farmer in Jesus' parable? *Just when the farmer thought he had all he wanted, he died.*

3. When you die, can you take your riches with you? *No, you cannot take your riches with you when you die.*

4. Can riches give you eternal life? *No, riches cannot give you eternal life.*

5. Who is the only One who can give eternal life? *Only God can give eternal life.*

6. Can riches buy happiness and peace? *No, only God can give true peace and happiness.*

7. Why did the rich man in Jesus' story go to the place of suffering? *He went to the place of suffering because he did not trust in God while he lived on Earth.*

8. Why did Lazarus go to paradise when he died? *Lazarus went to paradise because while he was living on Earth he trusted in God to save him.*

9. After a person goes to the place of suffering, is there any way of escape? *No, once you enter the place of suffering you can never leave.*

10. Why did Abraham say it was useless to send Lazarus to the rich man's brothers to warn them about the terrible place of suffering? *Abraham said that if they did not believe the Bible they would not believe someone who came back from the dead.*

Biblical Worldviews

- Only God can give eternal life and true peace.
- All people are sinners.
- We cannot save ourselves. Only God can save us.
- God saves only those who believe Him.
- Those who believe God go to Heaven when they die; those who do not believe God go to the terrible place of suffering.
- Wherever a person goes at the time of death is where he or she will remain forever and ever.

Activity: Treasure Chest Craft

Supplies:

- Small cardboard boxes, shoe boxes, or envelopes
- Sheets of paper (cut in quarters if boxes are small)
- Pencils, crayons, markers
- Stickers, buttons, cheap jewelry, anything to decorate boxes or envelopes

Instructions:

- Students decorate the boxes or envelopes.
- Give each student one of the pieces of paper.
- Students (or the teacher) write the following verse on their papers: "For what will it profit a man if he gains the whole world, and loses his own soul?" Mark 8:36
- Students place the piece of paper in the treasure chest or envelope.

- Discuss the verse.
- Optional: Students can save their boxes and add other Bible verses to them in the weeks to come.

Extra Bible References

Psalm 23:14, 31:15, 49:6-20, 139:16; Jeremiah 9:23-24; Romans 6:23, 10:11; 2 Corinthians 5:8; Ephesians 5:3; 1 Timothy 3:3, 6:7; Hebrews 11:6-40; James 1:17; 1 John 2:15-17; Revelation 20:10, 15

66
A Dead Man Comes Back to Life
Jesus Raises Lazarus from the Dead

Memory Verse

Jesus said to her, "I am the resurrection and the life. He who believes in Me, though he may die, he shall live." John 11:25

Lesson

Near Jerusalem, in the town of Bethany, lived some of Jesus' close friends: Mary, Martha, and Lazarus. This Lazarus was not the poor beggar we read about earlier. This Lazarus was the brother to Mary and Martha.

One day Jesus heard that Lazarus was really sick.

Therefore the sisters sent to Him, saying, "Lord, behold, he whom You love is sick."

When Jesus heard that, He said, "This sickness is not unto death, but for the glory of God, that the Son of God may be glorified through it."

Now Jesus loved Martha and her sister and Lazarus. So, when He heard that he was sick, He stayed two more days in the place where He was. John 11:3-6

If Jesus truly loved Mary and Martha, why did He stay where He was two more days? He should have hurried to Lazarus. After all, Jesus is God; He could have healed Lazarus.

But Jesus waited because He knew God the Father had a special purpose for Lazarus' sickness.

Then after this He said to the disciples, "Let us go to Judea again."

The disciples said to Him, "Rabbi, lately the Jews sought to stone You, and are You going there again?"

Jesus answered, "...Our friend Lazarus sleeps, but I go that I may wake him up."

Then His disciples said, "Lord, if he sleeps he will get well." However, Jesus spoke of his death, but they thought that He was speaking about taking rest in sleep.

Then Jesus said to them plainly, "Lazarus is dead. And I am glad for your sakes that I was not there, that you may believe. Nevertheless let us go to him."

Then Thomas...said to his fellow disciples, "Let us also go, that we may die with Him." John 11:7-16

Jerusalem and Bethany (where Mary and Martha lived) were located in the region of Israel called Judea. Jesus' disciples were afraid to go to Judea because they knew the Jews in that area wanted to kill Jesus.

But when it was time to go, Jesus went anyway. When He and His disciples arrived at Mary and Martha's home, they found Lazarus had already been dead four days.

So when Jesus came, He found that he had already been in the tomb four days. Now Bethany was near Jerusalem, about two miles away. And many of the Jews had joined the women around Martha and Mary, to comfort them concerning their brother.

Now Martha, as soon as she heard that Jesus was coming, went and met Him, but Mary was sitting in the house. Now Martha said to Jesus, "Lord, if You had been here, my brother would not have died. But even now I know that whatever You ask of God, God will give You." John 11:17-22

Martha believed Jesus was God and that He could have healed her brother. She believed that even still God the Father would do whatever Jesus asked.

Jesus said to her, "Your brother will rise again."

Martha said to Him, "I know that he will rise again in the resurrection at the last day." John 11:23-24

From the writings of the prophets, the Jews knew that all people who have died will someday come back to life.

When a person dies, his body remains on Earth, but his soul goes immediately either to Heaven or to the place of suffering. In the future, the souls and spirits of all the dead will be joined to their bodies again. Every person who has ever lived will rise again to be judged by God.

> ...the hour is coming in which all who are in the graves will hear His voice and come forth—those who have done good, to the resurrection of life, and those who have done evil, to the resurrection of condemnation. John 5:28-29

"Those who have done good" are those who trusted in Jesus during their lifetime. These people will appear before God in Heaven to be judged for how they lived their lives while on Earth. They will receive rewards for the things they did that pleased God, and they will lose rewards for all they did that displeased God, but they will continue to live with God in Heaven forever.

> For we must all appear before the judgment seat of Christ, that each one may receive the things done in the body, according to what he has done, whether good or bad. 2 Corinthians 5:10

The Judgment Seat of Christ is for believers.

"Those who have done evil" are those who did not trust in the Savior while they lived on Earth. These people will be brought out of the terrible place of suffering to be judged. When God shows them all the bad things they thought and did while on Earth, they will understand why they deserve to be separated from God forever. They will realize they should have trusted in Jesus Christ to save them from sin and death.

> Then I saw a great white throne and Him who sat on it...And I saw the dead, small and great, standing before God, and books were opened. And another book was opened, which is the Book of Life. And the dead were judged according to their works, by the things which were written in the books. The sea gave up the dead who were in it, and Death and Hades delivered up the dead who were in them. And they were judged, each one according to his works. Then Death and Hades were cast into the lake of fire. This is the second death. And anyone not found written in the Book of Life was cast into the lake of fire. Revelation 20:11-15

The Great White Throne Judgment is for those who did not believe in Jesus while they lived on Earth.

The terrible place of suffering is called Hades or Hell.

After this Great White Throne Judgment, all those who never trusted in Jesus while they lived on Earth will be sent to the Lake of Fire to join Satan and his demons forever!

The devil, who deceived them, was cast into the lake of fire and brimstone where the beast and the false prophet are. And they will be tormented day and night forever and ever. Revelation 20:10

Some people do not believe a person's soul goes on living forever. They believe that when the body dies the person stops existing.

Other people believe that after a person dies, he or she comes back in a different body, maybe as an animal or a bird. They believe this happens over and over again until he or she finally becomes perfect.

These are lies from Satan. Satan wants to trick people into thinking there is no place of suffering. He wants them to think they will not be judged for their sin. Satan does not want people to trust in the Savior to save them from the terrible place of suffering.

Martha knew Lazarus would someday be raised to life again.

Jesus said to her, "I am the resurrection and the life. He who believes in Me, though he may die, he shall live. And whoever lives and believes in Me shall never die. Do you believe this?"

She said to Him, "Yes, Lord, I believe that You are the Christ, the Son of God, who is to come into the world." John 11:25-27

The word resurrection means to raise up. Jesus said He was "the resurrection and the life." Jesus is the only One who can raise dead people back to life. Even though all people die once, those who trust in Jesus will not die the second time to be separated from God forever. Instead, Jesus will give them life with God forever.

> The second death is when a person is sent to the Lake of Fire to be separated from God forever and ever.

Martha believed what Jesus said. She believed Jesus was God the Son, the promised Savior. She believed she was a sinner who deserved to die the second death, but she trusted in Jesus to save her from death and give her everlasting life.

And when she had said these things, she went her way and secretly called Mary her sister, saying, "The Teacher has come and is calling for you."

As soon as she heard that, she arose quickly and came to Him. Now Jesus had not yet come into the town, but was in the place where Martha met Him. Then the Jews who were with her in the house, and comforting her, when they saw that Mary rose up quickly and went out, followed her, saying, "She is going to the tomb to weep there."

Then, when Mary came where Jesus was, and saw Him, she fell down at His feet, saying to Him, "Lord, if You had been here, my brother would not have died."

Therefore, when Jesus saw her weeping, and the Jews who came with her weeping, He groaned in the spirit and was troubled. And He said, "Where have you laid him?"

They said to Him, "Lord, come and see."

Jesus wept.

Then the Jews said, "See how He loved him!"

And some of them said, "Could not this Man, who opened the eyes of the blind, also have kept this man from dying?"

Then Jesus, again groaning in Himself, came to the tomb. It was a cave, and a stone lay against it. John 11:28-38

Even though Jesus is God, He is also a human being. Jesus had the same feelings you and I do. When He saw Mary and the Jews weeping, He wept. It made Him very sad to see how much Lazarus' family and friends were hurting.

When God made people in the beginning, it was not His plan for them to die. In fact, He wanted Adam and Eve to eat from The Tree of Life and live forever. But Adam and Eve went against what God said, and as a result they died. This brought death to all people.

...through one man sin entered the world, and death through sin, and thus death spread to all men, because all sinned... Romans 5:12

473

Sin and death make God sad. God does not want people to die. That is why He planned to send the Savior. Jesus Christ came to save people from the second death.

When Jesus arrived at Lazarus' grave, He told the Jews to take the stone away from the entrance.

Jesus said, "Take away the stone."

Martha, the sister of him who was dead, said to Him, "Lord, by this time there is a stench, for he has been dead four days."

Jesus said to her, "Did I not say to you that if you would believe you would see the glory of God?"

Then they took away the stone from the place where the dead man was lying. And Jesus lifted up His eyes and said, "Father, I thank You that You have heard Me. And I know that You always hear Me, but because of the people who are standing by I said this, that they may believe that You sent Me." Now when He had said these things, He cried with a loud voice, "Lazarus, come forth!" And he who had died came out bound hand and foot with grave clothes, and his face was wrapped with a cloth. Jesus said to them, "Loose him, and let him go." John 11:39-44

In those days when people died, their entire body was wrapped in strips of cloth. Even though Lazarus had been dead four days, when Jesus called for him to come out of the tomb, he came out immediately with the strips of cloth still wrapped around him.

Only God has the power to give life to the dead. This miracle caused many of the Jews to believe that Jesus truly was God the Son.

Then many of the Jews who had come to Mary, and had seen the things Jesus did, believed in Him. But some of them went away to the Pharisees and told them the things Jesus did. Then the chief priests and the Pharisees gathered a council and said, "What shall we do? For this Man works many signs. If we let Him alone like this, everyone will believe in Him, and the Romans will come and take away both our place and nation." John 11:45-48

The Pharisees did not like it that so many Jews were believing in Jesus. If the Jews suddenly decided to make Jesus their leader, the Roman government would get upset, and the Pharisees and other Jewish leaders would be in trouble. The Pharisees could think of only one thing to do. We'll find out what that was real soon.

Remember

Someday you will die. What will happen to you then? Will you go to live with God, or will you be separated from Him forever in the terrible place of suffering?

Jesus is the only One who can rescue you from the second death. He is the only One who can give you life after you die.

Trust in Jesus. Those who trust in Him will not perish: they will not die the second time. Instead, all who trust in Jesus will receive eternal life.

For God so loved the world that He gave His only begotten Son, that whoever believes in Him should not perish but have everlasting life. John 3:16

Questions

1. Why did Jesus not heal Lazarus of his sickness? *Jesus did not heal Lazarus because He knew God had a purpose for Lazarus' death.*

2. Did Martha believe Jesus could raise Lazarus from the dead? *Yes, she did.*

3. Did Martha believe Jesus was God the Son, the promised Savior? *Yes, she did.*

4. In the beginning when God created people, did He plan for them to die? *No, it was never God's plan for people to die. He wanted people to live forever.*

5. What will happen to those who do not trust in Jesus while they are alive on Earth? *Those who do not trust in the Savior while they are still alive will be judged for their works and sent to the Lake of Fire where they will suffer forever and ever.*

6. What is the second death? *It is separation from God forever in the terrible place of suffering.*

7. Did the Jews believe Jesus was God the Son? *No, most of them did not believe Jesus was God.*

8. What did Jesus do that caused many of the Jews to believe in Him? *He raised Lazarus from the dead.*

9. Were the Pharisees happy about the Jews believing in Jesus? *No, they were not.*

10. Who is the only One who can save you from the second death and give you eternal life?
Only Jesus Christ, God the Son, can give you eternal life.

Biblical Worldviews

- God is in control of all that happens; He works out all things for His purposes.
- The moment a person dies, his or her soul goes immediately either to Heaven or to the place of suffering called Hell.
- At the end of time, the souls and spirits of all who have died will be joined to their bodies again; everyone will be raised up to be judged by God.
- All people are sinners. The penalty for sin is death.
- God saves only those who believe in Him.
- Jesus Christ is God.
- Jesus Christ is the only Savior; only Jesus can give eternal life.
- Jesus Christ is a human being.

Activity: Memory Verse Ball

Supplies:

- One or more mid-size balls
- Copy of memory verse: Jesus said to her, "I am the resurrection and the life. He who believes in Me, though he may die, he shall live." John 11:25

Instructions:

- Depending on the number of students, students either divide into teams or form one large circle.
- Students then practice the memory verse while throwing the ball to each other and catching it.
- For example: The teacher says the first part of the verse to be memorized. Then she throws the ball to one of the students, who repeats word for word what she just said and throws the ball to another student. Go around until everyone has had a chance to catch the ball and say the first part of the verse. Now add the second part of the verse and do the same thing. Then add the third part and so on until each student has memorized the entire verse, including the reference.
- If students have been working in small groups, they now come together to form a large circle and each one recites the verse and reference in front of the entire class with or without the balls.

Extra Bible References

Psalm 98:9; Daniel 12:2; Matthew 25:46; John 5:24, 28-29; Acts 17:25, 31; 24:15; Romans 5:12; 1 Corinthians 3:11-13; 2 Corinthians 1:3, 5:9-11; Colossians 1:16, 2:18; 1 Thessalonians 4:15-18; 1 Timothy 2:4; 2 Timothy 4:1; 1 Peter 1:17; 2 Peter 3:9; Hebrews 9:27, 10:35, 11:6; 2 John 1:8; Revelation 11:18, 20:11-15, 22:12

67
The Last Passover
Jesus Rides a Colt and Eats the Passover Meal

Memory Verse

All we like sheep have gone astray; we have turned, every one, to his own way; and the LORD has laid on Him the iniquity of us all. Isaiah 53:6

Lesson

After Jesus raised Lazarus from the dead, He and His disciples walked on to Jerusalem. In Jerusalem, the streets were crowded with Jews from many places. Everyone had come to celebrate the Passover Feast.

Long ago, God told the Israelites to celebrate the Passover every year. God wanted the Israelites to always remember how their firstborn sons had been saved by the blood of the lamb on the night He freed them from slavery in Egypt.

Jesus' disciples were afraid to go to Jerusalem because they knew the Jewish leaders there wanted to kill Jesus.

Now they were on the road, going up to Jerusalem, and Jesus was going before them; and they were amazed. And as they followed they were afraid. Then He took the twelve aside again and began to tell them the things that would happen to Him: "Behold, we are going up to Jerusalem, and the Son of Man will be betrayed to the chief priests and to the scribes; and they will condemn Him to death and deliver Him to the Gentiles; and they will mock Him, and scourge Him, and spit on Him, and kill Him. And the third day He will rise again."

For even the Son of Man did not come to be served, but to serve, and to give His life a ransom for many." Mark 10:32-34, 45

The prophet Isaiah said:

He is despised and rejected by men, a Man of sorrows and acquainted with grief...He was wounded for our transgressions, He was bruised for our iniquities...And by His stripes we are healed. Isaiah 53:3a, 5

In the Bible, Jesus is called both the Son of Man and the Son of God. As the son of Mary and Joseph, Jesus was the Son of Man. But, of course, Jesus was also the Son of God the Father, or God the Son.

Jesus knew everything that was going to happen to Him in Jerusalem. He came to Earth to be the Savior, and He knew that in order to save us from Satan and death, He would have to suffer and die, just like the Old Testament prophets predicted so long ago. But Jesus told His disciples that after three days, He would rise again.

As Jesus and His disciples neared Jerusalem, He sent His disciples to find a colt for Him to ride. Hundreds of years earlier, the prophet Zechariah wrote that the Savior would ride into Jerusalem on a donkey's colt. Jesus knew that this prophesy had to be fulfilled before He died.

Now when they drew near Jerusalem...at the Mount of Olives, He sent two of His disciples; and He said to them, "Go into the village opposite you; and as soon as you have entered it you will find a colt tied, on which no one has sat. Loose it and bring it. And if anyone says to you, 'Why are you doing this?' say, 'The Lord has need of it,' and immediately he will send it here."

So they went their way, and found the colt tied by the door outside on the street, and they loosed it. But some of those who stood there said to them, "What are you doing, loosing the colt?"

And they spoke to them just as Jesus had commanded. So they let them go. Mark 11:1-6

The prophet Zechariah wrote:

Rejoice greatly, O daughter of Zion! Shout, O daughter of Jerusalem! Behold, your King is coming to you; He is just and having salvation, lowly and riding on a donkey, a colt, the foal of a donkey. Zechariah 9:9

Since Jesus is God, He knew just where the disciples could find a colt that had never been ridden. The disciples brought the colt to Jesus.

Then they brought the colt to Jesus and threw their clothes on it, and He sat on it. And many spread their clothes on the road, and others cut down leafy branches from the trees and spread them on the road. Then those who went before and those who followed cried out, saying: "Hosanna! 'Blessed is He who comes in the name of the

LORD!' Blessed is the kingdom of our father David that comes in the name of the Lord! Hosanna in the highest!" Mark 11:7-10

The Jews were glad to accept Jesus as the promised king from King David's family line, but they did not want to accept Him as the promised Savior. They wanted Jesus to rescue them from the Roman government, but they did not think they needed to be rescued from Satan, sin, and death.

The religious leaders, on the other hand, did not even want Jesus to be king; they wanted Him put to death!

After two days it was the Passover and the Feast...And the chief priests and the scribes sought how they might take Him by trickery and put Him to death. Mark 14:1

The chief priests and the teachers of the law knew what was written in the Old Testament about the coming Savior. They should have recognized that everything the prophets said about the Savior was true of Jesus. They had no excuse for not accepting Jesus as the Christ, the promised Savior, but they were blind to the truth.

They hated Jesus because He told them they were sinners, and they were jealous of the huge crowds that followed Him.

One day they got the chance they were waiting for.

Then Judas Iscariot, one of the twelve, went to the chief priests to betray Him to them. Mark 14:10

Even though Judas was one of Jesus' followers, Judas never believed Jesus was God the Son. Judas never trusted in Jesus as his Savior. Since he was still in Adam's family, Judas was controlled by Satan and his own sinful nature.

Judas was happy to betray Jesus in exchange for money.

What King David foretold about Judas:

Even my own familiar friend in whom I trusted, who ate my bread, has lifted up his heel against me. Psalm 41:9

What the prophet Zechariah said:

... they weighed out for my wages thirty pieces of silver. Zechariah 11:12a

And when they heard it, they were glad, and promised to give him money. So he sought how he might conveniently betray Him.
Mark 14:11

Satan is the one who led Judas and the religious leaders to kill Jesus. Satan did not want Jesus to rescue people from his dominion; he wanted to control the people of the world. Satan wants people to be separated from God forever in the Lake of Fire God prepared for him and his demons.

Every year during the Passover Feast the Jews killed and ate a lamb just like they did on the night they left Egypt. Since they were entering Jerusalem right before the Passover, Jesus' disciples asked Him where He wanted to eat the Passover lamb.

Now on the first day...when they killed the Passover lamb, His disciples said to Him, "Where do You want us to go and prepare, that You may eat the Passover?"

And He sent out two of His disciples and said to them, "Go into the city, and a man will meet you carrying a pitcher of water; follow him. Wherever he goes in, say to the master of the house, 'The Teacher says, "Where is the guest room in which I may eat the Passover with My disciples?"' Then he will show you a large upper room, furnished and prepared; there make ready for us."

So His disciples went out, and came into the city, and found it just as He had said to them; and they prepared the Passover.

In the evening He came with the twelve. Now as they sat and ate, Jesus said, "Assuredly, I say to you, one of you who eats with Me will betray Me." Mark 14:12-18

It was God's plan for Jesus to die for us, but it was wrong for Judas to take part in Jesus' death.

This is what Jesus said:

He answered and said to them, "...The Son of Man indeed goes just as it is written of Him, but woe to that man by whom the Son of Man is betrayed! It would have been good for that man if he had never been born."

And as they were eating, Jesus took bread, blessed and broke it, and gave it to them and said, "Take, eat; this is My body."

Then He took the cup, and when He had given thanks He gave it to them, and they all drank from it. And He said to them, "This is My blood of the new covenant, which is shed for many. Assuredly, I say to you, I will no longer drink of the fruit of the vine until that day when I drink it new in the kingdom of God."

And when they had sung a hymn, they went out to the Mount of Olives.
Mark 14:21-26

When Jesus broke the bread and gave it to His followers it was a picture of how His body was about to be broken for them. The wine was a picture of the blood He was about to shed for them.

Jesus is God, the Creator of the world. He never did anything wrong; He did not deserve to die. But Jesus was going to die in our place as the perfect Lamb of God.

Questions

1. Why did God want the Jews to celebrate the Passover Feast? *God wanted the people of Israel always to remember how the blood of the lambs had saved their firstborn sons when their forefathers left Egypt so long ago.*

2. Why was Jesus sometimes called the Son of Man? *Jesus was sometimes called the Son of Man because those around Him knew Him as the son of Mary and Joseph. Jesus was both the Son of Man and the Son of God.*

3. Why did Jesus go to Jerusalem when He knew what was going to happen to Him there? *Jesus knew He was the promised Savior. He knew He had to suffer and die in order to save people from Satan's dominion and from the second death.*

4. Who was leading Judas and the religious leaders to kill Jesus? *Satan was leading the religious leaders, because Satan did not want Jesus to save people from his control and from the death penalty.*

5. How did Jesus know where the disciples could find a colt for Him to ride? *Jesus is God. He knows everything.*

6. Why did the Jews want Jesus to be their king? *The Jews wanted Jesus to be their king so He could deliver them from the cruel Roman government.*

7. Why did the Jews not accept Jesus as the promised Savior? *The Jews did not think they were sinners separated from God; they did not think they needed the Savior to rescue them from the second death. They thought they were going to Heaven because they came from Abraham and tried to follow God's laws.*

8. Did the religious leaders know what was written in the Old Testament about the promised Savior? *Yes, they knew the prophecies about the Savior written in the Old Testament.*

9. Why did the religious leaders want to kill Jesus? *The religious leaders were jealous of Jesus because of the huge crowds of Jews that followed Him, and they were angry with Him because He told them they were sinners, so they wanted to get rid of Him.*

10. Did Judas trust in Jesus as His Savior? *No, Judas did not believe Jesus was God the Son, the promised Savior.*

11. When Jesus was eating the Passover meal with the disciples, why did He break the bread and give it to them? *The broken bread was a picture of how Jesus's body was going to be broken for them.*

12. What did the cup of wine Jesus gave His disciples at the Passover supper represent? *The wine was a picture of the blood Jesus was going to shed in order to pay for our sin.*

Biblical Worldviews

- Jesus Christ is a human being.
- Jesus Christ is God.
- God knows everything; Jesus knew all that was going to happen to Him.
- God is in charge of the world; everything happens according to His plan.
- God is a God of love; He sent Jesus to suffer and die for us.
- Jesus Christ is the only Savior.
- Satan hates God and people.
- Satan is powerful, but he cannot win against God. Satan cannot ruin God's plans.
- All people are born into Adam's family. Those in Adam's family cannot please God; they are controlled by Satan and their own sinful nature.
- Jesus saves only those who believe in Him.

Activity: Bible Hangman

Supplies:

- Chalkboard or dry erase board
- Chalk or dry erase markers

Instructions:

- Draw a large hangman tree on the board.
- Draw lines and spaces under the tree to correspond to the letters and spaces in the key phrase.

- **Key phrase**: Since Jesus is God, He knew everything that what was going to happen to Him in Jerusalem.
- **Key phrase for younger students:** Jesus is God; He knows everything.
- Ask the lesson review questions, one at a time. Call on one student or one team to answer each question.
- If answer is correct, the student or team gets to pick a letter, i.e., the letter b.
- If the letter picked is in the key phrase, the teacher fills it in on the board each time it occurs.
- If the letter picked is not in the key phrase, the teacher draws one part of a stick figure on the hangman tree, i.e., a head, an arm, a stick body, etc.
- When a student (or team) thinks he knows the key phrase, he may try to solve the puzzle on his turn. The game is over when a student or team solves the puzzle or the teacher draws all the parts of the stick man, whichever comes first.

Extra Bible References

Exodus 12:21-27; Deuteronomy 16:1-8; Matthew 21:1-11, 26:1-30; Luke 3:23-31, 4:22; Luke 19:28-40, 22:1-23; John 12:12-19; 13:1-2, 21-30

486

68
Condemned
Jesus Accused and Condemned

Memory Verse

> *All we like sheep have gone astray; we have turned, every one, to his own way; and the LORD has laid on Him the iniquity of us all. Isaiah 53:6*

Lesson

After Jesus and His disciples ate the Passover meal, they went out to a nearby olive orchard called Gethsemane. Gethsemane was on the Mount of Olives.

Then they came to a place which was named Gethsemane; and He said to His disciples, "Sit here while I pray." And He took Peter, James, and John with Him, and He began to be troubled and deeply distressed. Then He said to them, "My soul is exceedingly sorrowful, even to death. Stay here and watch."

He went a little farther, and fell on the ground, and prayed that if it were possible, the hour might pass from Him. And He said, "Abba, Father, all things are possible for You. Take this cup away from Me; nevertheless, not what I will, but what You will." Mark 14:32-36

And being in agony, He prayed...earnestly. Then His sweat became like great drops of blood falling down to the ground. Luke 22:44

Jesus knew what was about to happen; He knew the terrible torment He would have to suffer in order to pay the death penalty for everyone in the world.

As a human being, Jesus could not bear the thought of such terrible agony, but at the same time, He was willing to do whatever God the Father wanted Him to do. He was willing to do what was needed to save us from Satan and the second death.

As soon as Jesus finished praying, Judas arrived.

Then He...said to [His disciples], "...The hour has come; behold, the Son of Man is being betrayed into the hands of sinners. Rise, let us be going. See, My betrayer is at hand."

And immediately, while He was still speaking, Judas, one of the twelve, with a great multitude with swords and clubs, came from the chief priests and the scribes and the elders. Now His betrayer had given them a signal, saying, "Whomever I kiss, He is the One; seize Him and lead Him away safely."

As soon as he had come, immediately he went up to Him and said to Him, "Rabbi, Rabbi!" and kissed Him.

Then they laid their hands on Him and took Him. Mark 14:41-46

Judas had been Jesus' disciple for a long time. It was terrible for Judas to hand Jesus over to those who wanted Him killed!

Then Jesus answered and said to them, "Have you come out, as against a robber, with swords and clubs to take Me? I was daily with you in the temple teaching, and you did not seize Me. But the Scriptures must be fulfilled." Mark 14:48-49

The religious leaders sent a huge crowd of soldiers carrying swords and clubs to arrest Jesus. They must have been afraid of Jesus' power. After all, they had seen Him cast out demons, heal diseases, and raise the dead back to life. Instead of arresting Jesus, the religious leaders should have believed in Him! Only God could do the great things they had seen Jesus do.

But even though Jesus could have destroyed them all with one word, He let them arrest Him because He knew the time had come for Him to die.

The soldiers took Jesus to the courtyard of the high priest where the religious leaders were gathered. Peter, one of Jesus' disciples, followed the soldiers into the courtyard.

And they led Jesus away to the high priest; and with him were assembled all the chief priests, the elders, and the scribes. But Peter followed Him at a distance, right into the courtyard of the high priest. Mark 14:53-54a

Now when they had kindled a fire in the midst of the courtyard and sat down together, Peter sat among them. And a certain servant girl, seeing him as he sat by the fire, looked intently at him and said, "This man was also with Him."

But he denied Him, saying, "Woman, I do not know Him."

And after a little while another saw him and said, "You also are of them."

But Peter said, "Man, I am not!"

Then after about an hour had passed, another confidently affirmed, saying, "Surely this fellow also was with Him, for he is a Galilean."

But Peter said, "Man, I do not know what you are saying!"

Immediately, while he was still speaking, the rooster crowed. And the Lord turned and looked at Peter. Then Peter remembered the word of the Lord, how He had said to him, "Before the rooster crows, you will deny Me three times." So Peter went out and wept bitterly. Luke 22:55-62

> The prophet Isaiah wrote this about Jesus:
>
> He was oppressed and He was afflicted, yet He opened not His mouth; He was led as a lamb to the slaughter, and as a sheep before its shearers is silent, so He opened not His mouth. Isaiah 53:7

Jesus had told Peter earlier he would deny Him, but Peter didn't believe Jesus. After Peter betrayed Jesus and realized what he had done, he was terribly sad.

Many people in the court accused Jesus of crimes, but since their stories did not agree, the religious leaders could find no reason to have Jesus put to death.

Now the chief priests and all the council sought testimony against Jesus to put Him to death, but found none. For many bore false witness against Him, but their testimonies did not agree. Mark 14:55-56

> Over a thousand years before this time, King David wrote this about Jesus:
>
> ...false witnesses have risen against me, and such as breathe out violence. Psalm 27:12

The truth is that Jesus never did anything wrong. He never broke any of God's rules.

489

The Bible says that He...

...committed no sin, nor was deceit found in His mouth.
1 Peter 2:22

Even though Jesus had not done any of the crimes of which they accused Him, He kept quiet. Jesus did not get angry; He did not defend Himself.

And the high priest stood up in the midst and asked Jesus, saying, "Do You answer nothing? What is it these men testify against You?" But He kept silent and answered nothing.

Again the high priest asked Him, saying to Him, "Are You the Christ, the Son of the Blessed?"

Jesus said, "I am." Mark 14:60-62a

Finally, the high priest asked Jesus if He was the Christ, the Son of God.

Jesus said, "I am."

Remember when God told Moses His name?

And God said to Moses, "I AM WHO I AM." And He said, "Thus you shall say to the children of Israel, 'I AM has sent me to you.'"
Exodus 3:14

The Jews knew the Old Testament Scriptures. They knew "I AM" was another name for God. When Jesus said He was "I am," all the religious leaders knew Jesus was saying, "I am God."

Then the high priest tore his clothes and said, "What further need do we have of witnesses? You have heard the blasphemy! What do you think?"

And they all condemned Him to be deserving of death.

Then some began to spit on Him, and to blindfold Him, and to beat Him, and to say to Him, "Prophesy!" And the officers struck Him with the palms of their hands. Mark 14:63-65

When Jesus said He was God, the religious leaders became enraged. They said Jesus was guilty of blasphemy because He claimed to be God when He was only a human being. For this crime they said Jesus should be put to death.

Although the Jewish religious leaders wanted Jesus put to death, they did not have the authority to put a criminal to death without permission from the Roman governor. At that time, the Roman governor was Pilate.

Immediately, in the morning, the chief priests held a consultation with the elders and scribes and the whole council; and they bound Jesus, led Him away, and delivered Him to Pilate. Then Pilate asked Him, "Are You the King of the Jews?"

He answered and said to him, "It is as you say." Mark 15:1-2

Jesus was the Christ; He was God's Chosen One. Jesus was the One God chose to be a prophet, a priest, and a king.

In the Garden of Eden God said Satan would strike Jesus' heal. Just like a snake strikes its victim to cause its death, Satan was about to cause Jesus' death. But remember, Jesus was going to bruise Satan's head. No matter what the Jews did to Him, Jesus was going to destroy Satan's control over people, and someday He was going to be king forever just like the prophets foretold.

As Jesus stood before the Roman governor, the Jews continued to accuse Him of imaginary crimes.

And the chief priests accused Him of many things, but He answered nothing. Then Pilate asked Him again, saying, "Do You answer nothing? See how many things they testify against You!" But Jesus still answered nothing, so that Pilate marveled. Mark 15:3-5

Jesus remained silent; He knew He must suffer and die in order to be the Savior.

Pilate realized Jesus did not deserve to die. Since it was his custom to free one Jewish prisoner during the Passover Feast, Pilate offered to release Jesus.

Now at the feast he was accustomed to releasing one prisoner to them, whomever they requested. And there was one named Barabbas, who was chained with his fellow rebels; they had committed murder in the rebellion. Then the multitude, crying aloud, began to ask him to do just as he had always done for them. But Pilate answered them, saying, "Do you want me to release to you the King of the Jews?" For he knew that the chief priests had handed Him over because of envy.

But the chief priests stirred up the crowd, so that he should rather release Barabbas to them.

Pilate answered and said to them again, "What then do you want me to do with Him whom you call the King of the Jews?"

So they cried out again, "Crucify Him!"

Then Pilate said to them, "Why, what evil has He done?"

But they cried out all the more, "Crucify Him!"

So Pilate, wanting to gratify the crowd, released Barabbas to them; and he delivered Jesus, after he had scourged Him, to be crucified. Mark 15:6-15

The Jews did not want Jesus to be freed; they wanted Pilate to sentence Jesus to death.

In those days the death penalty was not carried out by lethal injection or the electric chair; it was carried out by crucifixion. Death by crucifixion was the most disgraceful and painful way to die imaginable.

Before Jesus was crucified, Pilate had Him flogged. To be flogged means to be whipped. The Roman soldiers took off Jesus' clothes and tied his hands to a pole above his head. Then they whipped Him over and over again with a long whip. The whip was made of strips of leather with pieces of metal or bone at the ends.

> The prophet Isaiah also wrote this about Jesus:
>
> He is despised and rejected by men, a Man of sorrows and acquainted with grief. Isaiah 53:3a
>
> I gave My back to those who struck Me, and My cheeks to those who plucked out the beard; I did not hide My face from shame and spitting. Isaiah 50:6

With each blow the whip cut deeper and deeper into Jesus' back. Though the blood flowed out, Jesus did not die.

Then the soldiers led Him away into the hall called Praetorium, and they called together the whole garrison. And they clothed Him with purple; and they twisted a crown of thorns, put it on His head, and began to salute Him, "Hail, King of the Jews!" Then they struck Him on the head with a reed and spat on Him; and bowing the knee, they worshiped Him. Mark 15:16-19

Afterwards the soldiers dressed Jesus in a purple robe as though He were a king and made fun of Him. They put a painful crown of thorns on Jesus' head and hit Him with sticks. They spit on Jesus, all the while making fun of Him for saying He was king of the Jews.

This is how Jesus Christ, the perfect Son of God and Creator of the world, was treated. It is hard to imagine, but it is exactly what Jesus told His disciples would happen. This was God's plan.

From the beginning of time, God decided that He Himself would come to Earth as the promised Savior and free mankind from Satan, sin, and death by dying in our place. Because of His great love for us, Jesus was willing to suffer incredible torture and disgrace.

He indeed was foreordained before the foundation of the world...
1 Peter 1:20a

Questions

1. How did Jesus know everything that was going to happen to Him before it happened? *Jesus is God. He knows everything. He knew that in order to save mankind from Satan, sin, and death He would have to suffer and die.*

2. What did Jesus mean when he asked God the Father, "Take this cup away from Me"? *Jesus was asking God to keep Him from having to go through the terrible suffering He was about to face.*

3. Even though as a human being Jesus dreaded taking the sin of the world on Himself, was He willing to do whatever God the Father asked Him to do? *Yes, He was.*

4. During His lifetime, did Jesus ever do anything wrong? *No, Jesus never broke any of God's laws. He never even had a bad thought.*

5. What did Jesus say when Pilate asked Him if He was the Christ? *Jesus said, "I am."*

6. Why did the Jews get angry when Jesus answered their question about Him being God's Son with, "I am"? *The Jews knew the story of Moses and the burning bush. They knew that "I AM" is God's name. They thought Jesus was just a man and that He was blaspheming by saying He was God.*

7. What did the religious leaders say was the punishment Jesus deserved for calling Himself God? *They said He deserved to die.*

8. What did Jesus do when He was accused of things He never did? *He remained quiet. He did not get angry or defend Himself.*

9. Was it true that Jesus was the King of the Jews? *Yes, it was. God had chosen Jesus to be the One from King David's family line who would be king forever.*

10. Could Satan destroy God's plans? *No, he could not. It may have seemed as though Satan was going to win, but in the end Jesus was going to bruise Satan's head. Jesus was going to inflict a fatal wound on Satan so that someday Satan's power would be totally destroyed and Jesus would become king of the world forever.*

11. Did everything the prophets wrote about the Savior in the Old Testament come true? *Yes, every detail they foretold about the coming the Savior came true in Jesus.*

Biblical Worldviews

- Jesus Christ is a human being.
- Jesus Christ is God.
- Jesus Christ knows everything; He knew what was going to happen to Him.
- Jesus Christ always did what God the Father wanted Him to do; He never sinned.
- God always completes His plans.
- Jesus Christ is the only Savior.
- God is a God of love.
- Satan cannot win against God.
- All people are sinners.

Activity 1: Sheep Craft

Supplies:

- "Lamb" template (see appendix page 581)
- White cardstock or construction paper (regular white printing paper will work if you don't have the other)
- Black construction paper or black crayon
- Cotton balls
- Glue or stapler
- Scissors
- Hole-punch and yarn (optional)

Instructions:

- Copy template of lamb's body onto white cardstock (or trace template if you don't have a copy machine).

- Copy template of lamb's legs and head onto black paper, or trace template if you don't have a copy machine. Or, if you don't have black paper, use white paper and a crayon to color the legs black.
- Students cut out lamb's body, legs, and head.
- Students fold body along the dotted line.
- Students use glue or stapler to attach legs and head to body of lamb.
- Open up lamb. The teacher or the student writes the following on the inside: "He was led as a lamb to the slaughter." Isaiah 53:7
- Students can use a hole-punch and yarn to make their lambs into ornaments that can be hung.

Activity 2: Memory Verse Ball

Supplies:

- One or more mid-size balls
- Copy of memory verse: And those who know Your name will put their trust in You; For You, LORD, have not forsaken those who seek You. Psalm 9:10

Instructions:

- Depending on the number of students, students either divide into teams or form one large circle.
- Students then practice the memory verse while throwing the ball to each other and catching it.
- For example: The teacher says the first part of the verse to be memorized. Then she throws the ball to one of the students, who repeats word for word what she just said and throws the ball to another student. Go around until everyone has had a chance to catch the ball and say the first part of the verse. Now add the second part of the verse and do the same thing. Then add the third part and so on until each student has memorized the entire verse, including the reference.
- If students have been working in small groups, they now come together to form a large circle and each one recites the verse and reference in front of the entire class with or without the balls.

Extra Bible References

Genesis 3:15, 17-18; Zechariah 13:7; Matthew 26:36-27:30; Luke 22:39-23:4, 25; John 13:26-27, 18:1-19:15, 20:9; Acts 17:2-3; Philippians 2:5-8; 1 Peter 2:21-24

496

69
Executed
Jesus Crucified

Memory Verse

Christ has redeemed us from the curse of the law, having become a curse for us (for it is written, "Cursed is everyone who hangs on a tree"), Galatians 3:13

Lesson

After they whipped Jesus and made fun of Him, the soldiers led Him away to be crucified.

And when they had mocked Him, they took the purple off Him, put His own clothes on Him, and led Him out to crucify Him.

And they brought Him to the place Golgotha, which is translated, Place of a Skull. Then they gave Him wine mingled with myrrh to drink, but He did not take it. Mark 15:20, 22-23

When they arrived at the hill of Golgotha, the soldiers hung Jesus on a cross. They did this by laying the wooden cross on the ground and laying Jesus on top of the cross with His arms and legs spread out. After nailing His hands (right above the wrist) and His feet to the cross, they stood the cross in the ground. There, alongside two criminals, Jesus hung in agony until He died.

Someone tried to give Jesus wine to help take away the pain, but Jesus would not drink it.

And when they crucified Him, they divided His garments, casting lots for them to determine what every man should take. Mark 15:24

Every detail the prophets foretold about the Savior in the Old Testament came true; everything happened just as God said it would.

Many, many years before the Roman government existed and anyone ever thought of crucifixion, King David prophesied about Jesus' hands and feet being pierced. He even prophesied about the soldiers "casting lots," or gambling, for Jesus' clothes.

> For dogs have surrounded Me; the congregation of the wicked has enclosed Me. They pierced My hands and My feet; I can count all My bones. They look and stare at Me. They divide My garments among them, and for My clothing they cast lots.

497

Remember when Jesus told Nicodemus that in the same way Moses had put the bronze serpent up on a pole in the wilderness, He too would be lifted up on a pole? Jesus knew He would be hung on a wooden cross.

> And as Moses lifted up the serpent in the wilderness, even so must the Son of Man be lifted up. John 3:14

The Romans usually attached a sign to the top of the cross that stated what crime the crucified person had done.

> ...and they crucified Him. And the inscription of His accusation was written above: THE KING OF THE JEWS. Mark 15:25b, 26

Jesus was not a criminal; He never did anything wrong. He did not deserve to die. The sign Pilate hung on Jesus' cross simply said: THE KING OF THE JEWS.

The Jews did not like what was written on the sign.

> Then many of the Jews read this title, for the place where Jesus was crucified was near the city; and it was written in Hebrew, Greek, and Latin.
>
> Therefore the chief priests of the Jews said to Pilate, "Do not write, 'The King of the Jews,' but, 'He said, "I am the King of the Jews."'"
>
> Pilate answered, "What I have written, I have written." John 19:20-22

Even though the Jewish religious leaders had Jesus crucified, God was still in charge. It was God who had the Roman governor place this sign above Jesus' cross. The writing on the sign was in three languages. God wanted everyone to know that Jesus truly was the King of the Jews.

Jesus was (and is) the Christ. He was the One God chose to be a prophet, a priest, and a king. As God's special prophet, Jesus taught the Jews the true meaning of Moses' and the prophets' writings in the Old Testament. As a priest, Jesus was the last sacrifice that would ever need to be made for the sins of mankind. And as a king, Jesus was going to reign forever and ever. No matter what the Jews did to Jesus, they could never stop God's plans.

There were two criminals crucified on either side of Jesus. The prophet Isaiah predicted that Jesus would die alongside sinners.

With Him they also crucified two robbers, one on His right and the other on His left. So the Scripture was fulfilled which says, "And He was numbered with the transgressors." Mark 15:27-28

Even while Jesus hung on the cross, the Jews continued to make fun of Him.

And those who passed by blasphemed Him, wagging their heads and saying, "...save Yourself, and come down from the cross!"

Likewise the chief priests also, mocking among themselves with the scribes, said, "He saved others; Himself He cannot save. Let the Christ, the King of Israel, descend now from the cross, that we may see and believe."

Even those who were crucified with Him reviled Him. Mark 15:29-32

The Jews did not believe Jesus was God the Son. They did not believe Jesus was the Messiah, the One chosen by God to be the Savior. They were blinded by Satan's lies.

Jesus could have come down from the cross, but that was the very reason He had come to Earth. Jesus came to be sacrificed as the perfect Lamb of God. He took our sin on Himself and died our death for us.

Suddenly, right in the middle of the day as Jesus hung there on the cross, it became dark as night.

The prophet Isaiah wrote about Jesus being treated like a criminal:

... He poured out His soul unto death, and He was numbered with the transgressors [law-breakers; sinners], and He bore the sin of many... Isaiah 53:12

King David wrote about how people would make fun of Jesus:

But I am a worm, and no man; a reproach of men, and despised by the people. All those who see Me ridicule Me; they shoot out the lip, they shake the head, saying, "He trusted in the LORD, let Him rescue Him; let Him deliver Him, since He delights in Him!" Psalm 22:6-8

Now when the sixth hour had come, there was darkness over the whole land until the ninth hour. And at the ninth hour Jesus cried out with a loud voice, saying, "Eloi, Eloi, lama sabachthani?" which is translated, "My God, My God, why have You forsaken Me?" Mark 15:33-34

Do you know why it got dark for three hours in the middle of the day? It was because God the Father turned His back on Jesus.

On the cross, Jesus carried the sin of the whole world on Himself.

For He made Him who knew no sin to be sin for us...
2 Corinthians 5:21a

It is sin that separates us from God.

But your iniquities have separated you from your God; And your sins have hidden His face from you, So that He will not hear.
Isaiah 59:2

When Jesus took our sin on Himself, He had to be separated from God. God turned His back on Jesus. To be separated from God the Father was the most terrible suffering the Son of God, Jesus Christ, had to endure.

Right before Jesus died...

...He said, "It is finished!" And bowing His head, He gave up His spirit. John 19:30b

When Jesus said, "It is finished!" He did not mean, "I am dead; my life is over." Jesus said, "It is finished!" because He completed the work God sent Him to do. Jesus came to Earth as the Lamb of God to die in our place. Because Jesus was God and was therefore perfect, God the Father accepted His death as the payment for all sin forever.

Near the cross where Jesus died stood a centurion soldier, a commander in the Roman army. When the centurion saw the way Jesus died, he believed Jesus truly was God the Son.

So when the centurion, who stood opposite Him, saw that He cried out like this and breathed His last, he said, "Truly this Man was the Son of God!" Mark 15:39

Questions

1. What did Jesus tell Nicodemus that showed He knew how He was going to die? *Jesus told Nicodemus that in the same way Moses put the bronze serpent up on a pole, He too would be lifted up on a pole.*

2. Why did the Romans put a sign above the head of criminals who were crucified? *They put up a sign to show the crime the criminal had committed.*

3. What did the sign above Jesus' head say? *"THE KING OF THE JEWS" in three different languages.*

4. What do the names "Messiah" and "Christ" tell us about Jesus? *These names mean that Jesus was God's Chosen One. God chose Jesus to be His special prophet, to be the last high priest, and to be king forever.*

5. How was Jesus God's prophet? *While He was on Earth, Jesus taught the Jews the meaning of the Old Testament writings.*

6. How could God fulfill His plan for Jesus to be king if He was killed? *No one can defeat God. Everything God planned for Jesus has either already happened, or will happen in the future. Even though the Jews killed Jesus, He is still going to be king someday.*

7. How did the religious leaders make fun of Jesus on the cross? *They said that if Jesus was truly God He would have the power to come down from the cross.*

8. Why did Jesus choose not to come down from the cross? *Jesus came to Earth to be the Savior. He knew that in order to pay for the sin of all mankind, He, God the Son, would have to die in our place.*

9. Why did it become as dark as night for three hours while Jesus was on the cross? *It became dark because Jesus, the Son of God, was separated from God the Father. Our sin is what separates us from God. Because Jesus carried our sin on Himself, He had to be separated from God the Father.*

10. What did Jesus mean when He said, *"It is finished"* right before He died? *He meant He had finished the work God sent Him to do. Jesus came to Earth as the perfect Lamb of God to die in our place and pay the full price for all sin.*

Biblical Worldviews

- Jesus Christ is God.
- Jesus knew all that would happen to Him.
- God is in control; He works everything out according to His plans.
- God is more powerful than Satan; Satan can never stop God from completing His plans.
- All people are sinners.
- The penalty for sin is death; it is separation from God forever.
- Jesus Christ is the only Savior; He took our sin on Himself and died in our place.
- Jesus paid the full price for all sin forever; there never ever needs to be another sacrifice made for sin.
- God is a God of love; He is not selfish or self-seeking.

Activity: Bible Bingo

Supplies:

- Bingo cards and game tokens (Any set will do. You can buy an inexpensive set at the dollar store.)

Instructions:

- Give each student a bingo card and some tokens.

- Ask a question from the lesson review and call on a student to answer it. If the student answers it correctly, she calls the bingo square she wants to cover. Everyone else who has that square covers it as well.

- Continue to ask questions, calling on a different student each time. Allow everyone to answer at least one question and pick at least one bingo square.

- The game is over when the first student shouts BINGO because she has covered a complete row with tokens, either vertically, horizontally, or diagonally.

- Play the game several times until everyone has had a turn answering a question and/or all the questions from the review have been asked and answered.

Extra Bible References

Genesis 3:15; Numbers 21:4-9; Proverbs 19:21, 31:6; Matthew 1:21; Luke 1:33; Luke 23:26-49; John 1:29; Romans 6:23; Philippians 2:5-11; 1 Peter 2:21-24; Hebrews 1:1-4; 1 Peter 1:10-12, 18-20

70
Alive!
Jesus Comes Back to Life

Memory Verse

He is not here, but is risen! Remember how He spoke to you when He was still in Galilee, saying, "The Son of Man must be delivered into the hands of sinful men, and be crucified, and the third day rise again." Luke 24:6-7

Lesson

Jesus died on a Friday. Since the Jews were not allowed to work on Saturday (the Sabbath), Jesus' body needed to be buried right away. A man named Joseph asked Pilate's permission to take Jesus' body down from the cross.

After this, Joseph of Arimathea, being a disciple of Jesus, but secretly, for fear of the Jews, asked Pilate that he might take away the body of Jesus; and Pilate gave him permission. So he came and took the body of Jesus. And Nicodemus, who at first came to Jesus by night, also came, bringing a mixture of myrrh and aloes, about a hundred pounds.

Then they took the body of Jesus, and bound it in strips of linen with the spices, as the custom of the Jews is to bury. Now in the place where He was crucified there was a garden, and in the garden a new tomb in which no one had yet been laid. So there they laid Jesus...
John 19:38-42a

Nicodemus, the Pharisee who came to Jesus at night, and Joseph were both rich. They both believed in Jesus, but they kept it a secret because they were afraid of the Jewish religious leaders.

After Jesus died, Joseph and Nicodemus took care of Jesus' body. They covered it in spices and wrapped it in strips of cloth. Then they buried Jesus in a new tomb that belonged to Joseph. A tomb is a grave that is cut into the side of a rock; it is kind of like a cave. After placing Jesus' body in the tomb, a heavy stone was rolled in front of the entrance.

When Joseph had taken the body, he wrapped it in a clean linen cloth, and laid it in his new tomb which he had hewn out of the rock; and he rolled a large stone against the door of the tomb, and departed. Matthew 27:59-60

Once more everything happened just like the prophets in the Old Testament said it would. Isaiah said that even though the Savior would die alongside criminals, He would be buried in a rich person's tomb.

The women who had come to Jerusalem with Jesus followed Joseph and Nicodemus to the tomb. After Jesus was buried, they all went home to rest because the next day was the Sabbath.

> **The prophet Isaiah wrote:**
>
> And they made His grave with the wicked—but with the rich at His death... Isaiah 53:9a

And the women who had come with Him from Galilee followed after, and they observed the tomb and how His body was laid. Then they returned and prepared spices and fragrant oils. And they rested on the Sabbath according to the commandment. Luke 23:55-56

The chief priests and the Pharisees had heard Jesus say He would rise from the dead in three days. This bothered them, so they asked Pilate to have the tomb guarded.

On the next day, which followed the Day of Preparation, the chief priests and Pharisees gathered together to Pilate, saying, "Sir, we remember, while He was still alive, how that deceiver said, 'After three days I will rise.' Therefore command that the tomb be made secure until the third day, lest His disciples come by night and steal Him away, and say to the people, 'He has risen from the dead.' So the last deception will be worse than the first."

Pilate said to them, "You have a guard; go your way, make it as secure as you know how." So they went and made the tomb secure, sealing the stone and setting the guard. Matthew 27:62-66

Pilate gave permission to put soldiers by the tomb to guard it, but these strong soldiers could not stop the work of God.

Early on Sunday morning, there was a big earthquake and an angel from Heaven rolled the heavy stone away from the tomb.

And behold, there was a great earthquake; for an angel of the Lord descended from heaven, and came and rolled back the stone from the door, and sat on it. His countenance was like lightning, and his clothing as white as snow. And the guards shook for fear of him, and became like dead men. Matthew 28:2-4

After the Sabbath was over, the women brought more spices to put on Jesus' body. Imagine their surprise when they arrived at the tomb to find the stone rolled away and Jesus' body gone!

Then, suddenly, two angels appeared beside them saying Jesus was alive; He had risen from the dead just like He had said He would.

Now on the first day of the week, very early in the morning...certain...women...came to the tomb bringing the spices which they had prepared. But they found the stone rolled away from the tomb. Then they went in and did not find the body of the Lord Jesus.

And it happened, as they were greatly perplexed about this, that behold, two men stood by them in shining garments. Then, as they were afraid and bowed their faces to the earth, they said to them, "Why do you seek the living among the dead? He is not here, but is risen! Remember how He spoke to you when He was still in Galilee, saying, 'The Son of Man must be delivered into the hands of sinful men, and be crucified, and the third day rise again.'"

And they remembered His words. Luke 24:1-8

The women ran to tell Jesus' disciples the wonderful news, but as they turned to go, Jesus Himself appeared to them.

So they went out quickly from the tomb with fear and great joy, and ran to bring His disciples word.

And as they went to tell His disciples, behold, Jesus met them, saying, "Rejoice!" So they came and held Him by the feet and worshiped Him.

Then Jesus said to them, "Do not be afraid. Go and tell My brethren to go to Galilee, and there they will see Me." Matthew 28:8-10

Jesus truly had come back to life! He told the women to tell the disciples to meet Him in Galilee. While the women were on their way to tell the disciples the good news, some of the soldiers who had been guarding the tomb arrived in Jerusalem to tell the chief priests what had happened.

Now while they were going, behold, some of the guard came into the city and reported to the chief priests all the things that had happened.

When they had assembled with the elders and consulted together, they gave a large sum of money to the soldiers, saying, "Tell them, 'His disciples came at night and stole Him away while we slept.' And if this comes to the governor's ears, we will appease him and make you secure."

So they took the money and did as they were instructed; and this saying is commonly reported among the Jews until this day. Matthew 28:11-15

The Jewish religious leaders paid the soldiers a lot of money to say that Jesus' disciples had come at night and stolen Jesus' body while they were asleep. Of course, this was a lie. But the religious leaders did not want anyone to know that Jesus truly had risen from the dead.

When the women told the disciples Jesus was alive, they could not believe it.

It was Mary Magdalene, Joanna, Mary the mother of James, and the other women with them, who told these things to the apostles. And their words seemed to them like idle tales, and they did not believe them.

But Peter arose and ran to the tomb; and stooping down, he saw the linen cloths lying by themselves; and he departed, marveling to himself at what had happened. Luke 24:10-12

Even though Jesus had told the disciples He would rise again on the third day, they were surprised. Peter, the disciple who had denied Jesus, ran to see if Jesus really had risen from the dead. When Peter got to the tomb, he found it really was empty just like the women said.

507

Then Jesus appeared to Peter and the other disciples. After that, He was seen by more than five hundred of His followers. These people were witnesses to the fact that Jesus truly did rise from the dead.

...Christ...rose again the third day...He was seen by Cephas [Peter], then by the twelve. After that He was seen by over five hundred brethren at once...After that He was seen by James, then by all the apostles. 1 Corinthians 15:3-7

For forty days, Jesus stayed on Earth appearing to His followers and proving that He really was alive again.

...to whom He also presented Himself alive after His suffering by many infallible proofs, being seen by them during forty days... Acts 1:3

Remember how God told Abraham that the Savior would bring kindness and help to all the families in the world?

Before Jesus went back to Heaven, He told His followers to tell everyone in the world the good news about how He had made a way for them to be rescued from Satan, sin, and death. Jesus wanted everyone to know that He had made it possible for them to live with Him forever as God's friends.

"...and you shall be witnesses to Me in Jerusalem, and in all Judea and Samaria, and to the end of the earth."

Now when He had spoken these things, while they watched, He was taken up, and a cloud received Him out of their sight.

And while they looked steadfastly toward heaven as He went up, behold, two men stood by them in white apparel, who also said, "Men of Galilee, why do you stand gazing up into heaven? This same Jesus, who was taken up from you into heaven, will so come in like manner as you saw Him go into heaven." Acts 1:8b-11

Someday, Jesus will come in the clouds to take all who have believed His good news to be with Him in Heaven. Those believers who have already died will come out of the graves, and those who are still alive will be caught up together with them to meet Jesus in the air. From then on, all these believers will be with Jesus forever!

For the Lord Himself will descend from heaven with a shout, with the voice of an archangel, and with the trumpet of God. And the dead in Christ will rise first. Then we who are alive and remain shall be caught up together with them in the clouds to meet the Lord in the air. And thus we shall always be with the Lord. 1 Thessalonians 4:16-17

After Jesus takes these believers off the earth, there will be a terrible time of suffering on Earth that will last 7 years. When this time of suffering is over, God will restore the earth so that it will be a lot like it was in the Garden of Eden. At that time, God will once again give the land of Canaan to Abraham's descendants just like He promised long ago.

"for all the land which you see I give to you and your descendants forever." Genesis 13:15

Then, after 1,000 years, God will make a completely new heaven and earth.

Now I saw a new heaven and a new earth, for the first heaven and the first earth had passed away. Also there was no more sea. Revelation 21:1

When God makes the new heaven and the new earth, all believers from all time will live there forever and ever with Jesus as their king.

Questions

1. Who asked Pilate for permission to take Jesus' body down from the cross? *Joseph asked Pilate if he could take Jesus' body down.*

2. Was Joseph rich or poor? *He was a rich man.*

3. In whose tomb was Jesus buried? *Jesus was buried in Joseph's tomb.*

4. Who brought a hundred pounds of spices to put on Jesus' body? *Nicodemus, the man who came to Jesus by night, brought a hundred pounds of spices to put on Jesus' body.*

5. Why did the Jewish religious leaders want Pilate to put soldiers by the tomb? *The religious leaders were afraid Jesus' disciples would come at night and steal Jesus' body away to make it look like Jesus had risen from the dead.*

6. Could anyone stop Jesus from coming back to life? *No, no one could stop God from raising Jesus back to life.*

7. When the women went to Jesus' tomb on Sunday morning, what did they find? *They found the stone rolled away and the tomb empty. Two angels told them Jesus had risen from the dead and was alive.*

8. When they realized Jesus' body was gone, what did the religious leaders tell the soldiers to say about it? *The religious leaders told the soldiers to say Jesus' disciples had come at night while they were sleeping and taken Jesus' body away.*

9. What proof did God give us that Jesus really did come back to life? *After Jesus came back to life, He not only appeared to His disciples, He appeared to over five hundred believers. These people are witnesses to the fact that Jesus did come back to life.*

10. Before Jesus went back up to Heaven, what did He tell His disciples to do? *He told them to tell everyone the good news that He had died for their sins and risen again.*

11. Will Jesus be king on Earth someday? *Yes. When God makes the new heaven and the new earth, all believers from all time will live there forever and ever with Jesus as their king.*

Biblical World Views

- God knows everything; He knows what will happen in the future.
- No one can stop God from working out His plan.
- God can do anything; nothing is too hard for Him. God has power over death!
- All people are sinners.
- Angels are God's messengers; they do what God sends them to do.
- God is a God of love; He loves everyone.
- Jesus Christ is the only Savior.

Activity 1: Resurrection Drawing

Supplies:

- Pencils, colored pencils, crayons
- Paper, one piece per student
- Celebration stickers (optional)

Instructions:

- Students draw and color pictures of the resurrection.
- Students decorate their pictures to show celebration over Jesus rising from the dead.
- Students write the following verse on their papers: "He is not here, but is risen!" Luke 24:6a

Activity 2: Memory Verse Ball

Supplies:

- One or more mid-size balls

- Copy of memory verse: He is not here, but is risen! Remember how He spoke to you when He was still in Galilee, saying, "The Son of Man must be delivered into the hands of sinful men, and be crucified, and the third day rise again." Luke 24:6-7

Instructions:

- Students divide into teams or form one large circle, depending on the number of students in your group. Have them practice the memory verse while throwing the ball to each other and catching it.

- For example: The teacher will say the first part of the verse to be memorized. Once the teacher says it correctly, he throws the ball to one of the students, who must then try to also say it correctly and then throw it to another student.

- Go around until everyone has had a chance to catch the ball and say the first part of the verse. Now the teacher can add the second part of the verse and do the same thing. Finally, the students can say the entire verse and add the scripture reference as well.

- If students have been working in small groups, you can now bring them together into a large circle and have them recite it in front of the class with or without the balls.

Extra Bible References

Exodus 15:18; Psalm 2:1-12, 16:10, 146:10; Micah 4:7; Zechariah 14:1-4, 9-11; Acts 2:22-36, 10:40-41, 17:30-31; Matthew 24:27-30; Mark 14:61-62, 15:42-47; Mark 16:1-20; Luke 1:33, 24:1-48; Romans 1:4; Philippians 2:5-11; 1 Thessalonians 4:13-18; 1 Timothy 2:4; Hebrews 1:1-4; 1 Peter 1:10-12, 18-20

71
Accepted

Memory Verse

to the praise of the glory of His grace, by which He made us accepted in the Beloved.
Ephesians 1:6

Lesson

Let's go back to the beginning. God made Adam and Eve perfect in every way. Since they were perfect, God accepted them. Adam and Eve could be with God any time; there was nothing to keep them apart. Adam and Eve were God's friends.

But God wanted Adam and Eve to be His friends because they *wanted* to be, not because that was the only thing they could do. So He gave them a choice. God put two trees in the middle of the garden. One was the Tree of Life and the other was the Tree of the Knowledge of Good and Evil.

If Adam and Eve ate from The Tree of Life they would live forever, but if they ate from The Tree of the Knowledge of Good and Evil they would die and be separated from God forever. It was their choice.

Satan saw this as his chance to destroy Adam and Eve's relationship with God. He told Eve they would not die if they ate from The Tree of the Knowledge of Good and Evil. He said that if they ate from this tree they would become wise like God. Sadly, Adam and Eve chose to believe Satan instead of God.

Going against what God says to do is called sin. When Adam and Eve believed Satan instead of God and ate from The Tree of the Knowledge of Good and Evil, they became sinners. Because of their sin, Adam and Eve were no longer acceptable to God.

When Adam and Eve sinned, they suddenly realized they were naked. Quickly they sewed leaves together to make coverings for themselves. But God did not accept the clothes Adam and Eve made to cover their nakedness. Only He could make acceptable clothes for Adam and Eve. In His love, He killed an animal, made clothes from its skin, and put the clothes on Adam and Eve.

Also for Adam and his wife the LORD God made tunics of skin, and clothed them. Genesis 3:21

Since you were born into Adam's family, you were born a sinner.

Therefore, just as through one man sin entered the world, and death through sin, and thus death spread to all men, because all sinned. Romans 5:12

As a sinner, you are not acceptable to God and there is nothing you can do to please Him. In the same way God did not accept the clothes Adam and Eve made for themselves, God does not accept any work you do. To God, all your good deeds are like filthy rags.

But we are all like an unclean thing, and all our righteousnesses [good works] are like filthy rags... Isaiah 64:6a

Being kind to others, praying, being baptized, or going to church will not make you acceptable to God.

Just like God was the only One who could provide acceptable clothes for Adam and Eve, God is the only One who can make you acceptable to Him. In order to make acceptable clothes for Adam and Eve, God killed an animal and clothed them with its skin. In order to make you acceptable, God sent Jesus to die for you. The Bible says that all who trust in Jesus to save them are clothed with Jesus.

Just like God covered Adam and Eve with the skins of the animal He killed, when a person trusts in Jesus Christ, it is as though God covers them with Jesus.

For as many of you as were baptized into Christ have put on Christ. Galatians 3:27

In the same way you put on your clothes in the morning, the Bible says that whoever trusts in Jesus puts on Christ. Jesus Christ is pure and sinless and perfect.

"This is My beloved Son, in whom I am well pleased." Matthew 3:17b

If you have believed in Jesus, you are clothed with a perfect covering: Jesus Christ, God's dearly loved Son. Since, in God's eyes, you are clothed with His perfect, beloved Son, God accepts you as His perfect and dearly loved child.

to the praise of the glory of His grace, by which He made us accepted in the Beloved. Ephesians 1:6

Even though your sin made you unacceptable to God and separated you from Him, God made a way for you to be acceptable to Him by sending His perfect and beloved Son to die in your place so that He could clothe you with a perfect and acceptable covering: Jesus Christ!

Questions

1. Were Adam and Eve acceptable to God when He first made them? *Yes, when God first made Adam and Eve they were perfect and God accepted them.*

2. What happened to Adam and Eve when they believed Satan instead of God and ate from the Tree of the Knowledge of Good and Evil? *When Adam and Eve believed Satan instead of God and did what God said not to do, they became sinners.*

3. After Adam and Eve became sinners, were they still acceptable to God? *No, God is perfect. When Adam and Eve became sinners they were no longer acceptable to God.*

4. How did God make acceptable clothes for Adam and Eve? *God made acceptable clothes for Adam and Eve by killing an animal and clothing them with its skin.*

5. When you were born, were you born into God's family or Adam's family? *You were born into Adam's family. You were born a sinner separated from God.*

6. Can you make yourself acceptable to God by doing good works? *No, God does not accept your good works. God says your good works are like filthy rags to Him.*

7. Who is the only One who is acceptable and pleasing to God? *Only Jesus is acceptable to God. Jesus is pure and perfect; He never sinned.*

8. What did Jesus do for you so that you could be made acceptable to God? *Jesus died for your sin and rose again.*

9. If you have trusted in Jesus, does God see you as unacceptable? *If you have trusted in Jesus, you have been clothed, or covered, with Jesus Christ and God accepts you just like He accepts Jesus. You are now God's beloved just like Jesus is!*

10. Why did God make a way for you to be made acceptable to Him? *It was because of God's great love and kindness that He sent Jesus to be the Savior and make a way for you to be made acceptable to Him!*

Activity: Make a Hanging

Supplies:

- Pieces of colorful cardstock, approximately 8 ½ by 5 ½ , one per student
- Hole-punch
- Stickers
- Pencils, markers, and crayons
- Yarn

Instructions:

- Students write the following verse on the cardstock: "He made us accepted in the Beloved." Ephesians 1:6b
- Students decorate the cardstock in any way they like.
- When they are done, punch two holes in the top of the cardstock.
- Students thread the yarn through the holes and tie it to make a hanging.

Extra Bible References

Psalm 51:5, 143:2b; Isaiah 59:2, 61:10; Romans 5:19, 8:39; Galatians 3:26-27; Ephesians 1:4-5; Revelation 7:9-10

72
Eternal Life

Memory Verse

For as in Adam all die, even so in Christ all shall be made alive. 1 Corinthians 15:22

Lesson

When Adam and Eve ate from The Tree of the Knowledge of Good and Evil, their soul and spirit immediately became separated from God. This meant that someday their bodies would die and turn back into dust.

So all the days that Adam lived were nine hundred and thirty years; and he died. Genesis 5:5

When Adam and Eve's bodies died, the real them would then go to the terrible place of suffering to be separated from God forever. To be separated from God forever is called the second death.

Since Cain and Abel were Adam and Eve's children, they were born separated from God too. Cain and Abel were also going to die the second death.

> **Your soul and spirit are the real you. Your body is only the house for your soul and spirit.**

But God did not want Cain and Abel to be separated from Him forever, so He kindly showed them how they could come to Him by killing a lamb and bringing it to Him.

Sadly, Cain did not believe God; he did not believe he was a sinner who deserved to die. He did not believe that the only way for him to come to God was by killing a lamb and bringing it to Him. Because Cain did not believe God, he remained separated from God forever.

Abel, on the other hand, did believe God. Abel knew his sin separated him from God, and he knew that only God could save him from the second death he deserved. That is why Abel came to God in the way God had shown - by killing a lamb and offering it to God.

By faith Abel offered to God a more excellent sacrifice than Cain, through which he obtained witness that he was righteous... Hebrews 11:4a

Since Abel believed God, he did not die the second death. When his body died, instead of being separated from God forever, he went to live with God forever.

You were also born into Adam's family. You were also born a sinner separated from God.

And you...were dead in trespasses and sins, Ephesians 2:1

But even though your sin separates you from God, He loves you. God does not want you to be separated from Him. That is why He sent Jesus Christ, the Lamb of God, to die in your place. Just like Cain and Abel came to God by killing a lamb, God wants you to come to Him by believing in His Lamb, Jesus Christ.

...Jesus Christ...died for us, that...we should live together with Him. 1 Thessalonians 5:9b, 10

Jesus died on the cross to pay for your sin so that you do not have to die and pay for your own sin. Jesus died the death you should have died so you can live with Him forever.

God wanted Cain and Abel to kill a lamb to show that the penalty for sin is death. God also wanted them to understand that even though they deserved to die for their sin, He would accept a lamb to die in their place.

Since Cain did not offer a lamb as a sacrifice, he did not have a substitute to die in his place. Because Cain did not believe God, he would have to die for his own sin. But Abel did believe God and God accepted Abel's sacrifice.

Jesus Christ offered Himself as the sacrifice for your sin; He died in your place. You need to believe God like Abel did. If you believe God and come to Him in the way He has shown in the Bible, by believing in Jesus Christ, God promises to accept Jesus' death in place of your death.

God promises that those who believe in Jesus Christ will not be separated from God forever in the terrible place of suffering. Those who trust in Jesus' sacrifice for them will not die the second death but will live with God forever!

For God so loved the world that He gave His only begotten Son, that whoever believes in Him should not perish but have everlasting life. John 3:16

The Bible says that whoever believes in Jesus Christ moves from the place of death to the place of life.

Most assuredly, I say to you, he who hears My word and believes in Him who sent Me has everlasting life, and shall not come into judgment, but has passed from death into life. John 5:24

Questions

1. What happened to Adam and Eve's soul and spirit when they ate from The Tree of the Knowledge of Good and Evil? *Their soul and spirit immediately became separated from God.*

2. What was going to happen to Adam and Eve when their bodies died? *The real them would be separated from God forever in the terrible place of suffering.*

3. When Cain and Abel were born, were they separated from God? *Since Cain and Abel were born into Adam's family, they were born sinners separated from God.*

4. How did God show Cain and Abel that they could come to Him to be accepted? *God showed Cain and Abel that in order to be accepted they needed to come to Him by killing a lamb and bringing it to Him.*

5. Into whose family were you born? *You were born into Adam's family.*

6. When you were born, were you born separated from God? *Yes, you were born a sinner separated from God.*

7. What is the penalty for sin? *The penalty for sin is death.*

8. Who did God send to die in your place so that you do not have to die? *God sent Jesus Christ the Lamb of God to die in your place for your sin.*

9. What do you need to do in order to receive eternal life? *You need to trust in Jesus the Lamb of God who died as a sacrifice in your place. Whoever believes in Jesus will not perish but will have eternal life.*

Activity: Bible Hangman

Supplies:

- Chalkboard or dry erase board
- Chalk or dry erase markers

Instructions:

- Draw a large hangman tree on the board.
- Draw lines and spaces under the tree to correspond to the letters and spaces of the key phrase.
- **Key phrase**: Jesus, the perfect Lamb of God, died in your place so that you can live with God forever.
- **Optional key phrase for younger students**: Jesus died in your place.

- Ask the lesson review questions, one at a time. Call on one student or one team to answer each question.
- If answer is correct, the student or team gets to pick a letter, i.e., the letter b.
- If the letter picked is in the key phrase, the teacher fills it in on the board each time it occurs.
- If the letter picked is not in the key phrase, the teacher draws one part of a stick figure on the hangman tree, i.e., a head, an arm, a stick body, etc.
- When a student (or team) thinks he knows the key phrase, he may try to solve the puzzle on his turn. The game is over when a student or team solves the puzzle or the teacher draws all the parts of the stick man, whichever comes first.

Extra Bible References

Ezekiel 18:4; John 17:3; Romans 5:8, 12-21; 6:23; 1 Corinthians 15:3; Ephesians 2:5; 1 Thessalonians 5:10; 2 Timothy 1:10; 1 John 5:11-13

73
Jesus is the Only Door

Memory Verse

Salvation is found in no one else, for there is no other name under heaven given to men by which we must be saved. Acts 4:12

Lesson

The people in Noah's day did not care about God. Every day all they thought about was how bad they could be. Finally, the people became so wicked God had to destroy them with a flood.

Everyone except Noah and his family drowned in the flood. Even though Noah was a sinner and deserved to die, God saved him because he believed God.

God told Noah to build a big boat to protect him and his family. Noah was to put only one door in the boat. In order for Noah's family and the animals to be saved from death, they had to enter the boat through this one door.

This reminds us of the sheepfolds the shepherds built in Jesus' day. Just like the big boat was a place of safety for Noah's family, the sheepfolds were a place of safety for the sheep. There was only one entrance into a sheepfold. At night, the shepherd would sleep in this entrance to keep out wild animals and robbers. A good shepherd would die fighting off danger so that his sheep would be safe.

In the Bible, Jesus compared Himself to the good shepherd who slept in the doorway of the sheepfold.

Then Jesus said to them again, "...I am the door. If anyone enters by Me, he will be saved...The thief does not come except to steal, and to kill, and to destroy. I have come that they may have life...I am the good shepherd. The good shepherd gives His life for the sheep.
John 10:7-11

Just like a good shepherd in Jesus' day would die in order to protect his sheep from wild animals and robbers, Jesus died to save us from Satan's power and from the second death.

📖 ...that through death he might destroy the one who has the power of death, that is, the devil, Hebrews 2:14

In the same way there was only one entrance into the big boat and into the sheepfolds of Jesus' day, Jesus is the only door, or way, to God. The only way for you to be able to live with God the Father in Heaven is to believe in Jesus.

📖 Jesus said to him, "I am the way...No one comes to the Father except through Me." John 14:6

Jesus Christ is the only Savior; He is the only One who can save you from Satan and death. A priest cannot save you, your religion cannot save you, and you cannot save yourself.

Jesus Christ is the only One who can make you acceptable to God so that you can live with Him forever. You cannot make yourself acceptable to God by being kind and good, by getting baptized, by going to church, or by reading the Bible.

Jesus Christ is the one and only door; He is the only One who can save you from death and make you acceptable to God. Only those who believe in Him are saved from death and receive everlasting life. So believe in Him!

📖 Salvation is found in no one else, for there is no other name under heaven given to men by which we must be saved. Acts 4:12

Questions

1. How many doors were there into Noah's big boat? *There was only one door into the ark.*

2. How many entrances were there into a sheepfold? *There was only one entrance into the sheepfold.*

3. How many ways are there for you to be saved from Satan and death? *There is only one way you to be saved from Satan and death and that is by believing in Jesus Christ.*

4. Is there anything you can do to make yourself acceptable to God so that you can live with Him forever? *No, there is nothing you can do to make yourself acceptable to God.*

5. How is Jesus like the good shepherd? *Jesus is the good shepherd because He gave His life to save us from Satan and death. Jesus gave His life so we could live.*

6. What must you do to be able to go to Heaven? *You must believe in Jesus Christ. You must admit you are a sinner and believe that Jesus died in your place and rose again, nothing else.*

Activity: Jesus is the Door Craft

Supplies:

- Construction paper, half a sheet per student
- Scissors
- Glue
- Pencils and/or crayons
- Small buttons

Instructions:

- Students fold the half sheet of construction paper in half to make a door.
- On the outside of the door students write: "I am the door."
- On the inside of the door they write the following verse: "If anyone enters by Me, he will be saved…" John 10:9a
- Students decorate the outside of the door with crayons and glue on a button for a doorknob.

Extra Bible References

John 10:1-17; 1 Timothy 2:5

74
Jesus Our Subsitute

Memory Verse

The next day John saw Jesus coming toward him, and said, "Behold! The Lamb of God who takes away the sin of the world!" John 1:29

Lesson

God promised to give Abraham so many descendants they could not be counted. God promised Abraham that one of his descendants would bring God's kindness and help to all the families in the world.

Even though Abraham and Sarah were already old and had no children when God made this promise, Abraham believed God. Finally when Abraham was one hundred years old, God gave Abraham and Sarah a son. Abraham and Sarah named their son Isaac.

Abraham knew that many descendants would come from Isaac and that one of them would be the promised Savior. But then one day God asked Abraham to do the unthinkable. God asked Abraham to sacrifice his only son on an altar.

How could God ask Abraham to kill his only son? If Abraham killed Isaac, he would not have any descendants! But Abraham had faith in God. Abraham believed that even if he killed Isaac, God would keep His promise to give him many descendants. Abraham believed that if he killed Isaac, God had the power to raise Isaac back to life.

Because Abraham believed God, he did what God asked him to do. He tied up his only son and laid him on an altar.

By faith Abraham...offered up Isaac...his only begotten son...
Hebrews 11:17

On the altar, Isaac was in a helpless position. He was tied up with ropes so that he could not get down.

Just like Isaac, you also are condemned to death because of your sin and helpless to save yourself. In the same way the ropes held Isaac on the altar, your sin holds you in the place of death. The Bible says that all who sin must die.

The soul who sins shall die. Ezekiel 18:4b

Remember God's commandments?

"You shall have no other gods before Me.

"You shall not make for yourself a carved image...you shall not bow down to them nor serve them...

"You shall not take the name of the LORD your God in vain...

"Honor your father and your mother...

"You shall not murder.

"You shall not commit adultery.

"You shall not steal.

"You shall not bear false witness against your neighbor.

"You shall not covet... Exodus 20:3-17

Have you ever been angry with anyone? God says getting mad is like committing murder.

Whoever hates his brother is a murderer... 1 John 3:15a

Have you ever gotten in trouble with your mom or dad? If so, it was probably because you did not honor, or respect, them. What about coveting? If you have ever wanted something that belongs to someone else, you have coveted. If you have ever stolen anything, or told a lie about someone, or loved anything more than you love God, you have broken God's commands.

The penalty for breaking God's commands is death. Even if you break just one command, you are guilty and must die.

For whoever shall keep the whole law, and yet stumble in one point, he is guilty of all. James 2:10

You cannot hide your sin from God. God knows about all your sin, even the sin in your heart.

📖...for the LORD searches all hearts, and understands every intent of the thoughts. 1 Chronicles 28:9

In the same way Isaac could not free himself from the ropes that held him in the place of death, you cannot free yourself from your sin. Because of your sin you should die; there is nothing you can do to escape the penalty for your sin. You are as helpless as Isaac was on the altar.

Only God could save Isaac. In His love, God provided a ram to die in Isaac's place. Abraham named that place "The Lord Will Provide."

📖...Abraham called the name of the place, The-LORD-Will-Provide; Genesis 22:14a

The ram God provided to die in Isaac's place was caught in the bushes by its horns so that it did not have any scratches or bruises. God could accept only a perfect lamb as a substitute for Isaac. If the ram would have had any scratches or bruises, God would not have accepted it in Isaac's place.

In the same way, God is the only One who can save you from sin and death. Just like God provided a perfect ram to die in Isaac's place, God provided Jesus Christ, the perfect Lamb of God, to die in your place.

📖 The next day John saw Jesus coming toward him, and said, "Behold! The Lamb of God who takes away the sin of the world!" John 1:29

The Bible says that Jesus Christ did not have any spots or blemishes.

📖...Christ...a lamb without blemish and without spot. . 1 Peter 1:19

Jesus never sinned; He never broke any of God's commands. Jesus was perfect in every way.

📖Who committed no sin... 1 Peter 2:22

Only Someone who had none of His own sin to pay for could pay for the sin of the world.

God provided the perfect Lamb to take your place. Jesus Christ, the perfect Lamb of God, died the death you should have died. He was your substitute.

Trust in Him and you will be saved from the second death!

Questions

1. What held Isaac on the altar so that he could not get off? *The ropes tied around Isaac kept him from being able to get off the altar.*

2. Who was the only One who could save Isaac from death? *God was the only One who could save Isaac from death.*

3. What kind of substitute did God provide to die in Isaac's place? *God provided a perfect male sheep to die in Isaac's place.*

4. In what way is your sin like the ropes that were tied around Isaac on the altar? *Just like the ropes kept Isaac from being able to escape, your sin makes it so that you have to die.*

5. Can you free yourself from your sin? *No, just like Isaac could not free himself from the ropes around him, you cannot free yourself from your sin.*

6. Who is the only One who can provide a way for you to be saved from death? *Only God can provide a way for you to be saved from death.*

7. Who did God provide to die in your place? *God provided Jesus, the perfect Lamb of God, to be your substitute and die in your place.*

Activity : Foam Cross Mosaic

Supplies:

- 8 ½ by 11 sheets of black foam board (one sheet will make two crosses)
- A lot of small pieces of foam of various colors
- Glue
- Scissors
- "Cross" template (see appendix page 582)
- "Verse" printouts (see appendix page 583)
- Hole-punch (optional)
- Ribbon or yarn (optional)

Instructions:

- Photocopy "Verse" templates so there is one verse cut-out per student.
- Cut out crosses from "Cross" template and use to trace crosses onto black foam (two crosses per piece of foam, one cross per student).
- Teacher or students cut out crosses.
- Students glue various colored pieces of foam onto one side of black foam cross to form mosaic pattern, being careful to use small amounts of glue to avoid excess.
- Teacher or the students cut out the verses on the dotted lines.
- Turn cross over and glue verse onto back of cross.
- Optional: Magnets can be attached to back of cross to make refrigerator magnets, or a hole can be punched on top of the cross and yarn or ribbon strung through so it can be hung as an ornament.

Extra Bible References

Genesis 22:13; Jeremiah 17:9-10; Matthew 5:21-23; Romans 3:10-18; Galatians 3:22

75
The Last Passover Lamb

Memory Verse

For indeed Christ, our Passover, was sacrificed for us. 1 Corinthians 5:7b

Lesson

The last plague God sent on Egypt when He freed the Israelites from slavery was the death of their firstborn sons, but God made a way for the Israelites to escape this plague.

This is what God told the Israelites to do: He told every Israelite family to pick out a perfect boy lamb.

Your lamb shall be without blemish, a male of the first year. Exodus 12:5a

After waiting four days, each family was to kill the lamb it had chosen.

Then the whole assembly of the congregation of Israel shall kill it at twilight. Exodus 12:6b

The Israelites were not to break any of the lamb's bones when they killed it.

...nor shall you break one of its bones. Exodus 12:46

After they sprinkled the blood of the lambs on the doorframes of their homes, the Israelites were to stay inside. God promised to pass over every home where He saw the blood of the lamb sprinkled on the doorframe. The firstborn son in that home would not die.

And you shall...strike the lintel and the two doorposts with the blood...And none of you shall go out of the door of his house until morning.

> For the LORD will pass through to strike the Egyptians; and when He sees the blood on the lintel and on the two doorposts, the LORD will pass over the door and not allow the destroyer to come into your houses to strike you. Exodus 12:22-23

God wanted the Israelites always to remember that night in Egypt when He saved their firstborn sons from death. That is why, once a year, the Israelites celebrated the Passover Feast in Jerusalem. It was a time to remember how their sons had been saved by the blood of the lamb.

Remember how Jesus died during the Passover Feast in Jerusalem? John the Baptist said Jesus was the Lamb of God. The Bible says that Jesus Christ is our Passover Lamb who was sacrificed for us.

For indeed Christ, our Passover, was sacrificed for us.
1 Corinthians 5:7

In the same way the firstborn sons of the Israelites were saved from death by the blood of the lamb, Jesus shed His blood to save us from eternal death.

At the very first Passover, God told Moses that the Israelites were not to break the bones of the lamb when they killed it. This was because the Passover lamb was a picture of the coming Savior.

The Roman soldiers often broke the legs of those being crucified to speed up their death, but when Jesus, the Passover Lamb of God, died, the soldiers did not break His legs.

But when they came to Jesus and saw that He was already dead, they did not break His legs. John 19:33

Just like God accepted only a perfect lamb to die in the place of the Israelites' firstborn sons, the Bible says that Jesus did not have any spots or blemishes. Jesus was the perfect Lamb of God. Jesus never did anything that displeased God.

...you were...redeemed...with the precious blood of Christ, as of a lamb without blemish and without spot. . 1 Peter 1:18-19

God accepted only a perfect Savior to die in our place.

In Egypt, God passed over every home where the blood of the lamb was sprinkled on the doorframe. The blood shed by the Passover lamb protected the firstborn son in that house from death.

In the same way, Jesus is our Passover Lamb. Jesus died so that you could be saved from the second death. Just like the blood on the doorframes showed that a lamb had been killed, protecting the firstborn son in that home, if you trust in Jesus Christ you are protected from eternal death because Jesus the Passover Lamb was killed for you.

Questions

1. What was the last plague God sent on Egypt? *It was the death of their firstborn sons.*

2. How could the firstborn sons of the Israelites be saved from death? *They could be saved from death if a perfect lamb was killed and the blood sprinkled on the doorframe of the houses where they lived.*

3. Why did God tell the Israelites to stay inside their homes after they sprinkled the blood on the doorframes? *God said He would not enter any home where He saw the blood of the lamb sprinkled on the doorframe. Those who were hidden behind the blood of the lamb would be saved from death.*

4. Why were the Israelites not to break any of the bones of the lamb they killed? *They were not to break the bones of the lamb because the lamb was a picture of Jesus the coming Savior. When Jesus died on the cross, His bones were not broken.*

5. Could the lambs chosen by the Israelites have any spots or blemishes? *No, God told the Israelites to choose a perfect lamb to die in the place of the firstborn son.*

6. Did Jesus ever sin? *No, Jesus was perfect in every way.*

7. What did John the Baptist call Jesus? *He called Jesus the Lamb of God.*

8. During what Jewish feast did Jesus die? *He died during the Passover Feast.*

9. How is Jesus our a Passover Lamb? *Jesus died and shed His blood so that you could be saved from the second death. If you trust in Jesus, it is as though you are hidden behind His blood, and you will not die.*

Activity: Christ our Passover Craft

Supplies:
-   "Heart" templates, one per student (see appendix page 584)
-   White cardstock or construction paper, one sheet per student
-   Pencils and red and black crayons
-   Tape or staples

Instructions:

- Students use "Heart" template to trace hearts onto cardstock or construction paper (two hearts per sheet).
- Next, students cut out the hearts.
- On one heart, students write their names and draw a picture of themselves.
- Students color this heart black around the edges to represent their sinfulness.
- On the other heart students draw a cross and write on it: Christ our Passover.
- Students color this heart red around the edges to represent Christ's death and shed blood.
- Staple or tape the red heart over the black heart to show that whoever trusts in Jesus is hiding behind Jesus' blood and will be saved from death because Jesus died in his or her place.
- Discuss: Christ is our Passover Lamb. When God looks at the person who has trusted in Jesus, He sees that person hidden behind the shed blood and death of Jesus, and so He passes over that person and he or she does not have to die.

Extra Bible References

Exodus 12; 1 Peter 1:19

76
Friends, Not Enemies

But now in Christ Jesus you who once were far off have been brought near by the blood of Christ. Ephesians 2:13

Lesson

Remember when God came down to Mount Sinai to give His commands to the Israelites? Moses had to put a fence around the mountain so no one would go near it. If anyone even touched the mountain where God was, that person would die!

You shall set bounds for the people all around, saying, 'Take heed to yourselves that you do not go up to the mountain or touch its base. Whoever touches the mountain shall surely be put to death.
Exodus 19:12

Sin keeps us away from God; it makes us God's enemies.

But your iniquities have separated you from your God; And your sins have hidden His face from you.... Isaiah 59:2a

After God gave His commandments to Israel, He came to live among the Israelites so that if anyone broke a command he could come to God to be forgiven.

But just because God was living among them did not mean the Israelites could go visit Him any time they wanted.

No, just like Cain and Abel were to approach God by killing a lamb and bringing it to Him, the only way for the sinful Israelites to come to God was by bringing a lamb and killing it there in front of the tabernacle where God lived.

The blood of the lambs covered the Israelites' sins so they could come near to God and so that God did not have to destroy them.

Of course, the Israelites were never allowed to go into the tabernacle. Only the priests were allowed into the tabernacle to do their work.

But no one was ever allowed into the Most Holy Place where God was.

Both in the tabernacle, and later in the temple, there was a heavy curtain that hid God's presence from view.

The veil shall be a divider for you between the holy place and the Most Holy. Exodus 26:33b

There was a divider between the Holy Place and the Most Holy Place. God lived above the mercy seat in the Most Holy Place in the form of a brilliant light.

No sinful person could approach God there. The Bible says that God lives...

...in unapproachable light, whom no man has seen or can see, to whom be honor and everlasting power. Amen. 1 Timothy 6:16

There was only one exception. Once a year the high priest was to go into God's presence in the Most Holy Place with the blood of a special sacrifice. This sacrifice was for his sins and for the sins the Israelites had unknowingly committed that year.

But if the high priest did not enter the Most Holy Place according to the way God said, he would die.

and the LORD said to Moses: "Tell Aaron your brother not to come at just any time into the Holy Place inside the veil, before the mercy seat which is on the ark, lest he die; for I will appear in the cloud above the mercy seat." Leviticus 16:2

Over and over again the Israelites made sacrifices to God for their sins. Every time an Israelite sinned, he had to bring a lamb to the bronze altar in front to the tabernacle, lay his hand on it, and kill it. Then the priest burned it on the altar.

Once a year the high priest brought the blood of the special sacrifice.

And every priest stands ministering daily and offering repeatedly the same sacrifices, which can never take away sins. Hebrews 10:11

But these animal sacrifices were only a covering for the Israelites' sins so that they would not die. They were a temporary solution until a perfect sacrifice could be made that would completely take away sin once for all.

Finally Jesus Christ the Savior came into the world. Jesus Christ was God's Chosen One. God had chosen Jesus to be the last High Priest. But Jesus did not take the blood of a lamb into the Most Holy Place. No, Jesus was the Lamb. He sacrificed Himself and shed His own blood.

But Christ came as High Priest...Not with the blood of goats and calves, but with His own blood He entered the Most Holy Place once for all, having obtained eternal redemption. Hebrews 9:11-12

Do you know what happened to the heavy curtain in front of the Most Holy Place when Jesus died? The Bible tells us that it was "torn in two from top to bottom"!

Then the veil [curtain] of the temple was torn in two from top to bottom. Mark 15:38

Suddenly, anyone could go right into God's presence. Why? Well, do you remember what John the Baptist called Jesus?

John called Jesus the Lamb of God who "takes away the sin of the world!"

Behold! The Lamb of God who takes away the sin of the world! John 1:29b

Because Jesus Christ is God, and because He is absolutely perfect, His sacrifice was far better than any animal sacrifice! Jesus' death did not just cover sin; Jesus' death took away the sin of the world because it totally paid for all sin forever. Jesus' death paid for all sins that had ever been committed in the past and all sins that would ever be committed in the future.

Now, by trusting that Jesus' sacrifice is for their sins, people can freely approach God at any time. There will never need to be another animal sacrifice, because God said Jesus' sacrifice was enough. Jesus' sacrifice was so great it paid the penalty for all the sin of everyone in the world forever! That's why whoever trusts in Jesus' death can be brought near to God.

But now in Christ Jesus you who once were far off have been brought near by the blood of Christ. Ephesians 2:1

In the Garden of Eden when Adam and Eve went against what God said, they became sinful on the inside and were separated from God. Ever since that time, all Adam and Eve's children have been born sinners separated from God. Because you were born a sinner, you were God's enemy.

And you, who once were alienated and enemies in your mind by wicked works, yet now He has reconciled in the body of His flesh through death... Colossians 1:21-22a

But now, because God the Son came to Earth and died for your sin and rose again, you can be reconciled to God. To be reconciled means to be God's friend again when you used to be His enemy. Before, you were God's enemy because you were a sinner, but because Jesus Christ paid for all your sin, He made it possible for you to be brought back into friendship with God.

For Christ also suffered once for sins, the just for the unjust, that He might bring us to God.... 1 Peter 3:18a

That was God's plan from the very beginning. From the beginning, God planned for His Son Jesus Christ to be the Savior and rescue us from Satan's dominion so that we could be close to Him again.

Now that Jesus has completely taken care of the sin problem, you do not have to be God's enemy any longer. All who trust in Jesus can freely come to God with boldness and confidence, just like Adam and Eve did before they joined Satan's side.

according to the eternal purpose which He accomplished in Christ Jesus our Lord, in whom we have boldness and access with confidence through faith in Him. Ephesians 3:11-12

All who believe in Jesus have everlasting life. But those who do not trust in what Jesus did for them are still God's enemies and will be separated from Him forever.

He who believes in the Son has everlasting life; and he who does not believe the Son shall not see life, but the wrath of God abides on him. John 3:36

Believe in Jesus! He died on the cross for your sin and rose again so that you could be reconciled to God. Trust in Him so that you can be His friend rather than His enemy!

Questions

1. Why can sinful people not live with God? *Sinful people cannot live with God because God is perfect and pure. He cannot allow sin to be around Him.*

2. What was the only way for the Israelites to approach God? *The only way for the Israelites to approach God was to bring a lamb to the tabernacle where God lived and kill it there in His presence. The death of the lambs covered the Israelites' sins so that they could come near to God.*

3. How often did the Israelites have to sacrifice lambs? *Every time an Israelite broke one of God's commands, he had to sacrifice another lamb. And once a year the high priest had to make a special sacrifice for himself and for all the sins the Israelites had committed without knowing it.*

4. Who did God choose to be the last High Priest? *Jesus Christ was chosen by God to be the last High Priest.*

5. How was Jesus' sacrifice better than the animal sacrifices? *The animal sacrifices only covered sins temporarily. Jesus is God and He is perfect. His sacrifice was so great it paid for all sin for all time; it completely paid for all sin that had ever been committed in the past and all sin that would ever be committed in the future.*

6. Why did the curtain in the temple rip in two when Jesus died on the cross? *The curtain tore because Jesus had paid for all the sin of the world. When Jesus paid for all sin, it opened the way for anyone who believes in Jesus to come near to God.*

7. Why were you God's enemy? *You were God's enemy because you were born into Adam's family and you were a sinner.*

8. What does it mean to be reconciled to God? *It means that you have been made God's friend when you were His enemy.*

9. Who made it possible for us sinners to be made God's friends? *Jesus did by dying on the cross for us and paying for our sin.*

10. Since Jesus paid for everyone's sin, does that mean everyone will go to Heaven? *No, only those who trust in Jesus are reconciled to God so that they can be His friends.*

Activity: Torn Curtain Craft

Supplies:

- Sheets of white, red, blue, or purple construction paper (see Exodus 26:31-33) cut in half, one half sheet per student
- Sheets of red, purple, or blue felt (optional)
- Glue
- Stapler or tape
- Scissors

- Pencils and crayons
- Gold glitter (optional)

Instructions:

- Students draw the mercy seat inside the Most Holy Place.
- Students illustrate the brilliant light of God's presence using yellow crayons or glue and glitter. They may want to write "God" in the center of the bright light.
- Students staple, glue, or tape a curtain (either of construction paper or felt) across the front of the mercy seat where God lived.
- Then have students either cut or tear the curtain to show the torn curtain.
- Discuss: Why did God tear the curtain when Jesus died on the cross?

Extra Bible References

Exodus 25:22; Leviticus 16:2-34; 2 Samuel 6:2; Psalm 7:11; Romans 5:10, 6:10; Ephesians 2:13, 18; 1 Timothy 6:16; Hebrews 2:17, 3:1, 4:14-15, 7:23-28, 9:6-15, 10:19

77
Redeemed

Memory Verse

...knowing that you were not redeemed with corruptible things, like silver or gold...but with the precious blood of Christ, as of a lamb without blemish and without spot
1 Peter 1:18-19

Lesson

God formed Adam from the dust of the ground and breathed life into him. God made Eve from Adam's rib and gave life to her too. Adam and Eve belonged to God.

God loved the people He created. They were wonderful and perfect in every way and they loved God too. God put them in a beautiful garden where they had everything they could ever want, but then Satan tricked Adam and Eve, and they believed His lie.

When Adam and Eve believed Satan instead of God, they joined Satan's side and came under his dominion. Satan is an evil leader. Life was not peaceful and joyful anymore. Adam and Eve had become sinners and they were going to be separated from God forever in the terrible place of suffering.

But God told Satan that one day He would send the Child of a woman to bruise his head. An injury to the head is fatal.

And I will put enmity between you and the woman, and between your seed and her Seed; He shall bruise your head, and you shall bruise His heel." Genesis 3:15

This was good news for Adam and Eve and their children. It meant that someday God would send Someone to rescue mankind from Satan's dominion and power.

At the right time, God did send Someone, just like He said He would. God sent His very own Son to be born of a woman. God sent his Son to pay the price to get us back.

But when the fullness of the time had come, God sent forth His Son, born of a woman...to redeem those who were under the law, that we might receive the adoption as sons. Galatians 4:4-5

There is a very old story about a boy and a sailboat. I don't know if it is true or not, but it is a good picture of what God did for us.

A boy built a sailboat and had it all fixed up, tarred and painted. He took it to the lake and pushed it in the water, hoping it would sail. Sure enough, a wisp of breeze filled the little sail and it billowed and went rippling along the waves. Suddenly, before the little boy knew it, the boat was out of his reach, even though he waded in fast and tried to grab it. As he watched it float away, he hoped maybe the breeze would shift and it would come sailing back to him. Instead, he watched it go farther and farther until it was gone. When he went home crying, his mother asked, "What's wrong, didn't it work?"

And he said, "It worked too well."

Sometime later, the little boy was downtown and walked past a second-hand store. There in the window he saw his boat. It was unmistakably his, so he went in and said to the shopkeeper, "That's my boat." He walked to the window, picked it up and started to leave with it.

The owner of the shop said, "Wait a minute, Sonny. That's my boat. I bought it from someone."

The boy said, "No, it's my boat. I made it. See." And the boy showed the owner the little scratches and the marks where he had hammered and filed.

The man said, "I'm sorry, Sonny. If you want it, you have to buy it."

The poor little guy didn't have any money, but he worked hard and saved his pennies. Finally, one day he had enough money. He went in and bought the little boat. As he left the store holding the boat close to him, he was heard saying, "You're twice my boat. First, you're my boat 'cause I made you and second, you're my boat 'cause I bought you!"

Just like the boat in this story rightfully belonged to the boy who made it, all people rightfully belong to God because God made them and gave them life.

...He gives to all life, breath, and all things. Acts 17:25b

But just like the boat floated away from the boy, Adam and Eve became separated from God. Because Adam and Eve were separated from God, all their children were separated from God too.

The Bible says that the payment for sin is death.

The soul who sins shall die. Ezekiel 18:4

Unlike the boy in the story, Jesus did not buy us back with money. He did not pay with silver or gold to redeem us. What Jesus redeemed mankind with was His own precious blood.

...you were not redeemed with...silver or gold...but with the precious blood of Christ, as of a lamb without blemish and without spot. 1 Peter 1:18-19

> It is important to understand that God did not pay anything to Satan. The payment for sin is death. Jesus paid the price we should have paid. You could say that Jesus paid the price for our sin to God.

To pay the penalty for our sin so that we could be rescued from Satan's dominion, Jesus Christ died on the cross and shed His blood.

For you were bought at a price; therefore glorify God in your body and in your spirit, which are God's. 1 Corinthians 6:20

> Redeem - to pay the price to get something back that belonged to you in the first place

If you have trusted in Jesus Christ to save you, God can say of you, "You're twice mine. First, you're mine because I made you, and second, you're mine because I bought you!"

One day two thousand years ago, Jesus Christ, God the Son, died on a cross. Three days later, He rose again. This was a true event. It was in the news of the day. Everyone talked about it.

Moreover, brethren, I declare to you the gospel...by which also you are saved...that Christ died for our sins according to the Scriptures, and that He was buried, and that He rose again the third day according to the Scriptures, 1 Corinthians 15:1-4

Gospel means good news. The good news is that Jesus' death on the cross paid for all our sin. God raised Jesus to life again because Jesus' work was done; He had completely paid for all sin for all time. God was satisfied with the payment Jesus made. Jesus had paid the full price to rescue us from Satan, sin, and death.

John, one of Jesus' disciples, wrote the book of Revelation, which is the last book in the Bible. God let John see the future. John wrote that someday people from all parts of the world will be in Heaven praising Jesus for redeeming them.

And they sang a new song, saying: "You are worthy...For You were slain, and have redeemed us to God by Your blood out of every tribe and tongue and people and nation, and have made us kings and priests to our God; and we shall reign on the earth." Revelation 5:9

Questions

1. Why do all people rightfully belong to God? *All people belong to God because God created them and gave them life.*

2. How did all the people in the world come to be under Satan's dominion? *Because Adam and Eve believed Satan instead of God and joined Satan's side, all their children (which is all the people in the world) are born on Satan's side.*

3. What did God tell Satan would happen to his head in the Garden of Eden? *God told Satan that someday He would send the Child of a woman to bruise Satan's head. This meant that one day God would send Someone to rescue mankind from Satan's dominion.*

4. Who did God send to redeem you? *God sent Jesus to redeem you.*

5. What is the payment for sin? *The payment for sin is death.*

6. What is the payment Jesus paid for your sin? *Jesus died and shed His blood for your sin.*

7. What does the word gospel mean? *It means good news.*

8. What is God's good news for you? *It is that two thousand years ago Jesus died on the cross to pay for the sin of the world. God was satisfied with the payment Jesus' made and raised Him from the dead.*

9. If you have trusted in Jesus as your Savior, who do you belong to? *You belong to Jesus. You are twice His, because first He created you, and second He bought you with His precious blood!*

Activity 1: Disappearing Memory Verse Game

Supplies:

- Chalkboard or white board
- Chalk or white board marker

Instructions:

- Write memory verse and scripture reference in large letters on chalkboard or white board.
- Have students repeat memory verse and scripture reference in unison two times
- Ask for a student volunteer to pick two words he would like for you to erase. Erase those two words (or you can have the student come up and erase them).

- Have the students repeat the memory verse in unison, including the two words that have been erased.
- Ask for a different student volunteer to pick two more words to erase. Erase the words as before.
- Have the students repeat the memory verse in unison.
- Repeat this process until all the words have been erased.
- See if the group can recite the verse in unison without any words on the board.
- If you like, you can ask for individual volunteers to recite the verse from memory.

Activity 2: Sailboat Story Skit

Supplies:

- Student volunteers

Instructions:

- Have groups of students take turns acting out the story of the boy and his sailboat.
- Discuss the meaning of the word redeem.

Extra Bible References

Galatians 3:12-14, 4:4-6; Ephesians 1:7; Colossians 1:13-14; Hebrews 9:13-15; Revelation 5:9

78
Declared Righteous

Memory Verse

...that we might be justified by faith in Christ and not by the works of the law; for by the works of the law no flesh shall be justified. Galatians 2:16b

Lesson

Remember the man who called Jesus "Good Teacher"? This man thought that by keeping God's commands he could be good enough to get to Heaven. But Jesus showed the man that in order to get to Heaven he would have to be perfect. Not only would he have to keep all the Ten Commandments, he would have to love people and love God more than he loved himself. This made the man sad, because he knew he could not be that good!

Now behold, one came and said to Him, "Good Teacher, what good thing shall I do that I may have eternal life?"

So He said to him, "Why do you call Me good? No one is good but One, that is, God. But if you want to enter into life, keep the commandments."

He said to Him, "Which ones?"

Jesus said, "'You shall not murder,' 'You shall not commit adultery,' 'You shall not steal,' 'You shall not bear false witness,' 'Honor your father and your mother,' and, 'You shall love your neighbor as yourself.'"

The young man said to Him, "All these things I have kept from my youth. What do I still lack?"

Jesus said to him, "If you want to be perfect, go, sell what you have and give to the poor, and you will have treasure in heaven; and come, follow Me." Matthew 19:16-21

God the Father is absolutely perfect and pure. Jesus told the Jews they needed to be as perfect as God is!

Therefore you shall be perfect, just as your Father in heaven is perfect. Matthew 5:48

But in order for you to be perfect enough to enter Heaven, you would have to keep all God's commands all the time. You could never break any of God's rules, not even in your mind or heart.

For whoever shall keep the whole law, and yet stumble in one point, he is guilty of all.

It is impossible for any human being to be that good!

There is none who does good, no, not one...for all have sinned and fall short of the glory of God... Romans 3:12b, 23

Everyone falls short of God's goodness; no one is good enough to live with God in Heaven. Because you were born into Adam's family, you were born a sinner and you cannot please God. Even the good things you do are filthy rags to Him.

But we are all like an unclean thing, And all our righteousnesses are like filthy rags... Isaiah 64:6a

The only way for you to get the righteousness you need so that you can live with God is for God to give it to you.

...the righteousness which is from God... Philippians 3:9b

Remember what God did for Abraham when Abraham believed in Him?

Abraham believed God, and it was accounted to him for righteousness. Romans 4:3b

When Abraham believed in the Lord, God gave him the gift of His perfect righteousness. Because Abraham trusted in God to send the Savior to rescue him from sin and death, God made Abraham perfectly righteous in His sight.

The Bible says that on the cross Jesus took your sin on Himself so that you could receive His perfect righteousness!

For He made Him who knew no sin to be sin for us, that we might become the righteousness of God in Him. 2 Corinthians 5:21

God is...

...the Judge of all the earth... Genesis 18:25b

God is the Judge of the world. He says the payment for sin is death. But since Jesus made this payment for us, God is able to give the gift of His perfect goodness to all who trust in Jesus and legally declare them righteous.

> **Justified - to be legally declared righteous**

God knew you could never keep His laws. So He made a way for you to be declared righteous, or perfect, by simply believing in Jesus Christ.

...that we might be justified by faith in Christ and not by the works of the law... Galatians 2:1

If you have believed in Jesus Christ, God has legally declared you righteous; in His eyes you are righteous even if you still do things that displease Him. Those who receive the gift of God's perfect righteousness are acceptable to Him. All who have been legally declared righteous by God are no longer His enemies, but are at peace with God and will live with Him in Heaven.

Therefore, having been justified by faith, we have peace with God through our Lord Jesus Christ... Romans 5:1

Questions

1. How did the man who called Jesus Good Teacher think he could earn eternal life? *He thought he could earn eternal life for himself by keeping God's commandments.*

2. How good does a person have to be in order to live with God in Heaven? *In order to be good enough to live with God, you have to be perfect. You have to obey all God's commands, all the time, even in your thoughts.*

3. Is there anyone who can be good enough to live with God? *No, all people are sinners separated from God. Even the good deeds we do are filthy rags to God.*

4. What is the only way for you to get the righteousness you need to be able to live with God in Heaven? *The only way for you to get the righteousness you need is for God to give it to you.*

5. When Jesus died on the cross, He took your sin on Himself so that He could give you His what? *Jesus took your sin on Himself so that He could give you His righteousness.*

6. Who is the Judge of all the earth? *God is the judge of all the Earth.*

7. What does the word justify mean? *It means to be legally declared righteous, or perfect, by God.*

8. How can God legally declare you righteous when you are a sinner? *God is the Judge of the world. Since Jesus Christ died and paid for the sin of the world, God can declare all who believe in Him righteous, or perfect.*

9. How can you be declared righteous by God so that you can live with Him in Heaven? *You can be declared righteous, or perfect, by believing in Jesus Christ.*

Activity 1: Gavel Craft

Supplies:
- Light brown cardstock or construction paper, one sheet per student
- Pencils and crayons
- Chalkboard or dry erase board
- Chalk or dry erase marker

Instructions:
- Students draw a big gavel on their papers.
- Students write the following on the gavel: Justified = to be legally declared righteous.

Extra Bible References

Matthew 19:20-22; Romans 3:9-30; 4:1-8, 23-25; 5:1-9, 12-21; Galatians 2:16, 3:21; Ephesians 1:3-4; Colossians 1:21-22, 2:13-15; Titus 3:7; Hebrews 9:9; 10:1-4; Hebrews 11:4, 7, 39-40

79
Safe and Secure

Memory Verse

And I give them eternal life, and they shall never perish; neither shall anyone snatch them out of My hand. John 10:28

Lesson

Every person in the world has a mom and a dad. Nothing can change that fact. You may not like your parents, but they are still your parents. You may not live with one or the other of your parents, but you cannot change the fact that they are your parents.

Sometimes people do not know who their parents are, but it is easy to find out by getting a blood test to check your DNA. Your DNA will only match the DNA of your real mom and dad. No one can change his or her DNA. In that way, you will always be connected to your real parents.

The Bible says that...

...as many as received Him, to them He gave the right to become children of God, to those who believe in His name: who were born, not of blood, nor of the will of the flesh, nor of the will of man, but of God. John 1:12-13

The day you received Jesus Christ by believing that He died for your sins and rose again, you were born again into God's family. You became God's child, and His Holy Spirit came to live inside you. You cannot take this spiritual DNA out of yourself any more than you can take your parents' DNA out of your blood. Once you are God's child, you will always be God's child.

...who also has sealed us and has given us the Spirit in our hearts as a guarantee. 2 Corinthians 1:22

The Bible says that God's spiritual DNA inside you is "incorruptible." That means it is indestructible. You can think of it like this: the DNA you received from God is everlasting; it can never be destroyed. That is what God says in the Bible.

...having been born again, not of corruptible seed but incorruptible... 1 Peter 1:23a

This is really good news for you as a child of God. Nothing can make you become "unborn" out of the family of God. Once you have become God's child, you will always be God's child. God will never cast off any of His children.

📖 And all that the Father gives Me will come to Me, and the one who comes to Me I will by no means cast out. John 6:37

The moment you were born into God's family, you were given a special kind of life.

📖 ...the gift of God is eternal life in Christ Jesus our Lord. Romans 6:23b

When you were born the second time into God's family, He gave you eternal life. "Eternal" means endless. The life God gave you will never end. You will live with God for infinity; you will never go to the place of suffering.

📖 Jesus said to her, "I am the resurrection and the life. He who believes in Me, though he may die, he shall live." John 11:25

Jesus said that whoever believes in Him will live forever even though his or her body may die.

The eternal life God gives is a completely free gift.

📖 For the gifts and the calling of God are irrevocable. Romans 1:29

"Irrevocable" means God's gifts can't be reversed; they are permanent. When God gives gifts, He will never take them back! Even if you try to give them back, God will not take them; once God has given a person eternal life, it is permanent. You do not have to worry that God will one day change His mind.

You do not pay for a gift. If you have to pay for a gift, it is not a gift.

📖 And if by grace, then it is no longer of works; otherwise grace is no longer grace. Romans 11:6a

In the same way you do not pay to get a gift, you do not pay to keep a gift. If you do, it is not a true gift.

For by grace you have been saved through faith, and that not of yourselves; it is the gift of God, not of works, lest anyone should boast. Ephesians 2:8-9

God did not ask you to work for eternal life. He did not ask you to promise to be good, or to pray a prayer, or to be baptized, or to go to church in order to receive His gift of eternal life. God gave you eternal life as a gift because of His grace. You did not work to receive this gift, and you do not have to work to keep this gift. You do not have to continue to be good to make God keep accepting you. You do not have to keep God's rules to make Him love you. God keeps you as His child because of His kindness, not because of anything good in you.

Of course, this does not mean God wants His children to break His rules. God trains His children to do what is right.

For whom the Lord loves He corrects, just as a father the son in whom he delights. Proverbs 3:12

God corrects His children when they go against what He wants them to do. God trains and corrects all His children, but He never disowns them.

Even if you are not true to God (faithless), even if you stop believing in God, God will always be true to you. He will never break a promise or take back a gift.

If we are faithless, He remains faithful; He cannot deny Himself. 2 Timothy 2:13

God loves you because of what Jesus did for you. Jesus paid for your sin so that you could be made acceptable to God and become His child. Nothing can separate you from the love of God which is in Christ Jesus.

For I am persuaded that neither death nor life, nor angels nor principalities nor powers, nor things present nor things to come, nor height nor depth, nor any other created thing, shall be able to separate us from the love of God which is in Christ Jesus our Lord. Romans 8:38-39

Nothing will ever be able to separate you from God's love: not death, not Satan or his demons, not you, or any other "created thing." Nothing in the whole world can separate you from God's love for you as His child.

Jesus has given you eternal life. He holds you in His hand. No one is strong enough to steal you from Jesus.

And I give them eternal life, and they shall never perish; neither shall anyone snatch them out of My hand. John 10:28

There is no safer place to be held than the hand of Jesus. You did not put yourself in Jesus' hand, and you do not keep yourself there. God does.

Not only are you safe in Jesus' hand, the Bible says you are hidden inside of God.

When you trusted in the Savior, God the Holy Spirit placed you into Jesus Christ. The old you that was part of Adam's family died, and you were born as a new person into the family of God. The new you and Jesus are hidden inside of God.

For you died, and your life is hidden with Christ in God. Colossians 3:3

How could Satan, or anyone else, ever find you? First, he would have to "break into" God. Then he would have to find where you are hidden with Jesus inside of God. After he found you, he would have to overpower Jesus in order to steal you away. Satan could not do that, nor could anyone else. It is impossible!

There is simply no way you will ever stop being God's child. God promised that whoever believes in Him will not perish; whoever believes in God will not go to the terrible place of suffering. Not only that, but God also promised that whoever believes in Him will have everlasting life. God never lies. You can depend on what God says.

For God so loved the world that He gave His only begotten Son, that whoever believes in Him should not perish but have everlasting life. John 3:16

Listen to the beautiful words of Jesus.

For He Himself has said, "I will never leave you nor forsake you." Hebrews 13:5b

If Jesus promises never to leave you, you can trust what He says.

The Bible says that God placed the Holy Spirit inside of you as a guarantee that you will go to Heaven when you die.

...having believed, you were sealed with the Holy Spirit of promise, who is the guarantee of our inheritance... Ephesians 1:13-14

God always finishes what He starts. When you believed in Jesus, you became God's child. Now you have eternal life with God, and God's Holy Spirit lives inside of you.

...being confident of this very thing, that He who has begun a good work in you will complete it until the day of Jesus Christ. Philippians 1:6

Even though God has already legally declared you to be righteous, you still sin, but every day God is at work in your life to make you more and more like Himself. Someday, His work will be complete. On the day God takes you to Heaven, you will be completely freed from sin. Finally you will be perfect through and through.

...we shall be like Him, for we shall see Him as He is. 1 John 3:2b

Questions

1. Who comes to live inside of you when you trust Jesus as your Savior? *God the Holy Spirit comes to live inside of you.*

2. Once you are born into God's family, can you become unborn? *No, once you are a child of God and His Holy Spirit lives in you, you will always be God's child.*

3. Will God ever cast out any of His children? *No, Jesus said He will not cast out any of His children.*

4. How long is eternal life? *Eternal life is eternal; it begins the day you become a child of God and lasts forever and ever. It will never end.*

5. If God gives you a gift, will He take it back? *No, God does not change His mind. If He gives you a gift, it is permanently yours. He will not take it back even if you try to give it back to Him.*

6. If you have to work for or pay for something, is it a gift? *No, a gift is always free. You do not have to work to get it nor do you have to work to keep it.*

7. Will God disown His children if they do not keep His rules? *No, God will not disown His children no matter what happens. Just like you did not do any work in order to first become God's child, you do not have to do any work to continue to be God's child. You do not have to keep God's rules in order to stay in His family.*

8. As God's child, where does God hide you? *You are hidden with Jesus inside of God.*

9. Could Satan and his demons, or anyone else, ever steal you away from God? *No, Satan would first of all have to find you inside of God and then he would have to overpower Jesus. That is impossible; Satan could never do that.*

10. What two promises does God make to whoever believes in Jesus? *God says that whoever believes in Jesus will first of all never perish, and secondly, will have eternal life.*

11. Does God always keep His word? *Yes, God always does what He says He will do.*

12. Does God always finish what He starts? *Yes, God always finishes what He starts.*

13. What is the work God is doing in your life? *Now that you are God's child, God is at work in your life to make you more and more like Himself.*

14. Since you are God's child, where will you go when you die? *All God's children will go to Heaven when they die.*

Activity: Envelope Craft

Supplies:

- Paper, one sheet per student
- Two different sizes of envelopes, i.e., business and letter, one of each per student
- Pencils or markers
- Scissors
- Sealing wax and stamp, optional

Instructions:

- Students draw and cut out a picture of themselves.
- Students label their drawings with their name and then cut them out.
- Students label the smaller envelope "Christ" and slip the drawing of themselves into it.
- They seal the "Christ" envelope with "them" in it.
- Next, students label the larger envelope "God."
- Then they place the "Christ" envelope inside the "God" envelope and seal it.
- If you have a seal, you can now seal the envelopes.
- Students write the following verse on the outside of the larger envelope: "Your life is hidden with Christ in God." Colossians 3:3

- Discuss how it would be impossible for Satan, or anyone else, to steal you from God, because first of all you are hidden inside Christ, and Christ would never let you go. Secondly, together with Christ, you are hidden inside of God. Thirdly, you are sealed with the Holy Spirit. God the Holy Spirit living inside of you is God's guarantee that you will most certainly live with God forever in Heaven.

80
A New Identity

Memory Verse

Therefore, if anyone is in Christ, he is a new creation; old things have passed away; behold, all things have become new. 2 Corinthians 5:17

Lesson

When God looks down on the world, He sees only two kinds of people. It is not important to God whether you are rich or poor, tall or short, brown or black. What matters to God is which family you are in. Every person in the world is either in Adam's family or in God's family.

When you were born into this world as a baby, you were born into Adam's family. Everyone in Adam's family is dead to God because of sin. Everyone in Adam's family is on Satan's side and is God's enemy. Those who are in Adam's family cannot please God and someday they will die the second death.

And you...were dead in...sins, in which you once walked according to the course of this world, according to the prince of the power of the air...and were by nature children of wrath... Ephesians 2:1-3

But when you trusted in Jesus as your Savior, you were born again into God's family. The old you that was part of Adam's family died, and you were born as a new person into the family of God.

Therefore, if anyone is in Christ, he is a new creation; old things have passed away; behold, all things have become new. 2 Corinthians 5:17

Just as certain things were true of you in Adam, certain things are true about the new you in Christ. In Christ, you are blessed. In Christ, you have been legally declared righteous. In Christ, you have been adopted into God's family. In Christ, you are not only acceptable to God, but you are greatly loved. In Christ, you have been redeemed and your sins are forgiven. In Christ, you have everlasting life with God!

Blessed be the God and Father of our Lord Jesus Christ, who has blessed us with **every spiritual blessing** in the heavenly places <u>in Christ</u>, just as He chose us <u>in Him</u> before the foundation of the world, that we should be **holy and without blame before Him** in love, having predestined us to **adoption as sons** by Jesus Christ to Himself...He made us **accepted in the Beloved.** <u>In Him</u> **we have redemption** through His blood, the **forgiveness of sins**, according to the riches of His grace... Ephesians 1:3-7 (highlights and underlining mine)

When you were born into God's family, you also received a new nature that cannot sin. Now you can please God and have a relationship with Him.

God wants you to get to know Him. You can do this by reading His letter to you, the Bible. Through the true stories of the Bible, God shows you what He is like. In the Bible, God tells you that He sent the Savior to rescue you from Satan, sin, and death. He also tells you what His will for you is. Everything God wants you to know about Him and about being a new creation in Christ is written in the Bible.

God loves you and wants to take care of you. In the same way God wanted Adam and Eve to depend on Him for all their needs, God wants you to depend on Him for all your needs.

casting all your care upon Him, for He cares for you. 1 Peter 5:7

God wants you to talk to Him about everything. We call that praying. You can talk to God anywhere, anytime. You can talk to Him out loud, or in your mind.

Because you are His child, God hears you when you pray. Isn't that incredible? God loves you so much!

Behold what manner of love the Father has bestowed on us, that we should be called children of God! 1 John 3:1a

But even though you are a new creation in Christ, there is still a part of you that always wants to sin. This part of you is called your sin nature. Although you were born again as a new person into God's family, until you die and go to Heaven, you will have this old sinful nature you received from Adam.

Because of this sin nature, you must always depend on God to keep you from sinning. He has provided the solution for this problem.

First of all, God has given you His Holy Spirit to live inside of you. That means God, the all-powerful Creator, lives in you!

But if the Spirit of Him who raised Jesus from the dead dwells in you, He...will also give life to your mortal bodies through His Spirit who dwells in you. Romans 8:11

God the Holy Spirit is always there to give you the strength to do what is right.

...strengthened with might through His Spirit in the inner man, Ephesians 3:16b

When you trusted in Jesus as your Savior, God the Holy Spirit placed you into Christ. The Bible says you were "baptized into Christ Jesus." The word "baptize" means to place into. Because you were placed into Christ, in God's eyes you died on the cross together with Jesus.

...do you not know that as many of us as were baptized into Christ Jesus were baptized into His death? Romans 6:3

Baptize - to dip, or to place into

When Jesus died on the cross, He not only died for sin, He also died to sin. That means He not only paid for your sin, He also died to destroy sin's power in your life. When you were in Adam, your sinful nature controlled you. But when you died with Jesus Christ on the cross, you died to sin. That means your sinful nature lost its power to control you.

Here is a little story to help you understand what it means to be dead to sin.

Let's say your sister works at a restaurant, and her manager is really mean. Every day before she gets off work, he makes her clean the bathrooms and wash the floors. Then one day she arrives at work to find that her manager was fired. Now she has a new manager who treats her much better. But one day her old manager enters the restaurant and starts bossing her around again. Does she have to do what her old manager says? No, she does not. Since she is no longer under his authority, she does not have to do what he says.

That is how it is with you. Although your sin nature still tries to tell you what to do, it no longer has authority over you. The Bible says that when you died with Christ you were set free from sin.

For he who has died has been freed from sin. Romans 6:7

Not only are you dead to sin, but you are alive to God.

Likewise you also, reckon yourselves to be dead indeed to sin, but alive to God in Christ Jesus our Lord. Romans 6:11

You have a new nature that is alive to God. This new nature is good and wants to please God. The Holy Spirit inside of you gives your new nature the power to do what is right.

...the new self, which in the likeness of God has been created in righteousness... Ephesians 4:24

God has given you everything you need to live a life that pleases Him. First of all, on the cross Jesus died to sin for you so that sin no longer has authority over you. Secondly, you have a new nature that is good and wants to please God. And finally, God the Holy Spirit lives inside of you and gives you strength.

But although your sinful nature does not have any authority to tell you what to do, sometimes you will do what it tells you to do anyway.

When that happens, God wants you simply to agree with Him about what you did; He wants you to admit you were wrong.

If we confess our sins, He is faithful and just to forgive us our sins and to cleanse us from all unrighteousness. 1 John 1:9

> Confess - to agree with God that what you did was wrong

The moment you confess your sin to God, your close relationship with Him is restored so that you can continue to live the way God wants you to.

God created people to be His friends; He wanted us to know and enjoy Him. God wanted Adam and Eve to depend on Him for everything so that He could pour out His love and goodness on them.

But then Satan came along and persuaded Adam and Eve that God was keeping something good from them and that God really did not love them. When Adam and Eve believed Satan instead of God, they caused the whole human race to join Satan's side and become separated from God.

Yet Satan cannot win against God. God still loved the people He created. He had an incredible solution to mankind's problem. In God's plan, He Himself would come to Earth to pay the death penalty for all mankind! What a huge sacrifice! Jesus Christ, God the Son, took the sin of the world on Himself and died the death you and I should have died so that we could once again have the relationship with Him that Adam and Eve lost when they sinned.

When Adam and Eve believed Satan instead of God, they died; they became separated from God, their Creator. But Jesus Christ, the promised Savior, came to give us life again. Because Jesus our Savior rose from the dead, we are alive to God right now, and someday we will live with Him in Heaven forever.

I have come that they may have life, and that they may have it more abundantly. John 10:10b

Questions

1. What was true of you in Adam? *In Adam you were dead to God. You were God's enemy. You were unable to please God. Because of your sin, you were condemned to die the second death.*

2. What are some things that are true of you now that you are a new creation in Christ? *In Christ you are blessed. In Christ, you are righteous before God. In Christ, you have been adopted into God's family. In Christ, you are not only acceptable to God, you are greatly loved by God. In Christ, you have been redeemed and your sins are forgiven. In Christ, you have everlasting life with God.*

3. How does God communicate with you? *God communicates with you through His letter, the Bible.*

4. How can you communicate with God? *You can communicate with God by praying. You can talk to God anytime, anywhere.*

5. What does it mean to be dead to sin? *It means that sin no longer has the authority to tell you what to do; you do not have to obey your sin nature.*

6. Now that you have trusted in Jesus Christ to save you, are you dead to God or alive to God? *You are alive to God. You have a relationship with God and are able to please Him.*

7. Who lives inside of you to give you the strength to do what is right? *God the Holy Spirit lives inside of you. He gives you the strength to do what pleases God.*

8. What does the word confess mean? *The word confess means to agree with God, or admit, that what you did was wrong.*

9. When you realize you have done something that displeases God, what does God want you to do? *He wants you to agree with Him that you are wrong. Then your friendship with God can be close again.*

10. Does God stop loving you when you do something that displeases Him? *No, now that you are God's child, nothing can separate you from His love.*

Activity: In Adam/In Christ Craft

Supplies:

- Construction paper, one piece per student
- In "Adam/In Christ" printouts, one per student (see appendix page 585)
- Scissors
- Glue

Instructions:

- Students fold a piece of construction paper in half lengthwise.
- Students label one side "In Christ" and the other side "In Adam."
- Students cut out the boxes in the printout and glue each box under the right heading.
- Discuss: You are now a new creation in Christ. All that was true of you in Adam is no longer true of you in Christ. You have a new identity. How does this affect your life?

Extra Bible References

Isaiah 26:3; Psalm 34:8; Habakkuk 2:4; John 1:1-32, 10:10, 15:1-14, 17:3; Romans 1:17; Romans 6-8:17, 28-30; 7:21-25; 1 Corinthians 3:16, 12:13; Galatians 2:20; 5:16-25; Ephesians 1:18; 2:1, 4-5; 3:14-17, 20; 4:20-32; Colossians 1:11, 26-28; 2:6-15; 3:1-3; 1 Thessalonians 5:23-24; 2 Timothy 1:1, 9-10; Hebrews 2:14; 3:12, 19; 10:38; 11:6; James 1:13-15; 1 Peter 1:19-21, 2:24; 2 Peter 1:3; 1 John 1:8; 3:1-9

APPENDIX

Lesson 2 Attribute Printout

Has always lived. Will keep living forever.	Was born and will die someday.
Is spirit	Has a body.
Always stays the same.	Everywhere at the same time.
Needs food, water and sunshine to stay alive.	Only one place at a time.
Is a real person.	Is a real person.
In charge of the world.	Should listen to God.
Changes; grows older.	Needs nothing.

Lesson 3 Coloring Picture Printout

Lesson 3 Memory Verse Printout

Before the mountains were brought forth, Or ever You had formed the earth and the world, Even from everlasting to everlasting, You are God.

Psalm 90:2

Lesson 4 Days of Creation Printout

	DAY 1
DAY 2	DAY 3
DAY 4	DAY 5
DAY 6	DAY 7

Lesson 6 Angel Printout

God made the

_____

to be His

_____.

Lesson 25 Nile River Printout

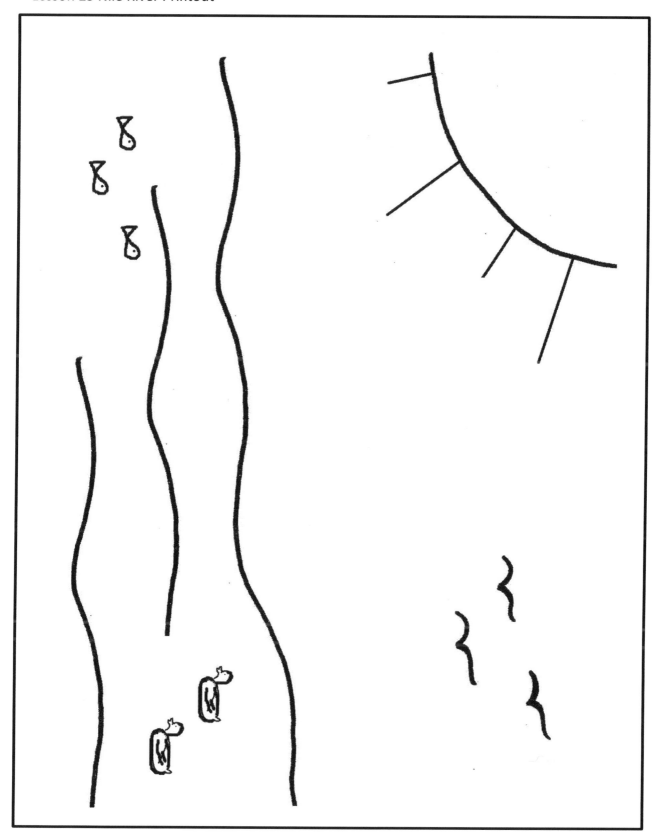

Lesson 25 Grass and Basket Printout

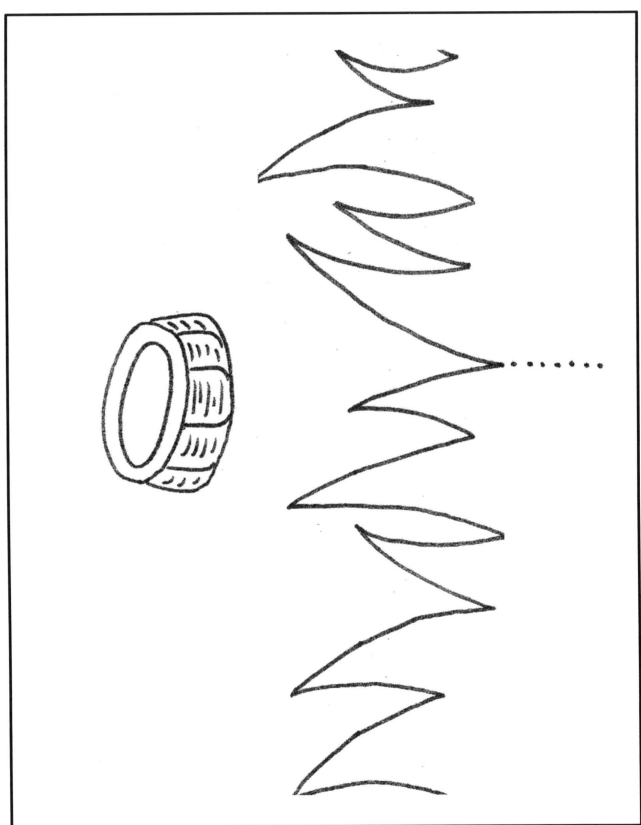